The Expositor's Bible
The Book Of Leviticus

by
Samuel H. Kellogg

The Expositor's Bible
The Book Of Leviticus
by Samuel H. Kellogg

Copyright © 2024

All Rights reserved.

No part of this publication may be reproduced, stored in a retrieval system, or transmitted in any form or by any means, electronic, mechanical, photocopying or Otherwise, without the written permission of the publisher.
The author/editor asserts the moral right to be identified as the author/editor of this work.

ISBN: 978-93-61150-75-3

Published by
DOUBLE 9 BOOKS
2/13-B, Ansari Road
Daryaganj, New Delhi – 110002
info@double9books.com
www.double9books.com
Tel. 011-40042856

This book is under public domain

ABOUT THE AUTHOR

Samuel H. Kellogg is an outstanding writer recognised for his masterpiece book, "The Expositor's Bible: The Book of Leviticus." In this exceptional paintings, Kellogg affords a complete and insightful evaluation of the biblical book of Leviticus, offering readers a deeper information of its ancient and spiritual importance. "The Expositor's Bible: The Book of Leviticus" delves into the problematic details of the Levitical laws and rituals, as recorded within the 0.33 book of the Old Testament. Kellogg's meticulous studies and profound interpretation shed mild at the cause and symbolism behind the various offerings, sacrifices, and ceremonies defined in Leviticus. With his knowledge in biblical studies, Kellogg explores the topics of holiness, atonement, and the connection among God and His people. He examines the significance of the priesthood, the regulations for worship, and the moral ideas outlined within the book. Additionally, Kellogg highlights the relevance of these historical laws and rituals to the religious existence of believers nowadays. Through his enticing writing style, Kellogg invitations readers to delve into the wealthy symbolism and spiritual insights determined within the book of Leviticus. His paintings serves as a valuable useful resource for pupils, theologians, and individuals seeking a deeper understanding of the Old Testament and its relevance to contemporary life.

CONTENTS

PART I
THE TABERNACLE WORSHIP

CHAPTER I
INTRODUCTORY..9

CHAPTER II
SACRIFICE: THE BURNT-OFFERING 25

CHAPTER III
THE BURNT-OFFERING (CONCLUDED) 36

CHAPTER IV
THE MEAL-OFFERING..46

CHAPTER V
THE PEACE-OFFERING 58

CHAPTER VI
THE SIN-OFFERING..76

CHAPTER VII
THE RITUAL OF THE SIN-OFFERING 92

CHAPTER VIII
THE GUILT-OFFERING..106

CHAPTER IX
THE PRIESTS' PORTIONS 118

CHAPTER X
THE CONSECRATION OF AARON AND HIS SONS,
AND OF THE TABERNACLE 122

CHAPTER XI
    THE INAUGURATION OF THE
    TABERNACLE SERVICE..146

CHAPTER XII
    NADAB'S AND ABIHU'S "STRANGE FIRE" 157

CHAPTER XIII
    THE GREAT DAY OF ATONEMENT 170

PART II
THE LAW OF THE DAILY LIFE

CHAPTER XIV
    CLEAN AND UNCLEAN ANIMALS,
    AND DEFILEMENT BY DEAD BODIES......................182

CHAPTER XV
    OF THE UNCLEANNESS OF ISSUES 199

CHAPTER XVI
    THE UNCLEANNESS OF CHILD-BEARING 204

CHAPTER XVII
    THE UNCLEANNESS OF LEPROSY..............................213

CHAPTER XVIII
    THE CLEANSING OF THE LEPER................................224

CHAPTER XIX
    OF HOLINESS IN EATING...238

CHAPTER XX
    THE LAW OF HOLINESS: CHASTITY 245

CHAPTER XXI
    THE LAW OF HOLINESS (CONCLUDED).................252

CHAPTER XXII
    PENAL SANCTIONS 269

CHAPTER XXIII
    THE LAW OF PRIESTLY HOLINESS............................278

CHAPTER XXIV
    THE SET FEASTS OF THE LORD 287

CHAPTER XXV
    THE HOLY LIGHT AND THE SHEW-BREAD:
    THE BLASPHEMER'S END 305

We must not, indeed, put more into these words than is truly there. They simply and only declare the Mosaic origin and the inspired authority of the legislation which the book contains. They say nothing as to whether or not Moses wrote every word of this book himself; or whether the Spirit of God directed and inspired other persons, in Moses' time or afterward, to commit this Mosaic law to writing. They give us no hint as to when the various sections which make up the book were combined into their present literary form, whether by Moses himself, as is the traditional view, or by men of God in a later day. As to these and other matters of secondary importance which might be named, the book records no statement. The words used in the text, and similar expressions used elsewhere, simply and only declare the legislation to be of Mosaic origin and of inspired authority. Only, be it observed, so much as this they do affirm in the most direct and uncompromising manner.

It is of great importance to note all this: for in the heat of theological discussion the issue is too often misapprehended on both sides. The real question, and, as every one knows, the burning Biblical question of the day, is precisely this, whether the claim this book contains, thus exactly defined, is true or false.

A certain school of critics, comprising many of the greatest learning, and of undoubted honesty of intention, assures the Church and the world that a strictly scientific criticism compels one to the conclusion that this claim, even as thus sharply limited and defined, is, to use plain words, not true; that an enlightened scholarship must acknowledge that Moses had little or nothing to do with what we find in this book; that, in fact, it did not originate till nearly a thousand years later, when, after the Babylonian captivity, certain Jewish priests, desirous of magnifying their authority with the people, fell on the happy expedient of writing this book of Leviticus, together with certain other parts of the Pentateuch, and then, to give the work a prestige and authority which on its own merits or over their own names it could not have had, delivered it to their countrymen as nearly a thousand years old, the work of their great lawgiver. And, strangest of all, they not only did this, but were so successful in imposing this forgery upon the whole nation that history records not even an expressed suspicion of a single person, until modern times, of its non-Mosaic origin; that is, they succeeded in persuading the whole people of Israel that a law which they had themselves just promulgated had been in existence among them for nearly ten centuries, the very work of Moses, when, in reality, it was quite a new thing.

Astonishing and even incredible as all this may seem to the uninitiated, substantially this theory is held by many of the Biblical scholars of our day as presenting the essential facts of the case; and the discovery of these supposed facts we are called upon to admire as one of the chief literary triumphs of modern critical scholarship!

Now the average Christian, whether minister or layman, though intelligent enough in ordinary matters of human knowledge, or even a well-educated man, is not, and cannot be, a specialist in Hebrew and in the higher criticism. What is he then to do when such a theory is presented to him as endorsed by scholars of the highest ability and the most extensive learning? Must we, then, all learn Hebrew and study this higher criticism before we can be permitted to have any well-justified and decided opinion whether this book, this law of Leviticus, be the Word of God or a forgery? We think not. There are certain considerations, quite level to the understanding of every one; certain facts, which are accepted as such by the most eminent scholars, which ought to be quite sufficient for the maintenance and the abundant confirmation of our faith in this book of Leviticus as the very Word of God to Moses.

In the first place, it is to be observed that if any theory which denies the Mosaic origin and the inspired authority of this book be true, then the fifty-six assertions of such origin and authority which the book contains are unqualifiedly false. Further, however any may seek to disguise the issue with words, if in fact this Levitical ritual and code of laws came into existence only after the Babylonian captivity and in the way suggested, then the book of Leviticus can by no possibility be the Word of God in any sense, but is a forgery and a fraud. S<u>urely</u> this needs no demonstration. "The Lord spake unto Moses," reads, for instance, this first verse; "The Lord did *not* speak these things unto Moses," answer these critics; "they were invented by certain unscrupulous priests centuries afterwards." Such is the unavoidable issue.

Now who shall arbitrate in these matters? who shall settle these questions for the great multitude of believers who know nothing of Hebrew criticism, and who, although they may not well understand much that is in this book, have yet hitherto accepted it with reverent faith as being what it professes to be, the very Word of God through Moses? To whom, indeed, can we refer such a question as this for decision but to Jesus Christ of Nazareth, our Lord and Saviour, confessed of all believers to be in verity the only-begotten Son of God from the bosom of the Father? For He declared that "the Father showed unto Him," the Son, "all things that He Himself did;" He will therefore be sure to know the truth of this matter, sure to know the Word of His Father from the word of man, if He will but speak.

And He has spoken on this matter, He, the Son of God. What was the common belief of the Jews in the time of our Lord as to the Mosaic origin and Divine authority of this book, as of all the Pentateuch, every one knows. Not a living man disputes the statement made by a recent writer on this subject, that "previous to the Christian era, there are no traces of a second opinion" on this question; the book "was universally ascribed to Moses." Now, that Jesus Christ shared and repeatedly endorsed this belief of His contemporaries should be perfectly clear to any ordinary reader of the Gospels.

The facts as to His testimony, in brief, are these. As to the Pentateuch in general, He called it (Luke xxiv. 44) "the law of Moses;" and, as regards its authority, He declared it to be such that "till heaven and earth pass away, one jot or one tittle shall in no wise pass away from the law, till all be fulfilled" (Matt. v. 18). Could this be truly said of this book of Leviticus, which is undoubtedly included in this term, "the law," if it were not the Word of God, but a forgery, so that its fifty-six affirmations of its Mosaic origin and inspired authority were false? Again, Christ declared that Moses in his "writings" wrote of Him,—a statement, which, it should be observed, imputes to Moses foreknowledge, and therefore supernatural inspiration; and further said that faith in Himself was so connected with faith in Moses, that if the Jews had believed Moses, they would have also believed Him (John v. 46, 47). Is it conceivable that Christ should have spoken thus, if the "writings" referred to had been forgeries?

But not only did our Lord thus endorse the Pentateuch in general, but also, on several occasions, the Mosaic origin and inspired authority of Leviticus in particular. Thus, when He healed the lepers (Matt. viii. 4) He sent them to the priests on the ground that Moses had commanded this in such cases. But such a command is found only in this book of Leviticus (xiv. 3-10). Again, in justifying His disciples for plucking the ears of corn on the Sabbath day, He adduces the example of David, who ate the shew-bread when he was an hungered, "which was not lawful for him to eat, but only for the priests" (Matt. xii. 4); thus referring to a law which is only found in Leviticus (xxiv. 9). But the citation was only pertinent on the assumption that He regarded the prohibition of the shew-bread as having the same inspired authority as the obligation of the Sabbath. In John vii. 32, again, He refers to Moses as having renewed the ordinance of circumcision, which at the first had been given to Abraham; and, as usual, assumes the Divine authority of the command as thus given. But this renewal of the ordinance of circumcision is recorded only in Leviticus (xii. 3). Yet once more, rebuking the Pharisees for their ingenious justification of the hard-hearted neglect of parents by undutiful children, He reminds them that Moses had said that he who cursed father or mother should be put to death; a law which is only found in the so-called priest-code, Exod. xxi. 17 and Lev. xx. 9. Further, He is so far from merely assuming the truth of the Jewish opinion for the sake of an argument, that He formally declares this law, equally with the fifth commandment, to be "a commandment of God," which they by their tradition had made void (Matt. xiv. 3-6).

One would suppose that it had been impossible to avoid the inference from all this, that our Lord believed, and intended to be understood as teaching, that the law of Leviticus was, in a true sense, of Mosaic origin, and of inspired, and therefore infallible, authority.

We are in no way concerned, indeed,—nor is it essential to the argument,—to press this testimony of Christ as proving more than the very least which the words fairly imply. For instance, nothing in His words, as we read them, any more than in the language of Leviticus itself, excludes the supposition that in the preparation of the law, Moses, like the Apostle Paul, may have had co-labourers or amanuenses, such as Aaron, Eleazar, Joshua, or others, whose several parts of the work might then have been issued under his endorsement and authority; so that Christ's testimony is in no wise irreconcilable with the fact of differences of style, or with the evidence of different documents, if any think that they discover this, in the book.[1]

We are willing to go further, and add that in the testimony of our Lord we find nothing which declares against the possibility of one or more redactions or revisions of the laws of Leviticus in post-Mosaic times, by one or more *inspired* men; as, *e.g.*, by Ezra, described (Ezra vii. 6) as "a ready scribe in the law of Moses, which the Lord, the God of Israel, had given;" to whom also ancient Jewish tradition attributes the final settlement of the Old Testament canon down to his time. Hence no words of Christ touch the question as to when the book of Leviticus received its present form, in respect of the order of its chapters, sections, and verses. This is a matter of quite secondary importance, and may be settled any way without prejudice to the Mosaic origin and authority of the laws it contains.

Neither, in the last place, do the words of our Lord, carefully weighed, of necessity exclude even the possibility that such persons, acting under Divine direction and inspiration, may have first reduced some parts of the law given by Moses to writing;[2] or even, as an extreme supposition, may have entered here and there, under the unerring guidance of the Holy Ghost, prescriptions which, although new as to the letter, were none the less truly Mosaic, in that by necessary implication they were logically involved in the original code.[3]

We do not indeed here argue either for or against any of these suppositions, which were apart from the scope of the present work. We are only concerned here to remark that Christ has not incontrovertibly settled these questions. These things may be true or not true; the decision of such matters properly belongs to the literary critics. But decide them as one will, it will still remain true that the law is "the law of Moses," given by revelation from God.

So much as this, however, is certain. Whatsoever modifications may conceivably have passed upon the text, all work of this kind was done, as all agree, long before the time of our Lord; and the text to which He refers as of Mosaic origin and of inspired authority, was therefore essentially the text of Leviticus as we have it to-day. We are thus compelled to insist that whatever modifications may have been made in the original Levitical law, they cannot have been, according to the testimony of our Lord, such as in any way conflicted with His affirmation of its Mosaic origin and its inspired authority. They can thus, at the very utmost, only have been, as suggested, in the way of legitimate logical development and application to successive circumstances, of the Levitical law as originally given to Moses; and that, too, under the administration of a priesthood endowed with the possession of the Urim and Thummim, so as to give such official deliverances, whenever required, the sanction of inerrant Divine authority, binding on the conscience as from God. Here, at least, surely, Christ by His testimony has placed an immovable limitation upon the speculations of the critics.

And yet there are those who admit the facts as to Christ's testimony, and nevertheless claim that without any prejudice to the absolute truthfulness of our Lord, we may suppose that in speaking as He did, with regard to the law of Leviticus, He merely conformed to the common usage of the Jews, without intending thereby to endorse their opinion; any more than, when, conforming to the ordinary mode of speech, He spoke of the sun as rising and setting, He meant thereby to be understood as endorsing the common opinion of men of that time that the sun actually passed round the earth every twenty-four hours. To which it is enough to reply that this illustration, which has so often been used in this argument, is not relevant to the case before us. For not only did our Lord use language which implied the truth of the Jewish belief regarding the origin and authority of the Mosaic law, but He formally teaches it; and—what is of still more moment—He rests the obligation of certain duties upon the fact that this law of Leviticus was a revelation from God to Moses for the children of Israel. But if the supposed facts, upon which He bases His argument in such cases, are, in reality, not facts, then His argument becomes null and void. How, for instance, is it possible to explain away the words in which He appeals to one of the laws of Exodus and Leviticus (Matt. xv. 3-6) as being *not* a Jewish opinion, but, instead, in explicit contrast with the traditions of the Rabbis, "a commandment of God"? Was this expression merely "an accommodation" to the mistaken notions of the Jews? If so, then what becomes of His argument?

Others, again, feeling the force of this, and yet sincerely and earnestly desiring to maintain above possible impeachment the perfect truthfulness of Christ, still assuming that the Jews were mistaken, and admitting that, if so, our Lord must have shared their error, take another line of argument. They remind us of what, however mysterious, cannot be denied, that our Lord, in virtue of His incarnation, came under certain limitations in knowledge; and then urge that without any prejudice to His character we may suppose that, not only with regard to the time of His advent and kingdom (Matt. xxiv. 36), but also with respect to the authorship and the Divine authority of this book of Leviticus, He may have shared in the ignorance and error of His countrymen.

But, surely, the fact of Christ's limitation in knowledge cannot be pressed so far as the argument of such requires, without by logical necessity nullifying Christ's mission and authority as a religious teacher. For it is certain that according to His own word, and the universal belief of Christians, the supreme object of Christ's mission was to reveal unto men through His life and teachings, and especially through His death upon the cross, the Father; and it is certain that He claimed to have, in order to this end, perfect knowledge of the Father. But how could this most essential claim of His be justified, and how could He be competent to give unto men a perfect and inerrant knowledge of the Father, if the ignorance of His humiliation was so great that He was unable to distinguish from His Father's Word a book which, by the hypothesis, was not the Word of the Father, but an ingenious and successful forgery of certain crafty post-exilian priests?

It is thus certain that Jesus must have known whether the Pentateuch, and, in particular, this book of Leviticus, was the Word of God or not; certain also that, if the Word of God, it could not have been a forgery; and equally certain that Jesus could not have intended in what He said on this subject to accommodate His speech to a common error of the people, without thereby endorsing their belief. It thus follows that critics of the radical school referred to are directly at issue with the testimony of Christ regarding this book. It is of immense consequence that Christians should see this issue clearly. While Jesus taught in various ways that Leviticus contains a law given by revelation from God to Moses, these teach that it is a priestly forgery of the days after Ezra. Both cannot be right; and if the latter are in the right, then— we speak with all possible deliberation and reverence—Jesus Christ was mistaken, and was therefore unable even to tell us with inerrant certainty whether this or that is the Word of God or not. But if this is so, then how can we escape the final inference that His claim to have a perfect knowledge of the Father must have been an error; His claim to be the incarnate Son of God, therefore, a false pretension, and Christianity, a delusion, so that mankind has in Him no Saviour?

But against so fatal a conclusion stands the great established fact of the resurrection of Jesus Christ from the dead; whereby He was with power declared to be the Son of God, so that we may know that His word on this, as on all subjects where He has spoken, settles controversy, and is a sufficient ground of faith; while it imposes upon all speculations of men, literary or philosophical, eternal and irremovable limitations.

Let no one think that the case, as regards the issue at stake, has been above stated too strongly. One could not well go beyond the often cited words of Kuenen on this subject: "We must either cast aside as worthless our dearly bought scientific method, or we must for ever cease to acknowledge the authority of the New Testament in the domain of the exegesis of the Old." With good reason does another scholar exclaim at these words, "The Master must not be heard as a witness! We treat our criminals with more respect." So then stands the question this day which this first verse of Leviticus brings before us: In which have we more confidence? in literary critics, like a Kuenen or Wellhausen, or in Jesus Christ? Which is the more likely to know with certainty whether the law of Leviticus is a revelation from God or not?

The devout Christian, who through the grace of the crucified and risen Lord "of whom Moses, in the law, and the prophets did write," and who has "tasted the good word of God," will not long hesitate for an answer. He will not indeed, if wise, timidly or fanatically decry all literary investigation of the Scriptures; but he will insist that the critic shall ever hold his reason in reverent subjection to the Lord Jesus on all points where the Lord has spoken. Such everywhere will heartily endorse and rejoice in those admirable words of the late venerable Professor Delitzsch; words which stand almost as of his last solemn testament:—"The theology of glory which prides itself upon being its own highest authority, bewitches even those who had seemed proof against its enchantments; and the theology of the Cross, which holds Divine folly to be wiser than men, is regarded as an unscientific lagging behind the steps of progress.... But the faith which I professed in my first sermons, ... remains mine to-day, undiminished in strength, and immeasurably higher than all earthly knowledge. Even if in many Biblical questions I have to oppose the traditional opinion, certainly my opposition rests on this side of the gulf, on the side of the theology of the Cross, of grace, of miracles!... By this banner let us stand; folding ourselves in it, let us die!"[4] To which truly noble words every true Christian may well say, Amen!

We then stand without fear with Jesus Christ in our view of the origin and authority of the book of Leviticus.

The Occasion and Order of Leviticus.

Before proceeding to the exposition of this book, a few words need to be said regarding its occasion and plan, and its object and present use.

The opening words of the book, "And the Lord said," connect it in the closest manner with the preceding book of Exodus, at the contents of which we have therefore to glance for a moment. The kingdom of God, rejected by corporate humanity in the founding of the Babylonian world-power, but continuing on earth in a few still loyal souls in the line of Abraham and his seed, at last, according to promise, had been formally and visibly re-established on earth at Mount Sinai. The fundamental law of the kingdom contained in the ten commandments and certain applications of the same, had been delivered in what is called the Book of the Covenant, amid thunders and lightnings, at the holy mount. Israel had solemnly entered into covenant with God on this basis, saying, "All these things will we do and be obedient," and the covenant had been sealed by the solemn sprinkling of blood.

This being done, Jehovah now issued commandment for the building of the tabernacle or "tent of meeting," where He might manifest His glory and from time to time communicate His will to Israel. As mediators between Him and the people, the priesthood was appointed, their vestments and duties prescribed. All this having been done as ordered, the tent of meeting covering the interior tabernacle was set up; the Shekinah cloud covered it, and the glory of Jehovah filled the tabernacle,—the manifested presence of the King of Israel!

Out of the tent of meeting, from this excellent glory, Jehovah now called unto Moses, and delivered the law as we have it in the first seven chapters of the book of Leviticus. To the law of offerings succeeds (viii.-x.) an account of the consecration of Aaron and his sons to the priestly office, and their formal public assumption of their functions, with an account of the very awful sanction which was given to the preceding law, by the death of Nadab and Abihu before the Lord, for offering as He had not commanded them.

The next section of the book contains the law concerning the clean and the unclean, under the several heads of food (xi.), birth-defilement (xii.), leprosy (xiii., xiv.), and unclean issues (xv.); and closes (xvi.) with the ordinance of the great day of atonement, in which the high priest alone, presenting the blood of a sin-offering in the Holy of Holies, was to make atonement once a year for the sins of the whole nation.[5]

The third section of the book contains the law of holiness,[6] first, for the people (xvii.-xx.), and then the special laws for the priests (xxi., xxii.). These are followed, first (xxiii.), by the order for the feasts of the Lord, or appointed times of public holy convocation; then (xxiv.), by a historical incident designed to show that the law, as given, must, in several respects noted, be applied in all its strictness no less to the alien than to the native-born Israelite; and finally (xxv.), by the remarkable ordinances concerning the sabbatic year, and the culmination of the sabbatic system of the law in the year of jubilee.

As a conclusion to the whole, the legislation thus given is now sealed (xxvi.) with promises from God of blessing to the nation if they will keep this law, and threats of unsparing vengeance against the people and the land, if they forsake His commandments and break the covenant, though still with a promise of mercy when, having thus transgressed, they shall at any time repent. The book then closes with a supplemental chapter on voluntary vows and dues (xxvii.).

The Purpose of Leviticus.

What now was the purpose of Leviticus? In general, as regards Israel, it was given to direct them how they might live as a holy nation in fellowship with God. The key-note of the book is "Holiness to Jehovah." More particularly, the object of the book was to furnish for the theocracy set up in Israel a code of law which should secure their physical, moral, and spiritual well-being. But the establishment of the theocracy in Israel was itself only a means to an end; namely, to make Israel a blessing to all nations, in mediating to the Gentiles the redemption of God. Hence, the Levitical laws were all intended and adapted to train and prepare the nation for this special historic mission to which God had chosen them.

To this end, it was absolutely necessary, first of all, that Israel should be kept separate from the heathen nations. To effect and maintain this separation, these laws of Leviticus were admirably adapted. They are of such a character, that obedience to them, even in a very imperfect way, has made the nation to this day to be, in a manner and degree perfectly unique, isolated and separate from all the peoples in the midst of whom they dwell.

The law of Leviticus was intended to effect this preparation of Israel for its world-mission, not only in an external manner, but also in an internal way; namely, by revealing in and to Israel the real character of God, and in particular His unapproachable holiness. For if Israel is to teach the nations the way of holiness, in which alone they can be blessed, the chosen nation must itself first be taught holiness by the Holy One. A lesson here for every one of us! The revelation of the holiness of God was made, first of all, in the sacrificial system. The great lesson which it must have kept before the most obtuse conscience was this, that "without shedding of blood there is no remission of sin;" that God therefore must be the Most Holy, and sin against Him no trifle. It was made, again, in the precepts of the law. If in some instances these seem to tolerate evils which we should have expected that a holy God would at once have swept away, this is explained by our Lord (Matt. xix. 8) by the fact that some things were of necessity ordained in view of the hardness of men's hearts; while, on the other hand, it is certainly quite plain that the laws of Leviticus constantly held before the Israelite the absolute holiness of God as the only standard of perfection.

The holiness of God was further revealed by the severity of the penalties which were attached to these Levitical laws. Men often call these harsh, forgetting that we are certain to underestimate the criminality of sin; forgetting that God must, in any case, have rights over human life which no earthly ruler can have. But no one will deny that this very severity of the law was fitted to impress the Israelite, as nothing else could, with God's absolute intolerance of sin and impurity, and make him feel that he could not trifle with God, and hope to sin with impunity.

And yet we must not forget that the law was adapted no less to reveal the other side of the Divine holiness; that "the Lord God is merciful and gracious, and of great kindness." For if the law of Leviticus proclaims that "without shedding of blood there is no remission," with equal clearness it proclaims that with shedding of blood there can be remission of sin to every believing penitent.

And this leads to the observation that this law was further adapted to the training of Israel for its world-mission, in that to every thoughtful man it must have suggested a secret of redeeming mercy yet to be revealed. Every such one must have often said in his heart that it was "not possible that the blood of bulls and of goats should take away sin;" and that as a substitute for human life, when forfeited by sin, more precious blood than this must be required; even though he might not have been able to imagine whence God should provide such a Lamb for an offering. And so it was that the law was fitted, in the highest degree, to prepare Israel for the reception of Him to whom all these sacrifices pointed, the High Priest greater than Aaron, the Lamb of God which should "take away the sins of the world," in whose person and work Israel's mission should at last receive its fullest realisation.

But the law of Leviticus was not only intended to prepare Israel for the Messiah by thus awakening a sense of sin and need, it was so ordered as to be in many ways directly typical and prophetic of Christ and His great redemption, in its future historical development. Modern rationalism, indeed, denies this; but it is none the less a fact. According to the Apostle John (v. 46) our Lord declared that Moses wrote of Him; and, according to Luke (xxiv. 27), when He expounded unto the two walking to Emmaus "the things concerning himself," He began His exposition with "Moses;" and (ver. 44) repeated what He had before His resurrection taught them, that all things "which were written in the law of Moses" concerning Him, must be fulfilled. And in full accord with the teaching of the Master taught also His disciples. The writer of the Epistle to the Hebrews, especially, argues from this postulate throughout, and also explicitly affirms the typical character of the ordinances of this book; declaring, for example, that the Levitical priests in the tabernacle service served "that which is a copy of the heavenly things" (Heb. viii. 5); that the blood with which "the copies of the things in the heavens" were cleansed, prefigured "better sacrifices than these," even the one offering of Him who "put away sin by the sacrifice of Himself" (Heb. ix. 23-6); and that the holy times and sabbatic seasons of the law were "a shadow of the things to come." The fact is familiar, and one need not multiply illustrations. Many, no doubt, in the interpretation of these types, have broken loose from the principles indicated in the New Testament, and given free rein to an unbridled fancy. But this only warns us that we the more carefully take heed to follow the intimations of the New Testament, and beware of mistaking our own imaginings for the teaching of the Holy Ghost. Such interpretations may bring typology into disrepute, but they cannot nullify it as a fact which must be recognised in any attempt to open up the meaning of the book.

Neither is the reality of this typical correspondence between the Levitical ritual and order and New Testament facts set aside, even though it is admitted that we cannot believe that Israel generally could have seen all in it which the New Testament declares to be there. For the very same New Testament which declares the typical correspondence, no less explicitly tells us this very thing: that many things predicted and prefigured in the Old Testament, concerning the sufferings and glory of Christ, were not understood by the very prophets through whom they were anciently made known (1 Peter i. 10-12). We have then carefully to distinguish in our interpretation between the immediate historical intention of the Levitical ordinances, for the people of that time, and their typical intention and meaning; but we are not to imagine with some that to prove the one, is to disprove the other.

The Present-day Use of Leviticus.

This very naturally brings us to the answer to the frequent question: Of what use can the book of Leviticus be to believers now? We answer, first, that it is to us, just as much as to ancient Israel, a revelation of the character of God. It is even a clearer revelation of God's character to us than to them; for Christ has come as the Fulfiller, and thus the Interpreter, of the law. And God has not changed. He is still exactly what He was when He called to Moses out of the tent of meeting or spoke to him at Mount Sinai. He is just as holy as then; just as intolerant of sin as then; just as merciful to the penitent sinner who presents in faith the appointed blood of atonement, as He was then.

More particularly, Leviticus is of use to us now, as holding forth, in a singularly vivid manner, the fundamental conditions of true religion. The Levitical priesthood and sacrifices are no more, but the spiritual truth they represented abides and must abide for ever: namely, that there is for sinful man no citizenship in the kingdom of God apart from a High Priest and Mediator with a propitiatory sacrifice for sin. These are days when many, who would yet be called Christians, belittle atonement, and deny the necessity of the shedding of substitutionary blood for our salvation. Such would reduce, if it were possible, the whole sacrificial ritual of Leviticus to a symbolic *self*-offering of the worshipper to God. But against this stands the constant testimony of our Lord and His apostles, that it is only through the shedding of blood *not his own* that man can have remission of sin.

But Leviticus presents not only a ritual, but also a body of civil law for the theocracy. Hence it comes that the book is of use for to-day, as suggesting principles which should guide human legislators who would rule according to the mind of God. Not, indeed, that the laws in their detail should be adopted in our modern states; but it is certain that the principles which underlie those laws are eternal. Social and governmental questions have come to the front in our time as never before. The question of the relation of the civil government to religion, the question of the rights of labour and of capital, of land-holding, that which by a suggestive euphemism we call "the social evil," with its related subjects of marriage and divorce,—all these are claiming attention as never before. There is not one of these questions on which the legislation of Leviticus does not cast a flood of light, into which our modern law-makers would do well to come and walk.

For nothing can be more certain than this; that if God has indeed once stood to a commonwealth in the relation of King and political Head, we shall be sure to discover in His theocratic law upon what principles infinite righteousness, wisdom, and goodness would deal with these matters. We shall thus find in Leviticus that the law which it contains, from beginning to end, stands in contradiction to that modern democratic secularism, which would exclude religion from government and order all national affairs without reference to the being and government of God; and, by placing the law of sacrifice at the beginning of the book, it suggests distinctly enough that the maintenance of right relation to God is fundamental to good government.

The severity of many of the laws is also instructive in this connection. The trend of public opinion in many communities is against capital punishment, as barbarous and inhuman. We are startled to observe the place which this has in the Levitical law; which exhibits a severity far removed indeed from the unrighteous and undiscriminating severity of the earlier English law, but no less so from the more undiscriminating leniency which has taken its place, especially as regards those crimes in which large numbers of people are inclined to indulge.

No less instructive to modern law-makers and political economists is the bearing of the Levitical legislation on the social question, the relations of rich and poor, of employer and employed. It is a legislation which, with admirable impartiality, keeps the poor man and the rich man equally in view; a body of law which, if strictly carried out, would have made in Israel either a plutocracy or a proletariat alike impossible. All these things will be illustrated in the course of exposition. Enough has been said to show that those among us who are sorely perplexed as to what government should do, at what it should aim in these matters, may gain help by studying the mind of Divine wisdom concerning these questions, as set forth in the theocratic law of Leviticus.

Further, Leviticus is of use to us now as a revelation of Christ. This follows from what has been already said concerning the typical character of the law. The book is thus a treasury of divinely-chosen illustrations as to the way of a sinner's salvation through the priestly work of the Son of God, and as to his present and future position and dignity as a redeemed man.

Finally, and for this same reason, Leviticus is still of use to us as embodying in type and figure prophecies of things yet to come, pertaining to Messiah's kingdom. We must not imagine with some that because many of its types are long ago fulfilled, therefore all have been fulfilled. Many, according to the hints of the New Testament, await their fulfilment in a bright day that is coming. Some, for instance, of the feasts of the Lord have been fulfilled; as passover, and the feast of Pentecost. But how about the day of atonement for the sin of corporate Israel? We have seen the type of the day of atonement fulfilled in the entering into heaven of our great High

Priest; but in the type He came out again to bless the people: has that been fulfilled? Has He yet proclaimed absolution of sin to guilty Israel? How, again, about the feast of trumpets, and that of the ingathering at full harvest? How about the Sabbatic year, and that most consummate type of all, the year of jubilee? History records nothing which could be held a fulfilment of any of these; and thus Leviticus bids us look forward to a glorious future yet to come, when the great redemption shall at last be accomplished, and "Holiness to Jehovah" shall, as Zechariah puts it (xiv. 20), be written even "on the bells of the horses."

CHAPTER II
SACRIFICE: THE BURNT-OFFERING

i. 2-4.

The voice of Jehovah which had spoken not long before from Sinai, now speaks from out "the tent of meeting." There was a reason for the change. For Israel had since then entered into covenant with God; and Moses, as the mediator of the covenant, had sealed it by sprinkling with blood both the Book of the Covenant and the people. And therewith they had professedly taken Jehovah for their God, and He had taken Israel for His people. In infinite grace, He had condescended to appoint for Himself a tabernacle or "tent of meeting," where He might, in a special manner, dwell among them, and manifest to them His will. The tabernacle had been made, according to the pattern shown to Moses in the mount; and it had been now set up. And so now, He who had before spoken amid the thunders of flaming, trembling Sinai, speaks from the hushed silence of "the tent of meeting." The first words from Sinai had been the holy law, forbidding sin with threatening of wrath: the first words from the tent of meeting are words of grace, concerning fellowship with the Holy One maintained through sacrifice, and atonement for sin by the shedding of blood. A contrast this which is itself a Gospel!

The offerings of which we read in the next seven chapters are of two kinds, namely, bloody and unbloody offerings. In the former class were included the burnt-offering, the peace-offering, the sin-offering, and the guilt-, or trespass-offering; in the latter, only the meal-offering. The book begins with the law of the burnt-offering.

In any exposition of this law of the offerings, it is imperative that our interpretation shall be determined, not by any fancy of ours as to what the offerings might fitly symbolise, nor yet, on the other hand, be limited by what we may suppose that any Israelite of that day might have thought regarding them; but by the statements concerning them which are contained in the law itself, and in other parts of Holy Scripture, especially in the New Testament.

First of all, we may observe that in the book itself the offerings are described by the remarkable expression, "the bread" or "food of God". Thus, it is commanded (xxi. 6) that the priests should not defile themselves, on this ground: "the offerings of the Lord made by fire, the bread of their God, do they offer." It was an ancient heathen notion that in sacrifice, food was provided for the Deity in order thus to show Him honour. And, doubtless, in Israel, ever prone to idolatry, there were many who rose no higher than this gross conception of the meaning of such words. Thus, in Psalm l. 8-15, God sharply rebukes Israel for so unworthy thoughts of Himself, using language at the same time which teaches the spiritual meaning of the sacrifice, regarded as the "food," or "bread," of God: "I will not reprove thee for thy sacrifices; and thy burnt-offerings are continually before Me.... I will take no bullock out of thy house, nor he-goats out of thy stalls.... If I were hungry, I would not tell thee; for the world is Mine, and the fulness thereof. Will I eat the flesh of bulls, or drink the blood of goats? Offer unto God the sacrifice of *thanksgiving*; and *pay thy vows* unto the Most High; and call upon Me in the day of trouble: I will deliver thee and thou shalt glorify Me."

Of which language the plain teaching is this. If the sacrifices are called in the law "the bread of God," God asks not this bread from Israel in any material sense, or for any material need. He asks that which the offerings symbolise; thanksgiving, loyal fulfilment of covenant engagements to Him, and that loving trust which will call on Him in the day of trouble. Even so! Gratitude, loyalty, trust! this is the "food of God," this the "bread" which He desires that we should offer, the bread which those Levitical sacrifices symbolised. For even as man, when hungry, craves food, and cannot be satisfied without it, so God, who is Himself Love, desires our love, and delights in seeing its expression in all those offices of self-forgetting and self-sacrificing service in which love manifests itself. This is to God even as is food to us. Love cannot be satisfied except with love returned; and we may say, with deepest humility and reverence, the God of love cannot be satisfied without love returned. Hence it is that the sacrifices, which in various ways symbolise the self-offering of love and the fellowship of love, are called by the Holy Ghost "the food," or "bread of God."

And yet we must, on no account, hasten to the conclusion, as many do, that therefore the Levitical sacrifices were *only* intended to express and symbolise the self-offering of the worshipper, and that this exhausts their significance. On the contrary, the need of infinite Love for this "bread of God" cannot be adequately met and satisfied by the self-offering of any creature, and, least of all, by the self-offering of a sinful creature, whose very sin lies just in this, that he has fallen away from perfect love. The symbolism of the sacrifice as "the food of God," therefore, by this very phrase points toward the self-offering in love of the eternal Son to the Father, and in behalf of sinners, for the Father's sake. It was the sacrifice on Calvary which first became, in innermost reality, that "bread of God," which the ancient sacrifices were only in symbol. It was this, not regarded as satisfying Divine justice (though it did this), but as satisfying the Divine love; because it was the supreme expression of the perfect love of the incarnate Son of God to the Father, in His becoming "obedient unto death, even the death of the cross."

And now, keeping all this in view, we may venture to say even more than at first as to the meaning of this phrase, "the bread of God," applied to these offerings by fire. For just as the free activity of man is only sustained in virtue of and by means of the food which he eats, so also the love of the God of love is only sustained in free activity toward man through the self-offering to the Father of the Son, in that atoning sacrifice which He offered on the cross, and in the ceaseless service of that exalted life which, risen from the dead, Christ now lives unto God for ever. Thus already, this expression, so strange to our ears at first, as descriptive of Jehovah's offerings made by fire, points to the person and work of the adorable Redeemer as its only sufficient explication.

But, again, we find another expression, xvii. 11, which is of no less fundamental consequence for the interpretation of the bloody offerings of Leviticus. In connection with the prohibition of blood for food, and as a reason for that prohibition, it is said: "The life of the flesh is in the blood; and I have given it to you upon the altar to make atonement for your souls; for it is the blood that maketh atonement,"—mark the expression; not, as in the received version, "*for* the soul," which were mere tautology, and gives a sense which the Hebrew cannot have, but, as the Revised Version has it,—"by reason of the life," or "soul" (marg.). Hence, wherever in this law we read of a sprinkling of blood upon the altar, this must be held fast as its meaning, whether it be formally mentioned or not; namely, atonement made for sinful man through the life of an innocent victim poured out in the blood. There may be, and often are, other ideas, as we shall see, connected with the offering, but this is always present. To argue, then, with so many in modern times, that because, not the idea of an atonement, but that of a sacrificial meal given by the worshipper to God, is the dominant conception in the sacrifices of the ancient nations, therefore we cannot admit the idea of atonement and expiation to have been intended in these Levitical sacrifices, is simply to deny, not only the New Testament interpretation of them, but the no less express testimony of the record itself.

But it is, manifestly, in the nature of the case "impossible that the blood of bulls and of goats should take away sins." Hence, we are again, by this phrase also, constrained to look beyond this Levitical shedding of sacrificial blood, for some antitype of which the innocent victims slain at that altar were types; one who, by the shedding of his blood, should do that in reality, which at the door of the tent of meeting was done in symbol and shadow.

What the New Testament teaches on this point is known to every one. Christ Jesus was the Antitype, to whose all-sufficient sacrifice each insufficient sacrifice of every Levitical victim pointed. John the Baptist struck the key-note of all New Testament teaching in this matter, when, beholding Jesus, he cried (John i. 29), "Behold the Lamb of God, which taketh away the sin of the world." Jesus Christ declared the same thought again and again, as in His words at the sacramental Supper: "This is My blood of the new covenant, which is shed for many for the remission of sins." Paul expressed the same thought, when he said (Eph. v. 2) that Christ "gave Himself up for us, an offering and a sacrifice to God, for an odour of a sweet smell;" and that "our redemption, the forgiveness of our trespasses," is "through His blood" (Eph. i. 7). And Peter also, speaking in Levitical language, teaches that we "were redeemed ... with precious blood, as of a lamb without blemish and without spot, even the blood of Christ;" to which he adds the suggestive words, of which this whole Levitical ritual is the most striking illustration, that Christ, although "manifested at the end of the times," "was foreknown" as the Lamb of God "before the foundation of the world" (1 Peter i. 18-20). John, in like manner, speaks in the language of Leviticus concerning Christ, when he declares (1 John i. 7) that "the blood of Jesus ... cleanseth us from all sin;" and even in the Apocalypse, which is the Gospel of Christ glorified, He is still brought before us as a Lamb that had been slain, and who has thus "purchased with His blood men of every tribe, and tongue, and people, and nation," "to be unto our God a kingdom and priests" (Rev. v. 6, 9, 10).

In this clear light of the New Testament, one can see how meagre also is the view of some who would see in these Levitical sacrifices nothing more than fines assessed upon the guilty, as theocratic penalties. Leviticus itself should have taught such better than that. For, as we have seen, the virtue of the bloody offerings is made to consist in this, that "the life of the flesh is in the blood;" and we are told that "the blood makes atonement for the soul," not in virtue of the monetary value of the victim, in a commercial way, but "by reason of the life" that is in the blood, and is therewith poured out before Jehovah on the altar, — the life of an innocent victim in the stead of the life of the sinful man.

No less inadequate, if we are to let ourselves be guided either by the Levitical or the New Testament teaching, is the view that the offerings only symbolised the self-offering of the worshipper. We do not deny, indeed, that the sacrifice — of the burnt-offering, for example — may have fitly represented, and often really expressed, the self-consecration of the offerer. But, in the light of the New Testament, this can never be held to have been the sole, or even the chief, reason in the mind of God for directing these outpourings of sacrificial blood upon the altar.

We must insist, then, on this, as essential to the right interpretation of this law of the offerings, that every one of these bloody offerings of Leviticus typified, and was intended to typify, our Saviour, Jesus Christ. The burnt-offering represented Christ; the peace-offering, Christ; the sin-offering, Christ; the guilt-, or trespass-offering, Christ. Moreover, since each of these, as intended especially to shadow forth some particular aspect of Christ's work, differed in some respects from all the others, while yet in all alike a victim's blood was shed upon the altar, we are by this reminded that in our Lord's redemptive work the most central and essential thing is this, that, as He Himself said (Matt. xx. 28), He "came to give His life a ransom for many."

Keeping this guiding thought steadily before us, it is now our work to discover, if we may, what special aspect of the one great sacrifice of Christ each of these offerings was intended especially to represent.

Only, by way of caution, it needs to be added that we are not to imagine that every minute circumstance pertaining to each sacrifice, in all its varieties, must have been intended to point to some correspondent feature of Christ's person or work. On the contrary, we shall frequently see reason to believe that the whole purpose of one or another direction of the ritual is to be found in the conditions, circumstances, or immediate intention of the offering. Thus, to illustrate, when a profound interpreter suggests that the reason for the command that the victim should be slain on the north side of the altar, is to be found in the fact that the north, as the side of shadow, signifies the gloom and joylessness of the sacrificial act, we are inclined rather to see sufficient reason for the prescription in the fact that the other three sides were already in a manner occupied: the east, as the place of ashes; the south, as fronting the entrance; and the west, as facing the tent of meeting and the brazen laver.

The Ritual of the Burnt-offering.

In the law of the offerings, that of the burnt-offering comes first, though in the order of the ritual it was not first, but second, following the sin-offering. In this order of mention we need, however, seek no mystic meaning. The burnt-offering was very naturally mentioned first, as being the most ancient, and also in the most constant and familiar use. We read of burnt-offerings as offered by Noah and Abraham; and of peace-offerings, too, in early times; while the sin-offering and the guilt-offering, in Leviticus treated last, were now ordered for the first time. So also the burnt-offering was still, by Divine ordinance, to be the most common. No day could pass in the tabernacle without the offering of these. Indeed, except on the great day of atonement for the nation, in the ritual for which, the sin-offering was the central act, the burnt-offering was the most important sacrifice on all the great feast-days.

The first law, which applies to bloody offerings in general, was this: that the victim shall be "of the cattle, even of the herd and of the flock" (ver. 2); to which is added, in the latter part of the chapter (ver. 14), the turtle-dove or young pigeon. The carnivora are all excluded; for these, which live by the death of others, could never typify Him who should come to give life. And among others, only clean beasts could be taken. Israel must not offer as "the food of God" that which they might not eat for their own food; nor could that which was held unclean be taken as a type of the Holy Victim of the future. And, even among clean animals, a further selection is made. Only domestic animals were allowed; not even a clean animal was permitted, if it were taken in hunting. For it was fitting that one should offer to God that which had become endeared to the owner as having cost the most of care and labour in its bringing up. For this, also, we can easily see another reason in the Antitype. Nothing was to mark Him more than this: that He should be subject and obey, and that not of constraint, as the unwilling captive of the chase, but freely and unresistingly.

And now follow the special directions for the burnt-offering. The Hebrew word so rendered means, literally, "that which ascends". It thus precisely describes the burnt-offering in its most distinctive characteristic. Of the other offerings, a part was burned, but a part was eaten; in some instances, even by the offerer himself. But in the burnt-offering all ascends to God in flame and smoke. For the creature is reserved nothing whatever.

The first specification in the law of the burnt-offering is this: "If his oblation be a burnt-offering of the herd, he shall offer it a male without blemish" (ver. 3). It must be a "male," as the stronger, the type of its kind; and "without blemish," that is, ideally perfect.

The reasons for this law are manifest. The Israelite was thereby taught that God claims the best that we have. They needed this lesson, as many among us do still. At a later day, we find God rebuking them by Malachi (i. 6, 13), with indignant severity, for their neglect of this law: "A son honoureth his father: ... if then I be a Father, where is My honour?... Ye have brought that which was taken by violence, and the lame, and the sick; ... should I accept this of your hand? saith the Lord." And as pointing to our Lord, the command was no less fitting. Thus, as in other sacrifices, it was foreshadowed that the great Burnt-offering of the future would be the one Man without blemish, the absolutely perfect Exemplar of what manhood should be, but is not.

And this brings us now to the ritual of the offering. In the ritual of the various bloody offerings we find six parts. These are: (1) the Presentation; (2) the Laying on of the Hand; (3) the Killing of the Victim; in which three the ritual was the same for all kinds of offerings. The remaining three are: (4) the Sprinkling of Blood; (5) the Burning; (6) the Sacrificial Meal. In these, differences appear in the various sacrifices, which give each its distinctive character; and, in the burnt-offering, the sacrificial meal is omitted,—the whole is burnt upon the altar.

First is given the law concerning

The Presentation of the Victim.

"He shall offer it at the door of the tent of meeting, that he may be accepted before the Lord" (ver. 3).

In this it was ordered, first, that the offerer should bring the victim himself. There were parts of the ceremony in which the priest acted for him; but this he must do for himself. Even so, he who will have the saving benefit of Christ's sacrifice must himself bring this Christ before the Lord. As by so doing, the Israelite signified his acceptance of God's gracious arrangements concerning sacrifice, so do we, bringing Christ in our act of faith before the Lord, express our acceptance of God's arrangement on our behalf; our readiness and sincere desire to make use of Christ, who is appointed for us. And this no man can do for another.

And the offering must be presented for a certain purpose; namely, "that he may be accepted before the Lord;"[7] and that, as the context tells us, not because of a present made to God, but through an atoning sacrifice. And so now it is not enough that a man make much of Christ, and mention Him in terms of praise before the Lord, as the One whom He would imitate and seek to serve. He must in his act of faith bring this Christ before the Lord, in such wise as to secure thus his personal acceptance through the blood of the Holy Victim.

And, finally, the *place* of presentation is prescribed. It must be "at the door of the tent of meeting." It is easy to see the original reason for this. For, as we learn from other Scriptures, the Israelites were ever prone to idolatry, and that especially at places other than the appointed temple or tent of meeting, in the fields and on high places. Hence the immediate purpose of this order concerning the place, was to separate the worship of God from the worship of false gods. There is now, indeed, no law concerning the place where we may present the great Sacrifice before God. At home, in the closet, in the church, on the street, wherever we will, we may present this Christ in our behalf and stead as a Holy Victim before God. And yet the principle which underlies this ordinance of place is no less applicable in this age than then. For it is a prohibition of all self-will in worship. It was not enough that an Israelite should have the prescribed victim; it is not enough that we present the Christ of God in faith, or what we think to be faith. But we must make no terms or conditions as to the mode or condition of the presentation, other than God appoints. And the command was also a command of publicity. The Israelite was therein commanded to confess publicly, and thus attest, his faith in Jehovah, even as God will now have us all make our confession of Christ a public thing.

The second act of the ceremonial was

The Laying on of the Hand.

It was ordered:

> "He shall lay his hand upon the head of the burnt offering; and it shall be accepted for him, to make atonement for him" (ver. 4).

The laying on of the hand was not, as some have maintained, a mere declaration of the offerer's property in that which he offered, as showing his right to give it to God. If this were true, we should find the ceremony also in the bloodless offerings; where the cakes of corn were no less the property of the offerer than the bullock or sheep of the burnt-offering. But the ceremony was confined to these bloody offerings.

It is nearer the truth when others say that this was an act of designation. It is a fact that the ceremony of the laying on of hands in Scripture usage does indicate a designation of a person or thing, as to some office or service. In this book (xxiv. 14), the witnesses are directed to lay their hands upon the blasphemer, thereby appointing him to death. Moses is said to have laid his hands on Joshua, thus designating him in a formal way as his successor; and, in the New Testament, Paul and Barnabas are set apart to the ministry by the laying on of hands. But, in all these cases, the ceremony symbolised more than mere designation; namely, a transfer or communication of something invisible, in connection with this visible act. Thus, in the New Testament the laying on of hands always denotes the communication of the Holy Ghost, either as an enduement for office, or for bodily healing. The laying of the hands of Moses on Joshua, in like manner, signified the transfer to him of the gifts, office, and authority of Moses. Even in the case of the execution of the blaspheming son of Shelomith, the laying on of the hands of the witnesses had the same significance. They thereby designated him to death, no doubt; but therewith thus symbolically transferred to the criminal the responsibility for his own death.

From the analogy of these cases we should expect to find evidence of an ideal transference of somewhat from the offerer to the victim here. And the context does not leave the matter doubtful. It is added (ver. 4), "It shall be accepted for him, to make atonement for him." Hence it appears that while, indeed, the offerer, by this laying on of his hand, did dedicate the victim to death, the act meant more than this. It symbolised a transfer, according to God's merciful provision, of an obligation to suffer for sin, from the offerer to the innocent victim. Henceforth, the victim stood in the offerer's place, and was dealt with accordingly.

This is well illustrated by the account which is given (Numb. viii.) of the formal substitution of the Levites in the place of all the first-born of Israel, for special service unto God. We read that the Levites were presented before the Lord; and that the children of Israel then laid their hands upon the heads of the Levites, who were thus, we are told, "offered as an offering unto the Lord," and were thenceforth regarded and treated as substitutes for the first-born of all Israel. Thus the obligation to certain special service was symbolically transferred, as the context tells us, from the first-born to the Levites; and this transfer of obligation from all the tribes to the single tribe of Levi was visibly represented by the laying on of hands. And just so here: the laying on of the hand designated, certainly, the victim to death; but it did this, in that it was the symbol of a transfer of obligation.

This view of the ceremony is decisively confirmed by the ritual of the great day of atonement. In the sin-offering of that day, in which the conception of expiation by blood received its fullest symbolic expression, it was ordered (xvi. 21) that Aaron should lay his hands on the head of one of the goats of the sin-offering, and "confess over him all the iniquities of the children of Israel." Thereupon the iniquity of the nation was regarded as symbolically transferred from Israel to the goat; for it is added, "and the goat shall bear upon him all their iniquities unto a solitary land." So, while in this ritual for the burnt-offering there is no mention of such confession, we have every reason to believe the uniform Rabbinical tradition, that it was the custom to make also upon the head of the victim for the burnt-offering a solemn confession of sin, for which they give the form to be used.

Such then was the significance of the laying on of hands. But the ceremony meant even more than this. For the Hebrew verb which is always used for this, as the Rabbis point out, does not merely mean to lay the hand upon, but so to lay the hand as to rest or lean heavily upon the victim.

This force of the word is well illustrated from a passage where it occurs, in Psalm lxxxviii. 7, "Thy wrath lieth hard upon me." The ceremony, therefore, significantly represented the offerer as resting or relying on the victim to procure that from God for which he presented him, namely, atonement and acceptance.

This part of the ceremonial of this and other sacrifices was thus full of spiritual import and typical meaning. By this laying on of the hand to designate the victim as a sacrifice, the offerer implied, and probably expressed, a confession of personal sin and demerit; as done "before Jehovah," it implied also his acceptance of God's penal judgment against his sin. It implied, moreover, in that the offering was made according to an arrangement ordained by God, that the offerer also thankfully accepted God's merciful provision for atonement, by which the obligation to suffer for sin was transferred from himself, the guilty sinner, to the sacrificial victim. And, finally, in that the offerer was directed so to lay his hand as to rest upon the victim, it was most expressively symbolised that he, the sinful Israelite, rested and depended on this sacrifice as the atonement for his sin, his divinely appointed substitute in penal death.

What could more perfectly set forth the way in which we are for our salvation to make use of the Lamb of God as slain for us? By faith, we lay the hand upon His head. In this, we do frankly and penitently own the sins for which, as the great Burnt-sacrifice, the Christ of God was offered; we also, in humility and self-abasement, thus accept the judgment of God against ourselves, that because of sin we deserve to be cast out from Him eternally; while, at the same time, we most thankfully accept this Christ as "the Lamb of God which taketh away the sins of the world," and therefore our sins also, if we will but thus make use of Him; and so lean and rest with all the burden of our sin on Him.

For the Israelite who should thus lay his hand upon the head of the sacrificial victim a promise follows. "It shall be accepted for him, to make atonement for him."

In this word "atonement" we are introduced to one of the key-words of Leviticus, as indeed of the whole Scripture. The Hebrew radical originally means "to cover," and is used once (Gen. vi. 14) in this purely physical sense. But, commonly, as here, it means "to cover" in a spiritual sense, that is, to cover the sinful person from the sight of the Holy God, who is "of purer eyes than to behold evil." Hence, it is commonly rendered "to atone," or "to make atonement;" also, "to reconcile," or "to make reconciliation." The thought is this: that between the sinner and the Holy One comes now the guiltless victim; so that the eye of God looks not upon the sinner, but on the offered substitute; and in that the blood of the substituted victim is offered before God for the sinner, atonement is made for sin, and the Most Holy One is satisfied.

And when the believing Israelite should lay his hand with confession of sin upon the appointed victim, it was graciously promised: "It shall be accepted for him, to make atonement for him." And just so now, whenever any guilty sinner, fearing the deserved wrath of God because of his sin, especially because of his lack of that full consecration which the burnt-sacrifice set forth, lays his hand in faith upon the great Burnt-offering of Calvary, the blessing is the same. For in the light of the cross, this Old Testament word becomes now a sweet New Testament promise: "When thou shalt rest with the hand of faith upon this Lamb of God, He shall be accepted for thee, to make atonement for thee."

This is most beautifully expressed in an ancient "Order for the Visitation of the Sick," attributed to Anselm of Canterbury, in which it is written:—

"The minister shall say to the sick man: Dost thou believe that thou canst not be saved but by the death of Christ? The sick man answereth, Yes. Then let it be said unto him: Go to, then, and whilst thy soul abideth in thee, put all thy confidence in this death alone; place thy trust in no other thing; commit thyself wholly to this death; cover thyself wholly with this alone.... And if God would judge thee, say: Lord! I place the death of our Lord Jesus Christ between me and Thy judgment; otherwise I will not contend or enter into judgment with Thee.

"And if He shall say unto thee that thou art a sinner, say: I place the death of our Lord Jesus Christ between me and my sins. If He shall say unto thee, that thou hast deserved damnation, say: Lord! I put the death of our Lord Jesus Christ between Thee and all my sins; and I offer His merits for my own, which I should have, and have not."

And whosoever of us can thus speak, to him the promise speaks from out the shadows of the tent of meeting: "This Christ, the Lamb of God, the true Burnt-offering, shall be accepted for thee, to make atonement for thee!"

CHAPTER III
THE BURNT-OFFERING (CONCLUDED)

Lev. i. 5-17; vi. 8-13.

After the laying on of the hand, the next sacrificial act was—

The Killing of the Victim.

"And he shall kill the bullock before the Lord" (ver. 5).

In the light of what has been already said, the significance of this killing, in a typical way, will be quite clear. For with the first sin, and again and again thereafter, God had denounced death as the penalty of sin. But here is a sinner who, in accord with a Divine command, brings before God a sacrificial victim, on whose head he lays his hand, on which he thus rests as he confesses his sins, and gives over the innocent victim to die instead of himself. Thus each of these sacrificial deaths, whether in the burnt-offering, the peace-offering, or the sin-offering, brings ever before us the death in the sinner's stead of that one Holy Victim who suffered for us, "the just for the unjust," and thus laid down His life, in accord with His own previously declared intention, "as a ransom for many."

In the sacrifices made by and for individuals, the victim was killed, except in the case of the turtle-dove or pigeon, by the offerer himself; but, very naturally, in the case of the national and public offerings, it was killed by the priest. As, in this latter case, it was impossible that all individual Israelites should unite in killing the victim, it is plain that the priest herein acted as the representative of the nation. Hence we may properly say that the fundamental thought of the ritual was this, that the victim should be killed by the offerer himself.

And by this ordinance we may well be reminded, first, how Israel,—for whose sake as a nation the antitypical Sacrifice was offered,—Israel itself became the executioner of the Victim; and, beyond that, how, in a deeper sense, every sinner must regard himself as truly causal of the Saviour's death, in that, as is often truly said, our sins nailed Christ to His cross. But whether such a reference were intended in this law of the offering or not, the great, significant, outstanding fact remains, that as soon as the offerer, by his laying on of the hand, signified the transfer of the personal obligation to die for sin from himself to the sacrificial victim, then came at once upon that victim the penalty denounced against sin.

And the added words, "before the Lord," cast further light upon this, in that they remind us that the killing of the victim had reference to Jehovah, whose holy law the offerer, failing of that perfect consecration which the burnt-offering symbolised, had failed to glorify and honour.

The Sprinkling of Blood.

> "And Aaron's sons, the priests, shall present the blood, and sprinkle the blood round about upon the altar that is at the door of the tent of meeting" (ver. 5).

And now follows the fourth act in the ceremonial, the Sprinkling of the Blood. The offerer's part is now done, and herewith the work of the priest begins. Even so must we, having laid the hand of faith upon the head of the substituted Lamb of God, now leave it to the heavenly Priest to act in our behalf with God.

The directions to the priest as to the use of the blood vary in the different offerings, according as the design is to give greater or less prominence to the idea of expiation. In the sin-offering this has the foremost place. But in the burnt-offering, as also in the peace-offering, although the conception of atonement by blood was not absent, it was not the dominant conception of the sacrifice. Hence, while the sprinkling of blood by the priest could in no wise be omitted, it took in this case a subordinate place in the ritual. It was to be sprinkled only on the sides of the altar of burnt-offering which stood in the outer court. We read (ver. 5): "Aaron's sons, the priests, shall present the blood, and sprinkle the blood round about upon the altar that is at the door of the tent of meeting."

It was in this sprinkling of the blood that the atoning work was completed. The altar had been appointed as a place of Jehovah's special presence; it had been designated as a place where God would come unto man to bless him. Thus, to present and sprinkle the blood upon the altar was symbolically to present the blood unto God. And the blood represented life,—the life of an innocent victim atoning for the sinner, because rendered up in the stead of his life. And the *priests* were to sprinkle the blood. So, while to bring and present the sacrifice of Christ, to lay the hand of faith upon His head, is our part, with this our duty ends. To sprinkle the blood, to use the blood God-ward for the remission of sin, this is the work alone of our heavenly Priest. We are then to leave that with Him.

Reserving a fuller exposition of the meaning of this sprinkling of blood for the exposition of the sin-offering, in which it was the central act of the ritual, we pass on now to the burning of the sacrifice, which in this offering marked the culmination of its special symbolism.

The Sacrificial Burning.

i. 6-9, 12, 13, 17.

"And he shall flay the burnt offering, and cut it into its pieces. And the sons of Aaron the priest shall put fire upon the altar, and lay wood in order upon the fire: and Aaron's sons, the priests, shall lay the pieces, the head, and the fat, in order upon the wood that is on the fire which is upon the altar: but its inwards and its legs shall he wash with water: and the priest shall burn the whole on the altar, for a burnt offering, an offering made by fire, of a sweet savour unto the Lord.... And he shall cut it into its pieces, with its head and its fat: and the priest shall lay them in order on the wood that is on the fire which is upon the altar: but the inwards and the legs shall he wash with water: and the priest shall offer the whole, and burn it upon the altar: it is a burnt offering, an offering made by fire, of a sweet savour unto the Lord.... And he shall rend it by the wings thereof, but shall not divide it asunder: and the priest shall burn it upon the altar, upon the wood that is upon the fire: it is a burnt offering, an offering made by fire, of a sweet savour unto the Lord."

It was the distinguishing peculiarity of the burnt-offering, from which it takes its name, that in every case the whole of it was burned, and thus ascended heavenward in the fire and smoke of the altar. The place of the burning, in this and other sacrifices, is significant. The flesh of the sin-offering, when not eaten, was to be burned in a clean place without the camp. But it was the law of the burnt-offering that it should be wholly consumed upon the holy altar at the door of the tent of meeting. In the directions for the burning we need seek for no occult meaning; the most of them are evidently intended simply as means to the end; namely, the consumption of the offering with the utmost readiness, ease, and completeness. Hence it must be flayed and cut into its pieces, and carefully arranged upon the wood. The inwards and the legs must be washed with water, that into the offering, as to be offered to the Holy One, might come nothing extraneous, nothing corrupt and unclean.

In vv. 10-13 and 14-17 provision is made for the offering of different victims, of the flock, or of the fowls. The reason for this permitted variation, although not mentioned here, was doubtless the same which is given for a similar permission in chap. v. 7, where it is ordered that if the offerer's means suffice not for a certain offering, he may bring one of less value. Poverty shall be no plea for not bringing a burnt-sacrifice; to the Israelite of that time it thus set forth the truth, that "if there first be a willing heart, it is accepted according to that a man hath, and not according to that he hath not."

The variations in the prescriptions regarding the different victims to be used in the sacrifice are but slight. The bird having been killed by the priest (why this change it is not easy to see), its crop, with its contents of food unassimilated, and therefore not a part of the bird, as also the feathers, was to be cast away. It was not to be divided, like the bullock, and the sheep or goat, simply because, with so small a creature, it was not necessary to the speedy and entire combustion of the offering. In each case alike, the declaration is made that the sacrifice, thus offered and wholly burnt upon the altar, is "an offering made by fire, of a sweet savour unto the Lord."

And now a question comes before us, the answer to which is vital to the right understanding of the burnt-offering, whether in its original or typical import. What was the significance of the burning? It has been very often answered that the consumption of the victim by fire symbolised the consuming wrath of Jehovah, utterly destroying the victim which represented the sinful person of the offerer. And, observing that the burning followed the killing and shedding of blood, some have even gone so far as to say that the burning typified the eternal fire of hell! But when we remember that, without doubt, the sacrificial victim in all the Levitical offerings was a type of our blessed Lord, we may well agree with one who justly calls this interpretation "hideous." And yet many, who have shrunk from this, have yet in so far held to this conception of the symbolic meaning of the burning as to insist that it must at least have typified those fiery sufferings in which our Lord offered up His soul for sin. They remind us how often, in the Scripture, fire stands as the symbol of the consuming wrath of God against sin, and hence argue that this may justly be taken here as the symbolic meaning of the burning of the victim on the altar.

But this interpretation is nevertheless, in every form, to be rejected. As regards the use of fire as a symbol in Holy Scripture, while it is true that it often represents the punitive wrath of God, it is equally certain that it has not always this meaning. Quite as often it is the symbol of God's purifying energy and might. Fire was not the symbol of Jehovah's vengeance in the burning bush. When the Lord is represented as sitting "as a refiner and a purifier of silver," surely the thought is not of vengeance, but of purifying mercy. We should rather say that fire, in Scripture usage, is the symbol of the intense energy of the Divine nature, which continually acts upon every person and on every thing, according to the nature of each person or thing; here conserving, there destroying; now cleansing, now consuming. The same fire which burns the wood, hay, and stubble, purifies the gold and the silver.

Hence, while it is quite true that fire often typifies the wrath of God punishing sin, it is certain that it cannot always symbolise this, not even in the sacrificial ritual. For in the meal-offering of chap. ii. it is impossible that the thought of expiation should enter since no life is offered and no blood is shed; yet this also is presented unto God in fire. The fire then in this case must mean something else than the Divine wrath, and presumably must mean one thing in all the sacrifices. And that not even in the burnt-offering can the burning of the sacrifice symbolise the consuming wrath of God, becomes plain, when we observe that, according to the uniform teaching of the sacrificial ritual, atonement is already fully accomplished, prior to the burning, in the sprinkling of the blood. That the burning, which follows the atonement, should have any reference to Christ's expiatory sufferings, is thus quite impossible.

We must hold, therefore, that the burning can only mean in the burnt-offering that which alone it can signify in the meal-offering; namely, the ascending of the offering in consecration to God, on the one hand; and, on the other, God's gracious acceptance and appropriation of the offering. This was impressively set forth in the case of the burnt-offering presented when the tabernacle service was inaugurated; when, we are told (ix. 24), the fire which consumed it came forth from before Jehovah, lighted by no human hand, and was thus a visible representation of God accepting and appropriating the offering to Himself.

The symbolism of the burning thus understood, we can now perceive what must have been the special meaning of this sacrifice. As regarded by the believing Israelite of those days, not yet discerning clearly the deeper truth it shadowed forth as to the great Burnt-sacrifice of the future, it must have symbolically taught him that complete consecration unto God is essential to right worship. There were sacrifices having a different special import, in which, while a part was burnt, the offerer might even himself join in eating the remaining part, taking that for his own use. But, in the burnt-offering, nothing was for himself: all was for God; and in the fire of the altar God took the whole in such a way that the offering for ever passed beyond the offerer's recall. In so far as the offerer entered into this conception, and his inward experience corresponded to this outward rite, it was for him an act of worship.

But to the thoughtful worshipper, one would think, it must sometimes have occurred that, after all, it was not himself or his gift that thus ascended in full consecration to God, but a victim appointed by God to represent him in death on the altar. And thus it was that, whether understood or not, the offering in its very nature pointed to a Victim of the future, in whose person and work, as the One only fully-consecrated Man, the burnt-offering should receive its full explication. And this brings us to the question, What aspect of the person and work of our Lord was herein specially typified? It cannot be the resultant fellowship with God, as in the peace-offering; for the sacrificial feast which set this forth was in this case wanting. Neither can it be expiation for sin; for although this is expressly represented here, yet it is not the chief thing. The principal thing, in the burnt-offering, was the burning, the complete consumption of the victim in the sacrificial fire. Hence what is represented chiefly here, is not so much Christ representing His people in atoning death, as Christ representing His people in perfect consecration and entire self-surrender unto God; in a word, in perfect obedience.

Of these two things, the atoning death and the representative obedience, we think, and with reason, much of the former; but most Christians, though without reason, think less of the latter. And yet how much is made of this aspect of our Lord's work in the Gospels! The first words which we hear from His lips are to this effect, when, at twelve years of age, He asked His mother (Luke ii. 49), "Wist ye not that I must be (lit.) in the things of My Father?" and after His official work began in the first cleansing of the temple, this manifestation of His character was such as to remind His disciples that it was written, "The zeal of Thy house shall eat me up";—phraseology which brings the burnt-offering at once to mind.[8] And His constant testimony concerning Himself, to which His whole life bare witness, was in such words as these: "I came down from heaven, not to do My own will, but the will of Him that sent Me." In particular, He especially regarded His atoning work in this aspect. In the parable of the Good Shepherd (John x. 1-18), for example, after telling us that because of His laying down His life for the sheep the Father loved Him, and that to this end He had received from the Father authority to lay down His life for the sheep, He then adds as the reason of this: "This commandment have I received from My Father." And so elsewhere (John xii. 49, 50) He says of all His words, as of all His works: "The Father hath given Me a commandment, what I should say, and what I should speak; ... the things therefore which I speak, even as the Father hath said unto Me, so I speak." And when at last His earthly work approaches its close, and we see Him in the agony of Gethsemane, there He appears, above all, as the perfectly consecrated One, offering Himself, body, soul, and spirit, as a whole burnt-offering unto God, in those never-to-be-forgotten words (Matt. xxvi. 39), "Father, if it be possible, let this cup pass away from Me; nevertheless, not as I will, but as Thou wilt." And, if any more proof were needed, we have it in that inspired exposition (Heb. x. 5-10) of Psalm xl. 6-8 wherein it is taught that this perfect obedience of Christ, in full consecration, was indeed the very thing which the Holy Ghost foresignified in the whole burnt-offerings of the law: "When He cometh into the world, He saith, Sacrifice and offering Thou wouldest not, but a body didst Thou prepare for Me; in whole burnt-offerings and sacrifices for sin Thou hadst no pleasure: then said I, Lo, I am come (in the roll of the book it is written of Me) to do Thy will, O God."

Thus the burnt-offering brings before us in type, for our faith, Christ as our Saviour in virtue of His being the One wholly surrendered to the will of the Father. Nor does this exclude, but rather defines, the conception of Christ as our substitute and representative. For He said that it was for our sakes that He "sanctified," or "consecrated" Himself (John xvii. 19); and while the New Testament represents Him as saving us by His death as an expiation for sin, it no less explicitly holds Him forth to us as having obeyed in our behalf, declaring (Rom. v. 19) that it is "by the obedience of the One Man" that "many are made righteous." And, elsewhere, the same Apostle represents the incomparable moral value of the atoning death of the cross as consisting precisely in this fact, that it was a supreme act of self-renouncing obedience, as it is written (Phil. ii. 6-9): "Being in the form of God, He yet counted it not a prize to be on an equality with God, but emptied Himself, taking the form of a servant, being made in the likeness of men; ... becoming obedient even unto death, yea, the death of the cross. Wherefore also God highly exalted Him, and gave unto Him the name which is above every name."

And so the burnt-offering teaches us to remember that Christ has not only died for our sins, but has also consecrated Himself for us to God in full self-surrender in our behalf. We are therefore to plead not only His atoning death, but also the transcendent merit of His life of full consecration to the Father's will. To this, the words, three times repeated concerning the burnt-offering (vv. 9, 13, 17), in this chapter, blessedly apply: it is "an offering made by fire, of a sweet savour," a fragrant odour, "unto the Lord." That is, this full self-surrender of the holy Son of God unto the Father is exceedingly delightful and acceptable unto God. And for this reason it is for us an ever-prevailing argument for our own acceptance, and for the gracious bestowment for Christ's sake of all that there is in Him for us.

Only let us ever remember that we cannot argue, as in the case of the atoning death, that as Christ died that we might not die, so He offered Himself in full consecration unto God, that we might thus be released from this obligation. Here the exact opposite is the truth. For Christ Himself said in His memorable prayer, just before His offering of Himself to death, "For their sakes I sanctify (marg. "consecrate") Myself, *that they also might be sanctified in truth.*" And thus is brought before us the thought, that if the sin-offering emphasised, as we shall see, the substitutionary death of Christ, whereby He became our righteousness, the burnt-offering, as distinctively, brings before us Christ as our sanctification, offering Himself without spot, a whole burnt-offering to God. And as by that one life of sinless obedience to the will of the Father He procured our salvation by His merit, so in this respect He has also become our one perfect Example of what consecration to God really is. A thought this is which, with evident allusion to the burnt-offering, the Apostle Paul brings before us, charging us (Eph. v. 2) that we "walk in love, as Christ also loved us, and gave Himself for us, an offering and a sacrifice to God for an odour of a sweet smell."

And the law further suggests that no extreme of spiritual need can debar any one from availing himself of our great Burnt-sacrifice. A burnt-offering was to be received even from one who was so poor that he could bring but a turtle-dove or a young pigeon (ver. 14). One might, at first thought, not unnaturally say: Surely there can be nothing in this to point to Christ; for the true Sacrifice is not many, but one and only. And yet the very fact of this difference allowed in the typical victims, when the reason of the allowance is remembered, suggests the most precious truth concerning Christ, that no spiritual poverty of the sinner need exclude him from the full benefit of Christ's saving work. Provision is made in Him for all those who, most truly and with most reason, feel themselves to be poor and in need of all things. Christ, as our sanctification, is for all who will make use of Him; for all who, feeling most deeply and painfully their own failure in full consecration, would take Him, as not only their sin-offering, but also their burnt-offering, both their example and their strength, unto perfect self-surrender unto God. We may well here recall to mind the exhortation of the Apostle to Christian believers, expressed in language which at once reminds us of the burnt-offering (Rom. xii. 1): "I beseech you, brethren, by the mercies of God, to present your bodies a living sacrifice, holy, acceptable to God, which is your reasonable service."

The Continual Burnt-offering.

vi. 8-13.

"And the Lord spake unto Moses, saying, Command Aaron and his sons, saying, This is the law of the burnt offering: the burnt offering shall be on the hearth upon the altar all night unto the morning; and the fire of the altar shall be kept burning thereon. And the priest shall put on his linen garment, and his linen breeches shall he put upon his flesh; and he shall take up the ashes whereto the fire hath consumed the burnt offering on the altar, and he shall put them beside the altar. And he shall put off his garments, and put on other garments, and carry forth the ashes without the camp unto a clean place. And the fire upon the altar shall be kept burning thereon, it shall not go out; and the priest shall burn wood on it every morning: and he shall lay the burnt offering in order upon it, and shall burn thereon the fat of the peace offerings. Fire shall be kept burning upon the altar continually; it shall not go out."

In chap. vi. 8-13 we have a "law of the burnt-offering" specially addressed to "Aaron and his sons," and designed to secure that the fire of the burnt-offering should be continually ascending unto God. In chap. i. we have the law regarding burnt-offerings brought by the individual Israelite. But besides these it was ordered, Exod. xxix. 38-46, that every morning and evening the priest should offer a lamb as a burnt-offering for the whole people,—an offering which primarily symbolised the constant renewal of Israel's consecration as "a kingdom of priests" unto the Lord. It is to this, the daily burnt-offering, that this supplementary law of chap. vi. refers. All the regulations are intended to provide for the uninterrupted maintenance of this sacrificial fire; first, by the regular removal of the ashes which would else cover and smother the fire; and, secondly, by the supply of fuel. The removal of the ashes from the fire is a priestly function; hence it was ordained that the priest for this service put on his robes of office, "his linen garment and his linen breeches," and then take up the ashes from the altar, and lay them by the side of the altar. But as from time to time it would be necessary to remove them from this place quite without the tent, it was ordered that he should carry them forth "without the camp unto a clean place," that the sanctity of all connected with Jehovah's worship might never be lost sight of; though, as it was forbidden to wear the priestly garments except within the tent of meeting, the priest, when this service was performed, must "put on other garments," his ordinary, unofficial robes. The ashes being thus removed from the altar each morning, then the wood was put on, and the parts of the lamb laid in order upon it to be perfectly consumed. And whenever during the day any one might bring a peace-offering unto the Lord, on this ever-burning fire the priest was to place also the fat, the richest part, of the offering, and with it also the various individual burnt-offerings and meal-offerings of each day. And thus it was arranged by the law that, all day long, and all night long, the smoke of the burnt-offering should be continually ascending unto the Lord.

The significance of this can hardly be missed. By this supplemental law which thus provided for "a continual burnt-offering" to the Lord, it was first of all signified to Israel, and to us, that the consecration which the Lord so desires and requires from His people is not occasional, but continuous. As the priest, representing the nation, morning by morning cleared away the ashes which had else covered the flame and caused it to burn dull, and both morning by morning and evening by evening, laid a new victim on the altar, so will God have us do. Our self-consecration is not to be occasional, but continual and habitual. Each morning we should imitate the priest of old, in putting away all that might dull the flame of our devotion, and, morning by morning, when we arise, and evening by evening, when we retire, by a solemn act of self-consecration give ourselves anew unto the Lord. So shall the word in substance, thrice repeated, be fulfilled in us in its deepest, truest sense: "The fire shall be kept burning on the altar continually; it shall not go out" (vv. 9, 12, 13).

But we must not forget that in this part of the law, as in all else, we are pointed to Christ. This ordinance of the continual burnt-offering reminds us that Christ, as our burnt-offering, *continually* offers Himself to God in self-consecration in our behalf. Very significant it is that the burnt-offering stands in contrast in this respect with the sin-offering. We never read of a continual sin-offering; even the great annual sin-offering of the day of atonement, which, like the daily burnt-offering, had reference to the nation at large, was soon finished, and once for all. And it was so with reason; for in the nature of the case, our Lord's offering of Himself for sin as an expiatory sacrifice was not and could not be a continuous act. But with His presentation of Himself unto God in full consecration of His person as our Burnt-offering, it is different. Throughout the days of His humiliation this self-offering of Himself to God continued; nor, indeed, can we say that it has yet ceased, or ever can cease. For still, as the High Priest of the heavenly sanctuary, He continually offers Himself as our Burnt-offering in constantly renewed and constantly continued devotement of Himself to the Father to do His will.

In this ordinance of the daily burnt-offering, ever ascending in the fire that never went out, the idea of the burnt-sacrifice reaches its fullest expression, the type its most perfect development. And thus the law of the burnt-offering leaves us in the presence of this holy vision: the greater than Aaron, in the heavenly place as our great Representative and Mediator, morning by morning, evening by evening, offering Himself unto the Father in the full self-devotement of His risen life unto God, as our "continual burnt-offering." In this, let us rejoice and be at peace.

CHAPTER IV
THE MEAL-OFFERING

Lev. ii. 1-16; vi. 14-23.

The word which in the original uniformly stands for the English "meal-offering" (A.V. "meat-offering," *i.e.*, "food-offering") primarily means simply "a present," and is often properly so translated in the Old Testament. It is, for example, the word which is used (Gen. xxxii. 13) when we are told how Jacob sent a present to Esau his brother; or, later, of the gift sent by Israel to his son Joseph in Egypt (Gen. xliii. 11); and, again (2 Sam. viii. 2), of the gifts sent by the Moabites to David. Whenever thus used of gifts to men, it will be found that it suggests a recognition of the dignity and authority of the person to whom the present is made, and, in many cases, a desire also to procure thereby his favour.

In the great majority of cases, however, the word is used of offerings to God, and in this use one or both of these ideas can easily be traced. In Gen. iv. 4, 5, in the account of the offerings of Cain and Abel, the word is applied both to the bloody and the unbloody offering; but in the Levitical law, it is only applied to the latter. We thus find the fundamental idea of the meal-offering to be this: it was a gift brought by the worshipper to God, in token of his recognition of His supreme authority, and as an expression of desire for His favour and blessing.

But although the meal-offering, like the burnt-offering, was an offering made to God by fire, the differences between them were many and significant. In the burnt-offering, it was always a life that was given to God; in the meal-offering, it was never a life, but always the products of the soil. In the burnt-offering, again, the offerer always set apart the offering by the laying on of the hand, signifying thus, as we have seen, a transfer of obligation to death for sin; thus connecting with the offering, in addition to the idea of a gift to God, that of expiation for sin, as preliminary to the offering by fire. In the meal-offering, on the other hand, there was no laying on of the hand, as there was no shedding of blood, so that the idea of expiation for sin is in no way symbolised. The conception of a gift to God, which, though dominant in the burnt-offering, is not in that the only thing symbolised, in the meal-offering becomes the *only* thought the offering expresses.

It is further to be noted that not only must the meal-offering consist of the products of the soil, but of such alone as grow, not spontaneously, but by cultivation, and thus represent the result of man's labour. Not only so, but this last thought is the more emphasised, that the grain of the offering was not to be presented to the Lord in its natural condition as harvested, but only when, by grinding, sifting, and often, in addition, by cooking in various ways, it has been more or less fully prepared to become the food of man. In any case, it must, at least, be parched, as in the variety of the offering which is last mentioned in the chapter (vv. 14-16).

With these fundamental facts before us, we can now see what must have been the primary and distinctive significance of the meal-offering, considered as an act of worship. As the burnt-offering represented the consecration of the life, the person, to God, so the meal-offering represented the consecration of the fruit of his labours.

If it be asked, why it was that when man's labours are so manifold, and their results so diverse, the product of the cultivation of the soil should be alone selected for this purpose, for this, several reasons may be given. In the first place, of all the occupations of man, the cultivation of the soil is that of by far the greatest number, and so, in the nature of the case, must continue to be; for the sustenance of man, so far as he is at all above the savage condition, comes, in the last analysis, from the soil. Then, in particular, the Israelites of those days of Moses were about to become an agricultural nation. Most natural and suitable, then, it was that the fruit of the activities of such a people should be symbolised by the product of their fields. And since even those who gained their living in other ways than by the cultivation of the ground, must needs purchase with their earnings grain and oil, the meal-offering would, no less for them than for others, represent the consecration to God of the fruit of their labour.

The meal-offering is no longer an ordinance of worship, but the duty which it signified remains in full obligation still. Not only, in general, are we to surrender our persons without reserve to the Lord, as in the burnt-offering, but unto Him must also be consecrated all our works.

This is true, first of all, regarding our religious service. Each of us is sent into the world to do a certain spiritual work among our fellow-men. This work and all the result of it is to be offered as a holy meal-offering to the Lord. A German writer has beautifully set forth this significance of the meal-offering as regards Israel. "Israel's bodily calling was the cultivation of the ground in the land given him by Jehovah. The fruit of his calling, under the

Divine blessing, was corn and wine, his bodily food, which nourished and sustained his bodily life. Israel's spiritual calling was to work in the field of the kingdom of God, in the vineyard of his Lord; this work was Israel's covenant obligation. Of this, the fruit was the spiritual bread, the spiritual nourishment, which should sustain and develop his spiritual life."[9] And the calling of the spiritual Israel, which is the Church, is still the same, to labour in the field of the kingdom of God, which is the world of men; and the result of this work is still the same, namely, with the Divine blessing, spiritual fruit, sustaining and developing the spiritual life of men. And in the meal-offering we are reminded that the fruit of all our spiritual labours is to be offered to the Lord.

The reminder might seem unneedful, as indeed it ought to be; but it is not. For it is sadly possible to call Christ "Lord," and, labouring in His field, do in His name many wonderful works, yet not really unto Him. A minister of the Word may with steady labour drive the ploughshare of the law, and sow continually the undoubted seed of the Word in the Master's field; and the apparent result of his work may be large, and even real, in the conversion of men to God, and a great increase of Christian zeal and activity. And yet it is quite possible that a man do this, and still do it for himself, and not for the Lord; and when success comes, begin to rejoice in his evident skill as a spiritual husbandman, and in the praise of man which this brings him; and so, while thus rejoicing in the fruit of his labours, neglect to bring of this good corn and wine which he has raised for a daily meal-offering in consecration to the Lord. Most sad is this, and humiliating, and yet sometimes it so comes to pass.

And so, indeed, it may be in every department of religious activity. The present age is without its like in the wonderful variety of its enterprise in matters benevolent and religious. On every side we see an ever-increasing army of labourers driving their various work in the field of the world. City Missions of every variety, Poor Committees with their free lodgings and soup-kitchens, Young Men's Christian Associations, Blue Ribbon Societies, the White Cross Army and the Red Cross Army, Hospital Work, Prison Reform, and so on;—there is no enumerating all the diverse improved methods of spiritual husbandry around us, nor can any one rightly depreciate the intrinsic excellence of all this, or make light of the work or of its good results. But for all this, there are signs that many need to be reminded that all such labour in God's field, however God may graciously make use of it, is not necessarily labour for God; that labour for the good of men is not therefore of necessity labour consecrated to the Lord. For can we believe that from all this the meal-offering is always brought to Him? The ordinance of this offering needs to be remembered by us all in connection with these things. The fruit of all these our labours must be offered daily in solemn consecration to the Lord.

But the teaching of the meal-offering reaches further than to what we call religious labours. For in that it was appointed that the offering should consist of man's daily food, Israel was reminded that God's claim for full consecration of all our activities covers everything, even to the very food we eat. There are many who consecrate, or think they consecrate, their religious activities; but seem never to have understood that the consecration of the true Israelite must cover the secular life as well,—the labour of the hand in the field, in the shop, the transactions of the office or on 'Change, and all their results, as also the recreations which we are able to command, the very food and drink which we use,—in a word, all the results and products of our labours, even in secular things. And to bring this idea vividly before Israel, it was ordered that the meal-offering should consist of food, as the most common and universal visible expression of the fruit of man's secular activities. The New Testament has the same thought (1 Cor. x. 31): "Whether ye eat or drink, or whatsoever ye do, do all to the glory of God."

And the offering was not to consist of any food which one might choose to bring, but of corn and oil, variously prepared. Not to speak yet of any deeper reason for this selection, there is one which lies quite on the surface. For these were the most common and universal articles of the food of the people. There were articles of food, then as now, which were only to be seen on the tables of the rich; but grain, in some form, was and is a necessity for all. So also the oil, which was that of the olive, was something which in that part of the world, all, the poor no less than the rich, were wont to use continually in the preparation of their food; even as it is used to-day in Syria, Italy, and other countries where the olive grows abundantly. Hence it appears that that was chosen for the offering which all, the richest and the poorest alike, would be sure to have; with the evident intent, that no one might be able to plead poverty as an excuse for bringing no meal-offering to the Lord.

Thus, if this ordinance of the meal-offering taught that God's claim for consecration covers all our activities and all their result, even to the very food that we eat, it teaches also that this claim for consecration covers all persons. From the statesman who administers the affairs of an Empire to the day-labourer in the shop, or mill, or field, all alike are hereby reminded that the Lord requires that the work of every one shall be brought and offered to Him in holy consecration.

And there was a further prescription, although not mentioned here in so many words. In some offerings, barley-meal was ordered, but for this offering the grain presented, whether parched, in the ear, or ground into meal, must be only wheat. The reason for this, and the lesson which it teaches, are plain. For wheat, in Israel, as still in most lands, was the best and most valued of the grains. Israel must not only offer unto God of the fruit of their labour, but the best result of their labours. Not only so, but when the offering was in the form of meal, cooked or uncooked, the best and finest must be presented. That, in other words, must be offered which represented the most of care and labour in its preparation, or the equivalent of this in purchase price. Which emphasises, in a slightly different form, the same lesson as the foregoing. Out of the fruit of our several labours and occupations we are to set apart especially for God, not only that which is best in itself, the finest of the wheat, but that which has cost us the most labour. David finely represented this thought of the meal-offering when he said, concerning the cattle for his burnt-offerings, which Araunah the Jebusite would have him accept without price: "I will not offer unto the Lord my God of that which doth cost me nothing."

But in the meal-offering it was not the whole product of his labour that the Israelite was directed to bring, but only a small part. How could the consecration of this small part represent the consecration of all? The answer to this question is given by the Apostle Paul, who calls attention to the fact that in the Levitical symbolism it was ordained that the consecration of a part should signify the consecration of the whole. For he writes (Rom. xi. 16), "If the first-fruit is holy, then the lump"—the whole from which the first-fruit is taken—"is also holy;" that is, the consecration of a part signifies and symbolically expresses the consecration of the whole from which that part is taken. The idea is well illustrated by a custom in India, according to which, when one visits a man of distinction, he will offer the guest a silver coin; an act of social etiquette which is intended to express the thought that all he has is at the service of the guest, and is therewith offered for his use. And so in the meal-offering. By offering to God, in this formal way, a part of the product of his labour, the Israelite expressed a recognition of His claim upon the whole, and professed a readiness to place, not this part merely, but the whole, at God's service.

But in the selection of the materials, we are pointed toward a deeper symbolism, by the injunction that in certain cases, at least, frankincense should be added to the offering. But this was not of man's food, neither was it, like the meal, and cakes, and oil, a product of man's labour. Its effect, naturally, was to give a grateful perfume to the sacrifice, that it might be, even in a physical sense, "an odour of a sweet smell." The symbolical meaning of incense, in which the frankincense was a chief ingredient, is very clearly intimated in Holy Scripture. It is suggested in David's prayer

(Psalm cxli. 2): "Let my prayer be set forth as incense; the lifting up of my hands, like the evening oblation." So, in Luke i. 10, we read of the whole multitude of the people praying without the sanctuary, while the priest Zacharias was offering incense within. And, finally, in the Apocalypse, this is expressly declared to be the symbolical significance of incense; for we read (v. 8), that the four-and-twenty elders "fell down before the Lamb, having ... golden bowls full of incense, which are the prayers of the saints." So then, without doubt, we must understand it here. In that frankincense was to be added to the meal-offering, it is signified that this offering of the fruit of our labours to the Lord must ever be accompanied by prayer; and, further, that our prayers, thus offered in this daily consecration, are most pleasing to the Lord, even as the fragrance of sweet incense unto man.

But if the frankincense, in itself, had thus a symbolical meaning, it is not unnatural to infer the same also with regard to other elements of the sacrifice. Nor is it, in view of the nature of the symbols, hard to discover what that should be.

For inasmuch as that product of labour is selected for the offering, which is the food by which men live, we are reminded that this is to be the final aspect under which all the fruit of our labours is to be regarded; namely, as furnishing and supplying for the need of the many that which shall be bread to the soul. In the highest sense, indeed, this can only be said of Him who by His work became the Bread of Life for the world, who was at once "the Sower" and "the Corn of Wheat" cast into the ground; and yet, in a lower sense, it is true that the work of feeding the multitudes with the bread of life is the work of us all; and that in all our labours and engagements we are to keep this in mind as our supreme earthly object. Just as the products of human labour are most diverse, and yet all are capable of being exchanged in the market for bread for the hungry, so are we to use all the products of our labour with this end in view, that they may be offered to the Lord as cakes of fine meal for the spiritual sustenance of man.

And the oil, too, which entered into every form of the meal-offering, has in Holy Scripture a constant and invariable symbolical meaning. It is the uniform symbol of the Holy Spirit of God. Isaiah lxi. 1 is decisive on this point, where in prophecy the Messiah speaks thus: "The Spirit of the Lord God is upon me; because the Lord God hath anointed me to preach good tidings." Quite in accord with this, we find that when Jesus reached thirty years of age,—the time for beginning priestly service,—He was set apart for His work, not as the Levitical priests, by anointing with symbolical oil, but by the anointing with the Holy Ghost descending on Him at His baptism. So, also, in the Apocalypse, the Church is symbolised by seven golden candlesticks, or lamp-stands, supplied with oil after the manner of that in the temple, reminding us that as the lamp can give light only as supplied with oil, so, if the Church is to be a light in the world, she must be continually supplied with the Spirit of God. Hence, the injunction that the meal of the offering be kneaded with oil, and that, of whatever form the offering be, oil should be poured upon it, is intended, according to this usage, to teach us, that in all work which shall be offered so as to be acceptable to God, must enter, as an inworking and abiding agent, the life-giving Spirit of God.

It is another direction as to these meal-offerings, as also regarding all offerings made by fire, that into them should never enter leaven (ver. 11). The symbolical significance of this prohibition is familiar to all. For in all leaven is a principle of decay and corruption, which, except its continued operation be arrested betimes in our preparation of leavened food, will soon make that in which it works offensive to the taste. Hence, in Holy Scripture, leaven, without a single exception, is the established symbol of spiritual corruption. It is this, both as considered in itself, and in virtue of its power of self-propagation in the leavened mass. Hence the Apostle Paul, using familiar symbolism, charged the Corinthians (1 Cor. v. 7) that they "purge out from themselves the old leaven; and that they keep festival, not with the leaven of malice and wickedness, but with the unleavened bread of sincerity and truth". Thus, in this prohibition is brought before us the lesson, that we take heed to keep out of those works which we present to God for consumption on His altar the leaven of wickedness in every form. The prohibition, in the same connection, of honey (ver. 11) rests upon the same thought; namely, that honey, like leaven, tends to promote fermentation and decay in that with which it is mixed.

The Revised Version—in this case doubtless to be preferred to the other—brings out a striking qualification of this universal prohibition of leaven or honey, in these words (ver. 12): "As an oblation of first-fruits ye shall offer them unto the Lord; but they shall not come up for a sweet savour on the altar."

Thus, as the prohibition of leaven and honey from the meal-offering burned by fire upon the altar reminds us that the Holy One demands absolute freedom from all that is corrupt in the works of His people; on the other hand, this gracious permission to offer leaven and honey in the first-fruits (which were *not* burned on the altar) seems intended to remind us that, nevertheless, from the Israelite in covenant with God through atoning blood, He is yet graciously pleased to accept even offerings in which sinful imperfection is found, so that only, as in the offering of first-fruits, there be the hearty recognition of His rightful claim, before all others, to the first and best we have.

In ver. 13 we have a last requisition as to the material of the meal-offering: "Every oblation of thy meal-offering shalt thou season with salt." As leaven is a principle of impermanence and decay, so salt, on the contrary, has the power of conservation from corruption. Accordingly, to this day, among the most diverse peoples, salt is the recognised symbol of incorruption and unchanging perpetuity. Among the Arabs of to-day, for example, when a compact or covenant is made between different parties, it is the custom that each eat of salt, which is passed around on the blade of a sword; by which act they regard themselves as bound to be true, each to the other, even at the peril of life. In like manner, in India and other Eastern countries, the usual word for perfidy and breach of faith is, literally, "unfaithfulness to the salt;" and a man will say, "Can you distrust me? Have I not eaten of your salt?" That the symbol has this recognised meaning in the meal-offering is plain from the words which follow (ver. 13): "Neither shalt thou suffer the salt of the covenant of thy God to be wanting from thy meal-offering." In the meal-offering, as in all offerings made by fire, the thought was this: that Jehovah and the Israelite, as it were, partake of salt together, in token of the eternal permanence of the holy covenant of salvation into which Israel has entered with God.

Herein we are taught, then, that by the consecration of our labours to God we recognise the relation between the believer and his Lord, as not occasional and temporary, but eternal and incorruptible. In all our consecration of our works to God, we are to keep this thought in mind: "I am a man with whom God has entered into an everlasting covenant, 'a covenant of salt.'"

Three varieties of the meal-offering were prescribed: the first (vv. 1-3), of uncooked meal; the second (vv. 4-11), of the same fine meal and oil, variously prepared by cooking; the third (vv. 14-16), of the first and best ears of the new grain, simply parched in the fire. If any special significance is to be recognised in this variety of the offerings, it may possibly be found in this, that one form might be suited better than another to persons of different resources. It has been supposed that the different implements named—the oven, the baking-pan or plate, the frying-pan—represent, respectively, what different classes of the people might be more or less likely to have. This thought more certainly appears in the permission even of parched grain, which then, as still in the East, while used more or less by all, was especially the food of the poorest of the people; such as might even be too poor to own so much as an oven or a baking-pan.

In any case, the variety which was permitted teaches us, that whatever form the product of our labour may take, as determined either by our poverty or our riches, or by whatever reason, God is graciously willing to accept it, so the oil, frankincense, and salt be not wanting. It is our privilege, as it is our duty, to offer of it in consecration to our redeeming Lord, though it be no more than parched corn. The smallness or meanness of what we have to give, need not keep us back from presenting our meal-offering.

If we have rightly understood the significance of this offering, the ritual which is given will now easily yield us its lessons. As in the case of the burnt-offering, the meal-offering also must be brought unto the Lord by the offerer himself. The consecration of our works, like the consecration of our persons, must be our own voluntary act. Yet the offering must be delivered through the mediation of the priest; the offerer must not presume himself to lay it on the altar. Even so still. In this, as in all else, the Heavenly High Priest must act in our behalf with God. We do not, by our consecration of our works, therefore become able to dispense with His offices as Mediator between us and God. This is the thought of many, but it is a great mistake. No offering made to God, except in and through the appointed Priest, can be accepted of Him.

It was next directed that the priest, having received the offering at the hand of the worshipper, should make a twofold use of it. In the burnt-offering the whole was to be burnt; but in the meal-offering only a small part. The priest was to take out of the offering, in each case, "a memorial thereof, and burn it on the altar"; and then it is added (vv. 3-10), "that which is left of the meal offering" — which was always much the larger part — "shall be Aaron's and his sons'." The small part taken out by the priest for the altar was burnt with fire; and its consumption by the fire of the altar, as in the other offerings, symbolised God's gracious acceptance and appropriation of the offering.

But here the question naturally arises, if the total consecration of the worshipper and his full acceptance by God, in the case of the burnt-offering, was signified by the burning of the whole, how is it that, in this case, where also we must think of a consecration of the whole, yet only a small part was offered to God in the fire of the altar? But the difficulty is only in appearance. For, no less than in the burnt-offering, all of the meal-offering is presented to God, and all is no less truly accepted by Him. The difference in the two cases is only in the use to which God puts the offering. A part of the meal-offering is burnt on the altar as "a memorial," to signify that God takes notice of and graciously accepts the consecrated fruit of our labours. It is called "a memorial" in that, so to speak, it reminded the Lord of the service and devotion of His faithful servant. The thought is well illustrated by the words of Nehemiah (v. 19), who said: "Think upon me, O Lord, for good, according to all that I have done for this people;" and by the word of the angel to Cornelius (Acts x. 4): "Thy prayers and thine alms are gone up for a memorial before God;" for a memorial in such wise as to procure to him a gracious visitation.

The remaining and larger portion of the meal-offering was given to the priest, as being the servant of God in the work of His house. To this service he was set apart from secular occupations, that he might give himself wholly to the duties of this office. In this he must needs be supported; and to this end it was ordained by God that a certain part of the various offerings should be given him, as we shall see more fully hereafter.

In striking contrast with this ordinance, which gave the largest part of the meal-offering to the priest, is the law that of the frankincense he must take nothing; "all" must go up to God, with the "memorial," in the fire of the altar (vv. 2, 16). But in consistency with the symbolism it could not be otherwise. For the frankincense was the emblem of prayer, adoration, and praise; of this, then, the priest must take nought for himself. The manifest lesson is one for all who preach the Gospel. Of the incense of praise which may ascend from the hearts of God's people, as they minister the Word, they must take none for themselves. "Not unto us, O Lord, but unto Thy name be the glory."

Such then was the meaning of the meal-offering. It represents the consecration unto God by the grace of the Holy Spirit, with prayer and praise, of all the work of our hands; an offering with salt, but without leaven, in token of our unchanging covenant with a holy God. And God accepts the offerings thus presented by His people, as a savour of a sweet smell, with which He is well pleased. We have called this consecration a duty; is it not rather a most exalted privilege?

Only let us remember, that although our consecrated offerings are accepted, we are not accepted because of the offerings. Most instructive it is to observe that the meal-offerings were not to be offered alone; a bloody sacrifice, a burnt-offering or sin-offering, must always precede. How vividly this brings before us the truth that it is only when first our persons have been cleansed by atoning blood, and thus and therefore consecrated unto God, that the consecration and acceptance of our works is possible. We are not accepted because we consecrate our works, but our consecrated works themselves are accepted because first we have been "accepted in the Beloved" through faith in the blood of the holy Lamb of God.

The Daily Meal-Offering.

vi. 14-23.

"And this is the law of the meal-offering: the sons of Aaron shall offer it before the Lord, before the altar. And he shall take up therefrom his handful, of the fine flour of the meal-offering and of the oil thereof, and all the frankincense which is upon the meal-offering, and shall burn it upon the altar for a sweet savour, as the memorial thereof, unto the Lord. And that which is left thereof shall Aaron and his sons eat: it shall be eaten without leaven in a holy place: in the court of the tent of meeting they shall eat it. It shall not be baken with leaven. I have given it as their portion of My offerings made by fire; it is most holy, as the sin-offering, and as the guilt-offering. Every male among the children of Aaron shall eat of it, as a due for ever throughout your generations, from the offerings of the Lord made by fire: whosoever toucheth them shall be holy. And the Lord spake unto Moses, saying, This is the oblation of Aaron and of his sons, which they shall offer unto the Lord in the day when he is anointed; the tenth part of an ephah of fine flour for a meal-offering perpetually, half of it in the morning, and half thereof in the evening. On a baking-pan it shall be made with oil; when it is soaked, thou shalt bring it in: in baken pieces shalt thou offer the meal-offering for a sweet savour unto the Lord. And the anointed priest that shall be in his stead from among his sons shall offer it: by a statute for ever it shall be wholly burnt unto the Lord. And every meal-offering of the priest shall be wholly burnt: it shall not be eaten."

As there were not only the burnt-offerings of the individual Israelite, but also a daily burnt-offering, morning and evening, presented by the priest as the representative of the collective nation, so also with the meal-offering. The law concerning this daily meal-offering is given in chap. vi. 19. The amount in this case was prescribed, being apparently the amount regarded as a day's portion of food—"the tenth part of an ephah of fine flour," half of which was to be offered in the morning and half in the evening, made on a baking pan with oil, "for a sweet savour unto the Lord." Unlike the meal-offering of the individual, it is said, "by a statute for ever, it shall be wholly burnt unto the Lord.... Every meal-offering of the priest shall be wholly burnt; it shall not be eaten." This single variation from the ordinance of chap. ii. is simply an application of the principle which governs all the sacrifices except the peace-offering, that he who offered any sacrifice could never himself eat of it; and as the priest in this case was the offerer, the symbolism required that he should himself have nothing of the offering, as being wholly given by him to the Lord. And this meal-offering was to be presented, not merely, as some have inferred from ver. 20, on the day of the anointing of the high priest, but, as is expressly said, "perpetually."

The typical meaning of the meal-offering, and, in particular, of this daily meal-offering, which, as we learn from Exod. xxx. 39, 40, was offered with the daily burnt-offering, is very clear. Every meal-offering pointed to Christ in His consecration of all His works to the Father. And as the daily burnt-offering presented by Aaron and his sons typified our heavenly High Priest as offering His person in daily consecration unto God in our behalf, so, in the daily meal-offering, wholly burnt upon the altar, we see Him in like manner offering unto God in perfect consecration, day by day, perpetually, all His works for our acceptance. To the believer, often sorely oppressed with the sense of the imperfection of his own consecration of his daily works, in that because of this the Father is not glorified by him as He should be, how exceedingly comforting this view of Christ! For that which, at the best, we do so imperfectly and interruptedly, He does in our behalf perfectly, and with never-failing constancy; thus at once perfectly glorifying the Father, and also, through the virtue of the boundless merit of this consecration, constantly procuring for us daily grace unto the life eternal.

CHAPTER V
THE PEACE-OFFERING

Lev. iii. 1-17; vii. 11-34; xix. 5-8; xxii. 21-25.

In chap. iii. is given, though not with completeness, the law of the peace-offering. The alternative rendering of this term, "thank-offering" (marg. R.V.), precisely expresses only one variety of the peace-offering; and while it is probably impossible to find any one word that shall express in a satisfactory way the whole conception of this offering, it is not easy to find one better than the familiar term which the Revisers have happily retained. As will be made clear in the sequel, it was the main object of this offering, as consisting of a sacrifice terminating in a festive sacrificial meal, to express the conception of friendship, peace, and fellowship with God as secured by the shedding of atoning blood.

Like the burnt-offering and the meal-offering, the peace-offering had come down from the times before Moses. We read of it, though not explicitly named, in Gen. xxxi. 54, on the occasion of the covenant between Jacob and Laban, wherein they jointly took God as witness of their covenant of friendship; and, again, in Exod. xviii. 12, where "Jethro took a burnt-offering and sacrifices for God; and Aaron came and all the elders of Israel, to eat bread with Moses' father-in-law before God." Nor was this form of sacrifice, any more than the burnt-offering, confined to the line of Abraham's seed. Indeed, scarcely any religious custom has from the most remote antiquity been more universally observed than this of a sacrifice essentially connected with a sacrificial meal. An instance of the heathen form of this sacrifice is even given in the Pentateuch, where we are told (Exod. xxxii. 6) how the people, having made the golden calf, worshipped it with peace-offerings, and sat down to eat and to drink at the sacrificial meal which was inseparable from the peace-offering; while in 1 Cor. x. Paul refers to like sacrificial feasts as common among the idolaters of Corinth.

It hardly needs to be again remarked that there is nothing in such facts as these to trouble the faith of the Christian, any more than in the general prevalence of worship and of prayer among heathen nations. Rather, in all these cases alike, are we to see the expression on the part of man of a sense of need and want, especially, in this case, of friendship and fellowship with God; and, seeing that the conception of a sacrifice culminating in a feast was, in truth, most happily adapted to symbolise this idea, surely it were nothing strange that God should base the ordinances of His own worship upon such universal conceptions and customs, correcting in them only, as we shall see, what might directly or indirectly misrepresent truth. Where an alphabet, so to speak, is thus already found existing, whether in letters or in symbols, why should the Lord communicate a new and unfamiliar symbolism, which, because new and unfamiliar, would have been, for that reason, far less likely to be understood?

The plan of chap. iii. is very simple; and there is little in its phraseology requiring explanation. Prescriptions are given for the offering of peace-offerings, first, from the herd (vv. 1-5); then, from the flock, whether of the sheep (vv. 6-11) or of the goats (vv. 12-16). After each of these three sections it is formally declared of each offering that it is "a sweet savour," "an offering made by fire," or "the food of the offering made by fire unto the Lord." The chapter then closes with a prohibition, specially occasioned by the directions for this sacrifice, of all use by Israel of fat or blood as food.

The regulations relating to the selection of the victim for the offering differ from those for the burnt-offering in allowing a greater liberty of choice. A female was permitted, as well as a male; though recorded instances of the observance of the peace-offering indicate that the male was even here preferred when obtainable. The offering of a dove or a pigeon is not, however, mentioned as permissible, as in the case of the burnt-offering. But this is no exception to the rule of greater liberty of choice, since these were excluded by the object of the offering as a sacrificial meal, for which, obviously, a small bird would be insufficient. Ordinarily, the victim must be without blemish; and yet, even in this matter, a larger liberty was allowed (chap. xxii. 23) in the case of those which were termed "free-will offerings," where it was permitted to offer even a bullock or a lamb which might have "some part superfluous or lacking." The latitude of choice thus allowed finds its sufficient explanation in the fact that while the idea of representation and expiation had a place in the peace-offering as in all bloody offerings, yet this was subordinate to the chief intent of the sacrifice, which was to represent the victim as food given by God to Israel in the sacrificial meal. It is to be observed that only such defects are therefore allowed in the victim as could not possibly affect its value as food. And so even already, in these regulations as to the selection of the victim, we have a hint that we have now to do with a type, in which the dominant thought is not so much Christ, the Holy Victim, our representative, as Christ the Lamb of God, the food of the soul, through participation in which we have fellowship with God.

As before remarked, the ritual acts in the bloody sacrifices are, in all, six, each of which, in the peace-offering, has its proper place. Of these, the first four, namely, the presentation, the laying on of the hand, the killing of the victim, and the sprinkling of the blood, are precisely the same as in the burnt-offering, and have the same symbolic and typical significance. In both the burnt-offering and the peace-offering, the innocent victim typified the Lamb of God, presented by the sinner in the act of faith to God as an atonement for sin through substitutionary death; and the sprinkling of the blood upon the altar signifies in this, as in the other, the application of that blood Godward by the Divine Priest acting in our behalf, and thereby procuring for us remission of sin, redemption through the blood of the slain Lamb.

In the other two ceremonies, namely, the burning and the sacrificial meal, the peace-offering stands in strong contrast with the burnt-offering. In the burnt-offering all was burned upon the altar; in the peace-offering all the fat, and that only. The detailed directions which are given in the case of each class of victims are intended simply to direct the selection of those parts of the animal in which the fat is chiefly found. They are precisely the same for each, except in the case of the sheep. With regard to such a victim, the particular is added, according to King James's version, "the whole rump;" but the Revisers have with abundant reason corrected this translation, giving it correctly as "the fat tail entire." The change is an instructive one, as it points to the idea which determined this selection of all the fat for the offering by fire. For the reference is to a special breed of sheep which is still found in Palestine, Arabia, and North Africa. With these, the tail grows to an immense size, sometimes weighing fifteen pounds or more, and consists almost entirely of a rich substance, in character between fat and marrow. By the Orientals in the regions where this variety of sheep is found it is still esteemed as the most valuable part of the animal for food. And thus, just as in the meal-offering the Israelite was required to bring out of all his grain the best, and of his meal the finest, so in the peace-offering he is required to bring the fat, and in the case of the sheep this fat tail, as the best and richest parts, to be burnt upon the altar to Jehovah. And the burning, as in the whole burnt-sacrifice, was, so to speak, the visible Divine appropriation of that which was placed upon the altar, the best of the offering, as appointed to be "the food of God." If the symbolism, at first thought, perplex any, we have but to remember how frequently in Scripture "fat" and "fatness" are used as the symbol of that which is richest and best; as, *e.g.*, where the Psalmist says, "They shall be abundantly satisfied with the fatness of Thy house;" and Isaiah, "Come unto Me, and let your soul delight itself in fatness." Thus when, in the peace-offering, of which the larger part was intended for food, it is ordered that the fat should be given to God in the fire of the altar, the same lesson is taught as in the meal-offering, namely, God is ever to be served first and with the best that we have. "All the fat is the Lord's."

In the burnt-offering, the burning ended the ceremonial: in the nature of the case, since all was to be burnt, the object of the sacrifice was attained when the burning was completed. But in the case of the peace-offering, to the burning of the fat upon the altar now followed the culminating act of the ritual, in the eating of the sacrifice. In this, however, we must distinguish from the eating by the offerer and his household, the eating by the priests; of which only the first-named properly belonged to the ceremonial of the sacrifice. The assignment of certain parts of the sacrifice to be eaten by the priests has the same meaning as in the meal-offering. These portions were regarded in the law as given, not by the offerer, but by God, to His servants the priests; that they might eat them, not as a ceremonial act, but as their appointed sustenance from His table whom they served. To this we shall return in a subsequent chapter, and therefore need not dwell upon it here.

This eating of the sacrifice by the priests has thus not yet taken us beyond the conception of the meal-offering, with a part of which they, in like manner, by God's arrangement, were fed. Quite different, however, is the sacrificial eating by the offerer which follows. He had brought the appointed victim; it had been slain in his behalf; the blood had been sprinkled for atonement on the altar; the fat had been taken off and burned upon the altar; the thigh and breast had been given back by God to the officiating priest; and now, last of all, the offerer himself receives back from God, as it were, the remainder of the flesh of the victim, that he himself might eat it before Jehovah. The chapter before us gives no directions as to this sacrificial eating; these are given in Deut. xii. 6, 7, 17, 18, to which passage, in order to the full understanding of that which is most distinctive in the peace-offering, we must refer. In the two verses last named, we have a regulation which covers, not only the peace-offerings, but with them all other sacrificial eatings, thus: "Thou mayest not eat within thy gates the tithe of thy corn, or of thy wine, or of thy oil, or the firstlings of thy herd or of thy flock, nor any of thy vows which thou vowest, nor thy free-will offerings, nor the heave-offering of thy hand: but thou shalt eat them before the Lord thy God in the place which the Lord thy God shall choose, thou and thy son, and thy daughter, and my man-servant, and thy maid-servant, and the Levite that is within thy gates; and thou shalt rejoice before the Lord thy God in all that puttest thy hand unto."

In these directions are three particulars; the offerings were to be eaten, by the offerer, not at his own home, but before Jehovah at the central sanctuary; he was to include in this sacrificial feast all the members of his family, and any Levite that might be stopping with him; and he was to make the feast an occasion of holy joy before the Lord in the labour of his hands. What was now the special significance of all this? As this was the special characteristic of the peace-offering, the answer to this question will point us to its true significance, both for Israel in the first place, and then for us as well, as a type of Him who was to come.

It is not hard to perceive the significance of a feast as a symbol. It is a natural and suitable expression of friendship and fellowship. He who gives the feast thereby shows to the guests his friendship toward them, in inviting them to partake of the food of his house. And if, in any case, there has been an interruption or breach of friendship, such an invitation to a feast, and association in it of the formerly alienated parties, is a declaration on the part of him who gives the feast, as also of those who accept his invitation, that the breach is healed, and that where there was enmity, is now peace.

So natural is this symbolism that, as above remarked, it has been a custom very widely spread among heathen peoples to observe sacrificial feasts, very like to this peace-offering of the Hebrews, wherein a victim is first offered to some deity, and its flesh then eaten by the offerer and his friends. Of such sacrificial feasts we read in ancient Babylonia and Assyria, in Persia, and, in modern times, among the Arabs, Hindoos, and Chinese, and various native races of the American continent; always having the same symbolic intent and meaning—namely, an expression of desire after friendship and intercommunion with the deity thus worshipped. The existence of this custom in Old Testament days is recognised in Isa. lxv. 11 (R.V.), where God charges the idolatrous Israelites with preparing "a table for the god Fortune," and filling up "mingled wine unto (the goddess) Destiny"—certain Babylonian (?) deities; and in the New Testament, as already remarked, the Apostle Paul refers to the same custom among the idolatrous Greeks of Corinth.

And because this symbolic meaning of a feast is as suitable and natural as it is universal, we find that in the symbolism of Holy Scripture, eating and drinking, and especially the feast, has been appropriated by the Holy Spirit to express precisely the same ideas of reconciliation, friendship, and intercommunion between the giver of the feast and the guest, as in all the great heathen religions. We meet this thought, for instance, in Psalm xxii. 5: "Thou preparest a table before me in the presence of my enemies;" and in Psalm xxxvi. 8, where it is said of God's people: "They shall be abundantly satisfied with the fatness of Thy house;" and again, in the grand prophecy in Isaiah, xxv., of the final redemption of all the long-estranged nations, we read that when God shall destroy in Mount Zion "the veil that is spread over all nations, and swallow up death for ever," then "the Lord of hosts shall make unto all peoples a feast of fat things, a feast of wines on the lees, of fat things full of marrow, of wines on the lees well refined." And in the New Testament, the symbolism is taken up again, and used repeatedly by our Lord, as, for example, in the parables of the Great Supper (Luke xiv. 15-24) and the Prodigal Son (Luke xv. 23), the Marriage of the King's Son (Matt. xxii. 1-14), concerning the blessings of redemption; and also in that ordinance of the Holy Supper, which He has appointed to be a continual reminder of our relation to Himself, and means for the communication of His grace, through our symbolic eating therein of the flesh of the slain Lamb of God.

Thus, nothing in the Levitical symbolism is better certified to us than the meaning of the feast of the peace-offering. Employing a symbol already familiar to the world for centuries, God ordained this eating of the peace-offering in Israel, to be the symbolic expression of peace and fellowship with Himself. In Israel it was to be eaten "before the Lord," and, as well it might be, "with rejoicing."

But, just at this point, the question has been raised: How are we to conceive of the sacrificial feast of the peace-offering? Was it a feast offered and presented by the Israelite to God, or a feast given by God to the Israelite? In other words, in this feast, who was represented as host, and who as guest? Among other nations than the Hebrews, it was the thought in such cases that the feast was given by the worshipper to his god. This is well illustrated by an Assyrian inscription of Esarhaddon, who, in describing his palace at Nineveh, says: "I filled with beauties the great palace of my empire, and I called it 'the Palace which rivals the World.' Ashur, Ishtar of Nineveh, and the gods of Assyria, all of them, I feasted within it. Victims, precious and beautiful, I sacrificed before them, and I caused them to receive my gifts."

But here we come upon one of the most striking and instructive contrasts between the heathen conception of the sacrificial feast and the same symbolism as used in Leviticus and other Scripture. In the heathen sacrificial feasts, it is man who feasts God; in the peace-offering of Leviticus, it is God who feasts man. Some have indeed denied that this is the conception of the peace-offering, but most strangely. It is true that the offerer, in the first instance, had brought the victim; but it seems to be forgotten by such, that prior to the feasting he had already given the victim to God, to be offered in expiation for sin. From that time the victim was no longer, any part of it, his own property, but God's. God having received the offering, now directs what use shall be made of it; a part shall be burned upon the altar; another part He gives to the priests, His servants; with the remaining part He now feasts the worshipper.

And as if to make this clearer yet, while Esarhaddon, for example, gives his feast to the gods, not in their temples, but in his own palace, as himself the host and giver of the feast, the Israelite, on the contrary,—that he might not, like the heathen, complacently imagine himself to be feasting God,—is directed to eat the peace-offering, not at his own house, but at God's house. In this way God was set forth as the host, the One who gave the feast, to whose house the Israelite was invited, at whose table he was to eat.

Profoundly suggestive and instructive is this contrast between the heathen custom in this offering, and the Levitical ordinance. For do we not strike here one of the deepest points of contrast between all of man's religion, and the Gospel of God? Man's idea always is, until taught better by God, "I will be religious and make God my friend, by doing something, giving something for God." God, on the contrary, teaches us in this symbolism, as in all Scripture, the exact reverse; that we become truly religious by taking, first of all, with thankfulness and joy, what He has provided for us. A breach of friendship between man and God is often implied in the heathen rituals, as in the ritual of Leviticus; as also, in both, a desire for its removal, and renewed fellowship with God. But in the former, man ever seeks to attain to this intercommunion of friendship by something that he himself will do for God. He will feast God, and thus God shall be well pleased. But God's way is the opposite! The sacrificial feast at which man shall have fellowship with God is provided not by man for God, but by God for man, and is to be eaten, not in our house, but spiritually partaken in the presence of the invisible God.

We can now perceive the teaching of the peace-offering for Israel. In Israel, as among all the nations, was the inborn craving after fellowship and friendship with God. The ritual of the peace-offering taught him how it was to be obtained, and how communion might be realised. The first thing was for him to bring and present a divinely-appointed victim; and then, the laying of the hand upon his head with confession of sin; then, the slaying of the victim, the sprinkling of its blood, and the offering of its choicest parts to God in the altar fire. Till all this was done, till in symbol expiation had been thus made for the Israelite's sin, there could be no feast which should speak of friendship and fellowship with God. But this being first done, God now, in token of His free forgiveness and restoration to favour, invites the Israelite to a joyful feast in His own house.

What a beautiful symbol! Who can fail to appreciate its meaning when once pointed out? Let us imagine that through some fault of ours a dear friend has become estranged; we used to eat and drink at his house, but there has been none of that now for a long time. We are troubled, and perhaps seek out one who is our friend's friend and also our friend, to whose kindly interest we entrust our case, to reconcile to us the one we have offended. He has gone to mediate; we anxiously await his return; but or ever he has come back again, comes an invitation from him who was estranged, just in the old loving way, asking that we will eat with him at his house. Any one of us would understand this; we should be sure at once that the mediator had healed the breach, that we were forgiven, and were welcome as of old to all that our friend's friendship had to give.

But God is the good Friend whom we have estranged; and the Lord Jesus, His beloved Son, and our own Friend as well, is the Mediator; and He has healed the breach; having made expiation for our sin in offering His own body as a sacrifice, He has ascended into heaven, there to appear in the presence of God for us; He has not yet returned. But meantime the message comes down from Him to all who are hungering after peace with God: "The feast is made; and ye all are invited; come! all things are now ready!" And this is the message of the Gospel. It is the peace-offering translated into words. Can we hesitate to accept the invitation? Or, if we have sent in our acceptance, do we need to be told, as in Deuteronomy, that we are to eat "with rejoicing."

And now we may well observe another circumstance of profound typical significance. When the Israelite came to God's house to eat before Jehovah, he was fed there with the flesh of the slain victim. The flesh of that very victim whose blood had been given for him on the altar, now becomes his food to sustain the life thus redeemed. Whether the Israelite saw into the full meaning of this, we may easily doubt; but it leads us on now to consider, in the clearer light of the New Testament, the deepest significance of the peace-offering and its ritual, as typical of our Lord and our relation to Him.

That the victim of the peace-offering, as of all the bloody offerings, was intended to typify Christ, and that the death of that victim, in the peace-offering, as in all the bloody offerings, foreshadowed the death of Christ for our sins,—this needs no further proof. And so, again, as the burning of the whole burnt-offering represented Christ as accepted for us in virtue of His perfect consecration to the Father, so the peace-offering, in that the fat is burned, represents Christ as accepted for us, in that He gave to God in our behalf the very best He had to offer. For in that incomparable sacrifice we are to think not only of the completeness of Christ's consecration for us, but also of the supreme excellence of that which He offered unto God for us. All that was best in Him, reason, affection, and will, as well as the members of His holy body,—nay, the Godhead as well as the Manhood, in the holy mystery of the Trinity and the Incarnation, He offered for us unto the Father.

This, however, has taken us as yet but little beyond the meaning of the burnt-offering. The closing act of the ritual, the sacrificial eating, however, reaches in its typical significance far beyond this or any of the bloody offerings.

First, in that he who had laid his hand upon the victim, and for whom the blood had been sprinkled, is now invited by God to feast in His house, upon food given by himself, the food of the sacrifice, which is called in the ritual "the bread of God," the eating of the peace-offering symbolically teaches us that if we have indeed presented the Lamb of God as our peace, not only has the Priest sprinkled for us the blood, so that our sin is pardoned, but, in token of friendship now restored, God invites the penitent believer to sit down at His own table,—in a word, to joyful fellowship with Himself! Which means, if our weak faith but take it in, that the Almighty and Most Holy God now invites us to fellowship in all the riches of His Godhead; places all that He has at the service of the believing sinner, redeemed by the blood of the slain Lamb. The prodigal has returned; the Father will now feast him with the best that He has. Fellowship with God through reconciliation by the blood of the slain Lamb,—this then is the first thing shadowed forth in this part of the ritual of the peace-offering. It is a sufficiently wonderful thought, but there is truth yet more wonderful veiled under this symbolism.

For when we ask, what then was the bread or food of God, of which He invited him to partake who brought the peace-offering, and learn that it was the flesh of the slain victim; here we meet a thought which goes far beyond atonement by the shedding of blood. The same victim whose blood was shed and sprinkled in atonement for sin is now given by God to be the redeemed Israelite's food, by which his life shall be sustained! Surely we cannot mistake the meaning of this. For the victim of the altar and the food of the table are one and the same. Even so He who offered Himself for our sins on Calvary, is now given by God to be the food of the believer; who now thus lives by "eating the flesh" of the slain Lamb of God. Does this imagery, at first thought, seem strange and unnatural? So did it also seem strange to the Jews, when in reply to our Lord's teaching they wonderingly asked (John vi. 52), "How can this man give us His flesh to eat?" And yet so Christ spoke; and when He had first declared Himself to the Jews as the Antitype of the manna, the true Bread sent down from heaven, He then went on to say, in words which far transcended the meaning of that type (John vi. 51), "The bread which I will give is My flesh, for the life of the world." How the light begins now to flash back from the Gospel to the Levitical law, and from this, again, back to the Gospel! In the one we read, "Ye shall eat the flesh of your peace-offerings before the Lord with joy;" in the other, the word of the Lord Jesus concerning Himself (John vi. 33, 55, 57): "The bread of God is that which cometh down out of heaven, and giveth life unto the world.... My flesh is meat indeed, and My blood is drink indeed.... As the living Father sent Me, and I live because of the Father, so he that eateth Me, he also shall live because of Me." And now the Shekinah light of the ancient tent of meeting begins to illumine even the sacramental table, and as we listen to the words of Jesus, "Take, eat! this is My body which was broken for you," we are reminded of the feast of the peace-offerings. The Israel of God is to be fed with the flesh of the sacrificed Lamb which became their peace.

Let us hold fast then to this deepest thought of the peace-offering, a truth too little understood even by many true believers. The very Christ who died for our sins, if we have by faith accepted His atonement and have been for His sake forgiven, is now given us by God for the sustenance of our purchased life. Let us make use of Him, daily feeding upon Him, that so we may live and grow unto the life eternal!

But there is yet one thought more concerning this matter, which the peace-offering, as far as was possible, shadowed forth. Although Christ becomes the bread of God for us only through His offering of Himself first for our sins, as our atonement, yet this is something quite distinct from atonement. Christ became our sacrifice once for all; the atonement is wholly a fact of the past. But Christ is now still, and will ever continue to be unto all His people, the bread or food of God, by eating whom they live. He was the propitiation, as the slain victim; but, in virtue of that, He is now become the flesh of the peace-offering. Hence He must be this, not as dead, but as living, in the present resurrection life of His glorified humanity. Here evidently is a fact which could not be directly symbolised in the peace-offering without a miracle ever repeated. For Israel ate of the victim, not as living, but as dead. It could not be otherwise. And yet there is a regulation of the ritual (chap. vii. 15-18; xix. 6, 7) which suggests this phase of truth as clearly as possible without a miracle. It was ordered that none of the flesh of the peace-offering should be allowed to remain beyond the third day; if any then was left uneaten, it was to be burned with fire. The reason for this lies upon the surface. It was doubtless that there might be no possible beginning of decay; and thus it was secured that the flesh of the victim with which God fed the accepted Israelite should be the flesh of a victim that was not to see corruption. But does not this at once remind us how it was written of the Antitype, "Thou wilt not suffer Thy Holy One to see corruption"? while, moreover, the extreme limit of time allowed further reminds us how it was precisely on the third day that Christ rose from the dead in the incorruptible life of the resurrection, that so He might through all time continue to be the living bread of His people.

And thus this special regulation points us not indistinctly toward the New Testament truth that Christ is now unto us the bread of God, not merely as the One who died, but as the One who, living again, was not allowed to see corruption. For so the Apostle argues (Rom. v. 11), that "being justified by faith," and so having "peace with God through our Lord Jesus Christ," our peace-offering, having been thus "reconciled by His death, we shall now be saved by His life." And thus, as we appropriate Christ crucified as our atonement, so by a like faith we are to appropriate Christ risen as our life, to be for us as the flesh of the peace-offering, our nourishment and strength by which we live.

The Prohibition of Fat and Blood.

iii. 16, 17; vii. 22-27; xvii. 10-16.

"And the priest shall burn them upon the altar: it is the food of the offering made by fire, for a sweet savour: all the fat is the Lord's. It shall be a perpetual statute throughout your generations in all your dwellings, that ye shall eat neither fat nor blood.... And the Lord spake unto Moses, saying, Speak unto the children of Israel, saying, Ye shall eat no fat, of ox, or sheep, or goat. And the fat of that which dieth of itself, and the fat of that which is torn of beasts, may be used for any other service: but ye shall in no wise eat of it. For whosoever eateth the fat of the beast, of which men offer an offering made by fire unto the Lord, even the soul that eateth it shall be cut off from his people. And ye shall eat no manner of blood, whether it be of fowl or of beast, in any of your dwellings. Whosoever it be that eateth any blood, that soul shall be cut off from his people.... And whatsoever man there be of the house of Israel, or of the strangers that sojourn among them, that eateth any manner of blood; I will set My face against that soul that eateth blood, and will cut him off from among his people. For the life of the flesh is in the blood: and I have given it to you upon the altar to make atonement for your souls: for it is the blood that maketh atonement by reason of the life. Therefore I said unto the children of Israel, No soul of you shall eat blood, neither shall any stranger that sojourneth among you eat blood. And whatsoever man there be of the children of Israel, or of the strangers that sojourn among them, which taketh in hunting any beast or fowl that may be eaten; he shall pour out the blood thereof, and cover it with dust. For as to the life of all flesh, the blood thereof is all one with the life thereof: therefore I said unto the children of Israel, Ye shall eat the blood of no manner of flesh: for the life of all flesh is the blood thereof: whosoever eateth it shall be cut off. And every soul that eateth that which dieth of itself, or that which is torn of beasts, whether he be homeborn or a stranger, he shall wash his clothes, and bathe himself in water, and be unclean until the even: then shall he be clean. But if he wash them not, nor bathe his flesh, then he shall bear his iniquity."

The chapter concerning the peace-offering ends (vv. 16, 17) with these words: "All the fat is the Lord's. It shall be a perpetual statute for you throughout your generations, that ye shall eat neither fat nor blood."

To this prohibition so much importance was attached that in the supplemental "law of the peace-offering" (vii. 22-27) it is repeated with added explanation and solemn warning, thus: "And the Lord spake unto Moses, saying, Speak unto the children of Israel, saying, Ye shall eat no manner of fat, of ox, or of sheep, or of goat. And the fat of the beast that dieth of itself, and the fat of that which is torn with beasts, may be used for any other service: but ye shall in no wise eat of it. For whosoever eateth the fat of the beast, of which men offer an offering made by fire unto the Lord, even the soul that eateth it shall be cut off from his people. And ye shall eat no manner of blood, whether it be of fowl or of beast, in any of your dwellings. Whosoever it be that eateth any blood, that soul shall be cut off from his people."

From which it appears that this prohibition of the eating of fat referred only to the fat of such beasts as were used for sacrifice. With these, however, the law was absolute, whether the animal was presented for sacrifice, or only slain for food. It held good with regard to these animals, even when, because of the manner of their death, they could not be used for sacrifice. In such cases, though the fat might be used for other purposes, still it must not be used for food.

The prohibition of the blood as food appears from xvii. 10 to have been absolutely universal; it is said, "Whatsoever man there be of the house of Israel, or of the strangers that sojourn among them, that eateth any manner of blood, I will set My face against that soul that eateth blood, and will cut him off from among his people."

The reason for the prohibition of the eating of blood, whether in the case of the sacrificial feasts of the peace-offerings or on other occasions, is given (xvii. 11, 12), in these words: "For the life of the flesh is in the blood: and I have given it to you upon the altar to make atonement for your souls: for it is the blood that maketh atonement by reason of the life. Therefore I said unto the children of Israel, No soul of you shall eat blood, neither shall any stranger that sojourneth among you eat blood."

And the prohibition is then extended to include not only the blood of animals which were used upon the altar, but also such as were taken in hunting, thus (ver. 13): "And whatsoever man there be of the children of Israel, or of the strangers that sojourn among them, which taketh in hunting any beast or fowl that may be eaten, he shall pour out the blood thereof, and cover it with dust," as something of peculiar sanctity; and then the reason previously given is repeated with emphasis (ver. 14): "For as to the life of all flesh, the blood thereof is all one with the life thereof: therefore I said unto the children of Israel, Ye shall eat the blood of no manner of flesh: for the life of all flesh is the blood thereof; whosoever eateth it shall be cut off."

And since, when an animal died from natural causes, or through being torn of a beast, the blood would be drawn from the flesh either not at all or but imperfectly, as further guarding against the possibility of eating blood, it is ordered (vv. 15, 16) that he who does this shall be held unclean: "Every soul that eateth that which dieth of itself, or that which is torn of beasts, whether he be home-born or a stranger, he shall wash his clothes, and bathe himself in water, and be unclean until the even. But if he wash them not nor bathe his flesh, then he shall bear his iniquity."

These passages explicitly state the reason for the prohibition by God of the use of blood for food to be the fact that, as the vehicle of the life, it has been appointed by Him as the means of expiation for sin upon the altar. And the reason for the prohibition of the fat is similar; namely, its appropriation for God upon the altar, as in the peace-offerings, the sin-offerings, and the guilt-offerings; "all the fat is the Lord's."

Thus the Israelite, by these two prohibitions, was to be continually reminded, so often as he partook of his daily food, of two things: by the one, of atonement by the blood as the only ground of acceptance; and by the other, of God's claim on the man redeemed by the blood, for the consecration of his best. Not only so, but by the frequent repetition, and still more by the heavy penalty attached to the violation of these laws, he was reminded of the exceeding importance that these two things had in the mind of God. If he eat the blood of any animal claimed by God for the altar, he should be cut off from his people; that is, outlawed, and cut off from all covenant privilege as a citizen of the kingdom of God in Israel. And even though the blood were that of the beast taken in the chase, still ceremonial purification was required as the condition of resuming his covenant position.

Nothing, doubtless, seems to most Christians of our day more remote from practical religion than these regulations touching the fat and the blood, which are brought before us with such fulness in the law of the peace-offering and elsewhere. And yet nothing is of more present-day importance in this law than the principles which underlie these regulations. For as with type, so with antitype. No less essential to the admission of the sinful man into that blessed fellowship with a reconciled God, which the peace-offering typified, is the recognition of the supreme sanctity of the precious sacrificial blood of the Lamb of God; no less essential to the life of happy communion with God, is the ready consecration of the best fruit of our life to Him.

Surely, both of these, and especially the first, are truths for our time. For no observing man can fail to recognise the very ominous fact that a constantly increasing number, even of professed preachers of the Gospel, in so many words refuse to recognise the place which propitiatory blood has in the Gospel of Christ, and to admit its pre-eminent sanctity as consisting in this, that it was given on the altar to make atonement for our souls. Nor has the present generation outgrown the need of the other reminder touching the consecration of the best to the Lord. How many there are, comfortable, easy-going Christians, whose principle—if one might speak in the idiom of the Mosaic law—would rather seem to be, ever to give the lean to God, and keep the fat, the best fruit of their life and activity, for themselves! Such need to be most urgently and solemnly reminded that in spirit the warning against the eating of the blood and the fat is in full force. It was written of such as should break this law, "that soul shall be cut off from his people." And so in the Epistle to the Hebrews (x. 26-29) we find one of its most solemn warnings directed to those who "count this blood of the covenant," the blood of Christ, "an unholy (*i.e.*, common) thing;" as exposed by this, their undervaluation of the sanctity of the blood, to a "sorer punishment" than overtook him that "set at nought Moses' law," even the retribution of Him who said, "Vengeance is Mine; I will repay, saith the Lord."

And so in this law of the peace-offerings, which ordains the conditions of the holy feast of fellowship with a reconciled God, we find these two things made fundamental in the symbolism: full recognition of the sanctity of the blood as that which atones for the soul; and the full consecration of the redeemed and pardoned soul to the Lord. So was it in the symbol; and so shall it be when the sacrificial feast shall at last receive its most complete fulfilment in the communion of the redeemed with Christ in glory. There will be no differences of opinion then and there, either as to the transcendent value of that precious blood which made atonement, or as to the full consecration which such a redemption requires from the redeemed.

Thank-Offerings, Vows, and Freewill-Offerings.

vii. 11-21.

"And this is the law of the sacrifice of peace-offerings which one shall offer unto the Lord. If he offer it for a thanksgiving, then he shall offer with the sacrifice of thanksgiving unleavened cakes mingled with oil, and unleavened wafers anointed with oil, and cakes mingled with oil, of fine flour soaked. With cakes of leavened bread he shall offer his oblation with the sacrifice of his peace-offerings for thanksgiving. And of it he shall offer one out of each oblation for an heave-offering unto the Lord; it shall be the priest's that sprinkleth the blood of the peace-offerings. And the flesh of the sacrifice of his peace-offerings for thanksgiving shall be eaten on the day of his oblation; he shall not leave any of it until the morning. But if the sacrifice of his oblation be a vow, or a freewill offering, it shall be eaten on the day that he offereth his sacrifice: and on the morrow that which remaineth of it shall be eaten: but that which remaineth of the flesh of the sacrifice on the third day shall be burnt with fire. And if any of the flesh of the sacrifice of his peace-offerings be eaten on the third day, it shall not be accepted, neither shall it be imputed unto him that offereth it: it shall be an abomination, and the soul that eateth of it shall bear his iniquity. And the flesh that toucheth any unclean thing shall not be eaten; it shall be burnt with fire. And as for the flesh, everyone that is clean shall eat thereof: but the soul that eateth of the flesh of the sacrifice of peace-offerings, that pertain unto the Lord, having his uncleanness upon him, that soul shall be cut off from his people. And when any one shall touch any unclean thing, the uncleanness of man, or an unclean beast, or any unclean abomination, and eat of the flesh of the sacrifice of peace-offerings, that soul shall be cut off from his people."

According to this supplemental section on the law of the peace-offerings, these were of three kinds; namely, "sacrifices of thanksgiving," "vows," and "freewill-offerings." The first were offered in token of gratitude for mercies received; as in Psalm cxvi. 16, 17, where we read: "Thou hast loosed my bonds; I will offer to Thee the sacrifice of thanksgiving." The second, like these, were offered also in grateful return for prayer answered and mercy received, but with the difference that they were promised before, upon the condition of the prayer for mercy being granted. Lastly, the freewill-offerings were those which had no special occasion, but were merely the spontaneous expression of the love of the offerer to God, and his desire to live in friendship and fellowship with Him. It is apparently these freewill-offerings that we are to recognise in the many instances recorded where the peace-offering was presented in connection with supplication for special help and favour from God; as, *e.g.*, when (Judges xx. 26) Israel supplicated mercy from God after their disastrous defeat in the civil war with the tribe of Benjamin; and when David entreated the Lord (2 Sam. xxiv. 25) for the staying of the plague in Israel.

With not only the thank-offering, but all peace-offerings, as is clear from Numb. xv. 2-4, a full meal-offering, consisting of three kinds of unleavened cakes, was to be offered, of each of which, one was to be presented as a heave-offering, with the heave-shoulder of the sacrifice, to the Lord (vii. 12). For the sacrificial feast, in which the offerer, his family, and friends were to partake, he was also to bring cakes of leavened bread, which, however, though eaten before God by the offerer, might not be presented unto God for a heave-offering, nor come upon the altar (ver. 13).

From what we have already seen, the spiritual meaning of this will be clear. Thus in symbol the Israelite offered unto God, with his life, the fruit of the labour of his hands, in gratitude to Him, and expressed his happy consciousness of friendship and fellowship with God through atonement, by feasting before Him. The leavened bread is offered simply, as Bähr suggests, as the usual accompaniment to a feast; though regard is still had to the fact, never once forgotten in Holy Scripture, that leaven is nevertheless an element and symbol of corruption; so that however the reconciled Israelite may eat his leavened bread before God, yet it cannot be allowed to come upon the altar of the Most Holy One.

Two slight differences appear in the ritual for the different kinds of peace-offerings. First, in the case of the freewill-offering, a single exception is allowed to the general rule that the victim must be without blemish, in the permission to offer what, otherwise perfect, might have "anything superfluous or lacking" in its parts (xxii. 23); a circumstance which could not affect its fitness as the symbol of spiritual food. For a vow (and, we may infer, for a thank-offering also) such a victim, however, could not be offered; evidently because it would seem peculiarly unsuitable, where the object of the offering was to make in some sense a return for the always perfect and most gracious gifts of God, that anything else than the absolutely perfect should be offered. In the case of the thank-offering, again, an exception is made to the general regulation permitting the eating of the offering on the first and second days, requiring that all be eaten on the day that it is presented, or else be burnt with fire (vii. 15). We need seek for no spiritual meaning in this. A sufficient reason for this special restriction in this case is probably to be found in the consideration that as this was the most common variety of the offering, there was the most danger that the flesh, by some oversight, might be kept too long. The flesh of the victim offered to God, the type of the Victim of Calvary, must on no account be allowed to see corruption; and to this end every needed precaution must be taken, that by no chance it shall remain unconsumed on the third day.

It is easy to connect the special characteristics of these several varieties of the peace-offering with the great Antitype. So may we use Him as our thank-offering; for what more fitting as an expression of gratitude and love to God for mercies received, than renewed and special fellowship with Him through feeding upon Christ as the slain Lamb? So also we may thus use Christ in our vows; as when, supplicating mercy, we promise and engage that if our prayer be heard we will renewedly consecrate our service to the Lord, as in the meal-offering, and anew enter into life-giving fellowship with Him through feeding by faith on the flesh of the Lord. And it is beautifully hinted in the permission of the use of leaven in this feast of the peace-offering, that while the work of the believer, as presented to God in grateful acknowledgment of His mercies, is ever affected with the taint of his native corruption, so that it cannot come upon the altar where satisfaction is made for sin, yet God is graciously pleased, for the sake of the great Sacrifice, to accept such imperfect service offered to Him, and make it in turn a blessing to us, as we offer it in His presence, rejoicing in the work of our hands before Him.

But there was one condition without which the Israelite could not have communion with God in the peace-offering. He must be clean! even as the flesh of the peace-offering must be clean also. There must be in him nothing which should interrupt covenant fellowship with God; as nothing in the type which should make it an unfit symbol of the Antitype. For it was ordered (vii. 19-21), as regards every possible occasion of uncleanness, thus: "The flesh that toucheth any unclean thing shall not be eaten; it shall be burnt with fire. As for the flesh, every one that is clean shall eat thereof; but the soul that eateth of the flesh of the sacrifice of peace-offerings, that pertain unto the Lord, having his uncleanness upon him, that soul shall be cut off from his people. And when any one shall touch any unclean thing, the uncleanness of man, or an unclean beast, or any unclean abomination, and eat of the flesh of the sacrifice of peace-offerings, that soul shall be cut off from his people."

In such cases, he must first go and purify himself, as provided in the law; and then, and then only, presume to come to eat before the Lord. And so

Israel was ever impressively reminded that he who would have fellowship with God, and eat in happy fellowship with Him at His table, must keep himself pure. So by the spirit of these commands are we no less warned that we take not encouragement from God's grace, in providing for us the flesh of the Lamb as our food, to be careless in walk and life. If we will use Christ as our peace-offering, we must keep ourselves "unspotted from the world;" must hate "even the garment spotted by the flesh," remembering ever that it is written in the New Testament (1 Peter i. 15, 16), with direct reference to the typical law of Leviticus: "As He which called you is holy, be ye yourselves also holy in all manner of living; because it is written, Ye shall be holy; for I am holy."

CHAPTER VI
THE SIN-OFFERING

Lev. iv. 1-35.

Both in the burnt-offering and in the peace-offering, Israel was taught, as we are, that all consecration and all fellowship with God must begin with, and ever depends upon, atonement made for sin. But this was not the dominant thought in either of these offerings; neither did the atonement, as made in these, have reference to particular acts of sin. For such, these offerings were never prescribed. They remind us therefore of the necessity of atonement, not so much for what we do or fail to do, as for what we are.

But the sin even of true believers, whether then or now, is more than sin of nature. The true Israelite was liable to be overtaken in some overt act of sin; and for all such cases was ordained, in this section of the law (iv. 1-v. 13), the sin-offering; an offering which should bring out into sole and peculiar prominence the thought revealed in other sacrifices more imperfectly, that in order to pardon of sin, there must be expiation. There was indeed a limitation to the application of this offering; for if a man, in those days, sinned wilfully, presumptuously, stubbornly, or, as the phrase is, "with a high hand," there was no provision made in the law for his restoration to covenant standing. "He that despised Moses' law died without mercy under two or three witnesses;" he was "cut off from his people." But for sins of a lesser grade, such as resulted not from a spirit of wilful rebellion against God, but were mitigated in their guilt by various reasons, especially ignorance, rashness, or inadvertence, God made provision, in a typical way, for their removal by means of the atonement of the sin- and the guilt-offerings. By means of these, accompanied also with full restitution of the wrong done, when such restitution was possible, the guilty one might be restored in those days to his place as an accepted citizen of the kingdom of God.

No part of the Levitical law is more full of deep, heart-searching truth than the law of the sin-offering. First of all, it is of consequence to observe that the sins for which this chief atoning sacrifice was appointed, were, for the most part, sins of ignorance. For so runs the general statement with which this section opens (ver. 2): "If any one shall sin unwittingly, in any of the things which the Lord hath commanded not to be done, and shall do any of them." And to these are afterwards added sins committed through rashness, the result rather of heat and hastiness of spirit than of deliberate purpose of sin; as, for instance, in chap. v. 4: "Whatsoever it be that a man shall utter rashly with an oath, and it be hid from him." Besides these, in the same section (vv. 1-4) as also in all the cases mentioned under the guilt-offering, and the special instance of a wrong done to a slave-girl (xix. 21), a number of additional offences are mentioned which all seem to have their special palliation, not indeed in the ignorance of the sinner, but in the nature of the acts themselves, as admitting of reparation. For all such it was also ordained that the offender should bring a sin- (or a guilt-) offering, and that by this, atonement being made for him, his sin might be forgiven.

All this must have brought before Israel, and is meant to bring before us, the absolute equity of God in dealing with His creatures. We think often of His stern justice in that He so unfailingly takes note of every sin. But here we may learn also to observe His equity in that He notes no less carefully every circumstance that may palliate our sin. We thankfully recognise in these words the spirit of Him of whom it was said (Heb. v. 2, marg.) that in the days of His flesh He could "reasonably bear with the ignorant;" and who said concerning those who know not their Master's will and do it not (Luke xii. 48), that their "stripes" shall be "few;" and who, again, with equal justice and mercy, said of His disciples' fault in Gethsemane (Matt. xxvi. 41), "The spirit indeed is willing, but the flesh is weak." We do well to note this. For in these days we hear it often charged against the holy religion of Christ, that it represents God as essentially and horribly unjust in consigning all unbelievers to one and the same unvarying punishment, the eternal lake of fire; and as thus making no difference between those who have sinned against the utmost light and knowledge, wilfully and inexcusably, and those who may have sinned through ignorance, or weakness of the flesh. To such charges as these we have simply to answer that neither in the Old Testament nor in the New is God so revealed. We may come back to this book of Leviticus, and declare that even in those days when law reigned, and grace and love were less clearly revealed than now, God made a difference, a great difference, between some sins and others; He visited, no doubt, wilful and defiant sin with condign punishment; but, on the other hand, no less justly than mercifully, He considered also every circumstance which could lessen guilt, and ordained a gracious provision for expiation and forgiveness. The God revealed in Leviticus, like the God revealed in the Gospel, the God "with whom we have to do," is then no hard and unreasonable tyrant, but a most just and equitable King. He is no less the Most Just, that He is the

Most Holy; but, rather, because He is most holy, is He therefore most just. And because God is such a God, in the New Testament also it is plainly said that ignorance, as it extenuates guilt, shall also ensure mitigation of penalty; and in the Old Testament, that while he who sins presumptuously and with a high hand against God, shall "die without mercy under two or three witnesses," on the other hand, he who sins unwittingly, or in some sudden rash impulse, doing that of which he afterward truly repents; or who, again, has sinned, if knowingly, still in such a way as admits of some adequate reparation of the wrong,—all these things shall be judged palliation of his guilt; and if he confess his sin, and make all possible reparation for it, then, if he present a sin- or a guilt-offering, atonement may therewith be made, and the sinner be forgiven.

This then is the first thing which the law concerning the sin-offering brings before us: it calls our attention to the fact that the heavenly King and Judge of men is righteous in all His ways, and therefore will ever make all the allowance that strict justice and righteousness demand, for whatever may in any way palliate our guilt.

But none the less for this do we need also to heed another intensely practical truth which the law of the sin-offering brings before us: namely, that while ignorance or other circumstances may palliate guilt, they do not and cannot nullify it. We may have sinned without a suspicion that we were sinning, but here we are taught that there can be no pardon without a sin-offering. We may have sinned through weakness or sudden passion, but still sin is sin, and we must have a sin-offering before we can be forgiven.

We may observe, in passing, the bearing of this teaching of the law on the question so much discussed in our day, as to the responsibility of the heathen for the sins which they commit through ignorance. In so far as their ignorance is not wilful and avoidable, it doubtless greatly diminishes their guilt; and the Lord Himself has said of such that their stripes shall be few. And yet more than this He does not say. Except we are prepared to cast aside the teaching alike of Leviticus and the Gospels, it is certain that their ignorance does not cancel their guilt. That the ignorance of any one concerning moral law can secure his exemption from the obligation to suffer for his sin, is not only against the teaching of all Scripture, but is also contradicted by all that we can see about us of God's government of the world. For when does God ever suspend the operation of physical laws, because the man who violates them does not know that he is breaking them? And so also, will we but open our eyes, we may see that it is with moral law. The heathen, for example, are ignorant of many moral laws; but do they therefore escape the terrible consequences of their law-breaking, even in this present life, where we can see for ourselves how God is dealing with them? And is there any reason to think it will be different in the life hereafter?

Does it seem harsh that men should be punished even for sins of ignorance, and pardon be impossible, even for these, without atonement? It would not seem so, would men but think more deeply. For beyond all question, the ignorance of men as to the fundamental law of God, to love Him with all the heart, and our neighbour as ourselves, which is the sum of all law, has its reason, not in any lack of light, but in the evil heart of man, who everywhere and always, until he is regenerated, loves self more than he loves God. The words of Christ (John iii. 20) apply: "He that doeth evil cometh not to the light;" not even to the light of nature.

And yet, one who should look only at this chapter might rejoin to this, that the Israelite was only obliged to bring a sin-offering, when afterward he came to the knowledge of his sin as sin; but, in case he never came to that knowledge, was not then his sin passed by without an atoning sacrifice? To this question, the ordinance which we find in chapter xvi. is the decisive answer. For therein it was provided that once every year a very solemn sin-offering should be offered by the high priest, for all the multitudinous sins of Israel, which were not atoned for in the special sin-offerings of each day. Hence it is strictly true that no sin in Israel was ever passed over without either penalty or shedding of blood. And so the law keeps it ever before us that our unconsciousness of sinning does not alter the fact of sin, or the fact of guilt, nor remove the obligation to suffer because of sin; and that even the sin of which we are quite ignorant, interrupts man's peace with God and harmony with him. Thus the best of us must take as our own the words of the Apostle Paul (1 Cor. iv. 4, R.V.): "I know nothing against myself; yet am I not hereby justified; He that judgeth me is the Lord."

Nor does the testimony of this law end here. We are by it taught that the guilt of sins unrecognised as sins at the time of their committal, cannot be cancelled merely by penitent confession when they become known. Confession must indeed be made, according to the law, as one condition of pardon, but, besides this, the guilty man must bring his sin-offering.

What truths can be more momentous and vital than these! Can any one say, in the light of such a revelation, that all in this ancient law of the sin-offering is now obsolete, and of no concern to us? For how many there are who are resting all their hopes for the future on the fact that they have sinned, if at all, then ignorantly; or that they "have meant to do right;" or that they have confessed the sin when it was known, and have been very sorry. And yet, if this law teach anything, it teaches that this is a fatal mistake, and that such hopes rest on a foundation of sand. If we would be forgiven, we must indeed confess our sin and we must repent; but this is not enough. We must have a sin-offering; we must make use of the great Sin-Offering which that of Leviticus typified; we must tell our compassionate High Priest how in ignorance, or in the rashness of some unholy, over-mastering impulse, we sinned, and commit our case to Him, that He may apply the precious blood in our behalf with God.

It is a third impressive fact, that after we include all the cases for which the sin-offering was provided, there still remain many sins for the forgiveness of which no provision was made. It was ordered elsewhere, for instance (Numb. xxxv. 31-33) that no satisfaction, should be taken for the life of a murderer. He might confess and bewail his sin, and be never so sorry, but there was no help for him; he must die the death. So was it also with blasphemy; so with adultery, and with many other crimes. This exclusion of so many cases from the merciful provision of the typical offering had a meaning. It was intended, not only to emphasise to the conscience the aggravated wickedness of such crimes, but also to develop in Israel the sense of need for a more adequate provision, a better sacrifice than any the Levitical law could offer; blood which should cleanse, not merely in a ceremonial and sacramental way, but really and effectively; and not only from some sins, but from all sins.

The law of the sin-offering is introduced by phraseology different from that which is used in the case of the preceding offerings. In the case of each of these, the language used implies that the Israelites were familiar with the offering before its incorporation into the Levitical sacrificial system. The sin-offering, on the other hand, is introduced as a new thing. And such, indeed, it was. While, as we have seen, each of the offerings before ordered had been known and used, both by the Shemitic and the other nations, since long before the days of Moses, before this time there is no mention anywhere, in Scripture or out of it, of a sacrifice corresponding to the sin- or the guilt-offering. The significance of this fact is apparent so soon as we observe what was the distinctive conception of the sin-offering, as contrasted with the other offerings. Without question, it was the idea of expiation of guilt by the sacrifice of a substituted victim. This idea, as we have seen, was indeed not absent from the other bloody offerings; but in those its place was secondary and subordinate. In the ritual of the sin-offering, on the contrary, this idea was brought out into almost solitary prominence;—sin pardoned on the ground of expiation made through the presentation to God of the blood of an innocent victim.

The introduction of this new sacrifice, then, marked the fact that the spiritual training of man, of Israel in particular, herewith entered on a new stadium; which was to be distinguished by the development, in a degree to that time without a precedent, of the sense of sin and of guilt, and the need therefore of atonement in order to pardon. This need had not indeed been unfelt before; but never in any ritual had it received so full expression. Not only is the idea of expiation by the shedding of blood almost the only thought represented in the ritual of the offering, but in the order afterward prescribed for the different sacrifices, the sin-offering, in all cases where others were offered, must go before them all; before the burnt-offering, the meal-offering, the peace-offering. So again, this new law insists upon expiation even for those sins which have the utmost possible palliation and excuse, in that at the time of their committal the sinner knew them not as sins; and thus teaches that even these so fatally interrupt fellowship with the holy God, that only such expiation can restore the broken harmony. What a revelation was this law, of the way in which God regards sin! and of the extremity, in consequence, of the sinner's need!

Most instructive, too, were the circumstances under which this new offering, with such a special purpose, embodying such a revelation of the extent of human guilt and responsibility, was first ordained. For its appointment followed quickly upon the tremendous revelation of the consuming holiness of God upon Mount Sinai. It was in the light of the holy mount, quaking and flaming with fire, that the eye of Moses was opened to receive from God this revelation of His will, and he was moved by the Holy Ghost to appoint for Israel, in the name of Jehovah, an offering which should differ from all other offerings in this—that it should hold forth to Israel, in solitary and unprecedented prominence, this one thought, that "without shedding of blood there is no remission of sin," not even of sins which are not known as sins at the time of their committal.

Our own generation, and even the Church of to-day, greatly needs to consider the significance of this fact. The spirit of our age is much more inclined to magnify the greatness and majesty of man, than the infinite greatness and holy majesty of God. Hence many talk lightly of atonement, and cannot admit its necessity to the pardon of sin. But can we doubt, with this narrative before us, that if men saw God more clearly as He is, there would be less talk of this kind? When Moses saw God on Mount Sinai, he came down to ordain a sin-offering even for sins of ignorance! And nothing is more certain, as a fact of human experience in all ages, than this, that the more clearly men have perceived the unapproachable holiness and righteousness of God, the more clearly they have seen that expiation of our sins, even of our sins of ignorance, by atoning blood, is the most necessary and fundamental of all conditions, if we will have pardon of sin and peace with a Holy God.

Man is indeed slow to learn this lesson of the sin-offering. It is quite too humbling and abasing to our natural, self-satisfied pride, to be readily received. This is strikingly illustrated by the fact that it is not until late in Israel's history that the sin-offering is mentioned in the sacred record; while even from that first mention till the Exile, it is mentioned only rarely. This fact is indeed often in our day held up as evidence that the sin-offering was not of Mosaic origin, but a priestly invention of much later days. But the fact is quite as well accounted for by the spiritual obtuseness of Israel. The whole narrative shows that they were a people hard of heart and slow to learn the solemn lessons of Sinai; slow to apprehend the holiness of God, and the profound spiritual truth set forth in the institution of the sin-offering. And yet it was not wholly unobserved, nor did every individual fail to learn its lessons. Nowhere in heathen literature do we find such a profound conviction of sin, such a sense of responsibility even for sins of ignorance, as in some of the earliest Psalms, and the earlier prophets. The self-excusing which so often marks the heathen confessions, finds no place in the confessions of those Old Testament believers, brought up under the moral training of that Sinaitic law which had the sin-offering as its supreme expression on this subject. "Search me, O God, and try my heart; and see if there be in me any wicked way" (Psalm cxxxix. 23, 24); "Cleanse Thou me from secret sins" (Psalm xix. 12); "Against Thee only have I sinned, and done this evil in Thy sight" (Psalm li. 4). Such words as these, with many other like prayers and confessions, bear witness to the deepening sense of sin, till at the last the sin-offering teaches, as its own chief lesson, its own inadequacy for the removal of guilt, in those words of the prophetic Psalm, (xl. 6) from the man who mourned iniquities more than the hairs of his head: "Sin-offering Thou hast not required."

But, according to the epistle to the Hebrews, we are to regard David in these words, speaking by the Holy Ghost, as typifying Christ; for we thus read, x. 5-10: "When He cometh into the world He saith, Sacrifice and offering Thou wouldest not, but a body didst Thou prepare for Me; in whole burnt-offerings and sin-offerings Thou hadst no pleasure. Then said I, Lo, I am come (in the roll of the book it is written of Me) to do Thy will, O God."

Which words are then expounded thus: "Saying above, Sacrifices and offerings, and whole burnt-offerings and sacrifices for sin Thou wouldest not, neither hadst pleasure therein (the which are offered according to the law); then hath He said, Lo, I am come to do Thy will. He taketh away the first that He may establish the second. By which will we have been sanctified through the offering of the body of Jesus Christ once for all."

And so, as the deepest lesson of the sin-offering, we are taught to see in it a type and prophecy of Christ, as the true and one eternally effectual sin-offering for the sins of His people; who, Himself at once High Priest and Victim, offering Himself for us, perfects us for ever, as the old sin-offering could not, giving us therefore "boldness to enter into the holy place by the blood of Jesus." May we all have grace by faith to receive and learn this deepest lesson of this ordinance, and thus in the law of the sin-offering discover Him who in His person and work became the Fulfiller of this law.

Graded Responsibility.

iv. 3, 13, 14, 22, 23, 27, 28.

"If the anointed priest shall sin so as to bring guilt on the people; then let him offer for his sin, which he hath sinned, a young bullock without blemish unto the Lord for a sin-offering.... And if the whole congregation of Israel shall err, and the thing be hid from the eyes of the assembly, and they have done any of the things which the Lord hath commanded not to be done, and are guilty; when the sin wherein they have sinned is known, then the assembly shall offer a young bullock for a sin-offering, and bring it before the tent of meeting.... When a ruler sinneth, and doeth unwittingly any one of all the things which the Lord his God hath commanded not to be done, and is guilty; if his sin, wherein he hath sinned, be made known to him, he shall bring for his oblation a goat, a male without blemish.... And if any one of the common people sin unwittingly, in doing any of the things which the Lord hath commanded not to be done, and be guilty; if his sin, which he hath sinned, be made known to him, then he shall bring for his oblation a goat, a female without blemish, for his sin which he hath sinned."

The law concerning the sin-offering is given in four sections, of which the last, again, is divided into two parts, separated by the division of the chapter. These four sections respectively treat of—first, the law of the sin-offering for the "anointed priest" (vv. 3-12); secondly, the law for the offering for the whole congregation (vv. 13-21); thirdly, that for a ruler (vv. 22-26); and lastly, the law for an offering made by a private person, one of "the common people" (iv. 27-v. 16). In this last section we have, first, the general law (iv. 27-35), and then are added (v. 1-16) special prescriptions having reference to various circumstances under which a sin-offering should be offered by one of the people. Under this last head are mentioned first, as requiring a sin-offering, in addition to sins of ignorance or inadvertence, which only were mentioned in the preceding chapter, also sins due to rashness or weakness (vv. 1-4); and then are appointed, in the second place, certain variations in the material of the offering, allowed out of regard to the various ability of different offerers (vv. 5-16).

In the law as given in chap. iv., it is to be observed that the selection of the victim prescribed is determined by the position of the persons who might have occasion to present the offering. For the whole congregation, the victim must be a bullock, the most valuable of all; for the high priest, as the highest religious official of the nation, and appointed also to represent them before God, it must also be a bullock. For the civil ruler, the offering must be a he-goat—an offering of a value less than that of the victim ordered for the high priest, but greater than that of those which were prescribed for the common people. For these, a variety of offerings were appointed, according to their several ability. If possible, it must be a female goat or lamb, or, if the worshipper could not bring that, then two turtle doves, or two young pigeons. If too poor to bring even this small offering, then it was appointed that, as a substitute for the bloody offering, he might bring an offering of fine flour, without oil or frankincense, to be burnt upon the altar.

Evidently, then, the choice of the victim was determined by two considerations: first, the rank of the person who sinned, and, secondly, his ability. As regards the former point, the law as to the victim for the sin-offering was this: the higher the theocratic rank of the sinning person might be, the more costly offering he must bring. No one can well miss of perceiving the meaning of this. The guilt of any sin in God's sight is proportioned to the rank and station of the offender. What truth could be of more practical and personal concern to all than this?

In applying this principle, the law of the sin-offering teaches, first, that the guilt of any sin is the heaviest, when it is committed by one who is placed in a position of religious authority. For this graded law is headed by the case of the sin of the anointed priest, that is, the high priest, the highest functionary in the nation.

We read (ver. 3): "If the anointed priest shall sin so as to bring guilt on the people, then let him offer for his sin which he hath committed, a young bullock without blemish, unto the Lord, for a sin-offering."

That is, the high priest, although a single individual, if he sin, must bring as large and valuable an offering as is required from the whole congregation. For this law there are two evident reasons. The first is found in the fact that in Israel the high priest represented before God the entire nation. When he sinned it was as if the whole nation sinned in him. So it is said that by his sin he "brings guilt on the people"—a very weighty matter.

And this suggests a second reason for the costly offering that was required from him. The consequences of the sin of one in such a high position of religious authority must, in the nature of the case, be much more serious and far-reaching than in the case of any other person.

And here we have another lesson as pertinent to our time as to those days. As the high priest, so, in modern time, the bishop, minister, or elder, is ordained as an officer in matters of religion, to act for and with men in the things of God. For the proper administration of this high trust, how indispensable that such a one shall take heed to maintain unbroken fellowship with God! Any shortcoming here is sure to impair by so much the spiritual value of his own ministrations for the people to whom he ministers. And this evil consequence of any unfaithfulness of his is the more certain to follow, because, of all the members of the community, his example has the widest and most effective influence; in whatever that example be bad or defective, it is sure to do mischief in exact proportion to his exalted station. If then such a one sin, the case is very grave, and his guilt proportionately heavy.

This very momentous fact is brought before us in an impressive way in the New Testament, where, in the epistles to the Seven Churches of Asia (Rev. ii., iii.), it is "the angel of the church," the presiding officer of the church in each city, who is held responsible for the spiritual state of those committed to his charge. No wonder that the Apostle James wrote (James iii. 1): "Be not many teachers, my brethren, knowing that we shall receive heavier judgment." Well may every true-hearted minister of Christ's Church tremble, as here in the law of the sin-offering he reads how the sin of the officer of religion may bring guilt, not only on himself, but also "on the whole people"! Well may he cry out with the Apostle Paul (2 Cor. ii. 16): "Who is sufficient for these things?" and, like him, beseech those to whom he ministers, "Brethren, pray for us!"

With the sin of the high priest is ranked that of the congregation, or the collective nation. It is written (vv. 13, 14): "If the whole congregation of Israel shall err, and the thing be hid from the eyes of the assembly, and they have done any one of the things which the Lord hath commanded not to be done, and are guilty, then the assembly shall offer a young bullock for a sin-offering."

Thus Israel was taught by this law, as we are, that responsibility attaches not only to each individual person, but also to associations of individuals in their corporate character, as nations, communities, and—we may add—all Societies and Corporations, whether secular or religious. Let us emphasise it to our own consciences, as another of the fundamental lessons of this law:

there is individual sin; there is also such a thing as a sin by "the whole congregation." In other words, God holds nations, communities—in a word, all associations and combinations of men for whatever purpose, no less under obligation in their corporate capacity to keep His law than as individuals, and will count them guilty if they break it, even through ignorance.

Never has a generation needed this reminder more than our own. The political and social principles which, since the French Revolution in the end of the last century, have been, year by year, more and more generally accepted among the nations of Christendom, are everywhere tending to the avowed or practical denial of this most important truth. It is a maxim ever more and more extensively accepted as almost axiomatic in our modern democratic communities, that religion is wholly a concern of the individual; and that a nation or community, as such, should make no distinction between various religions as false or true, but maintain an absolute neutrality, even between Christianity and idolatry, or theism and atheism. It should take little thought to see that this modern maxim stands in direct opposition to the principle assumed in this law of the sin-offering; namely, that a community or nation is as truly and directly responsible to God as the individual in the nation. But this corporate responsibility the spirit of the age squarely denies.

Not that all, indeed, in our modern so-called Christian nations have come to this. But no one will deny that this is the mind of the vanguard of nineteenth century liberalism in religion and politics. Many of our political leaders in all lands make no secret of their views on the subject. A purely secular state is everywhere held up, and that with great plausibility and persuasiveness, as the ideal of political government; the goal to the attainment of which all good citizens should unite their efforts. And, indeed, in some parts of Christendom the complete attainment of this evil ideal seems not far away.

It is not strange, indeed, to see atheists, agnostics, and others who deny the Christian faith, maintaining this position; but when we hear men who call themselves Christians—in many cases, even Christian ministers—advocating, in one form or another, governmental neutrality in religion as the only right basis of government, one may well be amazed. For Christians are supposed to accept the Holy Scriptures as the law of faith and of morals, private and public; and where in all the Scripture will any one find such an attitude of any nation or people mentioned, but to be condemned and threatened with the judgment of God?

Will any one venture to say that this teaching of the law of the sin-offering was only intended, like the offering itself, for the old Hebrews? Is it not rather the constant and most emphatic teaching of the whole Scriptures, that God dealt with all the ancient Gentile nations on the same principle? The history which records the overthrow of those old nations and empires does so, even professedly, for the express purpose of calling the attention of men in all ages to this principle, that God deals with all nations as under obligation to recognise Himself as King of nations, and submit in all things to His authority. So it was in the case of Moab, of Ammon, of Nineveh, and Babylon; in regard to each of which we are told, in so many words, that it was because they refused to recognise this principle of national responsibility to the one true God, which was brought before Israel in this part of the law of the sin-offering, that the Divine judgment came upon them in their utter national overthrow. How awfully plain, again, is the language of the second Psalm on this same subject, where it is precisely this national repudiation of the supreme authority of God and of His Christ, so increasingly common in our day, which is named as the ground of the derisive judgment of God, and is made the occasion of exhorting all nations, not merely to belief in God, but also to the obedient recognition of His only-begotten Son, the Messiah, as the only possible means of escaping the future kindling of His wrath.

No graver sign of our times could perhaps be named than just this universal tendency in Christendom, in one way or another, to repudiate that corporate responsibility to God which is assumed as the basis of this part of the law of the sin-offering. There can be no worse omen for the future of an individual than the denial of his obligations to God and to His Son, our Saviour; and there can be no worse sign for the future of Christendom, or of any nation in Christendom, than the partial or entire denial of national obligation to God and to His Christ. What it shall mean in the end, what is the future toward which these popular modern principles are conducting the nations, is revealed in Scripture with startling clearness, in the warning that the world is yet to see one who shall be in a peculiar and eminent sense *"the* Antichrist" (1 John ii. 18); who shall deny both the Father and Son, and be "the Lawless One," and the "Man of Sin," in that He shall "set Himself forth as God" (2 Thess. ii. 3-8); to whom authority will be given "over every tribe, and people, and tongue, and nation" (Rev. xiii. 7).

The nation, then, as such, is held responsible to God! So stands the law. And, therefore, in Israel, if the nation should sin, it was ordained that they also, like the high priest, should bring a bullock for a sin-offering, the most costly victim that was ever prescribed. This was so ordained, no doubt, in part because of Israel's own priestly station as a "kingdom of priests and a holy nation," exalted to a position of peculiar dignity and privilege before God, that they might mediate the blessings of redemption to all nations. It was because of this fact that, if they sinned, their guilt was peculiarly heavy.

The principle, however, is of present-day application. Privilege is the measure of responsibility, no less now than then, for nations as well as for individuals. Thus national sin, on the part of the British or American nation, or indeed with any of the so-called Christian nations, is certainly judged by God to be a much more evil thing than the same sin if committed, for example, by the Chinese or Turkish nation, who have had no such degree of Gospel light and knowledge.

And the law in this case evidently also implies that sin is aggravated in proportion to its universality. It is bad, for example, if in a community one man commit adultery, forsaking his own wife; but it argues a condition of things far worse when the violation of the marriage relation becomes common; when the question can actually be held open for discussion whether marriage, as a permanent union between one man and one woman, be not "a failure," as debated not long ago in a leading London paper; and when, as in many of the United States of America and other countries of modern Christendom, laws are enacted for the express purpose of legalising the violation of Christ's law of marriage, and thus shielding adulterers and adulteresses from the condign punishment their crime deserves. It is bad, again, when individuals in a State teach doctrines subversive of morality; but it evidently argues a far deeper depravation of morals when a whole community unite in accepting, endowing, and upholding such in their work.

Next in order comes the case of the civil ruler. For him it was ordered: "When a ruler sinneth, and doeth unwittingly any of the things which the Lord his God hath commanded not to be done, and is guilty; if his sin, wherein he hath sinned, be made known to him, he shall bring for his oblation a goat, a male without blemish" (ver. 22). Thus, the ruler was to bring a victim of less value than the high-priest or the collective congregation; but it must still be of more value than that of a private person; for his responsibility, if less than that of the officer of religion, is distinctly greater than that of a man in private life.

And here is a lesson for modern politicians, no less than for rulers of the olden time in Israel. While there are many in our Parliaments and like governing bodies in Christendom who cast their every vote with the fear of God before their eyes, yet, if there be any truth in the general opinion of men upon this subject, there are many in such places who, in their voting, have before their eyes the fear of party more than the fear of God; and who, when a question comes before them, first of all consider, not what would the law of absolute righteousness, the law of God, require, but how will a vote, one way or the other, in this matter, be likely to affect their party? Such certainly need to be emphatically reminded of this part of the law of the sin-offering, which held the civil ruler specially responsible to God for the execution of his trust. For so it is still; God has not abdicated His throne in favour of the people, nor will He waive His crown-rights out of deference to the political necessities of a party.

Nor is it only those who sin in this particular way who need the reminder of their personal responsibility to God. All need it who either are or may be called to places of greater or less governmental responsibility; and it is those who are the most worthy of such trust who will be the first to acknowledge their need of this warning. For in all times those who have been lifted to positions of political power have been under peculiar temptation to forget God, and become reckless of their obligation to Him as His ministers. But under the conditions of modern life, in many countries of Christendom, this is true as perhaps never before. For now it has come to pass that, in most modern communities, those who make and execute laws hold their tenure of office at the pleasure of a motley army of voters, Protestants and Romanists, Jews, atheists, and what not, a large part of whom care not the least for the will of God in civil government, as revealed in Holy Scripture. Under such conditions, the place of the civil ruler becomes one of such special trial and temptation that we do well to remember in our intercessions, with peculiar sympathy, all who in such positions are seeking to serve supremely, not their party, but their God, and so best serve their country. It is no wonder that the temptation too often to many becomes overpowering, to silence conscience with plausible sophistries, and to use their office to carry out in legislation, instead of the will of God, the will of the people, or rather, of that particular party which put them in power.

Yet the great principle affirmed in this law of the sin-offering stands, and will stand for ever, and to it all will do well to take heed; namely, that God will hold the civil ruler responsible, and more heavily responsible than any private person, for any sin he may commit, and especially for any violation of law in any matter committed to his trust. And there is abundant reason for this. For the powers that be are ordained of God, and in His providence are placed in authority; not as the modern notion is, for the purpose of executing the will of their constituents, whatever that will may be, but rather the unchangeable will of the Most Holy God, the Ruler of all nations, so far as revealed, concerning the civil and social relations of men. Nor must it be forgotten that this eminent responsibility attaches to them, not only in their official acts, but in all their acts as individuals. No distinction is made as to the sin for which the ruler must bring his sin-offering, whether public and official, or private and personal. Of whatsoever kind the sin may be, if committed by a ruler, God holds him specially responsible, as being a ruler; and reckons the guilt of that sin, even if a private offence, to be heavier than if it had been committed by one of the common people. And this, for the evident reason that, as in the case of the high priest, his exalted position gives his example double influence and effect. Thus, in all ages and all lands, a corrupt king or nobility have made a corrupt court; and a corrupt court or corrupt legislators are sure to demoralise all the lower ranks of society. But however it may be under the governments of men, under the equitable government of the Most Holy God, high station can give no immunity to sin. And in the day to come, when the Great Assize is set, there will be many who in this world stood high in authority, who will learn, in the tremendous decisions of that day, if not before, that a just God reckoned the guilt of their sins and crimes in exact proportion to their rank and station.

Last of all, in this chapter, comes the law of the sin-offering for one of the common people, of which the first part is given vv. 27-35. The victim which is appointed for those who are best able to give, a female goat, is yet of less value than those ordered in the cases before given; for the responsibility and guilt in the case of such is less. The first prescription for a sin-offering by one of the common people, is introduced by these words:—"If any one of the common people sin unwittingly, in doing any of the things which the Lord hath commanded not to be done, and be guilty; if his sin, which he hath sinned, be made known to him, then he shall bring for his oblation a goat, a female without blemish, for his sin which he hath sinned" (vv. 27, 28).

In case of his inability to bring so much as this, offerings of lesser value are authorised in the section following (v. 5-13), to which we shall attend hereafter.

Meanwhile it is suggestive to observe that this part of the law is expanded more fully than any other part of the law of the sin-offering. We are hereby reminded that if none are so high as to be above the reach of the judgment of God, but are held in that proportion strictly responsible for their sin; so, on the other hand, none are of station so low that their sins shall therefore be overlooked. The common people, in all lands, are the great majority of the population; but no one is to imagine that, because he is a single individual, of no importance in a multitude, he shall therefore, if he sin, escape the Divine eye, as it were, in a crowd. Not so. We may be of the very lowest social station; the provision in chapter v. 11 regards the case of such as might be so poor as that they could not even buy two doves. Men may judge the doings of such poor folk of little or no consequence; but not so God. With Him is no respect of persons, either of rich or poor. From all alike, from the anointed high priest, who ministers in the Holy of Holies, down to the common people, and among these, again, from the highest down to the very lowest, poorest, and meanest in rank, is demanded, even for a sin of ignorance, a sin-offering for atonement.

What a solemn lesson we have herein concerning the character of God! His omniscience, which not only notes the sin of those who are in some conspicuous position, but also each individual sin of the lowest of the people! His absolute equity, exactly and accurately grading responsibility for sin committed, in each case, according to the rank and influence of him who commits it! His infinite holiness, which cannot pass by without expiation even the transient act or word of rash hands or lips, not even the sin not known as sin by the sinner; a holiness which, in a word, unchangeably and unalterably requires, from every human being, nothing less than absolute moral perfection like His own!

CHAPTER VII
THE RITUAL OF THE SIN-OFFERING

Lev. iv. 4-35; v. 1-13; vi. 24-30.

According to the Authorised Version (v. 6, 7), it might seem that the section, v. 1-13, referred not to the sin-offering, but to the guilt-offering, like the latter part of the chapter; but, as suggested in the margin of the Revised Version, in these verses we may properly read, instead of "guilt-offering," "for his guilt." That the latter rendering is to be preferred is clear when we observe that in vv. 6, 7, 9 this offering is called a sin-offering; that, everywhere else, the victim for the guilt-offering is a ram; and, finally, that the estimation of a money value for the victim, which is the most characteristic feature of the guilt-offering, is absent from all the offerings described in these verses. We may safely take it therefore as certain that the marginal reading should be adopted in ver. 6, so that it will read, "he shall bring for his guilt unto the Lord;" and understand the section to contain a further development of the law of the sin-offering. In the law of the preceding chapter we have the direction for the sin-offering as graded with reference to the rank and station of the offerer; in this section we have the law for the sin-offering for the common people, as graded with reference to the ability of the offerer.

The specifications (v. 1-5) indicate several cases under which one of the common people was required to bring a sin-offering as the condition of forgiveness. As an exhaustive list would be impossible, those named are taken as illustrations. The instances selected are significant as extending the class of offences for which atonement could be made by a sin-offering, beyond the limits of sins of inadvertence as given in the previous chapter. For however some cases come under this head, we cannot so reckon sins of rashness (ver. 4), and still less, the failure of the witness placed under oath to tell the whole truth as he knows it. And herein it is graciously intimated that it is in the heart of God to multiply His pardons; and, on condition of the presentation of a sin-offering, to forgive also those sins in palliation of which no such excuse as inadvertence or ignorance can be pleaded. It is a faint foreshadowing, in the law concerning the type, of that which should afterward be declared concerning the great Antitype (1 John i. 7), "The blood of Jesus ... cleanseth from all sin."

When we look now at the various prescriptions regarding the ritual of the offering which are given in this and the foregoing chapter, it is plain that the numerous variations from the ritual of the other sacrifices were intended to withdraw the thought of the sinner from all other aspects in which sacrifice might be regarded, and centre his mind upon the one thought of sacrifice as expiating sin, through the substitution of an innocent life for the guilty. In many particulars, indeed, the ritual agrees with that of the sacrifices before prescribed. The victim must be brought by the guilty person to be offered to God by the priest; he must, as in other cases of bloody offerings, then lay his hand on the head of the victim, and then (a particular not mentioned in the other cases) he must confess the sin which he has committed, and then and thus entrust the victim to the priest, that he may apply its blood for him in atonement before God. The priest then slays the victim, and now comes that part of the ceremonial which by its variations from the law of other offerings is emphasised as the most central and significant in this sacrifice.

The Sprinkling of the Blood.

iv. 6, 7, 16-18, 25, 30; v. 9.

"And the priest shall dip his finger in the blood, and sprinkle of the blood seven times before the Lord, before the veil of the sanctuary. And the priest shall put of the blood upon the horns of the altar of sweet incense before the Lord, which is in the tent of meeting; and all the blood of the bullock shall he pour out at the base of the altar of burnt offering, which is at the door of the tent of meeting.... And the anointed priest shall bring of the blood of the bullock to the tent of meeting: and the priest shall dip his finger in the blood, and sprinkle it seven times before the Lord, before the veil. And he shall put of the blood upon the horns of the altar which is before the Lord, that is in the tent of meeting, and all the blood shall he pour out at the base of the altar of burnt offering, which is at the door of the tent of meeting.... And the priest shall take of the blood of the sin offering with his finger, and put it upon the horns of the altar of burnt offering, and the blood thereof shall he pour out at the base of the altar of burnt offering.... And the priest shall take of the blood thereof with his finger, and put it upon the horns of the altar of burnt offering, and all the blood thereof shall he pour out at the base of the altar.... And he shall sprinkle of the blood of the sin offering upon the side of the altar; and the rest of the blood shall be drained out at the base of the altar: it is a sin offering."

In the case of the burnt-offering and of the peace-offering, in which the idea of expiation, although not absent, yet occupied a secondary place in their ethical intent, it sufficed that the blood of the victim, by whomsoever brought, be applied to the sides of the altar. But in the sin-offering, the blood must not only be sprinkled on the sides of the altar of burnt-offering, but, even in the case of the common people, be applied to the horns of the altar, its most conspicuous and, in a sense, most sacred part. In the case of a sin committed by the whole congregation, even this is not enough; the blood must be brought even into the Holy Place, be applied to the horns of the altar of incense, and be sprinkled seven times before the Lord before the veil which hung immediately before the mercy seat in the Holy of Holies, the place of the Shekinah glory. And in the great sin-offering of the high priest once a year for the sins of all the people, yet more was required. The blood was to be taken even within the veil, and be sprinkled on the mercy seat itself over the tables of the broken law.

These several cases, according to the symbolism of these several parts of the tabernacle differ, in that atoning blood is brought ever more and more nearly into the immediate presence of God. The horns of the altar had a sacredness above the sides; the altar of the Holy Place before the veil, a sanctity beyond that of the altar in the outer court; while the Most Holy Place, where stood the ark, and the mercy-seat, was the very place of the most immediate and visible manifestation of Jehovah, who is often described in Holy Scripture, with reference to the ark, the mercy-seat, and the overhanging cherubim, as the God who "dwelleth between the cherubim."

From this we may easily understand the significance of the different prescriptions as to the blood in the case of different classes. A sin committed by any private individual or by a ruler, was that of one who had access only to the outer court, where stood the altar of burnt-offering; for this reason, it is there that the blood must be exhibited, and that on the most sacred and conspicuous spot in that court, the horns of the altar where God meets with the people. But when it was the anointed priest that had sinned, the case was different. In that he had a peculiar position of nearer access to God than others, as appointed of God to minister before Him in the Holy Place, his sin is regarded as having defiled the Holy Place itself; and in that Holy Place must Jehovah therefore see atoning blood ere the priest's position before God can be re-established.

And the same principle required that also in the Holy Place must the blood be presented for the sin of the whole congregation. For Israel in its corporate unity was "a kingdom of priests," a priestly nation; and the priest in the Holy Place represented the nation in that capacity. Thus because of this priestly office of the nation, their collective sin was regarded as defiling the Holy Place in which, through their representatives, the priests, they ideally ministered. Hence, as the law for the priests, so is the law for the nation. For their corporate sin the blood must be applied, as in the case of the priest who represented them, to the horns of the altar in the Holy Place, whence ascended the smoke of the incense which visibly symbolised accepted priestly intercession, and, more than this, before the veil itself; in other words, as near to the very mercy-seat itself as it was permitted to the priest to go; and it must be sprinkled there, not once, nor twice, but seven times, in token of the re-establishment, through the atoning blood, of God's covenant of mercy, of which, throughout the Scripture, the number seven, the number of sabbatic rest and covenant fellowship with God, is the constant symbol.

And it is not far to seek for the spiritual thought which underlies this part of the ritual. For the tabernacle was represented as the earthly dwelling-place, in a sense, of God; and just as the defiling of the house of my fellow-man may be regarded as an insult to him who dwells in the house, so the sin of the priest and of the priestly people is regarded as, more than that of those outside of this relation, a special affront to the holy majesty of Jehovah, criminal just in proportion as the defilement approaches more nearly the innermost shrine of Jehovah's manifestation.

But though Israel is at present suspended from its priestly position and function among the nations of the earth, the Apostle Peter (1 Peter ii. 5) reminds us that the body of Christian believers now occupies Israel's ancient place, being now on earth the "royal priesthood," the "holy nation." Hence this ritual solemnly reminds us that the sin of a Christian is a far more evil thing than the sin of others; it is as the sin of the priest, and defiles the Holy Place, even though unwillingly committed, and thus, even more imperatively than other sin, demands the exhibition of the atoning blood of the Lamb of God, not now in the Holy Place, but more than that, in the true Holiest of all, where our High Priest is now entered. And thus, in every possible way, with this elaborate ceremonial of sprinkling of blood does the sin-offering emphasise to our own consciences, no less than for ancient Israel, the solemn fact affirmed in the Epistle to the Hebrews (ix. 22), "Without shedding of blood there is no remission of sin."

Because of this, we do well to meditate much and deeply on this symbolism of the sin-offering, which, more than any other in the law, has to do with the propitiation of our Lord for sin. Especially does this use of the blood, in which the significance of the sin-offering reached its supreme expression, claim our most reverent attention. For the thought is inseparable from the ritual, that the blood of the slain victim must be presented, not before the priest, or before the offerer, but before Jehovah. Can any one mistake the evident significance of this? Does it not luminously hold forth the thought that atonement by sacrifice has to do, not only with man, but with God?

There is cause enough in our day for insisting on this. Many are teaching that the need for the shedding of blood for the remission of sin, lies only in the nature of man; that, so far as concerns God, sin might as well have been pardoned without it; that it is only because man is so hard and rebellious, so stubbornly distrusts the Divine love, that the death of the Holy Victim of Calvary became a necessity. Nothing less than such a stupendous exhibition of the love of God could suffice to disarm his enmity to God and win him back to loving trust. Hence the need of the atonement. That all this is true, no one will deny; but it is only half the truth, and the less momentous half,—which indeed is hinted in no offering, and in the sin-offering least of all. Such a conception of the matter as completely fails to account for this part of the symbolic ritual of the bloody sacrifices, as it fails to agree with other teachings of the Scriptures. If the only need for atonement in order to pardon is in the nature of the sinner, then why this constant insistence that the blood of the sacrifice should always be solemnly presented, not before the sinner, but before Jehovah? We see in this fact most unmistakably set forth, the very solemn truth that expiation by blood as a condition of forgiveness of sin is necessary, not merely because man is what he is, but most of all because God is what He is. Let us then not forget that the presentation unto God of an expiation for sin, accomplished by the death of an appointed substitutionary victim, was in Israel made an indispensable condition of the pardon of sin. Is this, as many urge, against the love of God? By no means! Least of all will it so appear, when we remember who appointed the great Sacrifice, and, above all, who came to fulfil this type. God does not love us because atonement has been made, but atonement has been made because the Father loved us, and sent His Son to be the propitiation for our sins.

God is none the less just, that He is love; and none the less holy, that He is merciful; and in His nature, as the Most Just and Holy One, lies this necessity of the shedding of blood in order to the forgiveness of sin, which is impressively symbolised in the unvarying ordinance of the Levitical law, that as a condition of the remission of sin, the blood of the sacrifice must be presented, not before the sinner, but before Jehovah. To this generation of ours, with its so exalted notions of the greatness and dignity of man, and its correspondingly low conceptions of the ineffable greatness and majesty of the Most Holy God, this altar truth may be most distasteful, so greatly does it magnify the evil of sin; but just in that degree is it necessary to the humiliation of man's proud self-complacency, that, whether pleasing or not, this truth be faithfully held forth.

Very instructive and helpful to our faith are the allusions to this sprinkling of blood in the New Testament. Thus, in the Epistle to the Hebrews (xii. 24), believers are reminded that they are come "unto the blood of sprinkling, that speaketh better than that of Abel." The meaning is plain. For we are told (Gen. iv. 10), that the blood of Abel cried out against Cain from the ground; and that its cry for vengeance was prevailing; for God came down, arraigned the murderer, and visited him with instant judgment. But in these words we are told that the sprinkled blood of the holy Victim of Calvary, sprinkled on the heavenly altar, also has a voice, and a voice which "speaketh better than that of Abel;" better, in that it speaks, not for vengeance, but for pardoning mercy; better, in that it procures the remission even of a penitent murderer's guilt; so that, "being now justified through His blood" we may all "be saved from wrath through Him" (Rom. v. 9). And, if we are truly Christ's, it is our blessed comfort to remember also that we are said (1 Peter i. 2) to have been chosen of God unto the sprinkling of this precious blood of Jesus Christ; words which remind us, not only that the blood of a Lamb "without blemish and without spot" has been presented unto God for us, but also that the reason for this distinguishing mercy is found, not in us, but in the free love of God, who chose us in Christ Jesus to this grace.

And as in the burnt-offering, so in the sin-offering, the blood was to be sprinkled by the priest. The teaching is the same in both cases. To present Christ before God, laying the hand of faith upon His head as our sin-offering, this is all we can do or are required to do. With the sprinkling of the blood we have nothing to do. In other words, the effective presentation of the blood before God is not to be secured by some act of our own; it is not something to be procured through some subjective experience, other or in addition to the faith which brings the Victim. As in the type, so in the Antitype, the sprinkling of the atoning blood—that is, its application Godward as a propitiation—is the work of our heavenly Priest. And our part in regard to it is simply and only this, that we entrust this work to Him. He will not disappoint us; He is appointed of God to this end, and He will see that it is done.

In a sacrifice in which the sprinkling of the blood occupies such a central and essential place in the symbolism, one would anticipate that this ceremony would never be dispensed with. Very strange it thus appears, at first sight, to find that to this law an exception was made. For it was ordained (ver. 11) that a man so poor that "his means suffice not" to bring even two doves or young pigeons, might bring, as a substitute, an offering of fine flour. From this, some have hastened to infer that the shedding of the blood, and therewith the idea of substituted life, was not essential to the idea of reconciliation with God; but with little reason. Most illogical and unreasonable it is to determine a principle, not from the general rule, but from an exception; especially when, as in this case, for the exception a reason can be shown, which is not inconsistent with the rule. For had no such exceptional offering been permitted in the case of the extremely poor man, it would have followed that there would have remained a class of persons in Israel whom God had excluded from the provision of the sin-offering, which He had made the inseparable condition of forgiveness. But two truths were to be set forth in the ritual; the one, atonement by means of a life surrendered in expiation of guilt; the other,—as in a similar way in the burnt-offering,—the sufficiency of God's gracious provision for even the neediest of sinners. Evidently, here was a case in which something must be sacrificed in the symbolism. One of these truths may be perfectly set forth; both cannot be, with equal perfectness; a choice must therefore be made, and is made in this exceptional regulation, so as to hold up clearly, even though at the expense of some distinctness in the other thought of expiation, the unlimited sufficiency of God's provision of forgiving grace.

And yet the prescriptions in this form of the offering were such as to prevent any one from confounding it with the meal-offering, which typified consecrated and accepted service. The oil and the frankincense which belonged to the latter, are to be left out (ver. 11); incense, which typifies accepted prayer,—thus reminding us of the unanswered prayer of the Holy Victim when He cried upon the cross, "My God! My God! why hast Thou forsaken Me?" and oil, which typifies the Holy Ghost,—reminding us, again, how from the soul of the Son of God was mysteriously withdrawn in that same hour all the conscious presence and comfort of the Holy Spirit, which withdrawment alone could have wrung from His lips that unanswered prayer. And, again, whereas the meal for the meal-offering had no limit fixed as to quantity, in this case the amount is prescribed—"the tenth part of an ephah" (ver. 11); an amount which, from the story of the manna, appears to have represented the sustenance of one full day. Thus it was ordained that if, in the nature of the case, this sin-offering could not set forth the sacrifice of life by means of the shedding of blood, it should at least point in the same direction, by requiring that, so to speak, the support of life for one day shall be given up, as forfeited by sin.

All the other parts of the ceremonial are in this ordinance made to take a secondary place, or are omitted altogether. Not all of the offering is burnt upon the altar, but only a part; that part, however, the fat, the choicest; for the same reason as in the peace-offering. There is, indeed, a peculiar variation in the case of the offering of the two young pigeons, in that, of the one, the blood only was used in the sacrifice, while the other was wholly burnt like a burnt-offering. But for this variation the reason is evident enough in the nature of the victims. For in the case of a small creature like a bird, the fat would be so insignificant in quantity, and so difficult to separate with thoroughness from the flesh, that the ordinance must needs be varied, and a second bird be taken for the burning, as a substitute for the separated fat of larger animals. The symbolism is not essentially affected by the variation. What the burning of the fat means in other offerings, that also means the burning of the second bird in this case.

The Eating and the Burning of the Sin-Offering without the Camp.

iv. 8-12, 19-21, 26, 31; v. 10, 12.

"And all the fat of the bullock of the sin offering he shall take off from it; the fat that covereth the inwards, and all the fat that is upon the inwards, and the two kidneys, and the fat that is upon them, which is by the loins, and the caul upon the liver, with the kidneys, shall he take away, as it is taken off from the ox of the sacrifice of peace offerings: and the priest shall burn them upon the altar of burnt offering. And the skin of the bullock, and all its flesh, with its head, and with its legs, and its inwards, and its dung, even the whole bullock shall he carry forth without the camp unto a clean place, where the ashes are poured out, and burn it on wood with fire: where the ashes are poured out shall it be burnt.... And all the fat thereof shall he take off from it, and burn it upon the altar. Thus shall he do with the bullock; as he did with the bullock of the sin offering, so shall he do with this: and the priest shall make atonement for them, and they shall be forgiven. And he shall carry forth the bullock without the camp, and burn it as he burned the first bullock: it is the sin offering for the assembly.... And all the fat thereof shall he burn upon the altar, as the fat of the sacrifice of peace offerings: and the priest shall make atonement for him as concerning his sin, and he shall be forgiven.... And all the fat thereof shall he take away, as the fat is taken away from off the sacrifice of peace offerings; and the priest shall burn it upon the altar for a sweet savour unto the Lord; and the priest shall make atonement for him, and he shall be forgiven.... And he shall offer the second for a burnt offering, according to the ordinance: and the priest shall make atonement for him as concerning his sin which he hath sinned, and he shall be forgiven.... And he shall bring it to the priest, and the priest shall take his handful of it as the memorial thereof, and burn it on the altar, upon the offerings of the Lord made by fire: it is a sin offering."

In the ritual of the sin-offering, sacrificial meal, such as that of the peace-offering, wherein the offerer and his house, with the priest and the Levite, partook together of the flesh of the sacrificed victim, there was none. The eating of the flesh of the sin-offerings by the priests, prescribed in chap. vi. 26, had, primarily, a different intention and meaning. As set forth elsewhere (vii. 35), it was "the anointing portion of Aaron and his sons;" an ordinance expounded by the Apostle Paul to this effect, that (1 Cor. ix. 13) they which wait upon the altar should "have their portion with the altar." Yet not of all the sin-offerings might the priest thus partake. For when he was himself the one for whom the offering was made, whether as an individual, or as included in the congregation, then it is plain that he for the time stood in the same position before God as the private individual who had sinned. It was a universal principle of the law that because of the peculiarly near and solemn relation into which the expiatory victim had been brought to God, it was "most holy," and therefore he for whose sin it is offered could not eat of its flesh. Hence the general law is laid down (vi. 30): "No sin offering, whereof any of the blood is brought into the tent of meeting to make atonement in the holy place, shall be eaten; it shall be burnt with fire."

And yet, although, because the priests could not eat of the flesh, it must be burnt, it could not be burnt upon the altar; not, as some have fancied, because it was regarded as unclean, which is directly contradicted by the statement that it is "most holy," but because so to dispose of it would have been to confound the sin-offering with the burnt-offering, which had, as we have seen, a specific symbolic meaning, quite distinct from that of the sin-offering. It must be so disposed of that nothing shall divert the mind of the worshipper from the fact that, not sacrifice as representing full consecration, as in the burnt-offering, but sacrifice as representing expiation, is set forth in this offering. Hence it was ordained that the flesh of these sin-offerings for the anointed priest, or for the congregation, which included him, should be "burnt on wood with fire without the camp" (iv. 11, 12, 21). And the more carefully to guard against the possibility of confounding this burning of the flesh of the sin-offering with the sacrificial burning of the victims on the altar, the Hebrew uses here and in all places where this burning is referred to, a verb wholly distinct from that which is used of the burnings on the altar, and which, unlike that, is used of any ordinary burning of anything for any purpose.

But this burning of the victim without the camp was not therefore empty of all typical significance. The writer of the Epistle to the Hebrews calls our attention to the fact that in this part of the appointed ritual there was also that which prefigured Christ and the circumstances of His death. For we read (Heb. xiii. 10-12), after an exhortation to Christians to have done with the ritual observances of Judaism regarding meats:—"We," that is, we Christian believers, "have an altar,"—the cross upon which Jesus suffered,—"whereof they have no right to eat which serve the tabernacle;" *i.e.*, they who adhere to the now effete Jewish tabernacle service, the unbelieving Israelites, derive no benefit from this sacrifice of ours. "For the bodies of those beasts whose blood is brought into the Holy Place by the high priest as an offering for sin, are burned without the camp;" the priesthood are debarred from eating them, according to the law we have before us. And then attention is called to the fact that in this respect Jesus fulfilled this part of the type of the sin-offering, thus: "Wherefore Jesus also, that He might sanctify the people with His own blood, suffered without the camp." That is, as Alford interprets (Comm. sub. loc.), in the circumstance that Jesus suffered without the gate, is seen a visible adumbration of the fact that He suffered outside the camp of legal Judaism, and thus, in that He suffered for the sin of the whole congregation of Israel, fulfilled the type of this sin-offering in this particular. Thus a prophecy is discovered here which perhaps we had not else discerned, concerning the manner of the death of the antitypical victim. He should suffer as a victim for the sin of the whole congregation, the priestly people, who should for that reason be debarred, in fulfilment of the type, from that benefit of His death which had else been their privilege. And herein was accomplished to the uttermost that surrender of His whole being to God, in that, in carrying out that full consecration, "He, bearing His cross went forth," not merely outside the gate of Jerusalem,—in itself a trivial circumstance,—but, as this fitly symbolised, outside the congregation of Israel, to suffer. In other words, His consecration of Himself to God in self-sacrifice found its supreme expression in this, that He voluntarily submitted to be cast out from Israel, despised and rejected of men, even of the Israel of God.

And so this burning of the flesh of the sin-offering of the highest grade in two places, the fat upon the altar, in the court of the congregation, and the rest of the victim outside the camp, set forth prophetically the full self-surrender of the Son to the Father, as the sin-offering, in a double aspect: in the former, emphasising simply, as in the peace-offering, His surrender of all that was highest and best in Him, as Son of God and Son of man, unto the Father as a Sin-offering; in the latter, foreshowing that He should also, in a special manner, be a sacrifice for the sin of the congregation of Israel, and that His consecration should receive its fullest exhibition and most complete expression in that He should die outside the camp of legal Judaism, as an outcast from the congregation of Israel.

Accordingly we find that this part of the type of the sin-offering was formally accomplished when the high priest, upon Christ's confession before the Sanhedrim of His Sonship to God, declared Him to be guilty of blasphemy; an offence for which it had been ordered by the Lord (Lev. xxiv. 14) that the guilty person should be taken "without the camp" to suffer for his sin.

In the light of these marvellous correspondences between the typical sin-offering and the self-offering of the Son of God, what a profound meaning more and more appears in those words of Christ concerning Moses: "He wrote of Me."

The Sanctity of the Sin-Offering.

vi. 24-30.

> "And the Lord spake unto Moses, saying, Speak unto Aaron and to his sons, saying, This is the law of the sin offering: in the place where the burnt offering is killed shall the sin offering be killed before the Lord: it is most holy. The priest that offereth it for sin shall eat it: in a holy place shall it be eaten, in the court of the tent of meeting. Whatsoever shall touch the flesh thereof shall be holy: and when there is sprinkled of the blood thereof upon any garment, thou shalt wash that whereon it was sprinkled in a holy place. But the earthen vessel wherein it is sodden shall be broken: and if it be sodden in a brasen vessel, it shall be scoured, and rinsed in water. Every male among the priests shall eat thereof: it is most holy. And no sin offering, whereof any of the blood is brought into the tent of meeting to make atonement in the holy place, shall be eaten: it shall be burnt with fire."

In chap. vi. 24-30 we have a section which is supplemental to the law of the sin-offering, in which, with some repetition of the laws previously given, are added certain special regulations, in fuller exposition of the peculiar sanctity attaching to this offering. As in the case of other offerings called "most holy," it is ordered that only the males among the priests shall eat of it; among whom, the officiating priest takes the precedence. Further, it is declared that everything that touches the offering shall be regarded as "holy," that is, as invested with the sanctity attaching to every person or thing specially devoted to the Lord.

Then by way of application of this principle to two of the most common cases in which it could apply, it is ordered, first (ver. 27), with regard to any garment which should be sprinkled with the blood, "thou shalt wash that whereon it was sprinkled in a holy place;" that so by no chance should the least of the blood which had been shed for the remission of sin, come into contact with anything unclean and unholy. And then, again, inasmuch as the flesh which should be eaten by the priest must needs be cooked, and the vessel used by this contact became holy, it is commanded (ver. 28) that, if a brazen vessel, "it shall be scoured" and "then rinsed with water;" that in no case should a vessel in which might remain the least of the sacrificial flesh, be used for any profane purpose, and so the holy flesh be defiled. And because when an (unglazed) earthen vessel was used, even such scouring and rinsing could not so cleanse it, but that something of the juices of the holy flesh should be absorbed into its substance, therefore, in order to preclude the possibility of its ever being used for any common purpose it is directed (ver. 28) that it shall be broken.[10]

By such regulations as these, it is plain that even in those days of little light the thoughtful Israelite would be impressed with the feeling that in the expiation of sin he came into a peculiarly near and solemn relation to the holiness of God, even though he might not be able to formulate his thought more exactly. In modern times, however, strange to say, these very regulations with regard to the sin-offering, when it has been taken as typical of Christ, have been used as an argument against the New Testament teaching as to the expiatory nature of His death as a true satisfaction to the holy justice of God for the sins of men. For it is argued, that if Christ was really, in a legal sense, regarded as a sinner, because standing in the sinner's place, to receive in His person the wrath of God against the sinner's sin, it could not have been ordered that the blood and the flesh of the typical offering should be thus regarded as of peculiar and pre-eminent holiness. Rather, we are told, should we, for example, have read in the ritual, "No one, and, least of all, the priests, shall eat of it; for it is most unclean." An extraordinary argument and conclusion! For surely it is an utter misapprehension both of the so-called "orthodox" view of the atonement, and of the New Testament teaching on the subject, to represent it as involving the suggestion that Christ, when for us "made sin," and suffering as our substitute, thereby must have been for the time Himself unclean. Surely, according to the constant use of the word, in imputation of sin, of any sin, to any one, there is no conveyance of character; it is only implied that such person is, for whatsoever reason, justly or unjustly, treated as if he were guilty of that sin which is imputed to him. Imputing falsehood to a man who is truth itself, does not make him a liar, though it does involve treating him as if he were. Just so it is in this case.

There is, then, in these regulations which emphasise the peculiar holiness of the sin-offering, nothing which is inconsistent with the strictest juridical view of the great atonement which in type it represented. On the contrary, one can hardly think of anything which should more effectively represent the great truth of the incomparable holiness of the victim of Calvary, than just this strenuous insistence that the blood and the flesh of the typical victim should be treated as of the most peculiar sanctity. If, when we see the victim of the sin-offering slain and its blood presented before God, we behold a vivid representation of Christ, the Lamb of God, "made sin in our behalf;" so when, in these regulations, we see how the flesh and blood of the offered victim is treated as of the most pre-eminent sanctity, we are as impressively reminded how it is written (2 Cor. v. 21) that it was "Him who knew no sin," that God "made to be sin on our behalf." Thus does the type, in order that nothing might be wanting in this law of the offering, insist in every possible way on the holiness of the great Victim who became the Antitype; and most of all in the sin-offering, because in this, where, not consecration of the person or the works, or the impartation and fellowship of the life of Christ, but expiation, was the central idea of the sacrifice, there was a special need for emphasising, in an exceptional way, this thought; that the Victim who bore our sins, although visibly laden with the curse of God, was none the less all the time Himself "most holy;" so that in that unfathomable mystery of Calvary, never was He more truly and really the well-beloved Son of the Father than when He cried out in the extremity of His anguish as "made sin for us," "My God, My God, why hast Thou forsaken Me?"

How wonderfully adapted in all its details was this law of the sin-offering, not only for the education of Israel, but, if we will meditate upon these things, also for our own! How the truths which underlie this law should humble us, even in proportion as they exalt to the uttermost the ineffable majesty of the holiness of God! And, if we will but yield to their teachings, how mightily should they constrain us, in grateful recognition of the love of the Holy One who was "made sin in our behalf," and of the love of the Father who sent Him for this end, to accept Him as our Sin-offering, set forth in the consummation of the ages, "to put away sin by the sacrifice of Himself." No more are offered the sin-offerings of the law of Moses: —

> "But Christ, the heavenly Lamb,
> Takes all our sins away;
> A sacrifice of nobler name,
> And richer blood, than they."

If, then, the law of the Levitical sin-offering abides in force no longer, this is not because God has changed, or because the truths which it set forth concerning sin, and expiation, and pardon, are obsolete, but only because the great Sin-offering which the ancient sacrifice typified, has now appeared. God hath "taken away the first, that He may establish the second" (Heb. x. 9). We have thus to do with the same God as the Israelite. Now, as then, He takes account of all our sins, even of sins committed "unwittingly;" He reckons guilt with the same absolute impartiality and justice as then; He pardons sin, as then, only when the sinner who seeks pardon, presents a sin-offering. But He has now Himself provided the Lamb for this offering, and now in infinite love invites us all, without distinction, with whatsoever sins we may be burdened, to make free use of the all-sufficient and most efficient blood of His well-beloved Son. Shall we risk neglecting this Divine provision, and undertake to deal with God by-and-bye, in the great day of judgment, on our own merits, without a sacrifice for sin? God forbid! Rather let us go on to say in the words of that old hymn:—

> "My faith would lay her hand
> On that dear Head of Thine,
> While like a penitent I stand,
> And there confess my sin."

CHAPTER VIII
THE GUILT-OFFERING

Lev. v. 14; vi. 7; vii. 1-7.

As in the English version, so also in the Hebrew, the special class of sins for which the guilt-offering[11] is prescribed, is denoted by a distinct and specific word. That word, like the English "trespass," its equivalent, always has reference to an invasion of the rights of others, especially in respect of property or service. It is used, for instance, of the sin of Achan (Josh. vii. 1), who had appropriated spoil from Jericho, which God had commanded to be set apart for Himself. Thus, also, the neglect of God's service, and especially the worship of idols, is often described by this same word, as in 2 Chron. xxviii. 22, xxix. 6, and many other places. The reason is evident; for idolatry involved a withholding from God of those tithes and other offerings which He claimed from Israel, and thus became, as it were, an invasion of the Divine rights of property. The same word is even applied to the sin of adultery (Numb. v. 12, 27), apparently from the same point of view, inasmuch as the woman is regarded as belonging to her husband, who has therefore in her certain sacred rights, of which adultery is an invasion. Thus, while every "trespass" is a sin, yet every sin is not a "trespass." There are, evidently, many sins of which this is not a characteristic feature. But the sins for which the guilt-offering is prescribed are in every case sins which *may*, at least, be specially regarded under this particular point of view, to wit, as trespasses on the rights of God or man in respect of ownership; and this gives us the fundamental thought which distinguishes the guilt-offering from all others, namely, that for any invasion of the rights of another in regard to property, not only must expiation be made, in that it is a sin, but also satisfaction, and, so far as possible, plenary reparation of the wrong, in that the sin is also trespass.

From this it is evident that, as contrasted with the burnt-offering, which pre-eminently symbolised full consecration of the person, and the peace-offering, which symbolised fellowship with God, as based upon reconciliation by sacrifice, the guilt-offering takes its place, in a general sense, with the sin-offering, as, like that, specially designed to effect the reinstatement of an offender in covenant relation with God. Thus, like the latter, and unlike the former offerings, it was only prescribed with reference to specific instances of failure to fulfil some particular obligation toward God or man. So also, as the express condition of an acceptable offering, the formal confession of such sin was particularly enjoined. And, finally, unlike the burnt-offering, which was wholly consumed upon the altar, or the peace-offering, of the flesh of which, with certain reservations, the worshipper himself partook, in the case of the guilt-offering, as in the sin-offering, the fat parts only were burnt on the altar, and the remainder of the victim fell to the priests, to be eaten by them alone in a holy place, as a thing "most holy." The law is given in the following words (vii. 3-7): "He shall offer of it all the fat thereof; the fat tail, and the fat that covereth the inwards, and the two kidneys, and the fat that is on them, which is by the loins, and the caul upon the liver, with the kidneys, shall he take away: and the priest shall burn them upon the altar for an offering made by fire unto the Lord: it is a guilt offering. Every male among the priests shall eat thereof: it shall be eaten in a holy place: it is most holy. As is the sin offering, so is the guilt offering: there is one law for them: the priest that maketh atonement therewith, he shall have it."

But while, in a general way, the guilt-offering was evidently intended, like the sin-offering, to signify the removal of sin from the conscience through sacrifice, and thus may be regarded as a variety of the sin-offering, yet the ritual presents some striking variations from that of the latter. These are all explicable from this consideration, that whereas the sin-offering represented the idea of atonement by sacrifice, regarded as an *expiation* of guilt, the guilt-offering represented atonement under the aspect of a *satisfaction* and *reparation* for the wrong committed. Hence, because the idea of expiation here fell somewhat into the background, in order to give the greater prominence to that of reparation and satisfaction, the application of the blood is only made, as in the burnt-offering and the peace-offering, by sprinkling "on the altar (of burnt-offering) round about" (vii. 1). Hence, again, we find that the guilt-offering always had reference to the sin of the individual, and never to the congregation; because it was scarcely possible that every individual in the whole congregation should be guilty in such instances as those for which the guilt-offering is prescribed.

Again, we have another contrast in the restriction imposed upon the choice of the victim for the sacrifice. In the sin-offering, as we have seen, it was ordained that the offering should be varied according to the theocratic rank of the offender, to emphasise thereby to the conscience gradations of guilt, as thus determined; also, it was permitted that the offering might be varied in value according to the ability of the offerer, in order that it might thus be signified in symbol that it was the gracious will of God that nothing in the personal condition of the sinner should exclude any one from the merciful provision of the expiatory sacrifice. But it was no less important that another aspect of the matter should be held forth, namely, that God is no respecter of persons; and that, whatever be the condition of the offender, the obligation to plenary satisfaction and reparation for trespass committed, cannot be modified in any way by the circumstances of the offender. The man who, for example, has defrauded his neighbour, whether of a small sum or of a large estate, abides his debtor before God, under all conceivable conditions, until restitution is made. The obligation of full payment rests upon every debtor, be he poor or rich, until the last farthing is discharged. Hence, the sacrificial victim of the guilt-offering is the same, whether for the poor man or the rich man, "a ram of the flock."

It was "a ram of the flock," because, as contrasted with the ewe or the lamb, or the dove and the pigeon, it was a valuable offering. And yet it is not a bullock, the most valuable offering known to the law, because that might be hopelessly out of the reach of many a poor man. The idea of value must be represented, and yet not so represented as to exclude a large part of the people from the provisions of the guilt-offering. The ram must be "without blemish," that naught may detract from its value, as a symbol of full satisfaction for the wrong done.

But most distinctive of all the requisitions touching the victim is this, that, unlike all other victims for other offerings, the ram of the guilt-offering must in each case be definitely appraised by the priest. The phrase is (v. 15), that it must be "according to thy estimation in silver by shekels, after the shekel of the sanctuary." This expression evidently requires, first, that the offerer's own estimate of the value of the victim shall not be taken, but that of the priest, as representing God in this transaction; and, secondly, that its value shall in no case fall below a certain standard; for the plural expression, "by shekels," implies that the value of the ram shall not be less than two shekels. And the shekel must be of full weight; the standard of valuation must be God's, and not man's, "the shekel of the sanctuary."

Still more to emphasise the distinctive thought of this sacrifice, that full satisfaction and reparation for all offences is with God the universal and unalterable condition of forgiveness, it was further ordered that in all cases where the trespass was of such a character as made this possible, that which had been unjustly taken or kept back, whether from God or man, should be restored "in full;" and not only this, but inasmuch as by this misappropriation of what was not his own, the offender had for the time deprived another of the use and enjoyment of that which belonged to him, he must add to that of which he had defrauded him "the fifth part more," a double tithe. Thus the guilty person was not allowed to have gained even any temporary advantage from the use for a while of that which he now restored; for "the fifth part more" would presumably quite overbalance all conceivable advantage or enjoyment which he might have had from his fraud. How admirable in all this the exact justice of God! How perfectly adapted was the guilt-offering, in all these particulars, to educate the conscience, and to preclude any possible wrong inferences from the allowance which was made, for other reasons, for the poor man, in the expiatory offerings for sin!

The arrangement of the law of the guilt-offering is very simple. It is divided into two sections, the first of which (v. 14-19) deals with cases of trespass "in the holy things of the Lord," things which, by the law or by an act of consecration, were regarded as belonging in a special sense to Jehovah; the second section, on the other hand (vi. 1-7), deals with cases of trespass on the property rights of man.

The first of these, again, consists of two parts. Verses 14-16 give the law of the guilt-offering as applied to cases in which a man, through inadvertence or unwittingly, trespasses in the holy things of the Lord, but in such manner that the nature and extent of the trespass can afterward be definitely known and valued; verses 17-19 deal with cases where there has been trespass such as to burden the conscience, and yet such as, for whatsoever reason, cannot be precisely measured.

By "the holy things of the Lord" are intended such things as, either by universal ordinance or by voluntary consecration, were regarded as belonging to Jehovah, and in a special sense His property. Thus, under this head would come the case of the man who, for instance, should unwittingly eat the flesh of the firstling of his cattle, or the flesh of the sin-offering, or the shew-bread; or should use his tithe, or any part of it, for himself. Even though he did this unwittingly, yet it none the less disturbed the man's relation to God; and therefore, when known, in order to his reinstatement in fellowship with God, it was necessary that he should make full restitution with a fifth part added, and, besides this, sacrifice a ram, duly appraised, as a guilt-offering. In that the sacrifice was prescribed over and above the restitution, the worshipper was reminded that, in view of the infinite majesty and holiness of God, it lies not in the power of any creature to nullify the wrong God-ward, even by fullest restitution. For trespass is not only trespass, but is also sin; an offence not only against the rights of Jehovah as Owner, but also an affront to Him as Supreme King and Lawgiver.

And yet, because the worshipper must not be allowed to lose sight of the fact that sin is of the nature of a debt, a victim was ordered which should especially bring to mind this aspect of the matter. For not only among the Hebrews, but among the Arabs, the Romans and other ancient peoples, sheep, and especially rams, were very commonly used as a medium of payment in case of debt, and especially in paying tribute.

Thus we read (2 Kings iii. 4), that Mesha, king of Moab, rendered unto the king of Israel "an hundred thousand lambs, and an hundred thousand rams, with the wool," in payment of tribute; and, at a later day, Isaiah (xvi. 1, R.V.) delivers to Moab the mandate of Jehovah: "Send ye the lambs for the ruler of the land ... unto the mount of the daughter of Zion."

And so the ram having been brought and presented by the guilty person, with confession of his fault, it was slain by the priest, like the sin-offering. The blood, however, was not applied to the horns of the altar of burnt-offering, still less brought into the Holy Place, as in the case of the sin-offering; but (vii. 2) was to be sprinkled "upon the altar round about," as in the burnt-offering. The reason of this difference in the application of the blood, as above remarked, lies in this, that, as in the burnt-offering, the idea of sacrifice as symbolising expiation takes a place secondary and subordinate to another thought; in this case, the conception of sacrifice as representing satisfaction for trespass.

The next section (vv. 17-19) does not expressly mention sins of trespass; for which reason some have thought that it was essentially a repetition of the law of the sin-offering. But that it is not to be so regarded is plain from the fact that the victim is still the same as for the guilt-offering, and from the explicit statement (ver. 19) that this "is a guilt-offering." The inference is natural that the prescription still has reference to "trespass in the holy things of the Lord;" and the class of cases intended is probably indicated by the phrase, "though he knew it not." In the former section, the law provided for cases in which though the trespass had been done unwittingly, yet the offender afterward came to know of the trespass in its precise extent, so as to give an exact basis for the restitution ordered in such cases. But it is quite supposable that there might be cases in which, although the offender was aware that there had been a probable trespass, such as to burden his conscience, he yet knew not just how much it was. The ordinance is only in so far modified as such a case would make necessary; where there was no exact knowledge of the amount of trespass, obviously there the law of restitution with the added fifth could not be applied. Yet, none the less, the man is guilty; he "bears his iniquity," that is, he is liable to the penalty of his fault; and in order to the re-establishment of his covenant relation with God, the ram must be offered as a guilt-offering.

It is suggestive to observe the emphasis which is laid upon the necessity of the guilt-offering, even in such cases. Three times, reference is explicitly made to this fact of ignorance, as not affecting the requirement of the guilt-offering: (ver. 17) "Though he knew it not, yet is he guilty, and shall bear his iniquity;" and again (ver. 18), with special explicitness, "The priest shall make atonement for him concerning the thing wherein he erred unwittingly and knew it not;" and yet again (ver. 19), "It is a guilt-offering: he is certainly guilty before the Lord." The repetition is an urgent reminder that in this case, as in all others, we are never to forget that however our ignorance of a trespass at the time, or even lack of definite knowledge regarding its nature and extent, may affect the degree of our guilt, it cannot affect the fact of our guilt, and the consequent necessity for satisfaction in order to acceptance with God.

The second section of the law of the guilt-offering (vi. 1-7) deals with trespasses against man, as also, like trespasses against Jehovah, requiring, in order to forgiveness from God, full restitution with the added fifth, and the offering of the ram as a guilt-offering. Five cases are named (vv. 2, 3,), no doubt as being common, typical examples of sins of this character.

The first case is trespass upon a neighbour's rights in "a matter of deposit;" where a man has entrusted something to another to keep, and he has either sold it or unlawfully used it as if it were his own. The second case takes in all fraud in a "bargain," as when, for example, a man sells goods, or a piece of land, representing them to be better than they really are, or asking a price larger than he knows an article to be really worth. The third instance is called "robbery;" by which we are to understand any act or process, even though it should be under colour of legal forms, by means of which a man may manage unjustly to get possession of the property of his neighbour, without giving him due equivalent therefor. The fourth instance is called "oppression" of his neighbour. The English word contains the same image as the Hebrew word, which is used, for instance, of the unnecessary retention of the wages of the *employé* by the employer (xix. 13); it may be applied to all cases in which a man takes advantage of another's circumstances to extort from him any thing or any service to which he has no right, or to force upon him something which it is to the poor man's disadvantage to take. The last example of offences to which the law of the guilt-offering applied, is the case in which a man finds something and then denies it to the rightful owner. The reference to false swearing which follows, as appears from ver. 5, refers not merely to lying and perjury concerning this last-named case, but equally to all cases in which a man may lie or swear falsely to the pecuniary damage of his neighbour. It is mentioned not merely as aggravating such sin, but because in swearing touching any matter, a man appeals to God as witness to the truth of his words; so that by swearing in these cases he represents God as a party to his falsehood and injustice.

In all these cases, the prescription is the same as in analogous offences in the holy things of Jehovah. First of all, the guilty man must confess the wrong which he has done (Numb. v. 7), then restitution must be made of all of which he has defrauded his neighbour, together with one-fifth additional. But while this may set him right with man, it has not yet set him right with God. He must bring his guilt-offering unto Jehovah (vv. 6, 7); "a ram without blemish out of the flock, according to the priest's estimation, for a guilt offering, unto the priest: and the priest shall make atonement for him before the Lord, and he shall be forgiven; concerning whatsoever he doeth so as to be guilty thereby."

And this completes the law of the guilt-offering. It was thus prescribed for sins which involve a defrauding or injuring of another in respect to material things, whether God or man, whether knowingly or unwittingly. The law was one and unalterable for all; the condition of pardon was plenary restitution for the wrong done, and the offering of a costly sacrifice, appraised as such by the priest, the earthly representative of God, in the shekel of the sanctuary, "a ram without blemish out of the flock."

There are lessons from this ordinance, so plain that, even in the dim light of those ancient days, the Israelite might discern and understand them. And they are lessons which, because man and his ways are the same as then, and God the same as then, are no less pertinent to all of us to-day.

Thus we are taught by this law that God claims from man, and especially from His own people, certain rights of property, of which He will not allow Himself to be defrauded, even through man's forgetfulness or inadvertence. In a later day Israel was sternly reminded of this in the burning words of Jehovah by the prophet Malachi (iii. 8, 9): "Will a man rob God? yet ye rob me. But ye say, Wherein have we robbed thee? In tithes and offerings. Ye are cursed with the curse; for ye rob me, even this whole nation." Nor has God relaxed His claim in the present dispensation. For the Apostle Paul charges the Corinthian Christians (2 Cor. viii. 7), in the name of the Lord, with regard to their gifts, that as they abounded in other graces, so they should "abound in this grace also." And this is the first lesson brought before us in the law of the guilt-offering. God claims His tithe, His first-fruit, and the fulfilment of all vows. It was a lesson for that time; it is no less a lesson for our time.

And the guilt-offering further reminds us that as God has rights, so man also has rights, and that Jehovah, as the King and Judge of men, will exact the satisfaction of those rights, and will pass over no injury done by man to his neighbour in material things, nor forgive it unto any man, except upon condition of the most ample material restitution to the injured party.

Then, yet again, if the sin-offering called especially for *faith* in an expiatory sacrifice as the condition of the Divine forgiveness, the guilt-offering as specifically called also for *repentance*, as a condition of pardon, no less essential. Its unambiguous message to every Israelite was the same as that of John the Baptist at a later day (Matt. iii. 8, 9): "Bring forth fruit worthy of repentance: and think not to say within yourselves, We have Abraham to our father."

The reminder is as much needed now as in the days of Moses. How specific and practical the selection of the particular instances mentioned as cases for the application of the inexorable law of the guilt-offering! Let us note them again, for they are not cases peculiar to Israel or to the fifteenth century before Christ. "If any one ... deal falsely with his neighbour in a matter of deposit;" as, *e.g.*, in the case of moneys entrusted to a bank or railway company, or other corporation; for there is no hint that the law did not apply except to individuals, or that a man might be released from these stringent obligations of righteousness whenever in some such evil business he was associated with others; the guilt-offering must be forthcoming, with the amplest restitution, or there is no pardon. Then false dealing in a "bargain" is named, as involving the same requirement; as when a man prides himself on driving "a good bargain," by getting something unfairly for less than its value, taking advantage of his neighbour's straits; or by selling something for more than its value, taking advantage of his neighbour's ignorance, or his necessity. Then is mentioned "robbery;" by which word is covered not merely that which goes by the name in polite circles, but all cases in which a man takes advantage of his neighbour's distress or helplessness, perhaps by means of some technicality of law, to "strip" him, as the Hebrew word is, of his property of any kind. And next is specified the man who may "have oppressed his neighbour," especially a man or woman who serves him, as the usage of the word suggests; grinding thus the face of the poor; paying, for instance, less for labour than the law of righteousness and love demands, because the poor man must have work or starve with his house. What sweeping specifications! And all such, in all lands and all ages, are solemnly reminded in the law of the guilt-offering that in these their sharp practices they have to reckon not with man merely, but with God; and that it is utterly vain for a man to hope for the forgiveness of sin from God, offering or no offering, so long as he has in his pocket his neighbour's money. For all such, full restoration with the added fifth, according to the law of the theocratic kingdom, was the unalterable condition of the Divine forgiveness; and we shall find that this law of the theocratic kingdom will also be the law applied in the adjudications of the great white throne.

Furthermore, in that it was particularly enjoined that in the estimation of the value of the guilt-offering, not the shekel of the people, often of light weight, but the full weight "shekel of the sanctuary" was to be held the invariable standard; we, who are so apt to ease things to our consciences by applying to our conduct the principles of judgment current among men, are plainly taught that if we will have our trespasses forgiven, the reparation and restitution which we make must be measured, not by the standard of men, but by that of God, which is absolute righteousness.

Yet again, in that in the case of all such trespasses on the rights of God or man it was ordained that the offering, unlike other sacrifices intended to teach other lessons, should be one and the same, whether the offender were rich or poor; we are taught that the extent of our moral obligations or the conditions of their equitable discharge are not determined by a regard to our present ability to make them good. Debt is debt by whomsoever owed. If a man have appropriated a hundred pounds of another man's money, the moral obligation of that debt cannot be abrogated by a bankrupt law, allowing him to compromise at ten shillings in the pound. The law of man may indeed release him from liability to prosecution, but no law can discharge such a man from the unalterable obligation to pay penny for penny, farthing for farthing. There is no bankrupt law in the kingdom of God. This, too, is evidently a lesson quite as much needed by Gentiles and nominal Christians in the nineteenth century after Christ, as by Hebrews in the fifteenth century before Christ.

But the spiritual teaching of the guilt-offering is not yet exhausted. For, like all the other offerings, it pointed to Christ. He is "the end of the law unto righteousness" (Rom. x. 4), as regards the guilt-offering, as in all else. As the burnt-offering prefigured Christ the heavenly Victim, in one aspect, and the peace-offering, Christ in another aspect, so the guilt-offering presents to our adoring contemplation yet another view of His sacrificial work. While, as our burnt-offering, He became our *righteousness* in full self-consecration; as our peace-offering, our *life*; as our sin-offering, the *expiation* for our sins; so, as our guilt-offering, He made *satisfaction* and plenary reparation in our behalf to the God on whose inalienable rights in us, by our sins we had trespassed without measure.

Nor is this an over-refinement of exposition. For in Isa. liii. 10, where both the Authorised and the Revised Versions read, "shall make his soul *an offering for sin*," the margin of the latter rightly calls attention to the fact that in the Hebrew the word here used is the very same which through all this Levitical law is rendered "guilt-offering." And so we are expressly told by this evangelic prophet, that the Holy Servant of Jehovah, the suffering Messiah, in this His sacrificial work should make His soul "a guilt-offering."

He became Himself the complete and exhaustive realisation of all that in sacrifice which was set forth in the Levitical guilt-offering.

A declaration this is which holds forth both the sin for which Christ atoned, and the Sacrifice itself, in a very distinct and peculiar light. In that Christ's sacrifice was thus a guilt-offering in the sense of the law, we are taught that, in one aspect, our sins are regarded by God, and should therefore be regarded by us, as debts which are due from us to God. This is, indeed, by no means the only aspect in which sin should be regarded; it is, for example, rebellion, high treason, a deadly affront to the Supreme Majesty, which must be expiated with the blood of the sin-offering. But our sins are also of the nature of debts. That is, God has claims on us for service which we have never met; claims for a portion of our substance which we have often withheld, or given grudgingly, trespassing thus in "the holy things of the Lord." Just as the servant who is set to do his master's work, if, instead, he take that time to do his own work, is debtor to the full value of the service of which his master is thus defrauded, so stands the case between the sinner and God. Just as with the agent who fails to make due returns to his principal on the moneys committed to him for investment, using them instead for himself, so stands the case between God and the sinner who has used his talents, not for the Lord, but for himself, or has kept them laid up, unused, in a napkin. Thus, in the New Testament, as the correlate of this representation of Christ as a guilt-offering, we find sin again and again set forth as a debt which is owed from man to God. So, in the Lord's prayer we are taught to pray, "Forgive us our debts;" so, twice the Lord Himself in His parables (Matt. xviii. 23-35; Luke vii. 41, 42) set forth the relation of the sinner to God as that of the debtor to the creditor; and concerning those on whom the tower of Siloam fell, asks (Luke xiii. 4), "Think ye that they were sinners (*Greek* 'debtors,') above all that dwelt in Jerusalem?" Indeed so imbedded is this thought in the conscience of man that it has been crystallised in our word "ought," which is but the old preterite of "owe;" as in Tyndale's New Testament, where we read (Luke vii. 41), "there was a certain lender, which ought him five hundred pence." What a startling conception is this, which forms the background to the great "guilt-offering"! Man a debtor to God! a debtor for service each day due, but no day ever fully and perfectly rendered! in gratitude for gifts, too often quite forgotten, oftener only paid in scanty part! We are often burdened and troubled greatly about our debts to men; shall we not be concerned about the enormous and ever accumulating debt to God! Or is He an easy creditor, who is indifferent whether these debts of ours be met or not? So think multitudes; but this is not the representation of Scripture, either in the Old or the New Testament. For in the law it was required, that if a man, guilty of any of these offences for the forgiveness of which the guilt-offering was prescribed, failed to confess and bring the offering, and make the restitution with the added fifth, as commanded by the law, he should be brought before the judges, and the full penalty of law exacted, on the principle of "an eye for an eye, a tooth for a tooth!" And in the New Testament, one of those solemn parables of the two debtors closes with the awful words concerning one of them who was "delivered to the tormentors," that he should not come out of prison till he had "paid the uttermost farthing." Not a hint is there in Holy Scripture, of forgiveness of our debts to God, except upon the one condition of full restitution made to Him to whom the debt is due, and therewith the sacrificial blood of a guilt-offering. But Christ is our Guilt-Offering. He is our Guilt-Offering, in that He Himself did that, really and fully, with respect to all our debts as sinful men to God, which the guilt-offering of Leviticus symbolised, but accomplished not. His soul He made a guilt-offering for our trespasses! Isaiah's words imply that He should make full restitution for all that of which we, as sinners, defraud God. He did this by that perfect and incomparable service of lowly obedience such as we should render, but have never rendered; in which He has made full satisfaction to God for all our innumerable debts. He has made such satisfaction, not by a convenient legal fiction, or in a rhetorical figure, or as judged by any human standard. Even as the ram of the guilt-offering was appraised according to "the shekel of the sanctuary," so upon our Lord, at the beginning of that life of sacrificial service, was solemnly passed the Divine verdict that with this antitypical Victim of the Guilt-Offering, God Himself was "well pleased" (Matt. iii. 17).

Not only so. For we cannot forget that according to the law, not only the full restitution must be made, but the fifth must be added thereto. So with our Lord. For who will not confess that Christ not only did all that we should have done, but, in the ineffable depth of His self-humiliation and obedience unto death, even the death of the cross, paid therewith the added fifth of the law. Said a Jewish Rabbi to the writer, "I have never been able to finish reading in the Gospel the story of the Jesus of Nazareth; for it too soon brings the tears to my eyes!" So affecting even to Jewish unbelief was this unparalleled spectacle, the adorable Son of God making Himself a guilt-offering, and paying, in the incomparable perfection of His holy obedience, the added fifth in our behalf! Thus has Christ "magnified this law" of the guilt-offering, and "made it honourable," even as He did all law (Isa. xlii. 21).

And, as is intimated, by the formal valuation of the sacrificial ram, in the type, even the death of Christ as the guilt-offering, in one aspect is to be regarded as the consummating act of service in the payment of debts Godward. Just as the sin-offering represented His death in its passive aspect, as meeting the demands of justice against the sinner as a rebel under sentence of death, by dying in his stead, so, on the other hand, the guilt-offering represents that same sacrificial death, rather in another aspect, no less clearly set forth in the New Testament; namely, the supreme act of obedience to the will of God, whereby He discharged "to the uttermost farthing," even with the added fifth of the law, all the transcendent debt of service due from man to God.

This representation of Christ's work has in all ages been an offence, "the offence of the cross." All the more need we to insist upon it, and never to forget, or let others forget, that Christ is expressly declared in the Word of God to have been "a guilt-offering," in the Levitical sense of that term; that, therefore, to speak of His death as effecting our salvation merely through its moral influence, is to contradict and nullify the Word of God. Well may we set this word in Isa. liii. 10, concerning the Servant of Jehovah, against all modern Unitarian theology, and against all Socinianising teaching; all that would maintain any view of Christ's death which excludes or ignores the divinely revealed fact that it was in its essential nature a guilt-offering; and, because a guilt-offering, therefore of the nature of the payment of a debt in behalf of those for whom He suffered.

Most blessed truth this, for all who can receive it! Christ, the Son of God, our Guilt-Offering! Like the poor Israelite, who had defrauded God of that which was His due, so must we do; coming before God, confessing that wherein we have wronged Him, and bringing forth fruit meet for repentance, we must bring and plead Christ in the glory of His person, in all the perfection of His holy obedience, as our Guilt-Offering. And therewith the ancient promise to the penitent Israelite becomes ours (vi. 7), "The priest shall make atonement for him before the Lord, and he shall be forgiven; concerning whatsoever he doeth so as to be guilty thereby."

CHAPTER IX
THE PRIESTS' PORTIONS

Lev. vi. 16-18, 26; vii. 6-10, 14, 31-36.

After the law of the guilt-offering follows a section (vi. 8-vii. 38) with regard to the offerings previously treated, but addressed especially to the priests, as the foregoing were specially directed to the people. Much of the contents of this section has already passed before us, in anticipation of its order in the book, as this has seemed necessary in order to a complete exposition of the several offerings. An important part of the section, however, relating to the portion of the offerings which was appointed for the priests, has been passed by until now, and must claim our brief attention.

In the verses indicated above, it is ordered that of the meal-offerings, the sin-offerings, and the guilt-offerings, all that was not burnt, as also the wave-breast and the heave-shoulder of the peace-offerings, should be for Aaron and his sons. In particular, it is directed that the priest's portion of the sin-offering and the guilt-offering shall be eaten by "the priest that maketh atonement therewith" (vii. 7); and that of the meal-offerings prepared in the oven, the frying-pan, or the baking-pan, all that is not burned upon the altar, according to the law of chap. ii., shall be eaten by "the priest that offereth it;" and that of every meal-offering mingled with oil, or dry, the same part "shall all the sons of Aaron have, one as well as another" (vii. 9, 10). Of the burnt-offering, all the flesh being burned, the hide alone fell to the officiating priest as his perquisite (vii. 8).

These regulations are explained in the concluding verses of the section (vii. 35, 36) as follows, "This is the anointing-portion of Aaron, and the anointing-portion of his sons, out of the offerings of the Lord made by fire, in the day when he presented them to minister unto the Lord in the priest's office; which the Lord commanded to be given them of the children of Israel, in the day that he anointed them. It is a due for ever throughout their generations."

Hence, it is plain that this use which was to be made of certain parts of certain offerings does not touch the question of the consecration of the whole to God. The whole of each offering is none the less wholly accepted and appropriated by God, that He designates a part of it to the maintenance of the priesthood. That even as thus used by the priest it is used by him as something belonging to God, is indicated by the phrase used, "it is most holy" (vi. 17); expressive words, which in the law of the offerings always have a technical use, as denoting those things of which only the sons of Aaron might partake, and that only in the holy place. In the case of the meal-offering, its peculiarly sacred character as belonging, the whole of it, exclusively to God, is further marked by the additional injunctions that it should be "eaten *without leaven* in a holy place" (vi. 16); and that whosoever touched these offerings should be holy (vi. 18); that is, he should be as a man separated to God, under all the restrictions (doubtless, without the privileges,) which belonged to the priesthood, as men set apart for God's service. In the eating of their portion of the various offerings by the priests, we are to recognise no official act: we simply see the servants of God supported by the bread of His table.

This last thought, which is absent in the case of no one of the offerings,[12] is brought out with special clearness and fulness in the ceremonial connected with the peace-offerings (vii. 28-34). In this case, certain parts, the right thigh (or shoulder?) and the breast, are set apart as the due of the priest. The selection of these is determined by the principle which marks all the Levitical legislation: God and those who represent Him are to be honoured by the consecration of the best of everything. In the animals used upon the altar, these were regarded as the choice parts, and are indeed referred to as such in other Scriptures. But, in order that neither the priest nor the people may imagine that the priest receives these as a man from his fellow-men, but may understand that they are given to God, and that it is from God that the priest now receives them, as His servant, fed from His table; to this end, certain ceremonies were ordained to be used with these parts; the breast was to be "heaved," the thigh was to be "waved," before the Lord. What was the meaning of these actions?

The breast was to be "heaved;" that is, elevated heavenward. The symbolic meaning of this act can scarcely be missed. By it, the priest acknowledged his dependence upon God for the supply of this sacrificial food, and, again, by this act consecrated it anew to Him as the One that sitteth in the heavens.

But God is not only the One that "sitteth in the heavens;" He is the God who has condescended also to dwell among men, and especially in the tent of meeting in the midst of Israel. And thus, as by the elevation of the breast heavenward, God, the Giver, was recognised as the One enthroned in heaven, so by the "waving" of the thigh, which, as the rabbis tell us, was a movement backward and forward, to and from the altar, He was recognised also as Jehovah, who had condescended from heaven to dwell in the midst of His people. Like the "heaving," so the "waving," then, was an act of acknowledgment and consecration to God; the former, to God, as in heaven, the God of creation; the other, to God, as the God of the altar, the God of redemption. And that this is the true significance of these acts is illustrated by the fact that in the Pentateuch, in the account of the gold and silver brought by the people for the preparation of the tabernacle (Exod. xxxv. 22), the same word is used to describe the presentation of these offerings which is here used of the wave-offering.

And so in the peace-offering the principle is amply illustrated upon which the priests received their dues. The worshippers bring their offerings, and present them, not to the priest, but through him to God; who, then, having used such parts as He will in the service of the sanctuary, gives again such parts of them as He pleases to the priests.

The lesson of these arrangements lies immediately before us. They were intended to teach Israel, and, according to the New Testament, are also designed to teach us, that it is the will of God that those who give up secular occupations to devote themselves to the ministry of His house should be supported by the free-will offerings of God's people. Very strange indeed it is to hear a few small sects in our day denying this. For the Apostle Paul argues at length to this effect, and calls the attention of the Corinthians (1 Cor. ix. 13, 14) to the fact that the principle expressed in this ordinance of the law of Moses has not been set aside, but holds good in this dispensation. "Know ye not that they which ... wait upon the altar have their portion with the altar? Even so did the Lord ordain that they which proclaim the Gospel should live of the Gospel." The principle plainly covers the case of all such as give up secular callings to devote themselves to the ministry of the Word, whether to proclaim the Gospel in any of the great mission fields, or to exercise the pastorate of the local church. Such are ever to be supported out of the consecrated offerings of God's people.

To point in disparagement of modern "hireling" ministers and missionaries, as some have done, to the case of Paul, who laboured with his own hands, that he might not be chargeable to those to whom he ministered, is singularly inapt, seeing that in the chapter above referred to he expressly vindicates his right to receive of the Corinthians his support, and in this Second Epistle to them even seems to express a doubt (2 Cor. xii. 13) whether in refusing, as he did, to receive support from them, he had not done them a "wrong," making them thus "inferior to the rest of the churches," from whom, in fact, he did receive such material aid (Phil. iv. 10, 16).

And if ever claims of this kind upon our benevolence and liberality seem to be heavy, and if to nature the burden is sometimes irksome, we shall do well to remember that the requirement is not of man, and not of the Church, but of God. It comes to us with the double authority of the Old and New Testament, of the Law and the Gospel. And it will certainly help us all to give to these ends the more gladly, if we keep that in mind which the Levitical law so carefully kept before Israel, that the giving was to be regarded by them as not to the priesthood, but to the Lord, and that in our giving outwardly to support the ministry of God's Word, we give, really, to the Lord Himself. And it stands written (Matt. x. 42): "Whosoever shall give to drink unto one of these little ones a cup of cold water only, ... he shall in no wise lose his reward."

CHAPTER X
THE CONSECRATION OF AARON AND HIS SONS, AND OF THE TABERNACLE

Lev. viii. 1-36.

The second section of the book of Leviticus (viii. 1-x. 20) is historical, and describes (viii.) the consecration of the tabernacle and of Aaron and his sons, (ix.) their induction into the duties of their office, and, finally (x.), the terrible judgment by which the high sanctity of the priestly office and of the tabernacle service was very solemnly impressed upon them and all the people.

First in order (chap. viii.) is described the ceremonial of consecration. We read (vv. 1-4): "And the Lord spake unto Moses, saying, Take Aaron and his sons with him, and the garments, and the anointing oil, and the bullock of the sin offering, and the two rams, and the basket of unleavened bread; and assemble thou all the congregation at the door of the tent of meeting. And Moses did as the Lord commanded him; and the congregation was assembled at the door of the tent of meeting."

These words refer us back to Exod. xxviii., xxix., in which are recorded the full directions previously given for the making of the garments and the oil of anointing, and for the ceremonial of the consecration of the priests. The law of offerings having been delivered, Moses now proceeds to consecrate Aaron and his sons to the priestly office, according to the commandment given; and to this end, by Divine direction, he orders "all the congregation" to be assembled "at the door of the tent of meeting." In this last statement some have seen a sufficient reason for rejecting the whole account as fabulous, insisting that it is palpably absurd to suppose that a congregation numbering some millions could be assembled at the door of a single tent! But, surely, if the words are to be taken in the ultra-literal sense required in order to make out this difficulty, the impossibility must have been equally evident to the supposed fabricator of the fiction; and it is yet more absurd to suppose that he should ever have intended his words to be pressed to such a rigid literality. Two explanations lie before us, either of which meets the supposed difficulty; the one, that endorsed by Dillmann,[13] that the congregation was gathered in their appointed representatives; the other, that which refuses to see in the words a statement that every individual in the nation was literally "at the door," and further reminds us that, inasmuch as the ceremonies of the consecration are said to have continued seven days, we are not, by the terms of the narrative, required to believe that all, in any sense, were present, either at the very beginning or at any one time during that week. It is not too much to say that by a captious criticism of this kind, any narrative, however sober, might be shown to be absurd.

The consecration ceremonial was introduced by a solemn declaration made by Moses to assembled Israel, that the impressive rites which they were now about to witness, were of Divine appointment. We read (ver. 5), "Moses said unto the congregation, This is the thing which the Lord hath commanded to be done."

Just here we may pause to note the great emphasis which the narrative lays upon this fact of the Divine appointment of all pertaining to these consecration rites. Not only is this Divine ordination of all thus declared at the beginning, but in connection with each of the chief parts of the ceremonial the formula is repeated, "as the Lord commanded Moses." Also, at the close of the first day's rites, Moses twice reminds Aaron and his sons that this whole ritual, in all its parts, is for them an ordinance of God, and is to be regarded accordingly, upon pain of death (vv. 34, 35). And the narrative of the chapter closes (ver. 36) with the words, "Aaron and his sons did all the things which the Lord commanded by the hand of Moses." Twelve times in this one chapter is reference thus made to the Divine appointment of these consecration rites.

This is full of significance and instruction. It is of the highest importance in an apologetic way. For it is self-evident that this twelvefold affirmation, twelve times directly contradicts the modern theory of the late origin and human invention of the Levitical priesthood. There is no evading of the issue which is thus placed squarely before us. To talk of the inspiration from God, in any sense possible to that word, of a writing containing such affirmations, so numerous, formal, and emphatic, if the critics referred to are right, and these affirmations are all false, is absurd. There is no such thing as inspired falsehood.

Again, a great spiritual truth is herein brought before us, which concerns believers in all ages. It is set forth in so many words in Heb. v. 4, where the writer, laying down the essential conditions of priesthood, specially mentions Divine appointment as one of these; which he affirms as satisfied in the high-priesthood of Christ: "No man taketh the honour unto himself, but when he is called of God, even as was Aaron. So Christ also glorified not

Himself to be made a high priest." Fundamental to Christian faith and life is this thought: priesthood is not of man, but of God. In particular, in all that Christ has done and is still doing as the High Priest, in the true holiest, He is acting under Divine appointment.

And we are hereby pointed to the truth of which some may need to be reminded, that the work of our Lord in our behalf, and that of the whole universe into which sin has entered, has its cause and origin in the mind and gracious will of the Father. It was in His incomprehensible love, who appointed the priestly office, that the whole work of atonement, and therewith purification and full redemption, had its mysterious origin. The thoughtful reader of the Gospels will hardly need to be reminded how constantly our blessed Lord, in the days of His high-priestly service upon earth, acted in all that He did under the consciousness, often expressed, of His appointment by the Father to this work. Thus, Aaron in the solemn ceremonial of those days of consecration, as ever afterward, doing "all the things which the Lord commanded by the hand of Moses," in so doing fitly represented Him who should come afterward, who said of Himself (John vi. 38), "I came down from heaven, not to do Mine own will, but the will of Him that sent Me."

The Levitical Priesthood and Tabernacle as Types.

In order to any profitable study of the following ceremonial, it is indispensable to have distinctly before us the New Testament teaching as to the typical significance of the priesthood and the tabernacle. A few words on this subject, therefore, seem to be needful as preliminary to more detailed exposition. As to the typical character of Aaron, as high priest, the New Testament leaves us no room for doubt. Throughout the Epistle to the Hebrews, Christ is held forth as the true and heavenly High Priest, of whom Aaron, with his successors, was an eminent type.

As regards the other priests, while it is true that, considered in themselves, and without reference to the high priest, each of them also, in the performance of his daily functions in the tabernacle, was a lesser type of Christ, as is intimated in Heb. x. 11, yet, as contrasted with the high priest, who was ever one, while they were many, it is plain that another typical reference must be sought for the ordinary priesthood. What that may be is suggested to us in several New Testament passages; as, especially, in Rev. v. 10, where the whole body of believers, bought by the blood of the slain Lamb, is said to have been made "unto our God a kingdom and priests;" with which may be compared Heb. xiii. 10, where it is said, "We have an altar, whereof they have no right to eat which serve the tabernacle"; words which plainly assume the priesthood of all believers in Christ, as the antitype of the priesthood of the Levitical tabernacle.[14]

As to the typical meaning of the tabernacle, which also is anointed in the consecration ceremonial, there has been much difference of opinion. That it was typical is declared, in so many words, in the Epistle to the Hebrews (viii. 5), where the Levitical priests are said to have served "that which is a copy and shadow of the heavenly things;" as also ix. 24, where we read, "Christ entered not into a holy place made with hands, like in pattern to the true; but into heaven itself, now to appear before the face of God for us." But when we ask what then were "the heavenly things" of which the tabernacle was "the copy and shadow," we have different answers.

Many have replied that the antitype of the tabernacle, as of the temple, was the Church of believers; and, at first thought, with some apparent Scriptural reason. For it is certain that Christians are declared (1 Cor. iii. 16) to be the temple of the living God; where, however, it is to be noted that the original word denotes, not the temple or tabernacle in general, but the "sanctuary" or inner shrine—the "holy of holies." More to the point is 1 Peter ii. 5, where it is said to Christians, "Ye also, as living stones, are built up a spiritual house." Such passages as these do certainly warrant us in saying that the tabernacle, and especially the inner sanctuary, as the special place of the Divine habitation and manifestation, did in so far typify the Church.

But when we consider the tabernacle, not in itself, but in relation to its priesthood and ministry, the explanation fails, and we fall into confusion. As when the priests are considered, not in themselves, but in their relation to the high priest, we are compelled to seek an antitype different from the Antitype of the high priest, so in this case. To identify the typical meaning of the tabernacle, considered as a part of a whole system and order, with that of the priesthood who serve in it, is to throw that whole typical system into confusion. Furthermore, this cannot be harmonised with a number of New Testament expressions with regard to the tabernacle and temple, as related to the high priesthood of our Lord. It is hard to see, for example, how the Church of believers could be properly described as "things in the heavens." Moreover, we are expressly taught (Heb. ix. 24), that the Antitype of the Holy Place into which the high priest entered every year, with blood, was "heaven itself," "the presence of God;" and again, His ascension to the right hand of God is described (Heb. iv. 14, R.V.), with evident allusion to the passing of the high priest through the Holy Place into the Holiest, as a passing "*through* the heavens;" and also (Heb. ix. 11), as an entering into the Holy Place, "through the greater and more perfect tabernacle." These expressions exclude reference to the Church of Christ as the antitype of the earthly tabernacle.

Others, again, have regarded the tabernacle as a type of the human nature of Christ, referring in proof to John ii. 19-21, where our Lord speaks of "the temple of His body;" and also to Heb. x. 19, 20, where it is said that believers have access to the Holiest "by a new and living way, which He dedicated for us through the veil, that is to say, His flesh."

As regards the first of these passages, we should note that the original word is, again, not the word for the temple in general, but that which is invariably used to denote the inner sanctuary, as the special shrine of Jehovah's presence: so that it really gives us no warrant for affirming that the tabernacle, *as a whole*, was a type of our Lord's humanity; nor, on that supposition, does it seem possible to explain the meaning of the three parts into which the tabernacle was divided. And the second passage referred to is no more to the point. For the writer had only a little before described the tabernacle as a "pattern of things in the heavens;" words which, surely, could not be applied to the humanity in which our Lord appeared in His incarnation and humiliation,—a humanity which was not a thing "of the heavens," but of the earth. The reference to the "flesh" of Christ, as being the veil through which He passed into the Holiest (Heb. x. 19, 20) is merely by way of illustration, and not of typical interpretation. The thought of the inspired writer appears to be this: Just as, in the Levitical tabernacle, the veil must be parted before the high priest could go into the Holiest Place, even so was it necessary that the flesh of our Lord should be rent in order that thus, through death, it might be possible for Him to enter into the true holiest. The thought has been happily expressed by Delitzsch, thus: "While He was with us here below, the weak, limit-bound, and mortal flesh which He had assumed for our sakes hung like a curtain between Him and the Divine sanctuary into which He would enter; and in order to such entrance, this curtain had to be withdrawn by death, even as the high priest had to draw aside the temple veil in order to make his entry to the Holy of Holies."[15]

Not to review other opinions on this matter, the various expressions used constrain us to regard the tabernacle as typifying the universe itself, measured and appointed in all its parts by infinite wisdom, as the abode of Him who "filleth immensity with His presence," the place of the Divine manifestation, and the abode of His holiness. In the outer court, where the victims were offered, we have this world of sense in which we live, in which our Lord was offered in the sight of all; in the Holy Place, and the Holy of Holies, the unseen and heavenly worlds, through the former of which our Lord is represented as having passed (Heb. iv. 14, ix. 11) that He might appear with His blood in the true Holiest, where God in the innermost shrine of His glory "covereth Himself with light as with a garment." For this cosmical dwelling-place of the Most High God has been defiled by sin, which, as it were, has profaned the whole sanctuary; for we read (Col. i. 20), that not only "things upon the earth," but also "things in the heavens," are to be "reconciled" through Christ, even "through the blood of His cross;" and, still more explicitly, to the same effect (Heb. ix. 23), that as the typical "copies of the things in the heavens" needed to be cleansed with the blood of bullocks and of goats, so "it was necessary that ... the heavenly things themselves should be cleansed with better sacrifices than these." And so, at this present time, Christ, as the High Priest of this cosmical tabernacle, "not made with hands," having offered His great sacrifice for sins for ever, is now engaged in carrying out His work of cleansing the people of God, and the earthly and the heavenly sanctuary, to the uttermost completion.

With these preliminary words, which have seemed essential to the exposition of these chapters, we are now prepared to consider the ceremonial of the consecration of the priesthood and tabernacle, and the spiritual meaning which it was intended to convey.

The Washing with Water.

viii. 6.

"And Moses brought Aaron and his sons, and washed them with water."

The consecration ceremonies consisted of four parts, namely, the Washing, the Investiture, the Anointing, and the Sacrifices. Of these, first in order was the *Washing*. We read that "Moses"—acting throughout, we must remember, as Mediator, representing God—"brought Aaron and his sons, and washed them with water." The meaning of this act is so evident as not to have been called in question. Washing ever signifies cleansing; the ceremonial cleansing of the body, therefore, in symbol ever represents the inward purification of the spirit.

Of this usage the Biblical illustrations are very numerous. Thus, the spiritual purification of Israel in the latter day is described (Isa. iv. 4) by the same word as is used here, as a washing away of "the filth of the daughters of Zion" by the Lord. So, again, in the New Testament, we read that Christ declared unto Nicodemus that in order to see the kingdom of God a man must be born again, "of water and the Spirit," and in the Epistle to Titus (iii. 5) we read of a cleansing of the Church "with the washing (*marg.*, laver) of water, by the Word," even the "washing of regeneration." The symbolism in this case, therefore, points to cleansing from the defilement of sin as a fundamental condition of priesthood. As regards our Lord indeed, such cleansing was no more needed for His high priesthood than was the sin-offering for Himself; for in His holy incarnation, though He took our nature indeed with all the consequences and infirmities consequent on sin He was yet "without sin." But all the more it was necessary in the symbolism that if Aaron was to typify the sinless Christ of God he must be cleansed with water, in type of the cleansing of human nature, without which no man can approach to God. And in that not only Aaron, but also his sons, the ordinary priests, were thus cleansed, we are in the ordinance significantly pointed to the deep spiritual truth that they who are called to be priests to God must be qualified for this office, first of all, by the cleansing of their human nature through the washing of regeneration, by the power of the Holy Ghost.

The Investiture.

viii. 7-9.

> "And he put upon him the coat, and girded him with the girdle, and clothed him with the robe, and put the ephod upon him, and he girded him with the cunningly woven band of the ephod, and bound it unto him therewith. And he placed the breastplate upon him: and in the breastplate he put the Urim and the Thummim. And he set the mitre upon his head: and upon the mitre, in front, did he set the golden plate, the holy crown; as the Lord commanded Moses."

The next ceremony of the consecration was the Investiture of Aaron with his official, high-priestly robes, as they had been appointed of God to be made (Exod. xxviii.). The investiture of the sons of Aaron significantly takes place only after the anointing of the tabernacle, and of Aaron as high priest. Of the investiture of Aaron we read in vv. 7-9, above.

As these garments were official, we must needs regard them as symbolical; a thought which is the more emphasised by the very minute and special directions given by the Lord for making them. Nothing was left to the fancy of man; all was prescribed by the Lord. The official robes of the high priest consisted of eight pieces, four of which, the coat, the girdle, the turban (or "mitre"), and the breeches, were, with the exception of the turban, of white linen, and identical in every respect with the official dress of the ordinary priests.

Four pieces more were peculiar to himself, the special insignia of his office, and unlike the dress of the ordinary priest, were richly made in gold and various colours, "garments for glory and for beauty." These were: the robe of the ephod, made all of blue, with a border of pendant pomegranates and golden bells in alternation; the ephod itself consisting of two pieces, broidered in gold and blue, purple, scarlet, and fine white linen, the one hanging in front, the other behind, over the robe of the ephod, and joined on the shoulders with two onyx stones, on which were graven the names of the twelve tribes, six on the one shoulder and six on the other; it was girt about him with a girdle of the same material and colours. The third was the breast-plate, which was a double square of the same material and colours as the ephod, within the fold of which, as it hung from his shoulders by golden chains, was placed the Urim and the Thummim, whatever these may have been, and upon the front of which were set twelve precious stones, on which, severally, were engraved the names of the twelve tribes of the children of Israel. And the fourth and last article of his attire was "the golden plate, the holy crown;" a band of gold bound about his forehead over the turban, with blue lace, on which were engraven the words, "Holiness to Jehovah."

This dress of the high priest represented him, in the first place, as the appointed minister of the *tabernacle*. The number of pieces, twice four, like the four of the common priests' attire, answered to the four which was represented in the ground plan of the tabernacle, quadrangular both in its form as a whole and in its several parts, the Holy of Holies being a perfect cube; four being in Scripture constantly the number which symbolises the universe, as created by God and bearing witness to Him. So also the garments of the high priest marked him as the minister of the tabernacle by their colours, also four in number, and the same as those of the latter, namely, blue, purple, scarlet, and white.

But the official robes of the high priest marked him, in the second place, as the servant of *the God of the tabernacle*, whose livery he wore. For these colours, various modifications of light, all thus had a symbolic reference to the God of light, who made the universe of which the Mosaic tabernacle was a type. Of these, the blue, the colour of the overarching heaven, has been in many lands and religions naturally regarded as the colour symbolising God, as the God of the heaven, bowing to the earth in condescending love and self-revelation. In like manner, we find it repeatedly recurring in the symbolic manifestations of Jehovah in the Holy Scriptures, where it always brings God before us with special reference to His condescending love as entering into covenant with man, and revealing for their good His holy law. [16] The purple, as will occur to every one, is everywhere recognised as the colour of royalty, and therefore symbolised the kingly exaltation and majesty of God, as the Ruler of heaven and earth. The scarlet reminds us at once of the colour of blood, which stands in the very foreground of the Mosaic symbolism as the symbol of life, and thus points us to the conception of God, as the essentially Living One, who is Himself the sole primal source of all life, whether physical or spiritual, in the creature. No one can mistake, again, the symbolic meaning of the white, which, not only in the Scripture, but among all nations, has ever been the symbol of purity and holiness, and thus represented the high priest as the minister of God, as the Most Holy One. By this investiture, therefore, Aaron was symbolically constituted the minister of the tabernacle, on the one hand, and of God, on the other; and, in particular, of God as the God of revelation, in covenant with Israel; of God as the Most High, the King of Israel; of God as the God of life, the Giver of life in the redemption of Israel; and, finally, of God as the Most Holy, the God "who is light," and "with whom is no darkness at all."

The "robe of the ephod" was woven in one piece, and all of blue. In that it was thus without seam, was symbolised the wholeness and absolute integrity necessary to him who should bear the high priestly office. In that it was made all of blue, the colour which symbolised the God of heaven as manifesting Himself to Israel in condescending love, in the holy law and covenant, this robe of the ephod specially marked the high priest as the minister of Jehovah and of His revealed law.

The ephod, which depended from the shoulders before and behind, according to the usage of Scripture, was the garment specially significant of rule and authority; a thought which reached full expression in the breast-plate which was fastened to it, which contained the Urim and Thummim, by which God's will was made known to Israel in times of perplexity, and was called "the breast-plate of judgment."

The ornamentation of these garments had also a symbolic meaning, though it may not be in each instance equally clear. In that the high priest, as thus robed, bore upon the ephod and the breast-plate of judgment, graven on precious stones, the names of the twelve tribes of Israel, he was marked as one who in all his high-priestly work before and with God, presented and represented Israel. In that the names were engraven upon precious stones was signified the exceeding preciousness of Israel in God's sight, as His "peculiar treasure." In that, again, they were worn upon his shoulders, Aaron was represented to Israel as upholding and bearing them before God in the strength of his office; in that he wore their names upon his breast, he was represented as also bearing them upon his heart in love and affection.

The symbolic meaning of the pomegranates and golden bells, which formed the border of the robe of the ephod, is not quite so clear. But we may probably find a hint as to their significance in the Divine direction as to the border of blue which every Israelite was to wear upon the bottom of his garment (Numb. xv. 39). The purpose of this is said to be that it might be for a continual reminder of the law: "It shall be unto you for a fringe, that ye may look upon it, and remember all the commandments of the Lord, and do them." If then this border in the garment of each individual member of the priestly nation was designed symbolically to mark them as the keepers of the law of the God of heaven, we may safely infer an analogous meaning in the similar border to the official garment of the high priest. And if so, then we shall perhaps not be far out of the way if in this case we follow Jewish tradition in regarding the pomegranate, a fruit distinguished by being filled to the full with seeds, as the symbol, *par excellence*, of the law of commandments, the words of the living God, as "incorruptible seed," endowed by Him with vital energy and power.[17]

As for the bells, we naturally think at once of the common use of the bell to give a signal, and announce what one may be concerned to know. So we read of these golden bells (Exod. xxviii. 35), "the sound thereof shall be heard when he goeth in unto the holy place before the Lord ... that he die not."

These golden bells in the border of his garment, between each pair of pomegranates, thus announced him as officially appearing before God as the fulfiller of the law of commandments, and as, for this reason, acceptable to God in the execution of his high-priestly functions.

As to the Urim and Thummim, "Light and Perfection," which were apparently placed within the fold of the breast-plate of judgment, as the tables of the law within the ark of the covenant, there has been in all ages much debate; but what they were cannot be said to have been certainly determined. Most probable appears the opinion that they were two sacred lots, which on solemn occasions were used by the high priest for determining the will of God. So much, in any case, is clear from the Scriptures, that in some way through them the will of God as the King of Israel was made known to the high priest, for the direction of the nation in doubtful matters. Most fitly, therefore, they were placed within the breast-plate of judgment, which, indeed, may have received this name from this circumstance. The high priest, therefore, as the bearer of the Urim and Thummim, was set forth, in accordance with the meaning of these words, as one who in virtue of his office received perfect enlightenment from God as to His will, in all that concerned Israel's action.

The plate of graven gold, called the "holy crown," was bound by Moses with a lace of blue upon the mitre of Aaron in front. The precious metal here, as elsewhere in the official garments of the high priest, and in the tabernacle, was symbolic of the boundless riches of the glory of the God of Israel, whose minister the high priest was. The special significance, however, of this holy crown, is found in the words which appeared upon it, "Holiness to Jehovah." This was a continual visible mark and reminder of the fact that the high priest, in all that he was, and in all that he did, was a person in the highest possible sense consecrated to Jehovah, the heavenly King of Israel, whose livery he wore. And in that this golden plate with this inscription is called his "crown," it is further suggested that in this last-named fact is found the crowning glory and dignity of the high priest's office. He is the minister of the God of Israel, Jehovah, whose own supreme glory is just this, that He is holy. In the directions given for this crown in Exod. xxviii. 36-38 it is said that in virtue of his wearing this, or, rather, in virtue of the fact thus set forth, "Aaron shall bear the iniquity of the holy things which the children of Israel shall hallow in all their holy gifts; and it shall always be upon his forehead, that they may be accepted before the Lord." That is, even Israel's consecrated things, their holiest gifts, are yet defiled by the ever abiding sinfulness of those who offer them; but they are nevertheless graciously accepted, as being offered by Aaron, himself "holy to the Lord."

Such then appears to have been the symbolic meaning of these "garments for glory and for beauty," with which Moses now robed Aaron, in token of his investiture with the manifold dignities of the exalted office to which God had called him. But we must not forget that we are not, in all this, dealing merely with matters of antiquarian or archæological interest. Nothing is plainer than the teaching of the New Testament, that Aaron, as the high priest, not by accident, but by Divine intention, prefigured Christ. In all the directions given concerning his investiture with his office, and the work which, as high priest, he had to do, the Holy Ghost intended to prefigure, directly or indirectly, something concerning the person, office, and work of Jesus Christ, as our heavenly High Priest, the Fulfiller of all these types. As Aaron appears in his fourfold high-priestly garments of four colours, which represented him as the minister, on the one hand, of the tabernacle, and, on the other, of the God of Israel, the Inhabitant of the tabernacle, so are we reminded how Christ is appointed as the "Minister of the greater and more perfect tabernacle, not made with hands" (Heb. ix. 11), the earth, the heaven, and the heaven of heavens, to reconcile, by the offering of His blood, "both the things which are on earth and those which are in the heavens" (Col. i. 20). We look upon the blue robe of the ephod, and remember how Christ is made a minister of "a better covenant, enacted upon better promises" (Heb. viii. 6), representing, as that old covenant did not, the fulness of the revelation of God's condescending love and saving mercy. So also the inwoven scarlet reminds us how Christ, again, as the great High Priest, is the minister of the God of life, and is also Himself life and the Giver of life to all His people. We look upon the high priest's purple and gold, and are reminded again that Christ, the High Priest, is also invested with regal power and dominion, all authority being given unto Him in heaven and on earth (Matt. xxviii. 18).

Again, we look on the ephod of fine linen, inwoven with blue, and scarlet, and purple, and gold, with its girdle, symbolising service, and its pendant breast-plate of judgment, and are reminded how Christ in all the relations thus pertaining to Him as High Priest, is the Ruler and the Judge of His people, who, as the bearer of the true Urim and Thummim, is not only Priest, and King, and Judge, but also, and in order to the salvation of His people, their Prophet, continually revealing unto those who seek Him, the will of God for their direction and guidance in every emergency of life. The girdle, the symbol of service, brings to mind, again, how in all this He is the Servant of the Lord, serving the Father in saving us.

The symbolism of the pomegranates and the golden bells reminds us, for the strengthening of our faith, how our exalted High Priest, who appears before God in our behalf in the Holiest, appears there as the great Preserver and Fulfiller of the Divine law, supremely qualified, no less by His supreme merit than by Divine appointment, to urge our needs with prevalence before God, His very presence in the heavenly sanctuary vocal with sweet music. Did Aaron bear the names of the twelve tribes of Israel on his shoulders and on his breast before God continually? Even so does his great Antitype bear continually all His people before God, as He executes His high-priestly office; and this, too, not merely in a vague and general way, but tribe by tribe, community by community, each with its peculiar case and special need; nay, we may say even more; each individual, as such, is thus borne continually on the shoulders and the breast of the heavenly Priest; on His shoulders He bears them, to support them by His power; on His heart, in tenderest love and sympathy. And so often as we are distressed and discouraged by the consciousness of defilement still pertaining even to the holiest of our holy things, consecration ever imperfect at the best, we may bethink ourselves of the golden crown which Aaron wore, and its inscription, and remember how the Lord Jesus is in fullest reality "holy to the Lord;" so that we may take heart of grace as, with full reason and right, we apply to Him what is said of this crown of holiness on Aaron's brow: "The crown of holiness is ever on His forehead, and He shall bear the iniquity of the holy things which we shall hallow in all our holy gifts; it is always on His forehead, that our works may be accepted before the Lord." And so we are taught by this symbolism ever to look away from all conscious defilement and sin to the infinite holiness of the person of the Lord Jesus, as He continually appears before God as High Priest in our behalf, the all-sufficient Surety for the acceptance of our persons and of our imperfect works, for His own sake.

The investiture, as also the anointing, of the sons of Aaron, followed the robing and anointing of Aaron. We read (ver. 13): "Moses brought Aaron's sons, and clothed them with coats, and girded them with girdles, and bound head-tires upon them; as the Lord commanded Moses."

To the three articles of their attire here mentioned, must be added the "linen breeches" (Exod. xxviii. 42, 43); so that they also, in the several parts of their official vestments, bore the number four, the signature of the creaturely, as represented in the tabernacle. All was of pure white linen, signifying the holiness and righteousness of those who should act as priests before God. So once and again in the Apocalypse, the same symbol is used to denote the spotless holiness and righteousness of the blood-bought saints, who are made "a kingdom and priests" unto God; as, for instance, it is said of that same holy body, symbolised as the bride of the Lamb, that "it was given unto her that she should array herself in fine linen, bright and pure: for the fine linen is the righteous acts of the saints" (Rev. xix. 8).

The Anointing.

viii. 10-12.

"And Moses took the anointing oil, and anointed the tabernacle and all that was therein, and sanctified them. And he sprinkled thereof upon the altar seven times, and anointed the altar and all its vessels, and the laver and its base, to sanctify them. And he poured of the anointed oil upon Aaron's head, and anointed him, to sanctify him."

Next in order came the anointing, first of the tabernacle and all that pertained to its service, and then the anointing of Aaron.

The anointing oil was made (Exod. xxx. 22-33) with a perfume of choice spices, their number, four, the sacred number so constantly recurring in the tabernacle. To make or use this oil, except for the sacred purposes of the sanctuary, was forbidden under penalty of being cut off from the holy people. The purpose of the anointing of the tabernacle and all within it, is declared to be its consecration thereby to the service of Jehovah. The altar, as a place of special sanctity, the place where God had covenanted to meet with Israel, was anointed seven times. For the number seven, compounded of three, the signet number of the Godhead, and four, the constant symbol of the creaturely, is thus by eminence the sacred number, the number, in particular, which is the sign and reminder of the covenant of redemption; and so here it is with special meaning that the altar, as being the place where God had specially covenanted to meet with Israel as reconciled through the blood of atonement, should receive a sevenfold anointing.

After this, the anointing oil was poured on the head of Aaron, to sanctify him.

As to the meaning of this part of the symbolic service, there is little room for doubt. The "anointing" is said to have been "to sanctify" or set apart to the service of Jehovah him that was anointed. And, inasmuch as oil, in the Holy Scriptures, is the constant symbol of the Holy Spirit, it is taught hereby that consecration is secured only through the anointing with the Holy Ghost.

The direct typical reference of this part of the ceremonial to Christ, will not be denied by any one for whom the Scripture any longer has authority. For Christ Himself quoted the words we find in Isa. lxi. 1, as fulfilled in Himself: "The Spirit of the Lord God is upon Me, because the Lord God hath anointed Me." And the Apostle Peter afterward taught (Acts x. 38) that God had "anointed Jesus with the Holy Ghost and with power;" while the most common title of our Lord, as "the Messiah" or "Christ," as we all know, though often forgetful of its meaning, simply means "the Anointed One." So every time we use the word, we unconsciously testify to the fulfilment of this type of the anointing of Aaron as priest, as, afterward, of the anointing of David as king, in Him. And as the anointing of Aaron took place in the sight of all Israel, assembled at the door of the tent of meeting, so in the fulness of time was Jesus, in the sight of all the multitude that waited on the baptism of John, after having been washed with water, "to fulfil all righteousness," anointed from heaven, as "the Holy Ghost descended in bodily form, as a dove," and abode upon him (Luke iii. 22). And while, according to Jewish tradition, the anointing oil was applied to the ordinary priests only in small quantity and by the finger, on the head of Aaron it was "poured;" in which word, as suggested in Psalm cxxxiii. 2, we are to understand a reference to the great copiousness with which it was used. In which, again, the type exactly corresponds to the Antitype. For while it is true of all believers that they "have an anointing from the Holy One" (1 John ii. 20), even as their Lord, yet of Him alone is it true that unto Him the Spirit "was not given by measure" (John iii. 34). And by this Divine anointing with the Holy Spirit without limit, was Jesus sanctified and qualified for the office of High Priest for all His people.

The anointing of the tabernacle with the same holy oil was according to a custom long before prevalent, and however it may seem strange to any of us now, will not have seemed strange to Israel. We read, for instance (Gen. xxviii. 18), of the anointing of the stone at Bethel by Jacob, by which he thus consecrated it to be a stone of remembrance of the revelation of God to him in that place. So by this anointing, the tabernacle, with all that it contained, was "sanctified;" that is, consecrated that so the use of these might be made, through the power of the Holy Ghost, a means of grace and blessing to Israel. And it was thus anointed, and for this purpose, as being a "copy and pattern of the heavenly things." By the ceremony is signified to us, that by the power of the Holy Ghost, through the high-priesthood of our Lord, the whole universe and all that is in it has been consecrated and endowed by God with virtue, to become a means of grace and blessing to all believers, by His grace and might who works "in all things and through all things" to this end.

The Consecration Sacrifices.

viii. 14-32.

"And he brought the bullock of the sin offering: and Aaron and his sons laid their hands upon the head of the bullock of the sin offering. And he slew it; and Moses took the blood, and put it upon the horns of the altar round about with his finger, and purified the altar, and poured out the blood at the base of the altar, and sanctified it, to make atonement for it. And he took all the fat that was upon the inwards, and the caul of the liver, and the two kidneys, and their fat, and Moses burned it upon the altar. But the bullock, and its skin, and its flesh, and its dung, he burnt with fire without the camp; as the Lord commanded Moses. And he presented the ram of the burnt offering: and Aaron and his sons laid their hands upon the head of the ram. And he killed it: and Moses sprinkled the blood upon the altar round about. And he cut the ram into its pieces; and Moses burnt the head, and the pieces, and the fat. And he washed the inwards and the legs with water; and Moses burnt the whole ram upon the altar: it was a burnt offering for a sweet savour: it was an offering made by fire unto the Lord; as the Lord commanded Moses. And he presented the other ram, the ram of consecration: and Aaron and his sons laid their hands upon the head of the ram. And he slew it; and Moses took of the blood thereof, and put it upon the tip of Aaron's right ear, and upon the thumb of his right hand, and upon the great toe of his right foot. And he brought Aaron's sons, and Moses put of the blood upon the tip of their right ear, and upon the thumb of their right hand, and upon the great toe of their right foot: and Moses sprinkled the blood upon the altar round about. And he took the fat, and the fat tail, and all the fat that was upon the inwards, and the caul of the liver, and the two kidneys and their fat, and the right thigh: and out of the basket of unleavened bread, that was before the Lord, he took one unleavened cake, and one cake of oiled bread, and one wafer, and placed them on the fat, and upon the right thigh: and he put the whole upon the hands of Aaron, and upon the hands of his sons, and waved them for a wave offering before the Lord. And Moses took them from off their hands, and burnt them on the altar upon the burnt offering: they were a consecration for a sweet savour: it was an offering made by fire unto the Lord. And Moses took the breast and waved it for a wave offering before the Lord: it was Moses' portion of the ram of consecration; as the Lord commanded Moses. And Moses took of the anointing oil, and of the blood which was upon the altar, and sprinkled it upon Aaron, upon his garments, and upon his sons, and upon his sons' garments with him; and sanctified Aaron, his garments, and his sons, and his sons' garments with him. And Moses said unto Aaron and to his sons, Boil the flesh at the door of the tent of meeting: and there eat it and the bread that is in the basket of consecration, as I commanded, saying, Aaron and his sons shall eat it. And that which remaineth of the flesh and of the bread shall ye burn with fire."

The last part of the consecration ceremonial was the sacrifices. Each of the chief sacrifices of the law were offered in order; first, a sin-offering; then, a burnt-offering; then, a peace-offering, with some significant variations from the ordinary ritual, adapting it to this occasion; with which was conjoined, after the usual manner, a meal-offering. A sin-offering was offered, first of all; there had been a symbolical cleansing with water, but still a sin-offering is required. It signified, what so many in these days seem to forget, that in order to our acceptableness before God, not only is needed a cleansing of the defilement of nature by the regeneration of the Holy Ghost, but also expiation for the guilt of our sins. The sin-offering was first, for the guilt of Aaron and his sons must be thus typically removed, before their burnt-offerings and their meal- and peace-offerings can be accepted.

The peculiarities of the offerings as rendered on this occasion are easily explained from the circumstances of their presentation. Moses officiates, for this time only, as specially delegated for this occasion, inasmuch as Aaron and his sons are not yet fully inducted into their office. The victim for the sin-offering is the costliest ever employed: a bullock, as ordered for the sin of the anointed priest. But the blood is not brought into the Holy Place, as in the ritual for the offering for the high priest, because Aaron is not yet fully inducted into his office. Nor do Aaron and his sons eat of the flesh of the sin-offering, as ordered in the case of other sin-offerings whose blood is not brought within the Holy Place; obviously, because of the principle which rules throughout the law, that he for whose sin the sin-offering is offered, must not himself eat of the flesh; it is therefore burnt with fire, without the camp, that it may not see corruption.

By this sin-offering, not only Aaron and his sons were cleansed, but we read that hereby atonement was also made "for the altar;" a mysterious type, reminding us that, in some way which we cannot as yet fully understand, sin has affected the whole universe: in such a sense, that not only for man himself who has sinned, is propitiation required, but, in some sense, even for the earth itself, with the heavens. That in expounding the meaning of this part of the ritual we do not go beyond the Scripture is plain from such passages as Heb. ix. 23, where it is expressly said that even as the tabernacle and the things in it were cleansed with the blood of the bullock, so was necessary that, not merely man, but "the heavenly things themselves," of which the tabernacle and its belongings were the "copies," should be cleansed with better sacrifices than these, even the offering of Christ's own blood. So also we read in Col. i. 20, before cited, that through Christ, even through the blood of His cross, not merely persons, "but all *things*, whether things on the earth, or things in the heavens," should be reconciled unto God. Mysterious words these, no doubt; but words which teach us at least so much as this, how profound and far-reaching is the mischief which sin has wrought, even our sin. Not merely the sinning man must be cleansed with blood before he can be made a priest unto God, but even nature, "made subject to vanity" (Rom. viii. 20), for man's sin, needs the reconciling blood before redeemed man can exercise his priesthood unto God in the heavenly places. Evidently we have here an estimate of the evil of sin which is incomparably higher than that which is commonly current among men; and we shall do well to conform our estimate to that of God, who required atonement to be made even for the earthen altar, to sanctify it.

Reconciliation being made by the sin-offering, next in order came the burnt-offering, symbolic, as we have seen, of the full consecration of the person of the offerer to God; in this case of the full consecration of Aaron and his sons to the service of God in the priesthood. The ritual was according to the usual law, and requires no further exposition.

The ceremonial culminated and was completed in the offering of "the ram of consecration." The expression is, literally, "the ram of fillings;" in which phrase there is a reference to the peculiar ceremony described in vv. 27, 28, in which certain portions of the victim and of the meal-offering were placed by Moses on the hands of Aaron and his sons, and waved by them for a wave-offering; and afterwards burnt wholly on the altar upon the burnt-offering, in token of their full devotement to the Lord. Of these it is then added, "they were a consecration" (*lit.* "fillings," *sc.* of hands, "were these"). The meaning of the phrase and the action it denoted is determined by its use in 1 Chron. xxix. 5 and 2 Chron. xxix. 31, where it is used of the bringing of the freewill-offerings by the people for Jehovah. The ceremonial in this case therefore signified the formal making over of the sacrifices into the charge of Aaron and his sons, which henceforth they were to offer; that they received them to offer them to and for Jehovah, was symbolised by their presentation to be waved before Jehovah, and further by their being burnt upon the altar, as a sacrifice of sweet savour.

Another thing peculiar to this special consecration sacrifice, was the use which was made of the blood, which (ver. 23) was put upon the tip of Aaron's right ear, upon the thumb of his right hand, and upon the great toe of his right foot. Although the solution is not without difficulty, we shall probably not err in regarding this as distinctively an act of consecration, signifying that in virtue of the sacrificial blood, Aaron and his sons were set apart to sacrificial service. It is applied to the ear, to the hand, and the foot, and to the most representative member in each case, to signify the consecration of the whole body to the Lord's service in the tabernacle; the ear is consecrated by the blood to be ever attentive to the word of Jehovah, to receive the intimations of His will; the hand, to be ever ready to do the Lord's work; and the foot, to run on His service.

Another peculiarity of this offering was in the wave-offering of Aaron and his sons. Not the breast, but the thigh, and that together with the fat (ver. 27) was waved before the Lord; and, afterward, not only the fat was burnt upon the altar, according to the law, but also the thigh, which in other cases was the portion of the priest, was burnt with the fat and the memorial of the meal-offering. The breast was afterward waved, as the law commanded in the case of the peace-offerings, but was given to Moses as his portion. The last particular is easy to understand; Moses in this ceremonial stands in the place of the officiating priest, and it is natural that he should thus receive from the Lord his reward for his service. As for the thigh, which, when the peace-offering was offered by one of the people, was presented to the Lord, and then given to the officiating priest to be eaten, obviously the law could not be applied here, as the priests themselves were the bringers of the offering; hence the only alternative was, as in the case of sin-offerings of the holy place, to burn the flesh with fire upon the altar, as "the food of Jehovah." The remainder of the flesh was to be eaten by the priests alone as the offerers, under the regulation for the thank-offering, except that whatever remained until the next day was to be burnt; a direction which is explained by the fact that the sacrifice was to be repeated for seven days, so that there could be no reason for keeping the flesh until the third day. Last of all, it is to be noted that whereas in the thank-offerings of the people, the offerer was allowed to bring leavened bread for the sacrificial feast, in the feast of the consecration of priests this was not permitted; no doubt to emphasise the peculiar sanctity of the office to which they were inducted.

With these modifications, it is plain that the sacrifice of consecration was essentially, not a guilt-offering, as some have supposed, but a peace-offering. It is true that a ram was enjoined as the victim instead of a lamb, but the correspondence here with the law of the guilt-offering is of no significance when we observe that rams were also enjoined or used for peace-offerings on other occasions of exceptional dignity and sanctity, as in the peace-offerings for the nation, mentioned in the following chapter, and the peace-offerings for the princes of the tribes (Numb. vii.). Unlike the guilt-offering, but after the manner of the other, the sacrifice was followed by a sacrificial feast. That participation in this was restricted to the priests, is sufficiently explained by the special relation of this sacrifice to their own consecration.

Before the sacrificial feast, however, one peculiar ceremony still remained. We read (ver. 30): "Moses took of the anointing oil, and of the blood (of the peace-offering) which was upon the altar, and sprinkled it upon Aaron, upon his garments, and upon his sons, and upon his sons' garments with him; and sanctified Aaron, his garments, and his sons, and his sons' garments with him."

This sprinkling signified that now, through the atoning blood which had been accepted before God upon the altar, and through the sanctifying Spirit of grace, which was symbolised by the anointing, thus inseparably associated each with the other, they had been brought into covenant relation with God regarding the office of the priesthood. That this their covenant relation to God concerned them, not merely as private persons, but in their official character, was intimated by the sprinkling, not only of their persons, but of the garments which were the insignia of their priestly office.

All this completed, now followed the sacrificial feast. We read that Moses now ordered Aaron and his sons (ver. 31): "Boil the flesh at the door of the tent of meeting: and there eat it and the bread that is in the basket of consecration, as I commanded, saying, Aaron and his sons shall eat it. And that which remaineth of the flesh and of the bread shall ye burn with fire."

This sacrificial feast most fitly marked the conclusion of the rites of consecration. Hereby it was signified, first, that by this solemn service they were now brought into a relation of peculiarly intimate fellowship with Jehovah, as the ministers of His house, to offer His offerings, and to be fed at His table. It was further signified, that strength for the duties of this office should be supplied to them by Him whom they were to serve, in that they were to be fed of His altar. And, finally, in that the ritual took the specific form of a thank-offering, was thereby expressed, as was fitting, their gratitude to God for the grace which had chosen them and set them apart to so holy and exalted service.

These consecration services were to be repeated for seven consecutive days, during which time they were not to leave the tent of meeting,—obviously, that by no chance they might contract any ceremonial defilement; so jealously must the sanctity of everything pertaining to the service be guarded.

The commandment was (vv. 33-35): "Ye shall not go out from the door of the tent of meeting seven days, until the days of your consecration be fulfilled: for he shall consecrate you seven days. As hath been done this day, so the Lord hath commanded to do, to make atonement for you. And at the door of the tent of meeting shall ye abide day and night seven days, and keep the charge of the Lord, that ye die not: for so I am commanded."

By the sevenfold repetition of the consecration ceremonies was expressed, in the most emphatic manner known to the Mosaic symbolism, the completeness of the consecration and qualification of Aaron and his sons for their office, and the fact also that, in virtue of this consecration, they had come into a special covenant relation with Jehovah concerning the priestly office.

That these consecration sacrifices by which Aaron and his sons were set apart to the priesthood, no less than the preceding part of the ceremonial, pointed forward to Christ and His priestly people as the Antitype, it will be easy to see. As regards our Lord, in Heb. vii. 28, the sacred writer applies to the consecration of our Lord as high priest the very term which the Seventy had used long before in this chapter of Leviticus to denote this formal consecration, and represents the consecration of the Son as the antitype of the consecration of Aaron by the law: "the law appointeth men high priests, having infirmity; but the word of the oath, which was after the law, appointeth a Son, perfected for evermore."

An exception, indeed, must be made, as regards our Lord, in the case of the sin-offering; of whom it is said (Heb. vii. 27), that He "needeth not ... like those high priests, to offer up sacrifices, first for His own sins." But as regards the other two sacrifices, we can see that in their distinctive symbolical import they each bring before us essential elements in the consecration of our Lord Jesus Christ as High Priest. In the burnt-offering, we see Him consecrating Himself by the complete self-surrender of Himself to the Father. In the offering of consecrations, we see Him in the meal-offering of unleavened bread, offering in like manner His most holy works unto the Father; and in the sacrifice of the peace-offering, wherein Aaron ate of the food of God's house in His presence, we see Jesus in like manner as qualified for His high-priestly work by His admission into terms of the most intimate fellowship with the Father, and sustained for His work by the strength given from Him, according to His own word: "The living Father hath sent Me, and I live because of the Father." In the formal "filling of the hands" of Aaron with the sacrificial material, in token of his endowment with the right to offer sacrifices for sin for the sake of sinful men, we are reminded how our Lord refers to the fact that He had received in like manner authority from the Father to lay down His life for His sheep, emphatically adding the words, (John x. 18), "This commandment have I received of My Father."

So also was the meaning of the collateral ceremonies fully realised in Him. If Aaron was anointed with the blood on ear, hand, and foot, by way of signifying that the members of his body should be wholly devoted unto God in priestly service, even so we are reminded (Heb. x. 5, 7), that "when He cometh into the world He saith, ... Sacrifice and offering thou wouldest not, but a body didst thou prepare for Me; ... Lo, I am come to do Thy will, O God."

And so, as Aaron was at the end of the sacrifice sprinkled with blood and oil, in token that God had now, through the blood and the oil, entered into a covenant of priesthood with him, so we find repeated reference to the fact of such a solemn covenant and compact between God and the High Priest of our profession summed up in the words of prophecy, "The Lord hath sworn, and will not repent, Thou art a priest for ever after the order of Melchizedek."

So did this whole consecration ceremony, with the exception only of such parts of it as had reference to the sin of Aaron, point forward to the future investiture of the Son of God with the high-priestly office, by God the Father, that He might act therein for our salvation in all matters between us and God. How can any who have eyes to see all this, as opened out for us in the New Testament, fail with fullest joy and thankfulness to accept Christ, the Son of God, now passed into the Holiest, as the High Priest of our profession? How naturally to all such come the words of exhortation with which is concluded the great argument upon Christ's high-priesthood in the Epistle to the Hebrews (x. 19-23): "Having therefore, brethren, boldness to enter into the holy place by the blood of Jesus; ... and having a great priest over the house of God; let us draw near with a true heart, in fulness of faith, having our hearts sprinkled from an evil conscience, and our body washed with pure water: let us hold fast the confession of our hope that it waver not; for He is faithful that promised."

But not only was Aaron thus consecrated to be high priest of the tabernacle, but his sons also, to be priests under him in the same service. In this also the type holds good. For when in Heb. ii. Christ is brought before us as "the High Priest of our confession," He is represented as saying (ver. 13), "Behold, I and the children which God hath given me!" As Aaron had his sons appointed to perform priestly functions under him in the earthly tabernacle, so also his great Antitype has "sons," called to priestly office under Him in the heavenly tabernacle. Accordingly, we find that in the New Testament, not any caste or class in the Christian Church, but all believers, are represented as "a holy priesthood, to offer up spiritual sacrifices, acceptable to God through Jesus Christ" (1 Peter ii. 5). To the testimony of Peter corresponds that of John in the Apocalypse, where in like manner believers are declared to be priests unto God, and represented as also acting as priests of God and of Christ in the age which is to come after "the first resurrection"[18] (Rev. xx. 6). Hence it is plain that according to the New Testament we shall rightly regard the consecration of the sons of Aaron as no less typical than that of Aaron himself. It is typical of the consecration of all believers to priesthood under Christ. It thus sets forth in symbol the fact and the manner of our own consecration to ministrations between lost men and God, in the age which now is and that which is to come, in things pertaining to sin and salvation, according to the measure to each one of the gift of Christ.

As the consecration of Aaron's sons began with the washing with pure water, so ours with "the washing of regeneration and the renewing of the Holy Ghost" (Titus iii. 5). As Aaron's sons, thus washed, were then invested in white linen, clean and pure, so for the believer must the word be fulfilled (Isa. lxi. 10): "He hath covered me with the robe of righteousness, as a bridegroom decketh himself" (marg. "decketh as a priest"). That is, the reality of our appointment of God unto this high dignity must be visibly attested unto men by the righteousness of our lives. But whereas the sons of Aaron were not clothed until first Aaron himself had been clothed and anointed, it is signified that the robing and anointing of Christ's people follows and depends upon the previous robing and anointing of their Head. Again, as Aaron's sons were also anointed with the same holy oil as was Aaron, only in lesser measure, so are believers consecrated to the priestly office, like their Lord, by the anointing with the Holy Ghost. The anointing of Pentecost follows and corresponds to the anointing of the High Priest at the Jordan with one and the same Spirit. This is another necessary consecration mark, on which the New Testament Scriptures constantly insist. As Jesus was "anointed with the Holy Ghost and (thereby) with power," so He Himself said to His disciples (Acts i. 8), "Ye shall receive power, when the

Holy Ghost is come upon you;" which promise being fulfilled, Paul could say (2 Cor. i. 21), "He that ... anointed us is God;" and John (1 John ii. 20), to all believers, "Ye have an anointing from the Holy One." And the sacrificial symbols are also all fulfilled in the case of the Lord's priestly people. For them, no less essential to their consecration than the washing of the Holy Ghost, is the removal of guilt by the great Sin-offering of Calvary; which same offering, and true Lamb of God, has also become their burnt-offering, their meal-offering, and their sacrifice of consecrations, as it is written (Heb. x. 10), that, by the will of God, "we have been sanctified through the offering of the body of Jesus Christ once for all:" and that He also is become "our peace," in that He has expiated our sins, and also given Himself to us as our spiritual food; that so we may derive daily strength for the daily service in the priest's office, by feeding on the Lamb of God, the true food of the altar, given by God for our support. Also, as the sons of Aaron, like Aaron himself, were anointed with the blood of the peace-offering of consecration, on the ear, the hand, and the foot, so has the blood of the Lamb, in that it has brought us into peace with God, set apart every true believer unto full surrender of all the members of his body unto Him; ears, that they may be quick to hear God's Word; hands, that they may be quick to do it; feet, that they may only run in the way of His commandments. And finally, whereas the solemn covenant of priesthood into which Aaron and his sons had entered with God, was sealed and ratified by the sprinkling with the oil and the blood, so by the unction of the Holy Spirit given to believers, and the cleansing of the conscience by the blood, is it witnessed and certified that they are a people called out to enter into covenant of priestly service with the God of all the earth and the heavens.

What searching questions as to personal experience all this raises! What solemn thoughts throng into the mind of every thoughtful reader! All this essential, if we are to be indeed members of that royal priesthood, who shall reign as priests of God and of Christ? Have we then the marks, all of them? Let us not shrink from the questions, but probe with them the innermost depths of our hearts. Have we had the washing of regeneration? If we think that we have had this, then let us also remember that after the washing came the investiture in white linen. Let us ask, Have we then put on these white garments of righteousness? All that were washed, were also clad in white; these were their official robes, without which they could not act as priests unto God. And there was also an anointing. Have we, in like manner, received the anointing with the Holy Ghost, endowing us with power and wisdom for service? Then, the sin-offering, the burnt-offering, the peace-offering of consecration,—has the Lamb of God been used by us in all these various ways, as our expiation, our consecration, our peace, and our life?

And has the blood which consecrates also been applied to ear, hand, and foot? Are we consecrated in all the members of our bodies?

What questions these are! Truly, it is no light thing to be a Christian; to be called and consecrated to be, with and under the great High Priest, Jesus Christ, a "priest unto God" in this life and in that of "the first resurrection;" to deal between God and men in matters of salvation. Have we well understood what is our "high calling," and what the conditions on which alone we may exercise our ministry? To this may God give us grace, for Jesus' sake. Amen.

CHAPTER XI
THE INAUGURATION OF THE TABERNACLE SERVICE

Lev. ix. 1-24.

Aaron and his sons having now been solemnly consecrated to the priestly office by the ceremonies of seven days, their formal assumption of their daily duties in the tabernacle was marked by a special service suited to the august occasion, signalised at its close by the appearance of the glory of Jehovah to assembled Israel, in token of His sanction and approval of all that had been done. It would appear that the daily burnt-offering and meal-offering had been indeed offered before this, from the time that the tabernacle had been set up; in which service, however, Moses had thus far officiated. But now that Aaron and his sons were consecrated, it was most fitting that a service should thus be ordered which should be a complete exhibition of the order of sacrifice as it had now been given by the Lord, and serve, for Aaron and his sons in all after time, as a practical model of the manner in which the divinely-given law of sacrifice should be carried out.

The order of the day began with a very impressive lesson of the inadequacy of the blood of beasts to take away sin. For seven consecutive days a bullock had been offered for Aaron and his sons, and so far as served the typical purpose, their consecration was complete. But still Aaron and his sons needed expiating blood; for before they could offer the sacrifices of the day for the people, they are ordered yet again first of all to offer a sin-offering for themselves. We read (vv. 1, 2): "And it came to pass on the eighth day, that Moses called Aaron and his sons, and the elders of Israel; and he said unto Aaron, Take thee a bull calf for a sin offering, and a ram for a burnt offering, without blemish, and offer them before the Lord."

And then Aaron was commanded (vv. 3-5): "Unto the children of Israel thou shalt speak, saying, Take ye a he-goat for a sin offering; and a calf and a lamb, both of the first year, without blemish, for a burnt offering; and an ox and a ram for peace offerings, to sacrifice before the Lord; and a meal offering mingled with oil: for to-day the Lord appeareth unto you. And they brought that which Moses commanded before the tent of meeting: and all the congregation drew near and stood before the Lord."

There is little in these directions requiring explanation. Because of the exceptional importance of the occasion, therefore, as in the feasts of the Lord, a special sin-offering was ordered, and a burnt-offering, besides the regular daily burnt-offering, meal-offering, and drink-offering; and, in addition, peculiar to this occasion, a peace-offering for the nation; which last was evidently intended to signify that now on the basis of the sacrificial worship and the mediation of a consecrated priesthood, Israel was privileged to enter into fellowship with Jehovah, the Lord of the tabernacle. No peace-offering was ordered for Aaron and his sons, as, according to the law of the peace-offering, they would themselves take part in that of the people. The sin-offering prescribed for the people was, not a kid, as in King James's version, but a he-goat, which, with the exception of the case of a sin of commission as described in chap. iv. 13, 14, appears to have been the usual victim. For the selection of such a victim, no reason appears more probable than that assigned by rabbinical tradition, namely, that it was intended to counteract the tendency of the people to the worship of shaggy he-goats, referred to in chap. xvii. 7, "They shall no more sacrifice their sacrifices unto the he-goats (R.V.), after whom they go a whoring."

The Order of the Offerings.

ix. 7-21.

"And Moses said unto Aaron, Draw near unto the altar, and offer thy sin offering, and thy burnt offering, and make atonement for thyself, and for the people: and offer the oblation of the people, and make atonement for them; as the Lord commanded. So Aaron drew near unto the altar, and slew the calf of the sin offering, which was for himself. And the sons of Aaron presented the blood unto him: and he dipped his finger in the blood, and put it upon the horns of the altar, and poured out the blood at the base of the altar: but the fat, and the kidneys, and the caul from the liver of the sin offering, he burnt upon the altar; as the Lord commanded Moses. And the flesh and the skin he burnt with fire without the camp. And he slew the burnt offering; and Aaron's sons delivered unto him the blood, and he sprinkled it upon the altar round about. And they delivered the burnt offering unto him, piece by piece, and the head: and he burnt them upon the altar. And he washed the inwards and the legs, and burnt them upon the burnt offering on the altar. And he presented the people's oblation, and took the goat of the sin offering which was for the people, and slew it, and offered it for sin, as the first. And he presented the burnt offering, and offered it according to the ordinance. And he presented the meal offering, and filled his hand therefrom, and burnt it upon the altar, besides the burnt offering of the morning. He slew also the ox and the ram, the sacrifice of peace offerings, which was for the people: and Aaron's sons delivered unto him the blood, and he sprinkled it upon the altar round about, and the fat of the ox; and of the ram, the fat tail, and that which covered the inwards, and the kidneys, and the caul of the liver: and they put the fat upon the breasts, and he burnt the fat upon the altar: and the breast and the right thigh Aaron waved for a wave offering before the Lord; as Moses commanded."

Verses 7-21 detail the way in which this commandment of Moses was carried out in the offerings, first, for Aaron and his sons, and then for all the people; but, as the peculiarities of these several offerings have been already explained, they need not here detain us. That which is new, and of profound spiritual and typical meaning, is the *order* of the sacrifices as here enjoined; an order, which as we learn from many Scriptures, represented what was intended to be the permanent and invariable law. The appointed order of the offerings was as follows: first, whenever presented, came the sin-offering, as here; then, the burnt-offering, with its meal-offering; and last, always, the peace-offering, with its characteristic sacrificial feast.

The significance of this order will readily appear if we consider the distinctive meaning of each of these offerings. The sin-offering had for its central thought, expiation of sin by the shedding of blood; the burnt-offering, the full surrender of the person symbolised by the victim, to God; the meal-offering, in like manner, the consecration of the fruit of his labours; the peace-offering, sustenance of life from God's table, and fellowship in peace and joy with God and with one another. And the great lesson for us now from this model tabernacle service is this: that this order is determined by a law of the spiritual life.

So much as this, even without clear prevision of the Antitype of all these sacrifices, the thoughtful Israelite might have discerned; and even though the truth thus symbolised is placed before us no more in rite and symbol, yet it abides, and ever will abide, a truth. Man everywhere needs fellowship with God, and cannot rest without it; to attain such fellowship is the object of all religions which recognise the being of a God at all. Even among the heathen, we are truly told, there are many who are feeling after God "if haply they may find Him;" and, among ourselves in Christian lands, and even in the external fellowship of Christian churches, there are many who with aching hearts are seeking after an unrealised experience of peace and fellowship with God. And yet God is "not far from any one of us;" and the whole Scripture represents Him as longing on His part with an incomprehensible condescension and love after fellowship with us, desiring to communicate to us His fulness; and still so many seek and find not!

We need not go further than this order of the offerings, and the spiritual truth it signifies regarding the order of grace, to discover the secret of these spiritual failures.

The peace-offering, the sacrificial feast of fellowship with God, the joyful banqueting on the food of His table, was always, as on this day, in order. Before this must ever come the burnt-offering. The ritual prescribed that the peace-offering should be burnt "upon the burnt-offering;" the presence of the burnt-offering is thus presupposed in every acceptable peace-offering. But what if one had ventured to ignore this divinely-appointed order, and had offered his peace-offering to be burnt alone; can we imagine that it would have been accepted?

These things are a parable, and not a hard one. For the burnt-offering with its meal-offering symbolised full consecration of the person and the works to the Lord. Remembering this, we see that the order is not arbitrary. For, in the nature of the case, full consecration to God must precede fellowship with God; he who would know what it is to have God give Himself to him, must first be ready to give himself to God. And that God should enter into loving fellowship with any one who is holding back from loving self-surrender is not to be expected. This is not merely an Old Testament law, still less merely a fanciful deduction from the Mosaic symbolism; everywhere in the New Testament is the thought pressed upon us, no longer indeed in symbol, but in plainest language. It is taught by precept in some of the most familiar words of the great Teacher. There is promise, for example, of constant supply of sufficient food and raiment, fellowship with God in temporal things; but only on condition that "we seek first the kingdom of God, and His righteousness," shall "all these things be added unto us" (Matt. vi. 33). There is a promise of "a hundred-fold in this life, and in the world to come, eternal life;" but it is prefaced by the condition of surrender of father, mother, brethren, sisters, of houses and lands, for the Lord's sake (Matt. xix. 29). Not, indeed, that the actual parting with these is enjoined in every case; but, certainly, it is intended that we shall hold all at the Lord's disposal, possessing, but "as though we possessed not;"—this is the least that we can take out of these words.

Full consecration of the person and the works, this then is the condition of fellowship with God; and if so many lament the lack of the latter, it is no doubt because of the lack of the former. We often act strangely in this matter; half unconsciously, searching, perhaps, every corner of our life but the right one, from looking into which by the clear light of God's Word we instinctively shrink, conscience softly whispering that just there is something about which we have a lurking doubt, and which therefore, if we will be fully consecrated, we must at once give up, till we are sure that it is right, and right for us; and for that self-denial, that renunciation unto God, we are not ready. Is it a wonder that, if such be our experience, we lack that blessed, joyful fellowship with the Lord, of which some tell us? Is it not rather the chief wonder that we should wonder at the lack, when yet we are not ready to consecrate all, body, soul, and spirit, with all our works, unto the Lord? Let us then remember the law of the offerings upon this point. No Israelite could have the blessed feast of the peace-offering, except, first, the burnt-offering and the meal-offering, symbolising full consecration, were smoking on the altar.

But this full consecration seems to many so exceeding hard,—nay, we may say more, to many it is utterly impossible. A consecration of some things, especially those for which they care little, this they can hear of; but a consecration of *all*, that the whole may be consumed upon the altar before and unto God, this they cannot think of. Which means—can we escape the conclusion?—that the love of God does not yet rule supreme. How sad! and how strange! But the law of the offerings will again declare the secret of the strange holding back from full consecration. For it was ordained, that wherever there was sin in the offerer, unconfessed and unforgiven, before even the burnt-offering must go the sin-offering, expiating sin by blood presented on the altar before God. And here we come upon another law of the spiritual life in all ages. If fellowship with God in peace and joy is conditioned by the full consecration of person and service to Him, this consecration, even as a possibility for us, is in turn conditioned by the expiation of sin through the great Sin-offering. So long as conscience is not satisfied that the question of sin has been settled in grace and righteousness with God, so long it is a spiritual impossibility that the soul should come into that experience of the love of God, manifested through atonement, which alone can lead to full consecration.

This truth is always of vital importance; but it is, if possible, more important than ever to insist upon it in our day, when, more and more, the doctrine of the expiation of sin through the blood of the Lamb of God is denied, and that, forsooth, under the claim of superior enlightenment. Men are well pleased to hear of a burnt-offering, so long especially as it is made to signify no more than the self-devotement of the offerer; but for a sin-offering, much modern theology has no place. So soon as we begin to speak of the sacrifice of our Lord for sin in the dialect of the ancient altar—which, it must never be forgotten, is that of Christ and His apostles—we are told that "it would be better for the world if the Christian doctrine of sacrifice could be presented to men apart from the old Jewish ideas and terms, which only serve to obscure the simplicity that is in Christ(!)" And so men, under the pretext of magnifying the love of God, and laying a truer basis for spiritual life, in effect deny the supreme and incomparable manifestation of that love, that God made "Him who knew no sin to be sin on our behalf" (2 Cor. v. 21).

Very different is the teaching, not merely of the law of Moses, but of the whole New Testament; which, in all it has to say of the Christian life as proceeding from full self-surrender, ever represents this full consecration as inspired by the believing recognition and penitent acceptance of Christ, not merely as the great Example of perfect consecration, but as a sin-offering, reconciling us first of all by His death, before He saves us by His life (Rom. v. 10). The expiation of sin by the sin-offering, before the consecration which burnt-offering and meal-offering typify,—this is the invariable order in both Testaments. The Apostle Paul, in his account of his own full consecration, is in full accord with the spiritual teaching of the Mosaic ritual when he gives this as the order. He describes himself, and that in terms of no undue exaggeration, as so under the constraint of the love of Christ as to seem to some beside himself; and then he goes on to explain the secret of this consecration, in which he had placed himself and all he had upon God's altar, as a whole burnt-sacrifice, as consisting just in this, that he had first apprehended the mystery of Christ's death, as a substitution so true and real of the sinless Victim in the place of sinful men, that it might be said that "one died for all, therefore all died;" whence he thus judged, "that they which live should no longer live unto themselves, but unto Him who for their sakes died and rose again" (2 Cor. v. 13-15). To the same effect is the teaching of the Apostle John. For all true consecration springs from the thankful recognition of the love of God; and, according to this Apostle also, the Divine love which inspires the consecration is manifest in this, that "He sent His Son to be the propitiation for our sins" (1 John iv. 10). The apprehension, then, of the reality of the expiation made by the great Sin-offering, and the believing appropriation of its virtue to the cancelling of our guilt, this is the inseparable previous condition of full consecration of person and work unto the Lord. It is so, because only the apprehension of the need of expiation by the blood of the Son of God, as the necessary condition of forgiveness, can give us any adequate measure of the depth of our guilt and ruin, as God sees it; and, on the other hand, only when we remember that God spared not His only-begotten Son, but sent Him to become, through death upon the cross, a propitiation for our sins, can we begin to have such an estimate of the love of God and of Christ His Son as shall make full consecration easy, or even possible.

Let us then, on no account, miss this lesson from the order of this ritual; before the peace-offering, the burnt-offering; before the burnt-offering, the sin-offering. Or, translating the symbolism, perfect fellowship with God in peace and joy and life, only after consecration; and the consecration only possible in fulness, and only accepted of God, in any case, when the great Sin-offering has been first believingly appropriated, according to God's ordination, as the propitiation for our sins, for the cancelling of our guilt.

But there is yet more in this order of the offerings. For, as the New Testament in every way teaches us, the Antitype of every offering was Christ. As we have already seen, in the Sin-offering we have the type of Christ as our propitiation, or expiation; in the burnt-offering, of Christ as consecrating Himself unto God in our behalf; in the meal-offering, as, in like manner, consecrating all His works in our behalf; in the peace-offering, as imparting Himself to us as our life, and thus bringing us into fellowship of peace and love and joy with the Father.

Now this last is, in fact, the ultimate aim of salvation; rather, indeed, we may say, it is salvation. For life in its fulness means the cancelling of death; death spiritual, and bodily death also, in resurrection from the dead; it means also perfect fellowship with the living God, and this, attained, is heaven. Hence it must needs be that the peace-offering which represents Christ as giving Himself to us as our life, and introducing us into this blessed state, comes last.

But before this, in order, not of time, but of grace, as also of logic, must be Christ as Sin-offering, and Christ as Burnt-offering. And, first of all, Christ as Sin-offering. For God's way of peace puts the cancelling of guilt, the satisfaction of His holy law and justice, and therewith the restoration of our right relation to Him, first, and in order to a holy life and fellowship; while man will ever put these last, and regard the latter as the means to obtaining a right standing with God. Hence, inasmuch as Christ, coming to save us, finds us under a curse, the first thing in order is, and must be, the removal of that curse of the holy wrath of God, against every one that "continueth not in all things that are written in the book of the law, to do them." And so, first in order in the typical ritual is the sin-offering which represents Christ as made "a curse for us," that He might thus redeem us from the curse of the law (Gal. iii. 13).

But this is not a complete account of the work of our Lord for us in the days of His flesh. His work indeed was one, but the Scriptures set it forth in a twofold aspect. On the one hand, He is the Sinless One bearing the curse for us; but also, in all His suffering for our sins, He is also manifested as the Righteous One, making many righteous by His obedience, even an obedience unto the death of the cross (Rom. v. 19; Phil. ii. 8). And if we ask what was the essence of this obedience of our Lord for us, what was it, indeed, but that which is the essence of all obedience to God, namely, full, unreserved, uninterrupted consecration and self-surrender to the will of the Father? And as, by His suffering, Christ endured the curse for us, so by all His obedience and suffering in full submission to the will of God, He became also "the Lord our righteousness." And this, as repeatedly remarked, is the central thought of the burnt-offering and the meal-offering,—full consecration of the person and the work to God.

In the sin-offering, then, we see Christ as our propitiation; in the burnt-offering, we see Him rather as our righteousness; but the former is presupposed in the latter; and apart from this, that in His death He became the expiation of our sins, His obedience could have availed us nothing. But given now Christ as our propitiation and also our righteousness, the whole question of the relation of Christ's people to God in law and righteousness is settled, and the way is now clear for the communication of life which the peace-offering symbolised. Thus, as by faith in Christ as the Sin-offering, our propitiation and righteousness, we are "justified freely by grace," "apart from the works of the law," so now the way is open, by the appropriation of Christ as our life in the peace-offering, for our sanctification and complete redemption. In a word, the law of the order of the offerings teaches, symbolically and typically, exactly what, in Rom. vi. and vii., the Apostle Paul teaches dogmatically, namely, that the order of grace is first justification, then sanctification; but both by the same crucified Christ, our propitiation, our righteousness, and our life: in whom we come to have fellowship in all good and blessing with the Father.

It is interesting to observe that after the analogy of this order of the offerings, is the most usual order of the development of Christian experience. For the awakened soul is usually first of all concerned about the question of forgiveness of sin and acceptance; and hence, most commonly, faith first apprehends Christ in this aspect, as the One who "bare our sins in His body," by whose stripes we are healed; and then, at a later period of experience, as the One who also, in lowly consecration to the Father's will, obeyed for us, that we might be made righteous through His obedience. But no one who is truly justified by faith in Christ as our propitiation and righteousness, can long rest with this. He very quickly finds what he had little thought of before, that the evil nature abides even in the justified and accepted believer; nay, more, that it has still a terrible strength to overcome him and lead him into sin, even often when he would not. And this prepares the believer, still in accord with the law of the order of grace here set forth, to lay hold also on Christ by faith as His Peace-offering, by feeding on whom we receive spiritual strength, so that He thus, in a word, becomes our sanctification and, at last, full redemption.

The Double Benediction.

ix. 22-24.

"And Aaron lifted up his hands toward the people, and blessed them; and he came down from offering the sin offering, and the burnt offering, and the peace offerings. And Moses and Aaron went into the tent of meeting, and came out, and blessed the people: and the glory of the Lord appeared unto all the people. And there came forth fire from before the Lord, and consumed upon the altar the burnt offering and the fat: and when all the people saw it, they shouted, and fell on their faces."

The sacrifices having now been made, and the offerings presented in this divinely-appointed order, by the ordained and consecrated priesthood, two things followed: a double benediction was pronounced upon the people, and Jehovah manifested to them His glory. We read (ver. 22), "And Aaron lifted up his hands toward the people, and blessed them; and he came down from offering the sin offering, and the burnt offering, and the peace offerings."

Presumably, the form of benediction which Aaron used was that which, according to Numb. vi. 24-27, the priests were commanded by the Lord to use: "The Lord bless thee, and keep thee: the Lord make His face to shine upon thee, and be gracious unto thee: the Lord lift up His countenance upon thee, and give thee peace." It was not an empty form; for the Lord at that time also promised Himself to make this blessing efficient, saying thereafter, "So shall they put My Name"—Jehovah, the name of God in covenant,—"upon the children of Israel; and I will bless them."

So also the Lord Jesus, just before withdrawing from the bodily sight of His disciples after the completion of His great sacrifice, "lifted up His hands, and blessed them;" and thereupon disappeared from their sight, ascending into heaven. Even so was it in the typical service of this day; for when Aaron had thus lifted up his hands and blessed the people (ver. 23), "Moses and Aaron went into the tent of meeting."

The work of Aaron in the outer court had been finished, and now he disappears from Israel's sight; for he must, in like manner, be inducted into the priestly work within the Holy Place. He must there be shown all those things to which, in his priestly ministrations, the blood must be applied; and, especially, must also offer the sweet incense at the golden altar which was before the veil which enshrined the immediate presence of Jehovah. But this offering of incense, as all have agreed, typifies the precious and most effective intercession of the great Antitype; so that thus it was shown in a figure, how the Christ of God, having finished His sacrificial work in the sight of men, and having ascended into heaven, should there for a season abide, hidden from human sight, making intercession for His waiting people.

After an interval—we are not told how long—Moses and Aaron again (vv. 23, 24), "came out, and blessed the people: and the glory of the Lord appeared unto all the people. And there came forth fire from before the Lord, and consumed upon the altar the burnt offering and the fat: and when all the people saw it, they shouted, and fell on their faces."

This second blessing by Moses and Aaron conjointly, followed Aaron's reappearance to Israel, and marked the completion of these inauguration services, the intercession within the veil, as well as the sacrifices. And the revelation in a visible way of the glory of the Lord added what now was alone required, the manifest attestation by the Lord of the tabernacle of His approval of all that had been done in these memorable eight days. This appearance of the Shekinah glory was followed by a flash of fire which, in token of the Divine appropriation of the sacrifices, consumed in an instant the burnt-offering on the altar with the fat of the sin-offering and the peace-offering, which had been laid upon it. We cannot follow here the Jewish tradition, which has it that with this act the sacrificial fire which was never to go out upon the altar, was originated. On the contrary, as we have seen, the offerings had before this been made by Moses, and even on this day the fire had been kindled before (ver. 10, *et seq.*). Nor is there any necessary inconsistency here; for we have but to suppose that the burning of the sacrifices which had been kindled by Aaron was not yet complete, when the flash from the cloud of glory in an instant consummated the burning, teaching in a most august and impressive manner the symbolic meaning of the burning of the sacrifices on the altar, as signifying the acceptance and appropriation of that which was offered, by the Lord who had commanded all, and thereby endorsing all that had been done, as according to His mind and will.

And even so, according to the sure Word of prophecy, our heavenly High Priest has yet in reserve for His people a second benediction. His first blessing upon leaving the world was followed by Pentecost; the second, on His reappearing, shall bring in resurrection and full salvation. And in that day, when He "shall appear a second time, apart from sin, to them that wait for Him unto salvation" (Heb. ix. 28), therewith shall appear the glory which on that day, long ago, appeared to Israel; for He "shall come in the glory of His Father," and thus shall God, the Most High and the Most Holy, testify before the universe His gracious acceptance of the service of the true Aaron and His "many sons," the priestly people of God, through all the Christian ages. Thus, the services and events of that day of induction, in their order from beginning to end, were not only a parable of the order of grace, but also, as it were, a typical epitome of the whole work of redemption. They are thus a prophecy that the work which began when Christ made His soul an offering for sin, and to perfect which He is now withdrawn from our sight for a season, shall be consummated at last by His reappearing in glory for the final blessing of His waiting people.

And if we look at other and subordinate aspects of this inauguration service, we shall still find this sequel of all, no less richly suggestive. Expiation, righteousness, fellowship in peace with God, shall bring with it the blessing of the Lord, and finally issue in the revelation of His glory in the sight of all who accept this great redemption through sacrifice. And so also in the personal life. As the trustful acceptance and use of the appointed Sin-offering leads to the consecration of the person and the life, and as by this consecration we come into conscious fellowship with God in joy and peace, as we feed on the flesh of the slain Lamb, so, as the blessed result, unto every true believer, according to the measure of his faith, this is followed by the double benediction of the Lord; one for this life, and a larger, for the life which is to come. The Lord blesses him, and keeps him: the Lord makes His face to shine upon him, and is gracious unto him: the Lord lifts up His countenance upon him, and gives him peace, according to that word of the great High Priest: "Peace I leave with you; My peace I give unto you" (John xiv. 27). And then, after the present peace, is yet to follow, as the final issue of the expiated sin, and the consecrated life, and fellowship in peace with the God of life and love, the beholding of the glory of the Lord; according to that high-priestly prayer of our Redeemer, "That which Thou hast given Me, I will that, where I am, they also may be with Me: that they may behold My glory" (John xvii. 24). Even here some know a little of this, and find that expiated sin and full consecration are followed here and now by bright glimpses of the glory of the Lord. But what is now seen thus in part shall then be seen fully and face to face. Who would not make sure of that beatific vision of the glory of the Lord?

CHAPTER XII
NADAB'S AND ABIHU'S "STRANGE FIRE"

Lev. x. 1-20.

The solemn and august ceremonies of the consecration of the priests and the tabernacle, and the inauguration of the tabernacle service, had a sad and terrible termination. The sacrifices of the inauguration day had been completed, the congregation had received the priestly benediction, the glory of Jehovah had appeared unto the people, and, in token of His acceptance of all that had been done, consumed the victims on the altar. This manifestation of the glory of the Lord so affected the people—as well it might—that when they saw it, "they shouted, and fell on their faces." It was, probably, under the influence of the excitement of this occasion that (vv. 1, 2), "Nadab and Abihu, the sons of Aaron, took each of them his censer, and put fire therein, and laid incense thereon, and offered strange fire before the Lord, which He had not commanded them. And there came forth fire from before the Lord, and devoured them, and they died before the Lord."

There has been no little speculation as to what it was, precisely, which they did. Some will have it, that they lighted their incense, not from the altar fire, but elsewhere. As to this, while it is not easy to prove that to light the incense at the altar fire was an invariable requirement, yet it is certain that this was commanded for the great day of atonement (xvi. 12); and also, that when Moses offered incense in connection with the plague which broke out upon the rebellion of Korah, Dathan, and Abiram, Moses commanded him to take the fire for the censer from off the altar (Numb. xvi. 46); so that, perhaps this is not unlikely to have been one element, at least, in their offence. Others, again, have thought that their sin lay in this, that they offered their incense at a time not commanded in the order of worship which God had just prescribed; and this, too, may very probably have been another element in their sin, for it is certain that the divinely-appointed order of worship for the day had been already completed. Yet again, others have supposed that they rashly and without Divine warrant pressed within the veil, into the immediate presence of the Shekinah glory of God, to offer their incense there. For this, too, there is evidence, in the fact that the institution of the great annual day of atonement, and the prohibition of entrance within the veil at any other time, even to the high priest himself, is said to have followed "after the death of the two sons of Aaron, when they drew near before the Lord, and died" (xvi. 1, 2).

It is perfectly possible, and even likely, that all these elements were combined in their offence. In any case, the gravamen of their sin is expressed in these words; they offered "fire which the Lord had not commanded them:" offered it, either in a way not commanded, or at a time not commanded, or in a place not commanded; or, perhaps, in each and all of these ways, offered "fire which the Lord had not commanded." This was their sin, and one which brought instant and terrible judgment.

It is easy enough to believe that yet they meant well in what they did. It probably seemed to them the right thing to do. After such a stupendous display as they had just witnessed, of the flaming glory of Jehovah, why should they not, in token of reverence and adoration, offer incense, even in the most immediate presence of Jehovah? And why should such minor variations from the appointed law, as to manner, or time, or place, matter very much, so the motive was worship? So may they probably have reasoned, if indeed they thought at all. But, nevertheless, this made no difference; all the same, "fire came forth from Jehovah, and devoured them." They had been but so lately consecrated! and—as we learn from ver. 5—their priestly robes were on them at the time, in token of their peculiar privilege of special nearness to God! But this, too, made no difference; "there came forth fire from before the Lord and devoured them."

Their sin, in the form in which it was committed, can never be repeated; but as regards its inner nature and essence, no sin has been in all ages more common. For the essence of their sin was this, that it was will-worship; worship in which they consulted not the revealed will of God regarding the way in which He would be served, but their own fancies and inclinations. The directions for worship had been, as we have seen, exceedingly full and explicit; but they apparently imagined that the fragrance of their incense, and its intrinsic suitableness as a symbol of adoration and prayer, was sufficient to excuse neglect of strict obedience to the revealed will of God touching His own worship. Their sin was not unlike that of Saul in a later day, who thought to excuse disobedience by the offering of enormous sacrifices. But he was sharply reminded that "to obey is better than sacrifice" (1 Sam. xv. 22); and the priesthood were in like manner on this occasion very terribly taught that obedience is also better than incense, even the incense of the sanctuary.

In all ages, men have been prone to commit this sin, and in ours as much as any. It is true that in the present dispensation the Lord has left more in

His worship than in earlier days to the sanctified judgment of His people, and has not minutely prescribed details for our direction. It is true, again, that there is, and always will be, room for some difference of judgment among good and loyal servants of the Lord, as to how far the liberty left us extends. But we are certainly all taught as much as this, that wherever we are not clear that we have a Divine warrant for what we do in the worship of God, we need to be exceeding careful, and to act with holy fear, lest possibly, like Nadab and Abihu, we be chargeable with offering "strange fire," which the Lord has not commanded. And when one goes into many a church and chapel, and sees the multitude of remarkable devices by which, as is imagined, the worship and adoration of God is furthered, it must be confessed that it certainly seems as if the generation of Nadab and Abihu was not yet extinct; even although a patient God, in the mystery of His long-suffering, flashes not instantly forth His vengeance.

This then is the first lesson of this tragic occurrence. We have to do with a God who is very jealous; who will be worshipped as He wills, or not at all. Nor can we complain. If God be such a Being as we are taught in the Holy Scripture, it must be His inalienable right to determine and prescribe how He will be served.

And it is a second lesson, scarcely less evident, that with God, intention of good, though it palliate, cannot excuse disobedience where He has once made known His will. No one can imagine that Nadab and Abihu meant wrong; but for all that, for their sin they died.

Again, we are herein impressively taught that, with God, high position confers no immunity when a man sins; least of all, high position in the Church. On the contrary, the greater the exaltation in spiritual honour and privilege, the more strictly will a man be held to account for every failure to honour Him who exalted him. We have seen this illustrated already by the law of the sin-offering; and this tragic story illustrates the same truth again.

But the question naturally arises, How could these men, who had been so exalted in privilege, who had even beheld the glory of the God of Israel in the holy mount (Exod. xxiv. 1, 9, 10), have ventured upon such a perilous experiment? The answer is probably suggested by the warning which immediately followed their death (vv. 8, 9): "The Lord spake unto Aaron, saying, Drink no wine nor strong drink, ... when ye go into the tent of the meeting, that ye die not." It is certainly distinctly hinted by these words, that it was under the excitement of strong drink that these men so fatally sinned.

If so, then, although their sin may not be repeated in its exact form among us, yet the fact points a very solemn warning, not only regarding the careless use of strong drink, but, more than that, against all religious worship and activity which is inspired by other stimulus than by the Holy Spirit of God. Of this every age of the Church's history has furnished sad examples. Sometimes we see it illustrated in "revivals," even in such as may be marked by some evidence of the presence of the Spirit of God; when injudicious speakers seek by various methods to work up what is, after all, merely a physical excitement of a strange, infectious kind, though too often mistaken for the work of the Holy Spirit of God. More subtle and yet more common is the sin of such as in preaching the Word find their chief stimulation in the excitement of a crowded house, or the visible signs of approbation on the part of the hearers; and perhaps sometimes mistake the natural effect of this influence for the quickening power of the Holy Ghost, and go on to offer before the Lord the incense of their religious service and worship, but with "strange fire." Of this all need to beware; and most of all, ministers of the Word.

The penalty of sin is often long delayed, but it did not lag in this case. The strange fire in the hands of Nadab and Abihu was met by a flash of flame that instantly withered their life; and, just as they were, their priestly robes upon them unconsumed, their censers in their hands, they dropped dead before the fatal bolt.

In reading this account and other similar narratives in Holy Scripture, of the deadly outbreak of God's wrath, many have felt not a little disquieted in mind because of the terrific severity of the judgment, which to them seems so out of all proportion to the guilt of the offender. And so, in many hearts, and even to many lips, the question has perforce arisen: Is it possible to believe that in this passage, for instance, we have a true representation of the character of God? In answering such a question we ought always to remember, first of all, that, apart from our imperfect knowledge, just because we all are sinners, we are, by that fact, all more or less disqualified and incapacitated for forming a correct and unbiassed judgment regarding the demerit of sin. It is quite certain that every sinful man is naturally inclined to take a lenient view of the guilt of sin, and, by necessary consequence, of its desert in respect of punishment. In approaching this question, here and elsewhere in God's Word, it is imperative that we keep this fact in mind.

Again, it is not unnecessary to remark, that we must be careful and not read into this narrative what, in fact, is not here. For it is often assumed without evidence, that when we read in the Bible of men being suddenly cut off by death for some special sin, we are therefore required to believe that the temporal judgment of physical death must have been followed, in each instance, by the judgment of the eternal fire. But always to infer this in such cases, when, as here, nothing of the kind is hinted in the text, is a great mistake, and introduces a difficulty which is wholly of our own making. That sometimes, at least, the facts are quite the opposite, is expressly certified to us in 1 Cor. xi. 30-32, where we are told that among the Christians of Corinth, many, because of their irreverent approach to the Holy Supper of the Lord, slept the sleep of death; but that these judgments from the Lord, of bodily death, instead of being necessarily intended for their eternal destruction, were sent that they might not finally perish. For the Apostle's words are most explicit; for it is with reference to these cases of sickness and death of which he had spoken, that he adds (ver. 32): "But when we are (thus) judged, we are chastened of the Lord, that we may not be condemned with the world."

What we have here before us, then, is not the question of the eternal condemnation of Nadab and Abihu for their thoughtless, though perhaps not so intended, profanation of God's worship,—a point on which the narrative gives us no information,—but, simply and only, the inflicting on them, for this sin, of the judgment of temporal death. And if this yet seem to some undue severity, as no doubt it will, there remain other considerations which deserve to have great weight here. In the first place, if this reveal God as terribly severe in His judgment, even upon what, compared with other crimes, may seem a small sin, we have to remember that, after all, this God of the Bible, this Jehovah of the Old Testament, is only herein revealed as in this respect like the God whose working we see in nature and in history. Was the God of Nadab and Abihu a severe God? Is not the God of nature a terribly severe God? Who then is it that has so appointed the economy of nature that even for one thoughtless indulgence by a young man, he shall be racked with pain all his life thereafter? It is a law of nature, one says. But what is a law of nature but the ordinary operation of the Divine Being who made nature? So let us not forget that the reasoning which, because of the confessed severity of this judgment on the sons of Aaron, argues God out of the tenth of Leviticus, and refuses to believe that this can be a revelation of His mind and character, by parity of reasoning must go on to argue God out of nature and out of history. But if one be not yet ready for the latter, let him take heed how he too hastily decide on this ground against the verity of the history and the truth of the revelation in the case before us.

Then, again, we need to be careful that we pass not judgment before considering all that was involved in this act of sin. We cannot look upon the case as if the act of Nadab and Abihu had been merely a private matter, personal to themselves alone. This it was not, and could not be. They did what they did in their official robes; moreover, it was a peculiarly public act: it took place before the sanctuary, where all the people were assembled. What was the influence of this their act, if it passed unrebuked and unpunished, likely to be? History shows that nothing was more inbred in the nature of the people than just this tendency to will-worship. For centuries after this, notwithstanding many like terrible judgments, it mightily prevailed, taking the form of numberless attempted improvements on the arrangements of worship appointed by God, and introducing, under such pretexts of expediency often the grossest idolatry. And although the Babylonian judgment made an end of the idolatrous form of will-worship, the old tendency persisted, and worked on under a new form till, as we learn from our Lord's words in the Gospel, the people were in His day utterly overwhelmed with "heavy burdens and grievous to be borne," rabbinical additions to the law, attempted improvements on Moses, under pretext of honouring Moses, all begotten of this same inveterate spirit of will-worship. Nor are such things of little consequence, as some seem to imagine, whether we find them among Jews or in Christian communions. On the contrary, all will-worship, in all its endless variety of forms, tends to confuse conscience, by confounding with the commandments of God the practices and traditions of men; and all history, no less of the Church than of Israel, shows that the tendency of all such will-worship is to the subversion alike of morality religion, occasioning, too often, total misapprehension as to what indeed is the essence of religion well pleasing to God.

Was the sin of the priests, Nadab and Abihu, then, committed in such a public manner, such a trifling matter after all? And when we further remember the peculiar circumstances of the occasion,—that the whole ceremonial of the day was designed in a special manner to instruct the people as to the manner in which Jehovah, their King and their God, would be worshipped,—it certainly is not so hard, after all, to see how it was almost imperative that in the very beginning of Israel's national history, God should give them a lesson on the sanctity of His ordinances and His hatred of will-worship, which should be remembered to all time.

The solemn lesson of the terrible judgment, Moses, as Prophet and Interpreter of God's will to the people, declares in these words (ver. 3): "This is it that the Lord spake, saying, I will be sanctified in them that come nigh Me, and before all the people I will be glorified."

If God separate a people to be specially near unto Him, it is that, admitted to such special nearness to Himself, they shall ever reverently recognise His transcendent exaltation in holiness, and take care that He be ever glorified in them before all men. But if any be careless of this, God will nevertheless not be defrauded. If they will recognise His august holiness, in the reverence of loyal service, well; God shall thus glorify Himself in them before all. But if otherwise, still God will be glorified in them before all people, though now in their chastisement and in retribution. The principle is that which is announced by Amos (iii. 2): "You only have I known of all the families of the earth; *therefore* I will visit upon you all your iniquities." And when we remember that the sons of Aaron typically represent the whole body of believers in Christ, as a priestly people, it is plain that the warning of this judgment comes directly home to us all. If, as Christians, we have been brought into a relation of special nearness and privilege with God, we have to remember that the place of privilege is, in this case, a place of peculiar danger. If we forget the reverence and honour due to His name, and insist on will-worship of any kind, we shall in some way suffer for it. God may wink at the sins of others, but not at ours. He is a God of love, and desires not our death, but that He may be glorified in our life; but if any will not have it so, He will not be robbed of His glory. Hence the warning of the Apostle Peter, who was so filled with these Old Testament conceptions of God and His worship: "It is written, Ye shall be holy, for I am holy. And if ye call on Him as Father, who without respect of persons judgeth according to each man's work, pass the time of your sojourning in fear" (1 Peter i. 17).

Ver. 3: "And Aaron held his peace."

For rebellion were useless; nay, it had been madness. Even the tenderest natural affection must be silent when God smites for sin; and in this case the sin was so manifest, and the connection therewith of the judgment so evident, that Aaron could say nothing, though his heart must have been breaking.

Mourning in Silence.

x. 4-7.

"And Moses called Mishael and Elzaphan, the sons of Uzziel the uncle of Aaron, and said unto them, Draw near, carry your brethren from before the sanctuary out of the camp. So they drew near, and carried them in their coats out of the camp; as Moses had said. And Moses said unto Aaron, and unto Eleazar and unto Ithamar, his sons, Let not the hair of your heads go loose, neither rend your clothes; that ye die not, and that He be not wroth with all the congregation:

but let your brethren, the whole house of Israel, bewail the burning which the Lord hath kindled. And ye shall not go out from the door of the tent of meeting, lest ye die: for the anointing oil of the Lord is upon you. And they did according to the word of Moses."

Even in ordinary cases, restrictions were placed upon Aaron and his sons as regards the outward signs of mourning; but exceptions were made in the case of the nearest relations, and, in particular, of the death of a son, or a brother (chap. xxi. 2). In this case, however, this permission could not be given; and they are warned that by public expressions of grief they would not only bring death from the Lord upon themselves, but also bring His wrath upon the whole congregation which they represented before God. They are not indeed forbidden to mourn in their hearts, but from all the outward and customary signs of mourning they must abstain. And the reason for this is given; "The anointing oil of the Lord is upon you." That is, by the anointing they had been set apart to represent God before Israel. Hence, when God had thus manifested His holy wrath against sin, for them to have exhibited the public signs of mourning for this, even though the stroke of wrath had fallen into their own family, would have been a visible contradiction between their actions and their priestly position. To others, indeed, these outward tokens of mourning are expressly permitted, for they stood in no such special relation to God; their brethren, "the whole house of Israel," might bewail the burning which the Lord had kindled, but they, although nearest of kin to the dead, are not permitted even to follow the slain of the Lord to the grave, and (vv. 4, 5) the sad duty is assigned to their cousins, who bear the dead, in their white priestly robes, just as they had fallen, out of the camp to burial, while Aaron and his sons mourn silently within the tent of meeting.

This has seemed hard to many, and has furnished some another illustration of the hardness and severity of the character of God as held up in the Pentateuch. But we shall do well to remember that in all this we have nothing which in any respect goes beyond the very solemn words of the tender-hearted and most compassionate Saviour, who said, for example, "If any man cometh unto Me, and hateth not his own father, and mother, and wife, and children, and brethren, and sisters, ... he cannot be My disciple" (Luke xiv. 26). In language such as this, we cannot but recognise the same character as in this command unto Aaron and his sons; and if such "hard sayings" are to be held reason for rejecting the revelation of the character of God as given in the Old Testament, the same logic, in the presence of similar words, will require us also to reject the revelation of God's character as given by Christ in the New Testament.

The teaching of both Testaments on this matter is plain. Natural affection is right; it is indeed implanted in our hearts by the God who made us in all our human relations. But none the less, whenever the feelings which belong even to the nearest and tenderest earthly relations come into conflict with absolute fealty and submission to the will of God, and unswerving loyalty to the will of Christ, then, hard though indeed it may be, natural affection must give way, and mourn within the tent in the silence of a holy submission to the Lord.

Carefulness after Judgment.

x. 8-20.

"And the Lord spake unto Aaron, saying, Drink no wine nor strong drink, thou, nor thy sons with thee, when ye go into the tent of meeting, that ye die not: it shall be a statute for ever throughout your generations: and that ye may put difference between the holy and the common, and between the unclean and the clean; and that ye may teach the children of Israel all the statutes which the Lord hath spoken unto them by the hand of Moses. And Moses spake unto Aaron, and unto Eleazar and unto Ithamar, his sons that were left, Take the meal offering that remaineth of the offerings of the Lord made by fire, and eat it without leaven beside the altar: for it is most holy: and ye shall eat it in a holy place, because it is thy due, and thy sons' due, of the offerings of the Lord made by fire: for so I am commanded. And the wave breast and the heave thigh shall ye eat in a clean place; thou, and thy sons, and thy daughters with thee: for they are given as thy due, and thy sons' due, out of the sacrifices of the peace offerings of the children of Israel. The heave thigh and the wave breast shall they bring with the offerings made by fire of the fat, to wave it for a wave offering before the Lord: and it shall be thine, and thy sons' with thee, as a due for ever; as the Lord hath commanded. And Moses diligently sought the goat of the sin offering, and, behold, it was burnt: and he was angry with Eleazar and with Ithamar, the sons of Aaron that were left, saying, Wherefore have ye not eaten the sin offering in the place of the sanctuary, seeing it is most holy, and He hath given it you to bear the iniquity of the congregation, to make atonement for them before the Lord?

Behold, the blood of it was not brought into the sanctuary within: ye should certainly have eaten it in the sanctuary, as I commanded. And Aaron spake unto Moses, Behold, this day have they offered their sin offering and their burnt offering before the Lord; and there have befallen me such things as these: and if I had eaten the sin offering to-day, would it have been well-pleasing in the sight of the Lord? And when Moses heard that, it was well-pleasing in his sight."

Such a judgment as the foregoing ought to have had a good effect, and it did. This appeared in renewed carefulness to secure the most exact obedience hereafter in all their official duties. To this end, the Lord Himself now laid down a law evidently designed to preclude, as far as possible, every risk of any such fault in the priestly service as might again bring down judgment. It is not only holiness, but considerate and anxious love, which speaks in the next words, addressed to Aaron (vv. 8, 9): "Drink no wine nor strong drink, thou, nor thy sons with thee, when ye go into the tent of meeting, that ye die not: it shall be a statute for ever throughout your generations."

And for this prohibition the reason is given (vv. 10, 11): "That ye may put difference between the holy and the common, and between the unclean and the clean; and that ye may teach the children of Israel all the statutes which the Lord hath spoken unto them by the hand of Moses."

It was not then that the use of wine was in itself sinful; for this is taught nowhere in the Old or New Testament, and as a doctrine of religion is characteristic, not of Judaism or Christianity, but only of Mohammedanism, of Buddhism and other heathen religions. The ground of this command of abstinence, as of the New Testament counsel (Rom. xiv. 20, 21), is that of expediency. Because, in the use of wine or strong drink, there was involved a certain risk, that by undue indulgence the judgment might be confused or the memory weakened, so that something might be done amiss; therefore the priests, who were specially commissioned to teach the statutes of the Lord to Israel, and this most of all, by their own carefulness to obey all the least of His commandments, are here warned to abstain whenever about engaging in their official duties. As suggested above, it is at least very natural to infer, from the historical setting of this prohibition, that the fatal offence of Nadab and Abihu was occasioned by such an indulgence in wine or strong drink as made it possible for impulse to get the better of knowledge and judgment.

But, however this may be, the lesson for us abides the same; a lesson which each one according to his circumstances must faithfully apply to his own case. For the Christian it is not enough that he shall abstain from what is in its own nature always sinful; it must be the law of our life that we abstain also from whatever may needlessly become occasion of sin. In this we cannot, indeed, lay down a universal code of law. Heathen reformers have done this, and their imitators in the Church, but never Christ or His Apostles. And this with reason. For that which for one carries with it inevitable risk of sin, is not always fraught with the same danger to another person with a different temperament, or even to the same person under different circumstances. In each instance we must judge for ourselves, taking heed not to abuse our liberty to another's harm; and also, on the other hand, being careful how we judge others in regard to things which in their essential nature are neither right nor wrong. But we shall be wise to recognise the fact that it is just in such things that many Christians do most harm, both to their own souls and to those of others. And in regard to the drinking of wine in particular, one must be blind indeed not to perceive it to be the fact that, whatever the reason may be, the English-speaking peoples seem to be peculiarly susceptible to the danger of undue indulgence in wine and strong drink. On both sides of the Atlantic, drunkenness must be set down as one of the most prevalent national sins.

In deciding the question of personal duty in this and like cases, all believers are bound, as the Lord's priestly people, to remember that He has appointed them that they should walk before Him as a separated people, who, by their daily walk, above all, are to teach others to "put a difference between holy and common, and unclean and clean, and to observe all the statutes which the Lord hath spoken."

In vv. 12-15 we have a repetition of the commandments previously given, concerning the use to be made of the meal-offering and the peace-offering. From this it appears that Moses himself, in view of the tragic occurrence of the day, was stirred up to charge Aaron and his sons anew on matters on which he had already commanded them. And with this intensified care on his part is evidently connected the incident recorded in the verses which follow, where we read that, having repeated the directions as to the meal-offering and the peace-offering (vv. 16, 17), "Moses diligently sought the goat of the sin offering, and, behold, it was burnt; and he was angry with Eleazar and with Ithamar, the sons of Aaron that were left, saying, Wherefore have ye not eaten the sin offering in the place of the sanctuary, seeing it is most holy, and He hath given it you to bear the iniquity of the congregation, to make atonement for them before the Lord?"

It had indeed been commanded, in the case of those sin-offerings of which the blood was brought into the holy place, that their flesh should not be eaten; but that the flesh of all others should be eaten, as belonging to the class of things "most holy," by the priests alone within the Holy Place. Hence Moses continued (ver. 18): "Behold, the blood of it was not brought into the sanctuary within: ye should certainly have eaten it in the sanctuary, as I commanded."

What had been done, as it appears, had been done with Aaron's knowledge and sanction; for Aaron then answered in behalf of his sons (ver. 19): "Behold, this day have they offered their sin offering and their burnt offering before the Lord; and there have befallen me such things as these: and if I had eaten the sin offering to-day, would it have been well-pleasing in the sight of the Lord?"

Of which answer, the intention seems to have been this. In this day of special exaltation and privilege, when for the first time they had performed their solemn priestly duties, when most of all there should have been the utmost care to please the Lord in the very smallest things, His holy Name had been profaned by the will-worship of his sons, and the wrath of God had broken out against them, and, in them, against their father's house. Could it be the will of God that a house in which was found the guilt of such a sin, should yet partake of the most holy things of God in the sanctuary?

From this it appears that the judgment sent into the house of Aaron had had a most wholesome spiritual effect. They had received such an impression of their own profound sinfulness as they had never had before. And it is very instructive to observe that they assume to themselves a part in the sinfulness which had been shown in the sin of Nadab and Abihu. It did not occur to Aaron or his remaining sons to say, in the spirit of Israel in the day of our Lord, "If we had been in their place, we would not have done so." Rather their consciences had been so awakened to the holiness of God and their own inborn evil, that they coupled themselves with the others as under the displeasure of God. Was it possible, even though they personally had not sinned, that such as they should eat that which was most holy unto God? They had thus in the letter disobeyed the law; but because their offence was begotten of a misapprehension, and only showed how deeply and thoroughly they had taken to heart the lesson of the sore judgment, we read that "when Moses heard" their explanation, "it was well pleasing in his sight."

All this which followed the sin of Nadab and Abihu, and the judgment which fell on them, and thus upon the whole house of Aaron, is a most instructive illustration of the working of the chastising judgments of the Lord, when rightly received. Its effect was to awaken the utmost solicitude that nothing else might be found about the tabernacle service, even through oversight, which was not according to the mind of God; and, in those immediately stricken, to produce a very profound sense of personal sinfulness and unworthiness before God. The New Testament gives us a graphic description of this effect of the chastisement of God on the believer, in the account which we have of the result of the discipline which the Apostle Paul inflicted on the sinning member of the Church of Corinth; concerning which he afterward wrote to them (2 Cor. vii. 11): "Behold, this selfsame thing, that ye were made sorry after a godly sort, what earnest care it wrought in you, yea, what clearing of yourselves, yea, what indignation, yea, what fear, yea, what longing, yea, what zeal, yea, what avenging!"

A good test is this, which, when we have passed under the chastising hand of God, we may well apply to ourselves: this "earnest care," this "clearing of ourselves," this holy fear of a humbled heart,—have we known what it means? If so, though we sorrow, we may yet rejoice that by grace we are enabled to sorrow "after a godly sort," with "a repentance which bringeth no regret."

CHAPTER XIII
THE GREAT DAY OF ATONEMENT

Lev. xvi. 1-34.

In the first verse of chapter xvi., which ordains the ceremonial for the great annual day of atonement, we are told that this ordinance was delivered by the Lord to Moses "after the death of the two sons of Aaron, when they drew near before the Lord, and died."[19] Because of the close historical connection thus declared between this chapter and chapter x., and also because in this ordinance the Mosaic sacrificial worship, which has been the subject of the book thus far, finds its culmination, it seems most satisfactory to anticipate the order of the book by taking up at this point the exposition of this chapter, before proceeding in chapter xi. to a wholly different subject.

This ordinance of the day of atonement was perhaps the most important and characteristic in the whole Mosaic legislation. In the law of the offerings, the most distinctive part was the law of the sin-offering; and it was on the great annual day of atonement that the conceptions embodied in the sin-offering obtained their most complete development. The central place which this day occupied in the whole system of sacred times is well illustrated in that it is often spoken of by the rabbis, without any more precise designation, as simply *"Yomà,"* "The Day." It was *"the* day" because, on this day, the idea of sacrificial expiation and the consequent removal of all sin, essential to the life of peace and fellowship with God, which was set forth imperfectly, as regards individuals and the nation, by the daily sin-offerings, received the highest possible symbolical expression. It is plain that countless sins and transgressions and various defilements must yet have escaped unrecognised as such, even by the most careful and conscientious Israelite; and that, for this reason, they could not have been covered by any of the daily offerings for sin. Hence, apart from this full, solemn, typical purgation and cleansing of the priesthood and the congregation, and the holy sanctuary, from the uncleannesses and transgressions of the children of Israel, "even all their sins" (ver. 16), the sacrificial system had yet fallen short of expressing in adequate symbolism the ideal of the complete removal of all sin. With abundant reason then do the rabbis regard it as the day of days in the sacred year.

It is insisted by the radical criticism of our day that the general sense of sin and need of expiation which this ordinance expresses could not have existed in the days of Moses; and that since, moreover, the later historical books of the Old Testament contain no reference to the observance of the day, therefore its origin must be attributed to the days of the restoration from Babylon, when, as such critics suppose, the deeper sense of sin, developed by the great judgment of the Babylonian captivity and exile, occasioned the elaboration of this ritual.

To this one might reply that the objection rests upon an assumption which the Christian believer cannot admit, that the ordinance was merely a product of the human mind. But if, as our Lord constantly taught, and as the chapter explicitly affirms, the ordinance was a matter of Divine, supernatural revelation, then naturally we shall expect to find in it, not man's estimate of the guilt of sin, but God's, which in all ages is the same.

But, meeting such objectors on their own ground, we need not go into the matter further than to refer to the high authority of Dillmann, who declares this theory of the post-exilian origin of this institution to be "absolutely incredible;" and in reply to the objection that the day is not alluded to in the whole Old Testament history, justly adds that this argument from silence would equally forbid us to assign the origin of the ordinance to the days of the return from Babylon, or any of the pre-Christian centuries! for "one would then have to maintain that the festival first arose in the first Christian century; since only out of that age do we first have any explicit testimonies concerning it."[20]

Again, the first verse of the chapter gives as the occasion of the promulgation of this law, "the death of the two sons of Aaron," Nadab and Abihu, "when they drew near before the Lord and died;" a historical note which is perfectly natural if we have here a narrative dating from Mosaic days, but which seems most objectless and unlikely to have been entered, if the law were a late invention of rabbinical forgers. On that occasion it was, as we read (v. 2), that "the Lord said unto Moses, Speak unto Aaron thy brother, that he come not at all times into the holy place within the veil, before the mercy-seat which is upon the ark; that he die not: for I will appear in the cloud upon the mercy-seat."

Into this place of Jehovah's most immediate earthly manifestation, even Aaron is to come only once a year, and then only with atoning blood, as hereinafter prescribed.

The object of the whole service of this day is represented as atonement; expiation of sin, in the highest and fullest sense then possible. It is said to be appointed to make atonement for Aaron and for his house (ver. 6), for the holy place, and for the tent of meeting (vv. 15-17); for the altar of burnt-offering in the outer court (vv. 18, 19); and for all the congregation of Israel (vv. 20-22, 33); and this, not merely for such sins of ignorance as had been afterward recognised and acknowledged in the ordinary sin-offerings of each day, but for "*all* the iniquities of the children of Israel, and *all* their transgressions, even all their sins:" even such as were still unknown to all but God (ver. 21). The fact of such an ordinance for such a purpose taught a most impressive lesson of the holiness of God and the sinfulness of man, on the one hand, and, on the other, the utter insufficiency of the daily offerings to cleanse from all sin. Day by day these had been offered in each year; and yet, as we read (Heb. ix. 8, 9), the Holy Ghost this signified by this ordinance, "that the way into the holy place hath not yet been made manifest;" it was "a parable for the time now present;" teaching that the temple sacrifices of Judaism could not "as touching the conscience, make the worshipper perfect" (Heb. ix. 9). We may well reverse the judgment of the critics, and say—not that the deepened sense of sin in Israel was the cause of the day of atonement; but rather, that the solemn observances of this day, under God, were made for many in Israel a most effective means to deepen the conviction of sin.

The time which was ordained for this annual observance is significant—the tenth day of the seventh month. It was appointed for the seventh month, as the sabbatic month, in which all the related ideas of rest in God and with God, in the enjoyment of the blessings of a now complete redemption, received in the great feast of tabernacles their fullest expression. It was therefore appointed for that month, and for a day which shortly preceded this greatest of the annual feasts, to signify in type the profound and most vital truth, that the full joy of the sabbatic rest of man with God, and the ingathering of the fruits of complete redemption, is only possible upon condition of repentance and the fullest possible expiation for sin. It was appointed for the tenth day of this month, no doubt, because in the Scripture symbolism the number ten is the symbol of completeness; and was fitly thus connected with a service which signified expiation completed for the sins of the year.

The observances appointed for the day had regard, first, to the people, and, secondly, to the tabernacle service. As for the former, it was commanded (ver. 29) that they should "do no manner of work," observing the day as a *Sabbath Sabbathon*, "a high Sabbath," or "Sabbath of solemn rest" (ver. 31); and, secondly, that they should "afflict their souls" (ver. 31), namely, by solemn fasting, in visible sign of sorrow and humiliation for sin. By which it was most distinctly taught, that howsoever complete atonement may be, and howsoever, in making that atonement through a sacrificial victim, the sinner himself have no part, yet apart from his personal repentance for his sins, that atonement shall profit him nothing; nay, it was declared (xxiii. 29), that if any man should fail on this point, God would cut him off from his people. The law abides as regards the greater sacrifice of Christ; except we repent, we shall, even because of that sacrifice, only the more terribly perish; because not even this supreme exhibition of the holy love and justice of God has moved us to renounce sin.

As regards the tabernacle service for the day, the order was as follows. First, as most distinctive of the ritual of the day, only the high-priest could officiate. The other priests, who, on other occasions, served continually in the holy place, must on this day, during these ceremonies, leave it to him alone; taking their place, themselves as sinners for whom also atonement was to be made, with the sinful congregation of their brethren. For it was ordered (ver. 17): "There shall be no man in the tent of meeting when the high priest goeth in to make atonement in the holy place, until he come out," and the work of atonement be completed.

And the high priest could himself officiate only after certain significant preparations. First (ver. 4), he must "bathe in water" his whole person. The word used in the original is different from that which is used of the partial washings in connection with the daily ceremonial cleansings; and, most suggestively, the same complete washing is required as that which was ordered in the law for the consecration of the priesthood, and for cleansing from leprosy and other specific defilements. Thus was expressed, in the clearest manner possible, the thought, that the high priest, who shall be permitted to draw near to God in the holiest place, and there prevail with Him, must himself be wholly pure and clean.

Then, having bathed, he must robe himself in a special manner for the service of this day. He must lay aside the bright-coloured "garments for glory and beauty" which he wore on all other occasions, and put on, instead, a vesture of pure, unadorned white, like that of the ordinary priest; excepting only that for him, on this day, unlike them, the girdle also must be white. By this substitution of these garments for his ordinary brilliant robes was signified, not merely the absolute purity which the white linen symbolised, but especially also, by the absence of adornment, humiliation for sin. On this day he was thus made in outward appearance essentially like unto the other members of his house, for whose sin, together with his own, he was to make atonement.

Thus washed and robed, wearing on his white turban the golden crown inscribed "Holiness to Jehovah" (Exod. xxviii. 38), he now took (vv. 3, 5-7), as a sin-offering for himself and for his house, a bullock; and for the congregation, "two he-goats for a sin offering;" with a ram for himself, and one for them, for a burnt offering. The two goats were set "before the Lord at the door of the tent of meeting." The bullock was the offering before prescribed for the sin-offering for the high priest (iv. 3), as being the most valuable of all sacrificial victims. For the choice of the goats many reasons have been given, none of which seem wholly satisfactory. Both of the goats are equally declared (ver. 5) to be "for a sin offering;" yet only one was to be slain.

The ceremonial which followed is unique; it is without its like either in Mosaism or in heathenism. It was ordered (ver. 8): "Aaron shall cast lots upon the two goats; one lot for the Lord, and the other lot for Azazel;" an expression to which we shall shortly return. Only the goat on whom the lot fell for the Lord was to be slain.

The two goats remain standing before the Lord; while now Aaron kills the sin-offering for himself and for his house (ver. 11); then enters, first, the Holy of Holies within the veil, having taken (ver. 12) a censer "full of coals of fire from off the altar before the Lord," with his hands full of incense (ver. 13), "that the cloud of the incense may cover the mercy-seat that is upon the testimony (*i.e.*, the two tables of the law within the ark), that he die not." Then (ver. 13) he sprinkles the blood "upon the mercy-seat on the east"—by which was signified the application of the blood God-ward, accompanied with the fragrance of intercession, for the expiation of his own sins and those of his house; and then "seven times, before the mercy-seat,"—evidently, on the floor of the sanctuary, for the symbolic cleansing of the holiest place, defiled by all the uncleannesses of the children of Israel, in the midst of whom it stood. Then, returning, he kills the goat of the sin-offering "for Jehovah," and repeats the same ceremony, now in behalf of the whole congregation, sprinkling, as before, the mercy-seat, and, seven times, the Holy of Holies, thus making atonement for it, "because of the uncleannesses of the children of Israel, and because of their transgressions, even all their sins" (ver. 16). In like manner, he was then to cleanse, by a seven-fold sprinkling, the Holy Place; and then again going into the outer court, also the altar of burnt-offering; this last, doubtless, as in other cases, by applying the blood to the horns of the altar.

In all this it will be observed that the difference from the ordinary sin-offerings and the wider reach of its symbolical virtue is found, not in that the offering is different from or larger than others, but in that, symbolically speaking, the blood is brought, as in no other offering, into the most immediate presence of God; even into the secret darkness of the Holy of Holies, where no child of Israel might tread. For this reason did this sin-offering become, above all others, the most perfect type of the one offering of Him, the God-Man, who reconciled us to God by doing that in reality which was here done in symbol, even entering with atoning blood into the very presence of God, there to appear in our behalf.

Azazel.

xvi. 20-28.

"And when he hath made an end of atoning for the holy place, and the tent of meeting, and the altar, he shall present the live goat: and Aaron shall lay both his hands upon the head of the live goat, and confess over him all the iniquities of the children of Israel, and all their transgressions, even all their sins; and he shall put them upon the head of the goat, and shall send him away by the hand of a man that is in readiness into the wilderness: and the goat shall bear upon him all their iniquities unto a solitary land: and he shall let go the goat in the wilderness. And Aaron shall come into the tent of meeting, and shall put off the linen garments, which he put on when he went into the holy place, and shall leave them there: and he shall bathe his flesh in water in a holy place, and put on his garments, and come forth, and offer his burnt offering and the burnt offering of the people, and make atonement for himself and for the people. And the fat of the sin offering shall he burn upon the altar. And he that letteth go the goat for Azazel shall wash his clothes, and bathe his flesh in water, and afterward he shall come into the camp. And the bullock of the sin offering, and the goat of the sin offering, whose blood was brought in to make atonement in the holy place, shall be carried forth without the camp; and they shall burn in the fire their skins, and their flesh, and their dung. And he that burneth them shall wash his clothes, and bathe his flesh in water, and afterward he shall come into the camp."

And now followed the second stage of the ceremonial, a rite of the most singular and impressive character. The live goat, during the former part of the ceremony, had been left standing before Jehovah, where he had been placed after the casting of the lot (ver. 10). The rendering of King James' version, that the goat was so placed, "to make an atonement *with* him," assumes a meaning to the Hebrew preposition here which it never has. Usage demands either that which is given in the text or the margin of the Revised Version, to make atonement "*for* him" or "*over* him." But to the former the objection seems insuperable that there is nothing in the whole rite suggesting an atonement as made for this living goat; while, on the other hand, if the rendering "over" be adopted from the margin, it may not unnaturally be understood of the performance *over* this goat of that part of the atonement ceremonial described as follows:—

Vv. 20-22: "When he hath made an end of atoning for the holy place, and the tent of meeting, and the altar, he shall present the live goat ... and confess over him all the iniquities of the children of Israel, and all their transgressions, even all their sins; and he shall put them upon the head of the goat, and shall send him away by the hand of a man that is in readiness into the wilderness: and the goat shall bear upon him all their iniquities unto a solitary land: and he shall let go the goat in the wilderness." And with this ceremony the atonement was completed. Aaron now laid aside the robes which he had put on for this service, bathed again, and put on again his richly coloured garments of office, came forth and offered the burnt-offering for himself and for the people, and burnt the fat of the sin-offering as usual on the altar (vv. 23-25), while its flesh was burned, according to the law for such sacrifices, without the camp (ver. 27).

What was the precise significance of this part of the service, is one of the most difficult questions which arises in the exposition of this book; the answer to which chiefly turns upon the meaning which is attached to the expression, "for Azazel" (O.V., "for a scapegoat"). What is the meaning of "Azazel"?

There are three fundamental facts which stand before us in this chapter, which must find their place in any explanation which may be adopted. 1. Both of the goats are declared to be "a sin-offering;" the live goat, no less than the other. 2. In consistency with this, the live goat, no less than the other, was consecrated to Jehovah, in that he was "set alive before the Lord." 3. The function expressly ascribed to him in the law is the complete removal of the transgressions of Israel, symbolically transferred to him as a burden, by the laying on of hands with confession of sin. Passing by, then, several interpretations, which seem intrinsically irreconcilable with one or other of these facts, or are, for other reasons, to be rejected, the case seems to be practically narrowed down to this alternative. Either Azazel is to be regarded as the name of an evil spirit, conceived of as dwelling in the wilderness, or else it is to be taken as an abstract noun, as in the margin (R.V.), signifying "removal," "dismissal." That the word may have this meaning is very commonly admitted even by those who deny that meaning here; and if, with Bähr[21] and others, we adopt it in this passage, all that follows is quite clear. The goat "for removal" bears away all the iniquities of Israel, which are symbolically laid upon him, into a solitary land; that is, they are taken wholly away from the presence of God and from the camp of His people. Thus, as the killing and sprinkling of the blood of the first goat visibly set forth the *means* of reconciliation with God, through the substituted offering of an innocent victim, so the sending away of the second goat, laden with those sins, the expiation of which had been signified by the sacrifice of the first, no less vividly set forth the *effect* of that sacrifice, in the complete removal of those expiated sins from the holy presence of Jehovah. That this effect of atonement should have been adequately represented by the first slain victim was impossible; hence the necessity for the second goat, ideally identified with the other, as jointly constituting with it one sin-offering, whose special use it should be to represent the blessed effect of atonement. The truth symbolised, as the goat thus bore away the sins of Israel, is expressed in those glad words (Psalm ciii. 12), "As far as the east is from the west, so far hath He removed our transgressions from us;" or, under another image, by Micah (vii. 19), "Thou wilt cast all their sins into the depths of the sea."

So far all seems quite clear, and this explanation, no doubt, will always be accepted by many.

And yet there remains one serious objection to this interpretation; namely, that the meaning we thus give this word "Azazel" is not what we would expect from the phrase which is used regarding the casting of the lots (ver. 8): "One lot for the Lord, and the other lot for Azazel." These words do most naturally suggest that Azazel is the name of a person, who is here contrasted with Jehovah; and hence it is believed by a large number of the best expositors that the term must be taken here as the name of an evil spirit, represented as dwelling in the wilderness, to whom this goat, thus laden with Israel's sins, is sent. In addition to this phraseology, it is urged, in support of this interpretation, that even the Scripture lends apparent sanction to the Jewish belief that demons are, in some special sense, the inhabitants of waste and desolate places; and, in particular, that Jewish demonology does in fact recognise a demon named Azazel, also called Sammael. It is admitted, indeed, that the name Azazel does not occur in the Scripture as the name of Satan or of any evil spirit; and, moreover, that there is no evidence that the Jewish belief concerning the existence of a demon called Azazel dates nearly so far back as Mosaic days; and, again, that even the rabbis themselves are not agreed on this interpretation here, many of them rejecting it, even on traditional grounds. Still the interpretation has secured the support of the majority of the best modern expositors, and must claim respectful consideration.

But if Azazel indeed denotes an evil spirit to whom the second goat of the sin-offering is thus sent, laden with the iniquities of Israel, the question then arises: How then, on this supposition, is the ceremony to be interpreted?

The notion of some, that we have in this rite a relic of the ancient demon-worship, is utterly inadmissible. For this goat is expressly said (ver. 5) to have been, equally with the goat that was slain, "a sin-offering," and (vv. 10, 20) it is placed "before the Lord," as an offering to Him; nor is there a hint, here or elsewhere, that this goat was sacrificed in the wilderness to this Azazel; while, moreover, in this very priest-code (xvii. 7-9, R.V.) this special form of idolatry is forbidden, under the heaviest penalty.

That the goat sent to Azazel personified, by way of warning and in a typical manner, Israel, as rejecting the great Sin-offering, and thus laden with iniquity, and therefore delivered over to Satan, is an idea equally untenable. For the goat, as we have seen, is regarded as ideally one with the goat which is slain; they jointly constitute one sin-offering. If, therefore, the slain goat represented in type Christ as the Lamb of God, our Sin-offering, so also must this goat represent Him as our Sin-offering. Further, the ceremonial which is performed over him is explicitly termed an "atonement;" that is, it was an essential part of a ritual designed to symbolise, not the condemnation of Israel for sin, but their complete deliverance from the guilt of their sins.

Not to speak of other explanations, more or less untenable, which have each found their advocates, the only one which, upon this understanding of the meaning of Azazel, the context and the analogy of the Scripture will both admit, appears to be the following. Holy Scripture teaches that Satan has power over man, only because of man's sin. Because of his sin, man is judicially left by God in Satan's power (1 John v. 19, R.V.). When as "the prince of this world" he came to the sinless Man, Jesus Christ, he had nothing in Him, because He was the Holy One of God; while, on the other hand, he is represented (Heb. ii. 14) as having over men under sin "the authority of death." In full accord with this conception, he is represented, both in the Old and the New Testament, as the accuser of God's people. He is said to have accused Job before God (Job i. 9-11; ii. 4, 5). When Zechariah (iii. 1) saw Joshua the high-priest standing before the angel of Jehovah, he saw Satan also standing at his right hand to be his "adversary." So, again, in the Apocalypse (xii. 10) he is called "the Accuser of our brethren, which accuseth them before our God day and night," and who is only overcome by means of "the blood of the Lamb."

To this Evil One, then, the Accuser and Adversary of God's people in all ages—if we assume the interpretation before us—the live goat was symbolically sent, bearing on him the sins of Israel. But does he bear their sins as forgiven, or as unforgiven? Surely, as forgiven; for the sins which he symbolically carries are those very sins of the bygone year for which expiating blood had just been offered and accepted in the Holy of Holies. Moreover, he is sent as being ideally one with the goat that was slain. As sent to Azazel, he therefore symbolically announces to the Evil One that with the expiation of sin by sacrificial blood the foundation of his power over forgiven Israel is gone. His accusations are now no longer in place; for the whole question of Israel's sin has been met and settled in the atoning blood. Thus, as the acceptance of the blood of the one goat offered in the Holiest symbolised the complete propitiation of the offended holiness of God and His pardon of Israel's sin, so the sending of the goat to Azazel symbolised the *effect* of this expiation, in the complete removal of all the penal effects of sin, through deliverance by atonement from the power of the Adversary as the executioner of God's wrath.

Which of these two interpretations shall be accepted must be left to the reader: that neither is without difficulty, those who have most studied this very obscure question will most readily admit; that either is at least consistent with the context and with other teachings of Scripture, should be sufficiently evident. In either case, the symbolic intention of the first part of the ritual, with the first goat, was to symbolise the *means* of reconciliation with God; namely, through the offering unto God of the life of an innocent victim, substituted in the sinner's place: in either case alike, the purpose of the second part of the ceremonial, with the second goat, was to symbolise the blessed *effect* of this expiation; either, if the reading of the margin be taken, in the complete removal of the expiated sin from the presence of the Holy God, or, if Azazel be taken as a proper name, in the complete deliverance of the sinner, through expiatory blood presented in the Holiest, from the power of Satan. If in the former case, we think of the words already cited, "As far as the east is from the west, so far hath He removed our transgressions from us;" in the latter the words from the Apocalypse (xii. 10, 11) come to mind, "The Accuser of our brethren is cast down, which accuseth them before our God day and night. And they overcame him because of the blood of the Lamb."

On other particulars in the ceremonial of the day we need not dwell, as they have received their exposition in earlier chapters of the law of the offerings. Of the burnt-offerings, indeed, which followed the dismissal of the living goat of the sin-offering, little is said; it is, emphatically, the sin-offering upon which, above all else, it was designed to centre the attention of Israel on this occasion.

And so, with an injunction to the perpetual observance of this day, this remarkable chapter closes. In it the sacrificial law of Moses attains its supreme expression; the holiness and the grace alike of Israel's God, their fullest revelation. For the like of the great day of atonement, we look in vain in any other people. If every sacrifice pointed to Christ, this most luminously of all. What the fifty-third of Isaiah is to his Messianic prophecies, that, we may truly say, is the sixteenth of Leviticus to the whole system of Mosaic types,—the most consummate flower of the Messianic symbolism. All the sin-offerings pointed to Christ, the great High Priest and Victim of the future; but this, as we shall now see, with a distinctness found in no other.

As the unique sin-offering of this day could only be offered by the one high-priest, so was it intimated that the High Priest of the future, who should indeed make an end of sin, should be one and only. As once only in the whole year, a complete cycle of time, this great atonement was offered, so did it point toward a sacrifice which should indeed be "once for all" (Heb. ix. 26; x. 10); not only for the lesser æon of the year, but for the æon of æons which is the lifetime of humanity. In that the high-priest, who was on all other occasions conspicuous among his sons by his bright garments made for glory and for beauty, on this occasion laid them aside, and assumed the same garb as his sons for whom he was to make atonement; herein was shadowed forth the truth that it behoved the great High Priest of the future to be "in all things made like unto His brethren" (Heb. ii. 17). When, having offered the sin-offering, Aaron disappeared from the sight of Israel within the veil, where in the presence of the unseen glory he offered the incense and sprinkled the blood, it was presignified how "Christ having come a High Priest of the good things to come, through the greater and more perfect tabernacle, not made with hands, ... nor yet through the blood of goats and calves, but through His own blood, entered in once for all into the holy place," even "into heaven itself, now to appear before the face of God for us" (Heb. ix. 11, 12, 24). And, in like manner, in that when the sin-offering had been offered, the blood sprinkled, and his work within the veil was ended, arrayed again in his glorious garments, he reappeared to bless the waiting congregation; it was again foreshown how yet that must be fulfilled which is written, that this same Christ, "having been once offered to bear the sins of many, shall appear a second time, apart from sin, to them that wait for Him, unto salvation" (Heb. ix. 28).

To all this yet more might be added of dispensational truth typified by the ceremonial of this day, which we defer to the exposition of chap. xxv., where its consideration more properly belongs. But even were this all, what a marvellous revelation here of the Lord Jesus Christ! The fact of these correspondences between the Levitical ritual and the New Testament facts, let it be observed, is wholly independent of the questions as to the date and origin of this law; and every theory on this subject must find a place for these correspondences and account for them. But how can any one believe that all these are merely accidental coincidences of a post-exilian forgery with the facts of the incarnation, and the high priestly work of Christ in death and resurrection as set forth in the Gospels? How can they all be adequately accounted for, except by assuming that to be true which is expressly taught in the New Testament concerning this very ritual: that in it the Holy Ghost presignified things that were to come; that, therefore, the ordinance must have been, not of man, but of God; not a mere product of the human mind, acting under the laws of a religious evolution, but a revelation from Him unto whom "known are all His works from the foundation of the world"?

Nor must we fail to take in the blessed truth so vividly symbolised in the second part of the ceremonial. When the blood of the sin-offering had been sprinkled in the Holiest, the sins of Israel were then, by the other goat of the sin-offering, borne far away. Israel stood there still a sinful people; but their sin, now expiated by the blood, was before God as if it were not. So does the Holy Victim in the Antitype, who first by His death expiated sin, then as the Living One bear away all the believer's sins from the presence of the Holy One into a land of forgetfulness. And so it is that, as regards acceptance with God, the believing sinner, though still a sinner, stands as if he were sinless; all through the great Sin-offering. To see this, to believe in it and rest in it, is life eternal; it is joy, and peace, and rest! It is the Gospel!

PART II
THE LAW OF THE DAILY LIFE

XI.-XV., XVII.-XXV.

Section 1. The Law Concerning the Clean and the Unclean: xi.-xv.

Section 2. The Law of Holiness: xvii.-xxii.

Section 3. The Law Concerning Sacred Times (with Episode, xxiv.): xxiii.-xxv.

CHAPTER XIV
CLEAN AND UNCLEAN ANIMALS, AND DEFILEMENT BY DEAD BODIES

Lev. xi. 1-47.

With chap. xi. begins a new section of this book, extending to the end of chap. xv., of which the subject is the law concerning various bodily defilements, and the rites appointed for their removal.

The law is given under four heads, as follows:—

I. Clean and Unclean Animals, and Defilement by Dead Bodies: chap. xi.

II. The Uncleanness of Child-birth: chap. xii.

III. The Uncleanness of Leprosy: chaps. xiii., xiv.

IV. The Uncleanness of Issues: chap. xv.

From the modern point of view this whole subject appears to many, with no little reason, to be encompassed with peculiar difficulties. We have become accustomed to think of religion as a thing so exclusively of the spirit, and so completely independent of bodily conditions, provided that these be not in their essential nature sinful, that it is a great stumbling-block to many that God should be represented as having given to Israel an elaborate code of laws concerning such subjects as are treated in these five chapters of Leviticus: a legislation which, to not a few, seems puerile and unspiritual, if not worse. And yet, for the reverent believer in Christ, who remembers that our blessed Lord did repeatedly refer to this book of Leviticus as, without any exception or qualification, the Word of His Father, it should not be hard, in view of this fact, to infer that the difficulties which most of us have felt are presumably due to our very imperfect knowledge of the subject. Remembering this, we shall be able to approach this part of the law of Moses, and, in particular, this chapter, with the spirit, not of critics, but of learners, who know as yet but little of the mysteries of God's dealings with Israel or with the human race.

Chap. xi. may be divided into two sections, together with a concluding appeal and summary (vv. 41-47). The first section treats of the law of the clean and the unclean in relation to eating (vv. 1-23). Under this head, the animals which are permitted or forbidden are classified, after a fashion not scientific, but purely empirical and practical, into (1) the beasts which are upon the earth (vv. 2-8); (2) things that are in the waters (vv. 9-12); (3) flying things,—comprising, first, birds and flying animals like the bat (vv. 13-19); and, secondly, insects, "winged creeping things that go upon all four" (vv. 20-23).

The second section treats of defilement by contact with the dead bodies of these, whether unclean (vv. 24-38), or clean (vv. 39, 40).

Of the living things among the beasts that are upon the earth (vv. 2-8), those are permitted for food which both chew the cud and divide the hoof; every animal in which either of these marks is wanting is forbidden. Of the things which live in the waters, those only are allowed for food which have both fins and scales; those which lack either of these marks, such as, for example, eels, oysters, and all the mollusca and crustacea, are forbidden (vv. 9-12). Of flying things (vv. 13-19) which may be eaten, no special mark is given; though it is to be noted that nearly all of those which are by name forbidden are birds of prey, or birds reputed to be unclean in their habits. All insects, "winged creeping things that go upon all four" (ver. 20), or "whatsoever hath many feet," or "goeth upon the belly," as worms, snakes, etc., are prohibited (ver. 42). Of insects, a single class, described as those "which have legs above their feet, to leap withal upon the earth," is excepted (vv. 21, 22): these are known to us as the order *Saltatoria*, including, as typical examples, the cricket, the grasshopper, and the migratory locust; all of which, it may be noted, are clean feeders, living upon vegetable products only. It is worthy of notice that the law of the clean and the unclean in food is not extended, as it was in Egypt, to the vegetable kingdom.

The second section of the chapter (vv. 24-40) comprises a number of laws relating chiefly to defilement by contact with the dead bodies of animals. In these regulations, it is to be observed that the dead body, even of a clean animal, except when killed in accordance with the law, so that its blood is all drained out (xvii. 10-16), is regarded as defiling him who touches it; while, on the other hand, even an unclean animal is not held capable of imparting defilement by mere contact, so long as it is living. Very minute charges are given (vv. 29-38) concerning eight species of unclean animals, of which six (vv. 29, 30, R.V.) appear to be different varieties of the lizard family. Regarding these, it is ordered that not only shall the person be held unclean who touches the dead body of one of them (ver. 31), but also anything becomes unclean on which such a dead body may fall, whether household utensil, or food, or drink (vv. 32-35). The exception only is made (vv. 36-38), that fountains, or wells of water, or dry seed for sowing, shall not be held to be by such defiled.

That which has been made unclean must be put into water, and be unclean until the even (ver. 32); with the exception that nothing which is made of earthenware, whether a vessel, or an oven, or a range, could be thus cleansed; for the obvious reason that the water could not adequately reach the interior of its porous material. It must therefore be broken in pieces (vv. 33, 34). If a person be defiled by any of these, he remained unclean until the even (ver. 31). No washing is prescribed, but, from analogy, is probably to be taken for granted.

Such is a brief summary of the law of the clean and the unclean as contained in this chapter. To preclude adding needless difficulty to a difficult subject, the remark made above should be specially noted,—that so far as general marks are given by which the clean is to be distinguished from the unclean, these marks are evidently selected simply from a practical point of view, as of easy recognition by the common people, for whom a more exact and scientific mode of distinction would have been useless. We are not therefore for a moment to think of cleanness or uncleanness as causally determined, for instance, by the presence or absence of fins or scales, or by the habit of chewing the cud, and the dividing of the hoof, or the absence of these marks, as if they were themselves the ground of the cleanness or uncleanness, in any instance. For such a fancy as this, which has diverted some interpreters from the right line of investigation of the subject, there is no warrant whatever in the words of the law, either here or elsewhere.

Than this law concerning things clean and unclean nothing will seem to many, at first, more alien to modern thought, or more inconsistent with any intelligent view of the world and of man's relation to the things by which he is surrounded. And, especially, that the strict observance of this law should be connected with religion, and that, upon what professes to be the authority of God, it should be urged on Israel on the ground of their call to be a holy people to a holy God,—this, to the great majority of Bible readers, certainly appears, to say the least, most extraordinary and unaccountable. And yet the law is here, and its observance is enforced by this very consideration; for we read (vv. 43, 44): "Ye shall not make yourselves abominable with any creeping thing that creepeth, neither shall ye make yourselves unclean with them, that ye should be defiled thereby. For I am the Lord your God: sanctify yourselves therefore, and be ye holy; for I am holy." And, in any case, explain the matter as we may, many will ask, How, since the New Testament formally declares this law concerning clean and unclean beasts to be no longer binding (Col. ii. 16, 20-23), is it possible to imagine that there should now remain anything in this most perplexing law which should be of spiritual profit still to a New Testament believer? To the consideration of these questions, which so naturally arise, we now address ourselves.

First of all, in approaching this subject it is well to recall to mind the undeniable fact, that a distinction in foods as clean and unclean, that is, fit and unfit for man's use, has a very deep and apparently irremovable foundation in man's nature. Even we ourselves, who stumble at this law, recognise a distinction of this kind, and regulate our diet accordingly; and also, in like manner, feel, more or less, an instinctive repugnance to dead bodies. As regards diet, it is true that when the secondary question arises as to what particular animals shall be reckoned clean or unclean, fit or unfit for food, nations and tribes differ among themselves, as also from the law of Moses, in a greater or less degree; nevertheless, this does not alter the fact that such a distinction is recognised among all nations of culture; and that, on the other hand, in those who recognise it not, and who eat, as some do, without discrimination, whatever chances to come to hand,—insects, reptiles, carrion, and so on,—this revolting indifference in the matter of food is always associated with gross intellectual and moral degradation. Certainly these indisputable facts should suffice to dispose of the charge of puerility, as sometimes made against the laws of this chapter.

And not only this, but more is true. For while even among nations of the highest culture and Christian enlightenment many animals are eaten, as, *e.g.*, the oyster, the turtle, the flesh of the horse and the hog, which the law of Moses prohibits; on the other hand, it remains true that, with the sole exception of creatures of the locust tribe, the animals which are allowed for food by the Mosaic code are reckoned suitable for food by almost the entire human family. A notable exception to the fact is indeed furnished in the case of the Hindoos, and also the Buddhists (who follow an Indian religion), who, as a rule, reject all animal food, and especially, in the case of the former, the flesh of the cow, as not to be eaten. But this exception is quite explicable by considerations into which we cannot here enter at length, but which do not affect the significance of the general fact.

And, again, on the other hand, it may also be said that, as a general rule, the appetite of the great majority of enlightened and cultivated nations revolts against using as food the greater part of the animals which this code prohibits. Birds of prey, for instance, and the carnivora generally, animals having paws, and reptiles, for the most part, by a kind of universal instinct among cultivated peoples, are judged unfit for human food.

The bearing of these facts upon our exposition is plain. They certainly suggest, at least, that this law of Lev. xi. may, after all, very possibly have a deep foundation both in the nature of man and that of the things permitted or forbidden; and they also raise the question as to how far exceptions and divergencies from this law, among peoples of culture, may possibly be due to a diversity in external physical and climatic conditions, because of which that which may be wholesome and suitable food in one place—the wilderness of Sinai, or Palestine, for instance—may not be wholesome and suitable in other lands, under different physical conditions. We do not yet enter into this question, but barely call attention to it, as adapted to check the hasty judgment of many, that such a law as this is necessarily puerile and unworthy of God.

But while it is of no small consequence to note this agreement in the fundamental ideas of this law with widely extended instincts and habits of mankind, on the other hand, it is also of importance to emphasise the contrast which it exhibits with similar codes of law among other peoples. For while, as has just been remarked, there are many most suggestive points of agreement between the Mosaic distinctions of clean and unclean and those of other nations, on the other hand, remarkable contrasts appear, even in the case of those people with whom, like the Egyptians, the Hebrews had been most intimately associated. In the Egyptian system of dietary law, for instance, the distinction of clean and unclean in food was made to apply, not only in the animal, but also in the vegetable world; and, again, while all fishes having fins and scales are permitted as food in the Mosaic law, no fishes whatever are permitted by the Egyptian code. But more significant than such difference in details is the difference in the religious conception upon which such distinctions are based. In Egypt, for example, animals were reckoned clean or unclean according as they were supposed to have more predominant the character of the good Osiris or of the evil Typhon. Among the ancient Persians, those were reckoned clean which were supposed to be the creation of Ormazd, the good Spirit, and those unclean whose origin was attributed to Ahriman, the evil Spirit. In India, the prohibition of flesh as food rests on pantheistic assumptions. Not to multiply examples, it is easy to see that, without anticipating anything here with regard to the principle which determined the Hebrew distinctions, it is certain that of such dualistic or pantheistic principles as are manifested in these and other instances which might be named, there is not a trace in the Mosaic law. How significant and profoundly instructive is the contrast here, will only fully appear when we see what in fact appears to have been the determining principle in the Mosaic legislation.

But when we now seek to ascertain upon what principle certain animals were permitted and others forbidden as food, it must be confessed that we have before us a very difficult question, and one to which, accordingly, very diverse answers have been given. In general, indeed, we are expressly told that the object of this legislation, as of all else in this book of laws, was moral and spiritual. Thus, we are told in so many words (vv. 43-45) that Israel was to abstain from eating or touching the unclean, on the ground that they were to be holy, because the Lord their God was holy. But to most this only increases the difficulty. What possible connection could there be between eating, or abstinence from eating, animals which do not chew the cud, or fishes which have not scales, and holiness of life?

In answer to this question, some have supposed a mystical connection between the soul and the body, such that the former is defiled by the food which is received and assimilated by the latter. In support of this theory, appeal has been made to ver. 44 of this chapter, which, in the Septuagint translation, is rendered literally: "Ye shall not defile your souls." But, as often in Hebrew, the original expression here is simply equivalent to our compound pronoun "yourselves," and is therefore so translated both in the Authorised and the Revised Versions. As for any other proof of such a mystical evil influence of the various kinds of food prohibited in this chapter, there is simply none at all.

Others, again, have sought the explication of these facts in the undoubted Divine purpose of keeping Israel separate from other nations; to secure which separation this special dietetic code, with other laws regarding the clean and the unclean, was given them. That these laws have practically helped to keep the children of Israel separate from other nations, will not be denied; and we may therefore readily admit, that inasmuch as the food of the Hebrews has differed from that of the nations among whom they have dwelt, this separation of the nation may therefore have been included in the purpose of God in these regulations. However, it is to be observed that in the law itself the separation of Israel from other nations is represented, not as the end to be attained by the observance of these food laws, but instead, as a fact already existing, which is given as a reason why they should keep these laws (xx. 24, 25). Moreover, it will be found impossible, by reference to this principle alone, to account for the details of the laws before us. For the question is not merely why there should have been food laws, but also why these laws should have been such as they are? The latter question is not adequately explained by reference to God's purpose of keeping Israel separate from the nations.

Some, again, have held that the explanation of these laws was to be found simply in the design of God, by these restrictions, to give Israel a profitable moral discipline in self-restraint and control of the bodily appetites; or to impose, in this way, certain conditions and limitations upon their approach to Him, which should have the effect of deepening in them the sense of awe and reverence for the Divine majesty of God, as their King. Of this theory it may be said, as of the last-named, that there can be no doubt that in fact these laws did tend to secure these ends; but that yet, on the other hand, the explanation is still inadequate, inasmuch as it only would show why restrictions of some kind should have been ordered, and not, in the least, why the restrictions should have been such, in detail, as we have here.

Quite different from any of these attempted explanations is that of many who have sought to explain the law allegorically. We are told by such that Israel was forbidden the flesh of certain animals, because they were regarded as typifying by their character certain sins and vices, as, on the other hand, those which were permitted as food were regarded as typifying certain moral virtues. Hence, it is supposed by such that the law tended to the holiness of Israel, in that it was, so to speak, a continual object-lesson, a perpetually acted allegory, which should continually remind them of the duty of abstaining from the typified sins and of practising the typified virtues. But, assuredly, this theory cannot be carried out. Animals are in this law prohibited as food whose symbolic meaning elsewhere in Scripture is not always bad, but sometimes good. The lion, for example, as having paws, is prohibited as food; and yet it is the symbol of our blessed Lord, "the Lion of the tribe of Judah." Nor is there the slightest evidence that the Hebrews ever attached any such allegorical significance to the various prescriptions of this chapter as the theory would require.

Other expositors allegorise in a different but no more satisfactory manner. Thus a popular, and, it must be added, most spiritual and devout expositor, sets forth the spiritual meaning of the required conjunction of the two marks in clean animals of the chewing of the cud and the dividing of the hoof in this wise: "The two things were inseparable in the case of every clean animal. And, as to the spiritual application, it is of the very last importance in a practical point of view.... A man may profess to love and feed upon, to study and ruminate over, the Word of God—the pasture of the soul; but if his footprints along the pathway of life are not such as the Word requires, he is not clean."

But it should be evident that such allegorising interpretation as this can carry with it no authority, and sets the door wide open to the most extravagant fancy in the exposition of Scripture.

Others, again, find the only principle which has determined the laws concerning defilement by the dead, and the clean and unclean meats, to be the presence in that which was reckoned unclean, of something which is naturally repulsive to men; whether in odour, or in the food of a creature, or its other habits of life. But while it is true that such marks distinguish many of the creatures reckoned unclean, they are wanting in others, and are also found in a few animals which are nevertheless permitted. If this had been the determining principle, surely, for example, the law which permitted for food the he-goat and forbade the horse, would have been exactly the opposite; while, as regards fishes and insects permitted and forbidden, it is hard to see any evidence whatever of the influence of this principle.

Much more plausible, at first sight, and indeed much more nearly approaching the truth, than any of the theories above criticised, is one which has been elaborated with no little learning and ingenuity by Sommer,[22] according to which the laws concerning the clean and the unclean, whether in regard to food or anything else, are all grounded in the antithesis of death and life. Death, everywhere in Holy Scripture, is set in the closest ethical and symbolical connection with sin. Bodily death is the wages of sin; and inasmuch as it is the outward physical expression and result of the inner fact that sin, in its very nature, is spiritual death, therefore the dead is always held to be unclean; and the various laws enforcing this thought are all intended to keep before the mind the fact that death is the visible representation and evidence of the presence of sin, and the consequent curse of God. Hence, also, it will follow that the selection of foods must be governed by a reference to this principle. The carnivora, on this principle, must be forbidden,—as they are,—because they live by taking the life of other animals; hence, also, is explained the exclusion of the multitudinous varieties of the insect world, as feeding on that which is dead and corrupt. On the other hand, the animals which chew the cud and divide the hoof are counted clean; inasmuch as the sheep and the cattle, the chief representatives of this class, were by every one recognised as at the furthest possible remove from any such connection with death and corruption in their mode of life; and hence the familiar marks which distinguish them, as a matter merely of practical convenience, were taken as those which must distinguish every animal lawful for food.

But while this view has been elaborated with great ability and skill, it yet fails to account for all the facts. It is quite overlooked that if the reason of the prohibition of carnivorous birds and quadrupeds is to be found in the fact that they live by the destruction of life, the same reason should have led to the prohibition of all fishes without exception, as in Egypt; inasmuch as those which have fins and scales, no less than others, live by preying on other living creatures. On the other hand, by the same principle, all insects which derive their sustenance from the vegetable world should have been permitted as food, instead of one order only of these.

Where so much learning and profound thought has been expended in vain, one might well hesitate to venture anything in exposition of so difficult a subject, and rest content, as some have, with declaring that the whole subject is utterly inexplicable. And yet the world advances in knowledge, and we are therefore able to approach the subject with some advantage in this respect over earlier generations. And in the light of the most recent investigations, we believe it highly probable that the chief principle determining the laws of this chapter will be found in the region of hygiene and sanitation, as relating, in this instance, to diet, and to the treatment of that which is dead. And this in view of the following considerations.

It is of much significance to note, in the first place, that a large part of the animals which are forbidden as food are unclean feeders. It is a well-ascertained fact that even the cleanest animal, if its food be unclean, becomes dangerous to health if its flesh be eaten. The flesh of a cow which has drunk water contaminated with typhoid germs, if eaten, especially if insufficiently cooked, may communicate typhoid fever to him who eats it. It is true, indeed, that not all animals that are prohibited are unclean in their food; but the fact remains that, on the other hand, among those which are allowed is to be found no animal whose ordinary habits of life, especially in respect of food, are unclean.

But, in the second place, an animal which is not unclean in its habits may yet be dangerous for food, if it be, for any reason, specially liable to disease. One of the greatest discoveries of modern science is the fact that a large number of diseases to which animals are liable are due to the presence of low forms of parasitic life. To such diseases those which are unclean in their feeding will be especially exposed, while none will perhaps be found wholly exempt.

Another discovery of recent times which has a no less important bearing on the question raised by this chapter is the now ascertained fact that many of these parasitic diseases are common to both animals and men, and may be communicated from the former to the latter. All are familiar with the fact that the smallpox, in a modified and mild form, is a disease of cattle as well as of men, and we avail ourselves of this fact in the practice of vaccination. Scarcely less familiar is the communication of the parasitic trichinæ, which often infest the flesh of swine, to those who eat such meat. And research is constantly extending the number of such diseases. Turkeys, we are now told, have the diphtheria, and may communicate it to men; men also sometimes take from horses the loathsome disease known as the glanders. Now in the light of such facts as these, it is plain that an ideal dietary law would, as far as possible, exclude from human food all animals which, under given conditions, might be especially liable to these parasitic diseases, and which, if their flesh should be eaten, might thus become a frequent medium of communicating them to men.

Now it is a most remarkable and significant fact that the tendency of the most recent investigations of this subject has been to show that the prohibitions and permissions of the Mosaic law concerning food, as we have them in this chapter, become apparently explicable in view of the above facts. Not to refer to other authorities, among the latest competent testimonies on this subject is that of Dr. Noel Gueneau de Mussy, in a paper presented to the Paris Academy of Medicine in 1885, in which he is quoted as saying: "There is so close a connection between the thinking being and the living organism in man, so intimate a solidarity between moral and material interests, and the useful is so constantly and so necessarily in harmony with the good, that these two elements cannot be separated in hygiene.... It is this combination which has exercised so great an influence on the preservation of the Israelites, despite the very unfavourable external circumstances in which they have been placed.... The idea of parasitic and infectious maladies, which has conquered so great a position in modern pathology, appears to have greatly occupied the mind of Moses, and to have dominated all his hygienic rules. He excludes from Hebrew dietary *animals particularly liable to parasites*; and as it is in the blood that the germs or spores of infectious disease circulate, he orders that they must be drained of their blood before serving for food."

If this professional testimony, which is accepted and endorsed by Dr. Behrends, of London, in his remarkable paper on "Diseases caught from Butcher's Meat,"[23] be admitted, it is evident that we need look no further for the explanation of the minute prescriptions of these dietary laws which we find here and elsewhere in the Pentateuch.

And, it may be added, that upon this principle we may also easily explain, in a rational way, the very minute prescriptions of the law with regard to defilement by dead bodies. For immediately upon death begins a process of corruption which produces compounds not only obnoxious to the senses, but actively poisonous in character; and what is of still more consequence to observe, in the case of all parasitic and infectious diseases, the energy of the infection is specially intensified when the infected person or animal dies. Hence the careful regulations as to cleansing of those persons or things which had been thus defiled by the dead; either by water, where practicable; or where the thing could not be thus thoroughly cleansed, then by burning the article with fire, the most certain of all disinfectants.

But if this be indeed the principle which underlies this law of the clean and the unclean as here given, it will then be urged that since the Hebrews have observed this law with strictness for centuries, they ought to show the evidence of this in a marked immunity from sickness, as compared with other nations, and especially from diseases of an infectious character; and a consequent longevity superior to that of the Gentiles who pay no attention to these laws. Now it is the fact, and one which evidently furnishes another powerful argument for this interpretation of these laws, that this is exactly what we see. In this matter we are not left to guessing; the facts are before the world, and are undisputed. Even so long ago as the days when the plague was desolating Europe, the Jews so universally escaped infection that, by this their exemption, the popular suspicion was excited into fury, and they were accused of causing the fearful mortality among their Gentile neighbours by poisoning the wells and springs. In our own day, in the recent cholera epidemic in Italy, a correspondent of the *Jewish Chronicle* testifies that the Jews enjoyed almost absolute immunity, at least from fatal attack.

Professor Hosmer says: "Throughout the entire history of Israel, the wisdom of the ancient lawgivers in these respects has been remarkably shown. In times of pestilence the Jews have suffered far less than others; as regards longevity and general health, they have in every age been noteworthy, and, at the present day, in the life-insurance offices, the life of a Jew is said to be worth much more than that of men of other stock."

Of the facts in the modern world which sustain these statements, Dr. Behrends gives abundant illustration in the article referred to, such as the following: "In Prussia, the mean duration of Jewish life averages five years more than that of the general population. In Furth, the average duration of Jewish life is 37, and of Christians 26 years. In Hungary, an exhaustive study of the facts shows that the average duration of life with the Croats is 20·2, of the Germans 26·7, but of the Jews 46·5 years, and that although the latter generally are poor, and live under much more unfavourable sanitary conditions than their Gentile neighbours."

In the light of such well-certified facts, the conclusion seems certainly to be warranted, that at least one chief consideration which, in the Divine wisdom, determined the allowance or prohibition, as the food of Israel, of the animals named in this chapter, has been their fitness or unfitness as diet from a hygienic point of view, especially regarding their greater or less liability to have, and to communicate to man, infectious, parasitic diseases.

From this position, if it be justified, we can now perceive a secondary reference in these laws to the deeper ethical truth which, with much reason, Sommer has so emphasised; namely, the moral significance of the great antithesis of death to life; the former being ever contrasted in Holy Scripture with the latter, as the visible manifestation of the presence of sin in the world, and of the consequent curse of God. For whatever tends to weakness or disease, by that fact tends to death,—to that death which, according to the Scriptures, is, for man, the penal consequence of sin. But Israel was called to be a people redeemed from the power of death to life, a life of full consecration to God. Hence, because redeemed from death, it was evidently fitting that the Israelite should, so far as possible in the flesh, keep apart from death, and all that in its nature tended, or might specially tend, to disease and death.

It is very strange that it should have been objected to this view, that since the law declares the reason for these regulations to have been religious, therefore any supposed reference herein to the principles of hygiene is by that fact excluded. For surely the obligation so to live as to conserve and promote the highest bodily health must be regarded, both from a natural, and a Biblical and Christian point of view, as being no less really a religious obligation than truthfulness or honesty. If there appear sufficient reason for believing that the details of these laws are to be explained by reference to hygienic considerations, surely this, so far from contradicting the reason which is given for their observance, helps us rather the more clearly to see how, just because Israel was called to be the holy people of a holy God, they must needs keep this law. For the central idea of the Levitical holiness was consecration unto God, as the Creator and Redeemer of Israel,—consecration in the most unreserved, fullest possible sense, for the most perfect possible service. But the obligation to such a consecration, as the essence of a holy character, surely carried with it, by necessary consequence, then, as now, the obligation to maintain all the powers of mind and body also in the highest possible perfection. That, as regards the body, and, in no small degree, the mind as well, this involves the duty of the preservation of health, so far as in our power; and that this, again, is conditioned by the use of a proper diet, as one factor of prime importance, will be denied by no one. If, then, sufficient reason can be shown for recognising the determining influence of hygienic considerations in the laws of this chapter concerning the clean and the unclean, this fact will only be in the fullest harmony with all that is said in this connection, and elsewhere in the law, as to the relation of their observance to Israel's holiness as a consecrated nation.

It may very possibly be asked, by way of further objection to this interpretation of these laws: Upon this understanding of the immediate purpose of these laws, how can we account for the selection of such test marks of the clean and the unclean as the chewing of the cud, and the dividing of the hoof, or having scales and fins? What can the presence or absence of these peculiarities have to do with the greater or less freedom from parasitic disease of the animals included or excluded in the several classes? To which question the answer may fairly be given, that the object of the law was not to give accurately distributed categories of animals, scientifically arranged, according to hygienic principles, but was purely practical; namely, to secure, so far as possible, the observance by the whole people of such a dietary as in the land of Palestine would, on the whole, best tend to secure perfect bodily health. It is not affirmed that every individual animal which by these tests may be excluded from permitted food is therefore to be held specially liable to disease; but only that the limitation of the diet by these test marks, as a practical measure, would, *on the whole*, secure the greatest degree of immunity from disease to those who kept the law.

It may be objected, again, by some who have looked into this question, that, according to recent researches, it appears that cattle, which occupy the foremost place in the permitted diet of the Hebrews, are found to be especially liable to tubercular disease, and capable, apparently, under certain conditions, of communicating it to those who feed upon their flesh. And it has been even urged that to this source is due a large part of the consumption which is responsible for so large part of our mortality. To which objection two answers may be given. First, and most important, is the observation that we have as yet no statistics as to the prevalence of disease of this kind among cattle in Palestine; and that, presumably, if we may argue from the climatic conditions of its prevalence among men, it would be found far less frequently there among cattle than in Europe and America. Further, it must be remembered that, in the case even of clean cattle, the law very strictly provides elsewhere that the clean animal which is slain for food shall be absolutely free from disease; so that still we see here, no less than elsewhere, the hygienic principles ruling the dietary law.

It will be perhaps objected, again, that if all this be true, then, since abstinence from unwholesome food is a moral duty, the law concerning clean and unclean meats should be of universal and perpetual obligation; whereas, in fact, it is explicitly abrogated in the New Testament, and is not held to be now binding on any one. But the abrogation of the law of Moses touching clean and unclean food can be easily explained, in perfect accord with all that has been said as to its nature and intent. In the first place, it is to be remembered that it is a fundamental characteristic of the New Testament law as contrasted with that of the Old, that on all points it leaves much more to the liberty of the individual, allowing him to act according to the exercise of an enlightened judgment, under the law of supreme love to the Lord, in many matters which, in the Old Testament day, were made a subject of specific regulation. This is true, for instance, regarding all that relates to the public worship of God, and also many things in the government and administration of the Church, not to speak of other examples. This does not indeed mean that it is of no consequence what a man or a Church may do in matters of this kind; but it is intended thus to give the individual and the whole Church a discipline of a higher order than is possible under a system which prescribes a large part of the details of human action. Subjection to these "rudiments" of the law, according to the Apostle, belongs to a condition of religious minority (Gal. iv. 1-3), and passes away when the individual, or the Church, so to speak, attains majority. Precisely so it is in the case of these dietary and other laws, which, indeed, are selected by the Apostle Paul (Col. ii. 20-22) in illustration of this characteristic of the new dispensation. That such matters of detail should no longer be made matter of specific command is only what we should expect according to the analogy of the whole system of Christian law. This is not, indeed, saying that it is of no consequence in a religious point of view what a man eats; whether, for instance, he eat carrion or not, though this, which was forbidden in the Old Testament, is nowhere expressly prohibited in the New. But still, as supplying a training of higher order, the New Testament uniformly refrains from giving detailed commandments in matters of this kind.

But, aside from considerations of this kind, there is a specific reason why these laws of Moses concerning diet and defilement by dead bodies, if hygienic in character, should not have been made, in the New Testament, of universal obligation, however excellent they might be. For it is to be remembered that these laws were delivered for a people few in number, living in a small country, under certain definite climatic conditions. But it is well known that what is unwholesome for food in one part of the world may be, and often is, necessary to the maintenance of health elsewhere. A class of animals which under the climatic conditions of Palestine may be specially liable to certain forms of parasitic disease, under different climatic conditions may be comparatively free from them. Abstinence from fat is commanded in the law of Moses (iii. 17), and great moderation in this matter is necessary to health in hot climates; but, on the contrary, to eat fat largely is necessary to life in the polar regions. From such facts as these it would follow, of necessity, that when the Church of God, as under the new dispensation, was now to become a world-wide organisation, still to have insisted on a dietetic law perfectly adapted only to Palestine would have been to defeat the physical object, and by consequence the moral end, for which that law was given. Under these conditions, except a special law were to be given for each land and climate, there was and could be, if we have before us the true conception of the ground of these regulations, no alternative but to abrogate the law.

This exposition has been much prolonged; but not until we have before us a definite conception as to the principle underlying these regulations, and the relation of their observance to the holiness of Israel, are we in a position to see and appreciate the moral and spiritual lessons which they may still have for us. As it is, if the conclusions to which our exposition has conducted be accepted, such lessons lie clearly before us. While we have here a law which, as to the letter, is confessedly abrogated, and which is supposed by the most to be utterly removed from any present-day use for practical instruction, it is now evident that, annulled as to the letter, it is yet, as to the spirit and intention of it, in full force and vital consequence to holiness of life in all ages.

In the first place, this exposition being granted, it follows, as a present-day lesson of great moment, that the holiness which God requires has to do with the body as well as the soul, even with such commonplace matters as our eating and drinking. This is so, because the body is the instrument and organ of the soul, with which it must do all its work on earth for God, and because, as such, the body, no less than the soul, has been redeemed unto God by the blood of His Son. There is, therefore, no religion in neglecting the body, and ignoring the requirements for its health, as ascetics have in all ages imagined. Neither is there religion in pampering, and thus abusing, the body, after the manner of the sensual in all ages. The principle which inspires this chapter is that which is expressed in the New Testament by the words: "Whether therefore ye eat, or drink, or whatsoever ye do, do all to the glory of God" (1 Cor. x. 31). If, therefore, a man needlessly eats such things, or in such a manner, as may be injurious to health, he sins, and has come short of the law of perfect holiness. It is therefore not merely a matter of earthly prudence to observe the laws of health in food and drink and recreation, in a word, in all that has to do with the appetite and desires of the body, but it is essential to holiness. We are in all these things to seek to glorify God, not only in our souls, but also in our bodies.

The momentous importance of this thought will the more clearly appear when we recall to mind that, according to the law of Moses (v. 2), if a man was defiled by any unclean thing, and neglected the cleansing ordered by this law, even though it were through ignorance or forgetfulness, he was held to have incurred guilt before God. For it was therein declared that when a man defiled by contact with the dead, or any unclean thing, should for any reason have omitted the cleansing ordered, his covenant relation with God could only be re-established on his presentation of a sin-offering. By parity of reasoning it follows that the case is the same now; and that God will hold no man guiltless who violates any of those laws which He has established in nature as the conditions of bodily health. He who does this is guilty of a sin which requires the application of the great atonement.

How needful it is even in our day to remind men of all this, could not be better illustrated than by the already mentioned argument of many expositors, that hygienic principles cannot have dominated and determined the details of these laws, because the law declares that they are grounded, not in hygiene, but in religion, and have to do with holiness. As if these two were exclusive, one of the other, and as if it made no difference in respect to holiness of character whether a man took care to have a sound body or not!

No less needful is the lesson of this law to many who are at the opposite extreme. For as there are those who are so taken up with the soul and its health, that they ignore its relation to the body, and the bearing of bodily conditions upon character; so there are others who are so preoccupied with questions of bodily health, sanitation and hygiene, regarded merely as prudential measures, from an earthly point of view, that they forget that man has a soul as well as a body, and that such questions of sanitation and hygiene only find their proper place when it is recognised that health and perfection of the body are not to be sought merely that man may become a more perfect animal, but in order that thus, with a sound mind in a sound body, he may the more perfectly serve the Lord in the life of holiness to which we are called. Thus it appears that this forgotten law of the clean and the unclean in food, so far from being, at the best, puerile, and for us now certainly quite useless, still teaches us the very important lesson that a due regard to wholeness and health of body is essential to the right and symmetrical development of holiness of character. In every dispensation, the law of God combines the bodily and the spiritual in a sacred synthesis. If in the New Testament we are directed to glorify God in our spirits, we are no less explicitly commanded to glorify God in our bodies (1 Cor. vi. 20). And thus is given to the laws of health the high sanction of the Divine obligation of the moral law, as summed up in the closing words of this chapter: "Be ye holy; for I am holy."

This law concerning things unclean, and clean and unclean animals, as thus expounded, is also an apologetic of no small value. It has a direct and evident bearing on the question of the Divine origin and authority of this part of the law. For the question will at once come up in every reflecting mind: Whence came this law? Could it have been merely an invention of crafty Jewish priests? Or is it possible to account for it as the product merely of the mind of Moses? It appears to have been ordered with respect to certain facts, especially regarding various invisible forms of noxious parasitic life, in their bearing on the causation and propagation of disease,—facts which, even now, are but just appearing within the horizon of modern science. Is it probable that Moses knew about these things three thousand years ago? Certainly, the more we study the matter, the more we must feel that this is not to be supposed.

It is common, indeed, to explain much that seems very wise in the law of Moses by referring to the fact that he was a highly educated man, "instructed in all the wisdom of the Egyptians." But it is just this fact of his Egyptian education that makes it in the last degree improbable that he should have derived the ideas of this law from Egypt. Could he have taken his ideas with regard, for instance, to defilement by the dead, from a system of education which taught the contrary, and which, so far from regarding those who had to do with the dead as unclean, held them especially sacred? And so with regard to the dietetic laws: these are not the laws of Egypt; nor have we any evidence that those were determined, like these Hebrew laws, by such scientific facts as those to which we have referred. In this day, when, at last, men of all schools, and those with most scientific knowledge, most of all, are joining to extol the exact wisdom of this ancient law, a wisdom which has no parallel in like laws among other nations, is it not in place to press this question? Whence had this man this unique wisdom, three thousand years in advance of his times? There are many who will feel compelled to answer, even as Holy Scripture answers; even as Moses, according to the record, answers. The secret of this wisdom will be found, not in the court of Pharaoh, but in the holy tent of meeting; it is all explained if we but assume that what is written in the first verse of this chapter is true: "The Lord spake unto Moses and unto Aaron."

CHAPTER XV
OF THE UNCLEANNESS OF ISSUES

Lev. xv. 1-33.

Inasmuch as the law concerning defilement from issues is presupposed and referred to in that concerning the defilement of child-bearing, in chap. xii., it will be well to consider this before the latter. For this order there is the more reason, because, as will appear, although the two sections are separated, in the present arrangement of the book, by the law concerning defilement by leprosy (xiii., xiv.), they both refer to the same general topic, and are based upon the same moral conceptions.

The arrangement of the law in chap. xv. is very simple. Verses 2-18 deal with the cases of ceremonial defilement by issues in men; vv. 19-30, with analogous cases in women. The principle in both classes is one and the same; the issue, whether normal or abnormal, rendered the person affected unclean; only, when abnormal, the defilement was regarded as more serious than in other cases, not only in a physical, but also in a ceremonial and legal aspect. In all such cases, in addition to the washing with water which was always required, it was commanded that on the eighth day from the time of the cessation of the issue, the person who had been so affected should come before the priest and present for his cleansing a sin-offering and a burnt-offering.

What now is the principle which underlies these regulations?

In seeking the answer to this question, we at once note the suggestive fact that this law concerning issues takes cognisance only of such as are connected with the sexual organisation. All others, however, in themselves, from a merely physical point of view, equally unwholesome or loathsome, are outside the purview of the Mosaic code. They do not render the person affected, according to the law, ceremonially unclean. It is therefore evident that the lawgiver must have had before him something other than merely the physical peculiarities of these defilements, and that, for the true meaning of this part of the law, we must look deeper than the surface. It should also be observed here that this characteristic of the law just mentioned, places the law of issues under the same general category with the law (chap. xii.)

concerning the uncleanness of child-bearing, as indeed the latter itself intimates (xii. 2). The question thus arises: Why are these particular cases, and such as these only, regarded as ceremonially defiling?

To see the reason of this, we must recur to facts which have already come before us. When our first parents sinned, death was denounced against them as the penalty of their sin. Such had been the threat: "In the day that thou eatest thereof, thou shalt die." The death denounced indeed affected the whole being, the spiritual as well as the physical nature of man; but it comprehended the death of the body, which thus became, what it still is, the most impressive manifestation of the presence of sin in every person who dies. Hence, as we have seen, the law kept this connection between sin and death steadily before the mind, in that it constantly applied the principle that the dead defiles. Not only so, but, for this reason, such things as tended to bring death were also reckoned unclean; and thus the regulations of the law concerning clean and unclean meats, while strictly hygienic in character, were yet grounded in this profound ethical fact of the connection between sin and death; had man not sinned, nothing in the world had been able to bring in death, and all things had been clean. For the same reason, again, leprosy, as exemplifying in a vivid and terrible way disease as a progressive death, a living manifestation of the presence of the curse of God, and therefore of the presence of sin, a type of all disease, was regarded as involving ceremonial defilement, and therefore as requiring sacrificial cleansing.

But in the curse denounced upon our first parents was yet more. It was specially taught that the curse should affect the generative power of the race. For we read (Gen. iii. 16): "Unto the woman He said, I will greatly multiply thy sorrow and thy conception; in sorrow thou shalt bring forth children." Whatever these words may precisely mean, it is plain that they are intended to teach that, because of sin, the curse of God fell in some mysterious way upon the sexual organisation. And although the woman only is specifically mentioned, as being "first in the transgression," that the curse fell also upon the same part of man's nature is plain from the words in Gen. v. 3, where the long mortuary record of the antediluvians is introduced by the profoundly significant statement that Adam began the long line, with its inheritance of death, by begetting a son "in his own likeness, after his image." Fallen himself under the curse of death, physical and spiritual, he therewith lost the capacity to beget a creature like himself in his original state, in the image of God, and could only be the means of bringing into the world a creature who was an inheritor of physical weakness and spiritual and bodily death.

In the light of this ancient record, which must have been before the mind of the Hebrew lawgiver, we can now see why the law concerning unclean issues should have had special relation to that part of man's physical organisation which has to do with the propagation of the race. Just as death defiled, because it was a visible representation of the presence of the curse of God, and thus of sin, as the ground of the curse, even so was it with all the issues specified in this law. They were regarded as making a man unclean, because they were manifestations of the curse in a part of man's nature which, according to the Word of God, sin has specially affected. For this reason they fell under the same law as death. They separated the person thus affected from the congregation, and excluded him from the public worship of a holy God, as making him "unclean."

It is impossible now to miss the spiritual meaning of these laws concerning issues of this class. In that these alone, out of many others, which from a merely physical point of view are equally offensive, were taken under the cognisance of this law, the fact was thereby symbolically emphasised that the fountain of life in man is defiled. To be a sinner were bad enough, if it only involved the voluntary and habitual practice of sin. But this law of issues testifies to us, even now, that, as God sees man's case, it is far worse than this. The evil of sin is so deeply seated that it could lie no deeper. The curse has in such manner fallen on our being, as that in man and woman the powers and faculties which concern the propagation of their kind have fallen under the blight. All that any son of Adam can now do is to beget a son in his own physical and moral image, an heir of death, and by nature unclean and unholy. Sufficiently distasteful this truth is in all ages; but in none perhaps ever more so than our own, in which it has become a fundamental postulate of much popular theology, and of popular politics as well, that man is naturally not bad, but good, and, on the whole, is doing as well as under the law of evolution, and considering his environment, can reasonably be expected. The spiritual principle which underlies the law concerning defilement by issues, as also that concerning the uncleanness of child-bearing, assumes the exact opposite.

It is indeed true that similar causes of ceremonial uncleanness have been recognised in ancient and in modern times among many other peoples. But this is no objection to the truth of the interpretation of the Mosaic law here given. For in so far as there is genuine agreement, the fact may rather confirm than weaken the argument for this view of the case, as showing that there is an ineradicable instinct in the heart of man which connects all that directly or indirectly has to do with the continuance of our race, in a peculiar degree, with the ideas of uncleanness and shame. And, on the other hand, the differences in such cases from the Mosaic law show us just what we should expect,—a degree of moral confusion and a deadening of the moral sense among the heathen nations, which is most significant. As has been justly remarked, the Hindoo has one law on this subject for the Brahman, another for others; the outcast for some deadly sin, often of a purely frivolous nature, and a new-born child, are reckoned equally unclean. Or,—to take the case of a people contemporary with the Hebrews,—among the ancient Chaldeans, while these same issues were accounted ceremonially defiling, as in the law of Moses, with these were also reckoned in the same category, as unclean, whatsoever was separated from the body, even to the cuttings of the hair and the parings of the nails. Evidently, we thus have here, not likeness, but a profound and most suggestive moral contrast between the Chaldean and the Hebrew law. Of the profound ethical truth which vitalises and gives deep significance to the law of Moses, we find no trace in the other system. And it is no wonder if, indeed, the one law is, as declared, a revelation from the holy God, and the other the work of sinful and sin-blinded man.

It is another moral lesson which is brought before us in these laws that, as God looks at the matter, sin pertains not only to action, but also to being. Not only actions, from which we can abstain, but operations of nature which we cannot help, alike defile; defile in such a manner and degree as to require, even as voluntary acts of sin, the cleansing of water, and the expiatory blood of a sin-offering. One could not avoid many of the defilements mentioned in this chapter, but that made no difference; he was unclean. For the lesser grades of uncleanness it sufficed that one be purified by washing with water; and a sin-offering was only required when this purification had been neglected; but in all cases where the defilement assumed its extreme form, the sin-offering and the burnt-offering must be brought, and be offered for the unclean person by the priest. So is it, we are taught, with that sin of nature which these cases symbolised; we cannot help it, and yet the washing of regeneration and the cleansing of the blood of Christ is required for its removal. Very impressive in its teaching now becomes the miracle in which our Lord healed the poor woman afflicted with the issue of blood (Mark v. 25-34), for which she had vainly sought cure. It was a case like that covered by the law in chap. xv. 25-27; and he who will read and consider the provisions of that law will understand, as otherwise he could not, how great her trial and how heavy her burden must have been. He will wonder also, as never before, at the boldness of her faith, who, although, according to the law, her touch should defile the Lord, yet ventured to believe that not only should this not be so, but that the healing power which went forth from Him should neutralise the defilement, and carry healing virtue to the very centre of her life. Thus, if other miracles represent our Lord as meeting the evil of sin in its various manifestations in action, this miracle represents His healing power as reaching to the very source and fountain of life, where it is needed no less.

The law concerning the removal of these defilements, after all that has preceded, will admit only of one interpretation. The washing of water is the uniform symbol of the cleansing of the soul from pollution by the power of the Holy Ghost; the sacrifices point to the sacrifice of Christ, in its twofold aspect as burnt-offering and sin-offering, as required by and availing for the removal of the sinful defilement which, in the mind of God, attaches even to that in human nature which is not under the control of the will. At the same time, whereas in all these cases the sin-offering prescribed is the smallest known to the law, it is symbolised, in full accord with the teaching of conscience, that the gravity of the defilement, where there has not been the active concurrence of the will, is less than where the will has seconded nature. In all cases of prolonged defilement from these sources, it was required that the affected person should still be regarded as unclean for seven days after the cessation of the infirmity, and on the eighth day came the sacrificial cleansing. The significance of the seven as the covenant number, the number also wherein was completed the old creation, has been already before us: that of "the eighth" will best be considered in connection with the provisions of chap. xii., to which we next turn our attention.

The law of this chapter has a formal closing, in which are used these words (ver. 31): "Thus shall ye separate the children of Israel from their uncleanness; that they die not in their uncleanness, when they defile My tabernacle that is in the midst of them."

Of which the natural meaning is this, that the defilements mentioned, as conspicuous signs of man's fallen condition, were so offensive before a holy God, as apart from these purifications to have called down the judgment of death on those in whom they were found. In these words lies also the deeper spiritual thought—if we have rightly apprehended the symbolic import of these regulations—that not only, as in former cases mentioned under the law of offerings, do voluntary acts of sin separate from God and if unatoned for call down His judgment, but that even our infirmities and the involuntary motions of sin in our nature have the same effect, and, apart from the cleansing of the Holy Spirit and the blood of the Lord Jesus Christ, ensure the final judgment of death.

CHAPTER XVI
THE UNCLEANNESS OF CHILD-BEARING

Lev. xii. 1-8.

The reference in xii. 2 to the regulations given in xv. 19, as remarked in the preceding chapter, shows us that the author of these laws regarded the circumstances attending child-birth as falling under the same general category, in a ceremonial and symbolic aspect, as the law of issues. As a special case, however, the law concerning child-birth presents some very distinctive and instructive features.

The period during which the mother was regarded as unclean, in the full comprehension of that term, was seven days, as in the analogous case mentioned in xv. 19, with the remarkable exception, that when she had borne a daughter this period was doubled. At the expiration of this period of seven days, her ceremonial uncleanness was regarded as in so far lessened that the restrictions affecting the ordinary relations of life, as ordered, xv. 19-23, were removed. She was not, however, yet allowed to touch any hallowed thing or to come into the sanctuary, until she had fulfilled, from the time of the birth of the child, if a son, forty days; if a daughter, twice forty, or eighty days. At the expiration of the longer period, she was to bring, as in the law concerning the prolonged issue of blood (xv. 25-30), a burnt-offering and a sin-offering unto the door of the tent of meeting, wherewith the priest was to make an atonement for her; when first she should be accounted clean, and restored to full covenant privileges. The only difference from the similar law in chap. xv. is in regard to the burnt-offering commanded, which was larger and more costly,—a lamb, instead of a turtle dove, or a young pigeon. Still, in the same spirit of gracious accommodation to the poor which was illustrated in the general law of the sin-offering, it was ordered (ver. 8.): "If her means suffice not for a lamb, then she shall take two turtledoves, or two young pigeons; the one for a burnt offering, and the other for a sin offering." The law then applied, according to xv. 29, 30. A gracious provision this was, as all will remember, of which the mother of our Lord availed herself (Luke ii. 22-24), as being one of those who were too poor to bring a lamb for a burnt-offering.

To the meaning of these regulations, the key is found in the same conceptions which we have seen to underlie the law concerning issues. In the birth of a child, the special original curse against the woman is regarded by the law as reaching its fullest, most consummate and significant expression. For the extreme evil of the state of sin into which the first woman, by that first sin, brought all womanhood, is seen most of all in this, that now woman, by means of those powers given her for good and blessing, can bring into the world only a child of sin. And it is, apparently, because we here see the operation of this curse in its most conspicuous form, that the time of her enforced separation from the tabernacle worship is prolonged to a period of forty or eighty days.

It has been usual to speak of the time of the mother's uncleanness, and subsequent continued exclusion from the tabernacle worship, as being doubled in the case of the birth of a daughter; but it were, perhaps, more accurate to regard the normal length of these periods as being respectively fourteen and eighty days, of which the former is double of that required in xv. 28. This normal period would then be more properly regarded as shortened by one half in the case of a male child, in virtue of his circumcision on the eighth day.

The Ordinance of Circumcision.

xii. 3.

"And in the eighth day the flesh of his foreskin shall be circumcised."

Although the rite of circumcision here receives a new and special sanction, it had been appointed long before by God as the sign of His covenant with Abraham (Gen. xvii. 10-14). Nor was circumcision, probably, even then a new thing. That the ancient Egyptians practised it is well known; so also did the Arabs and Phœnicians; in fact, the custom has been very extensively observed, not only by nations with whom the Israelites came in contact, but by others who have not had, in historic times, connection with any civilised peoples; as, for example, the Congo negroes, and certain Indian tribes in South America.

The fundamental idea connected with circumcision, by most of the peoples who have practised it, appears to have been physical purification; indeed, the Arabs call it by the name *tatur*, which has this precise meaning. And it deserves to be noticed that for this idea regarding circumcision there is so much reason in fact, that high medical authorities have attributed to it a real hygienic value, especially in warm climates.

No one need feel any difficulty in supposing that this common conception attached to the rite also in the minds of the Hebrews. Rather all the more fitting it was, if there was a basis in fact for this familiar opinion, that God should thus have taken a ceremony already known to the surrounding peoples, and in itself of a wholesome physical effect, and constituted it for Abraham and his seed a symbol of an analogous spiritual fact; namely, the purification of sin at its fountain-head, the cleansing of the evil nature with which we all are born. It should be plain enough that it makes nothing against this as the true interpretation of the rite, even if that be granted which some have claimed, that it has had, in some instances, a connection with the phallic worship so common in the East, or that it has been regarded by some as a sacrificial ceremony. Only the more noteworthy would it thus appear that the Hebrews should have held strictly to that view of its significance which had a solid basis in physical fact,—a fact, moreover, which made it a peculiarly fitting symbol of the spiritual grace which the Biblical writers connect with it. For that it was so regarded by them will not be disputed. In this very book (xxvi. 41) we read of an "uncircumcised heart;" as also in Deuteronomy, the prophecies of Jeremiah and Ezekiel, and other books of Scripture.

All this, as intimating the signification of circumcision as here enjoined, is further established by the New Testament references. Of these the most formal is perhaps that in Col. ii. 10, 11, where we read that believers in Christ, in virtue of their union with Him in whom the unclean nature has been made clean, are said to be "circumcised with a circumcision not made with hands, in the putting off of the body of the flesh, in the circumcision of Christ;" so that Paul elsewhere writes to the Philippians (iii. 3): "We are the circumcision, who worship by the Spirit of God, and glory in Christ Jesus, and have no confidence in the flesh."

And that God, in selecting this ancient rite to be the sign of His covenant in the flesh of Abraham and his seed (Gen. xvii. 13), had regard to the deep spiritual meaning which it could so naturally carry is explicitly declared by the Apostle Paul (Rom. iv. 11), who tells us that this sign of circumcision was "a seal of the righteousness of faith," even the righteousness and the faith concerning which, in the previous context, he was arguing; and which are still, for all men, the one, the ground, and the other, the condition, of salvation. It is truly strange that, in the presence of these plain words of the Apostle, any should still cling to the idea that circumcision had reference only to the covenant with Israel as a nation, and not, above all, to this profound spiritual truth which is basal to salvation, whether for the Jew or for the Gentile.

And so, when the Hebrew infant was circumcised, it signified for him and for his parents these spiritual realities. It was an outward sign and seal of the covenant of God with Abraham and with his seed, to be a God to him and to his seed after him; and it signified further that this covenant of God was to be carried out and made effectual only through the putting away of the flesh, the corrupt nature with which we are born, and of all that belongs to it, in order that, thus circumcised with the circumcision of the heart, every child of Abraham might indeed be an Israelite in whom there should be no guile.

And the law commands, in accord with the original command to Abraham, that the circumcision should take place on the eighth day. This is the more noticeable, that among other nations which practised, or still practise, the rite, the time is different. The Egyptians, for example, circumcised their sons between the sixth and tenth years, and the modern Mohammedans between the twelfth and fourteenth year. What is the significance of this eighth day?

In the first place, it is easy to see that we have in this direction a provision of God's mercy; for if delayed beyond infancy or early childhood, as among many other peoples, the operation is much more serious, and may even involve some danger; while in so early infancy it is comparatively trifling, and attended with no risk.

Further, by the administration of circumcision at the very opening of life, it is suggested that in the Divine ideal the grace which was signified thereby, of the cleansing of nature, was to be bestowed upon the child, not first at a late period of life, but from its very beginning, thus anticipating the earliest awakening of the principle of inborn sin. It was thus signified that before ever the child knew, or could know, the grace that was seeking to save him, he was to be taken into covenant relation with God. So even under the strange form of this ordinance we discover the same mind that was in Him who said concerning infant children (Luke xviii. 16): "Suffer the little children to come unto Me, and forbid them not: for of such is the kingdom of God." Thus we may well recollect, in passing, that, although the law has passed away in the Levitical form, the mind of the Lawgiver concerning the little children of His people, is still the same.

But the question still remains, Why was the eighth day selected, and not rather, for instance, the sixth or the seventh, which would have no less perfectly represented these ideas? The answer is to be found in the symbolic significance of the eighth day. As the old creation was completed in six days, with a following Sabbath of rest, so that six is ever the number of the old creation, as under imperfection and sin; the eighth day, which is the first day of a new week, everywhere in Scripture appears as the number symbolic of the new creation, in which all things shall be restored in the great redemption through the Second Adam. The thought finds its fullest expression in the resurrection of Christ, as the First-born from the dead, the Beginning and the Lord of the new creation, who in His resurrection-body manifested the first-fruits in physical life of the new creation, rising from the dead on the first, or, in other words, the day after the seventh, the eighth day. This gives the key to the use of the number eight in the Mosaic symbolism. Thus in the law of the cleansing of the man or the woman that had an issue, the sacrifices which effectuated their formal deliverance from the curse under which, through the weakness of their old nature, they had suffered, were to be offered on the eighth day (xv. 14, 29); the priestly cleansing of the leper from the taint of his living death was also effected on the eighth day (xiv. 10); so also the cleansing of the Nazarite who had been defiled by the dead (Numb. vi. 10). So also the holy convocation which closed the feast of tabernacles or ingathering—the feast which, as we shall see, typically prefigured the great harvest of which Christ was the First-fruits—was ordained, in like manner, for the eighth day (xxiii. 36). With good reason, then, was circumcision ordered for the eighth day, seeing that what it symbolically signified was precisely this: the putting off of the flesh with which we are born through the circumcision of Christ, and therewith the first beginning of a new and purified nature—a change so profound and radical, and in which the Divine efficiency is so immediately concerned, that Paul said of it that if any man was in Christ, in whose circumcision we are circised (Col. ii. 11), "there is a new creation" (2 Cor. v. 17, margin, R.V.).

Purification after Child-birth.

xii. 4-8.

"And she shall continue in the blood of her purifying three and thirty days; she shall touch no hallowed thing, nor come into the sanctuary, until the days of her purifying be fulfilled. But if she bear a maid child, then she shall be unclean two weeks, as in her impurity: and she shall continue in the blood of her purifying threescore and six days. And when the days of her purifying are fulfilled, for a son, or for a daughter, she shall bring a lamb of the first year for a burnt offering, and a young pigeon, or a turtledove, for a sin offering, unto the door of the tent of meeting, unto the priest: and he shall offer it before the Lord, and make atonement for her; and she shall be cleansed from the fountain of her blood. This is the law for her that beareth, whether a male or a female.

And if her means suffice not for a lamb, then she shall take two turtledoves, or two young pigeons; the one for a burnt offering, and the other for a sin offering: and the priest shall make atonement for her, and she shall be clean."

Until the circumcision of the new-born child, on the eighth day, he was regarded by the law as ceremonially still in a state of nature, and therefore as symbolically unclean. For this reason, again, the mother who had brought him into the world, and whose life was so intimately connected with his life, was regarded as unclean also. Unclean, under analogous circumstances, according to the law of xv. 19, she was reckoned doubly unclean in this case,—unclean because of her issue, and unclean because of her connection with this child, uncircumcised and unclean. But when the symbolic cleansing of the child took place by the ordinance of circumcision, then her uncleanness, so far as occasioned by her immediate relation to him, came to an end. She was not indeed completely restored; for, according to the law, in her still continuing condition, it was impossible that she should be allowed to come into the tabernacle of the Lord, or touch any hallowed thing; but the ordinance which admitted her child, admitted her also again to the fellowship of the covenant people.

The longer period of forty—or, in the case of the birth of a female child, of twice forty—days must also be explained upon symbolical grounds. Some have indeed attempted to account for these periods, as also for the difference in their length in the two cases, by a reference to beliefs of the ancients with regard to the physical condition of the mother during these periods; but such notions of the ancients are not justified by facts; nor, especially, would they by any means account for the greatly prolonged period of eighty days in the case of the female child. It is possible that in the forty, and twice forty, we may have a reference to the forty weeks during which the life of the unborn child had been identified with that of the mother,—a child which, it must be remembered, according to the uniform Biblical view, was not innocent, but conceived in sin; for each week of which connection of life, the mother suffered a judicial exclusion of one, or, in the case of the birth of a daughter, of two days; the time being doubled in the latter case with allusion to the double curse which, according to Genesis, rested upon the woman, as "first in the transgression." But, apart from this, however difficult it may be to give a satisfactory explanation of the fact, it is certain that throughout Scripture the number forty appears to have a symbolic meaning; and one can usually trace in its application a reference, more or less distinct, to the conception of trial or testing. Thus for forty days was Moses in the mount,—a time of testing for Israel, as for him: forty days, the spies explored the promised land; forty years, Israel was tried in the wilderness; forty days, abode Elijah in the wilderness; forty days, also, was our Lord fasting in the wilderness; and forty days, again, He abode in resurrection life upon the earth.

The forty (or eighty) days ended, the mother was now formally reinstated in the fulness of her privileges as a daughter of Israel. The ceremonial, as in the law of issues, consisted in the presentation of a burnt-offering and a sin-offering, with the only variation that, wherever possible, the burnt-offering must be a young lamb, instead of a dove or pigeon; the reason for which variation is to be found either in the fact that the burnt-offering was to represent not herself alone, but also her child, or, possibly, as some have suggested, it was because she had been so much longer excluded from the tabernacle service than in the other case.[25]

The teaching of this law, then, is twofold: it concerns, first, the woman; and, secondly, the child which she bears. As regards the woman, it emphasises the fact that, because "first in the trangression," she is under special pains and penalties in virtue of her sex. The capacity of motherhood, which is her crown and her glory, though still a precious privilege, has yet been made, because of sin, an inevitable instrument of pain, and that because of her relation to the first sin. We are thus reminded that the specific curse denounced against the woman, as recorded in the book of Genesis, is no dead letter, but a fact. No doubt, the conception is one which raises difficulties which in themselves are great, and to modern thought are greater than ever. Nevertheless, the fact abides unaltered, that even to this day woman is under special pains and disabilities, inseparably connected with her power of motherhood. Modern theorists, men and women with nineteenth-century notions concerning politics and education, may persist in ignoring this; but the fact abides, and cannot be got rid of by passing resolutions in a mass-meeting, or even by Act of Parliament or Congress.

And so, as it is useless to object to facts, it is only left to object to the Mosaic view of the facts, which connects them with sin, and, in particular, with the first sin. Why should all the daughters of Eve suffer because of her sin? Where is the justice in such an ordinance? A question this is to which we cannot yet give any satisfactory answer. But it does not follow that because in any proposition there are difficulties which at present we are unable to solve, therefore the proposition is false. And, further, it is important to observe that this law, under which womanhood abides, is after all only a special case under that law of the Divine government which is announced in the second commandment, by which the iniquities of the fathers are visited upon the children. It is most certainly a law which, to our apprehension, suggests great moral difficulties, even to the most reverent spirits; but it is no less certainly a law which represents a conspicuous and tremendous fact, which is illustrated, for instance, in the family of every drunkard in the world. And it is well worth observing, that while the ceremonial law, which was specially intended to keep this fact before the mind and the conscience, is abrogated, the fact that woman is still under certain Divinely imposed disabilities because of that first sin, is reaffirmed in the New Testament, and is by apostolic authority applied in the administration of Church government. For Paul wrote to Timothy (1 Tim. ii. 12, 13): "I permit not a woman to teach, nor to have dominion over a man.... For Adam was not beguiled, but the woman being beguiled hath fallen into transgression." Modern theorists, and so-called "reformers" in Church, State, and society, busy with their social, governmental, and ecclesiastical novelties, would do well to heed this apostolic reminder.

All the more beautiful, as against this dark background of mystery, is the word of the Apostle which follows, wherein he reminds us that, through the grace of God, even by means of those very powers of motherhood on which the curse has so heavily fallen, has come the redemption of the woman; so that "she shall be saved through the childbearing, if they continue in faith and love and sanctification with sobriety" (1 Tim. ii. 15, R.V.); seeing that "in Christ Jesus," in respect of the completeness and freeness of salvation, "there can be no male and female" (Gal. iii. 28, R.V.).

But, in the second place, we may also derive abiding instruction from this law, concerning the child which is of man begotten and of woman born. It teaches us that not only has the curse thus fallen on the woman, but that, because she is herself a sinful creature, she can only bring forth another sinful creature like herself; and if a daughter, then a daughter inheriting all her own peculiar infirmities and disabilities. The law, as regards both mother and child, expresses in the language of symbolism those words of David in his penitential confession (Psalm li. 5): "Behold, I was shapen in iniquity; and in sin did my mother conceive me." Men may contemptuously call this "theology," or even rail at it as "Calvinism;" but it is more than theology, more than Calvinism; it is a *fact*, to which until this present time history has seen but one exception, even that mysterious Son of the Virgin, who claimed, however, to be no mere man, but the Christ, the Son of the Blessed!

And yet many, who surely can think but superficially upon the solemn facts of life, still object to this most strenuously, that even the new-born child should be regarded as in nature sinful and unclean. Difficulty here we must all admit,—difficulty so great that it is hard to overstate it—regarding the bearing of this fact on the character of the holy and merciful God, who in the beginning made man. And yet, surely, deeper thought must confess that herein the Mosaic view of infant nature—a view which is assumed and taught throughout Holy Scripture—however humbling to our natural pride, is only in strictest accord with what the admitted principles of the most exact science compel us to admit. For whenever, in any case, we find all creatures of the same class doing, under all circumstances, any one thing, we conclude that the reason for this can only lie in the nature of such creatures, antecedent to any influence of a tendency to imitation. If, for instance, the ox everywhere and always eats the green thing of the earth, and not flesh, the reason, we say, is found simply in the nature of the ox as he comes into being. So when we see all men, everywhere, under all circumstances, as soon as ever they come to the time of free moral choice, always choosing and committing sin, what can we conclude—regarding this, not as a theological, but merely as a scientific question—but that man, as he comes into the world, must have a sinful nature? And this being so, then why must not the law of heredity apply, according to which, by a law which knows of no exceptions, like ever produces its like?

Least of all, then, should those object to the view of child-nature which is represented in this law of Leviticus, who accept these commonplaces of modern science as representing facts. Wiser it were to turn attention to the other teaching of the law, that, notwithstanding these sad and humiliating facts, there is provision made by God, through the cleansing by grace of the very nature in which we are born, and atonement for the sin which without our fault we inherit, for a complete redemption from all the inherited corruption and guilt.

And, last of all, especially should Christian parents with joy and thankfulness receive the manifest teaching of this law,—teaching reaffirmed by our blessed Lord in the New Testament,—that God our Father offers to parental faith Himself to take in hand our children, even from the earliest beginning of their infant days, and, purifying the fountain of their life through "a circumcision made without hands," receive the little ones into covenant relation with Himself, to their eternal salvation. And thus is the word of the Apostle fulfilled: "Where sin abounded, grace did abound more exceedingly: that, as sin reigned in death, even so might grace reign through righteousness unto eternal life through Jesus Christ our Lord."

CHAPTER XVII
THE UNCLEANNESS OF LEPROSY

Lev. xiii. 1-46.

The interpretation of this chapter presents no little difficulty. The description of the diseases with which the law here deals is not given in a scientific form; the point of view, as the purpose of all, is strictly practical. As for the Hebrew word rendered "leprosy," it does not itself give any light as to the nature of the disease thus designated. The word simply means "a stroke," as also does the generic term used in ver. 2 and elsewhere, and translated "plague." Inasmuch as the Septuagint translators rendered the former term by the Greek word *"lepra"* (whence our word "leprosy"), and as, it is said, the old Greek physicians comprehended under that term only such scaly cutaneous eruptions as are now known as *psoriasis* (*vulg.*, "salt-rheum"), and for what is now known as leprosy reserved the term "elephantiasis,"[26] it has been therefore urged by high authority that in these chapters is no reference to the leprosy of modern speech, but only to some disease or diseases much less serious, either psoriasis or some other, consisting, like that, of a scaly eruption on the skin.[27] To the above argument it is also added that the signs which are given for the recognition of the disease intended, are not such as we should expect if it were the modern leprosy; as, for example, there is no mention of the insensibility of the skin, which is so characteristic a feature of the disease, at least, in a very common variety; moreover, we find in this chapter no allusion to the hideous mutilation which so commonly results from leprosy.

When the use of the Hebrew term rendered "leprosy" is examined, in this law and elsewhere, it certainly seems to be used with great definiteness to describe a disease which had as a very characteristic feature a whitening of the skin throughout, together with other marks common to the early stages of leprosy as given in this chapter. Only in ver. 12 does the Hebrew word appear to be applied to a disease of a different character, though also marked by the whitening of the skin. As for the symptoms indicated, the undoubted absence of many conspicuous marks of leprosy may be accounted for by the following considerations. In the first place, with a single exception (vv. 9-11), the earliest stages of the disease are described; and, secondly, it may reasonably be assumed that, through the desire to ensure the earliest possible separation of a leprous man from the congregation, signs were to be noted and acted upon, which might also be found in other forms of skin disease. The aim of the law is that, if possible, the man shall be removed from the camp before the disease has assumed its most unambiguous and revolting form. As for the omission to mention the insensibility of the skin of the leper, this seems to be sufficiently explained when we remember that this symptom is characteristic of only one, and that not the most fatal, variety of the disease.

But, it has also been urged, that elsewhere in the Scripture the so-called lepers appear as mingling with other people—as, for example, in the case of Naaman and Gehazi—in a way which shows that the disease was not regarded as contagious; whence it is inferred, again, that the leprosy of which we read in the Bible cannot be the same with the disease which is so called in our time. But, in reply to this objection, it may be answered that even modern medical opinion has been by no means as confident of the contagiousness of the disease—at least, until quite recently—as were people in the middle ages; nor, moreover, can we assume that the prevention of contagion must have been the chief reason for the segregation of the leper, according to the Levitical law, seeing that a like separation was enjoined in many other cases of ceremonial uncleanness where any thought of contagion or infection was quite impossible.

In further support of the more common opinion, which identifies the disease chiefly referred to in this chapter with the leprosy of modern times, the following considerations appear to be of no little weight. In the first place, the words themselves which are applied to the disease in these chapters and elsewhere,—*tsara'ath* and *nega'*, both meaning, etymologically, "a stroke," *i.e.*, a stroke in some eminent sense,[28]—while peculiarly fitting if the disease be that which we now know as leprosy, seem very strangely chosen if, as Sir Risdon Bennett thinks, they only designate varieties of a disease of so little seriousness as *psoriasis*. Then, again, the words used by Aaron to Moses (Numb. xii. 12), referring to the leprosy of Miriam, deserve great weight here: "Let her not, I pray, be as one dead, of whom the flesh is half consumed." These words sufficiently answer the allegation that there is no certain reference in Scripture to the mutilation which is so characteristic of the later stages of the disease. It would not be easy to describe in more accurate language the condition of the leper as the plague advances; while, on the other hand, if the leprosy of the Bible be only such a light affection as "salt-rheum," these words and the evident horror which they express, are so exaggerated as to be quite unaccountable.

Then, again, we cannot lose sight of the place which the disease known in Scripture language as leprosy holds in the sight of the law. As a matter of fact, it is singled out from a multitude of diseases as the object of the most stringent and severe regulations, and the most elaborate ceremonial, known to the law. Now, if the disease intended be indeed the awful *elephantiasis Græcorum* of modern medical science, popularly known as leprosy, this is most natural and reasonable; but if, on the other hand, only some such non-malignant disease as *psoriasis* be intended, this fact is inexplicable. Further, the tenour of all references to the disease in the Scripture implies that it was deemed so incurable that its removal in any case was regarded as a special sign of the exercise of Divine power. The reference of the Hebrew maid of Naaman to the prophet of God (2 Kings v. 3), as one who could cure him, instead of proving that it was thought curable—as has been strangely urged—by ordinary means, surely proves the exact opposite. Naaman, no doubt, had exhausted medical resources; and the hope of the maid for him is not based on the medical skill of Elisha, but on the fact that he was a prophet of God, and therefore able to draw on Divine power. To the same effect is the word of the King of Israel, when he received the letter of Naaman (2 Kings v. 7): "Am I God, to kill and to make alive, that this man doth send unto me to recover a man of his leprosy?" In full accord with this is the appeal of our Lord (Matt. xi. 5) to His cleansing of the lepers, as a sign of His Messiahship which He ranks for convincing power along with the raising of the dead.

Nor is it a fatal objection to the usual understanding of this matter, that because the Levitical law prescribes a ritual for the ceremonial cleansing of the leper in case of his cure, therefore the disease so called could not be one of the gravity and supposed incurability of the true leprosy. For it is to be noted, in the first place, that there is no intimation that recovery from the leprosy was a common occurrence, or even that it was to be expected at all, apart from the direct power of God; and, in the second place, that the Scriptural narrative represents God as now and then—though very rarely—interposing for the cure of the leper. And it may perhaps be added, that while a recent authority writes, and with truth, that "medical skill appears to have been more completely foiled by this than by any other malady," it is yet remarked that, when of the anæsthetic variety, "some spontaneous cures are recorded."

The chapter before us calls for little detailed exposition. The diagnosis of the disease by the priest is treated under four different heads: (1) the case of a leprosy rising spontaneously (vv. 1-17, 38, 39); (2) leprosy rising out of a boil (vv. 18-24); (3) rising out of a burn (vv. 24-28); (4) leprosy on the head or beard (vv. 29-37, 40-44). The indications which are to be noted are described (vv. 2, 3, 24-27, etc.) as a rising of the surface, a scab (or scale), or a bright spot (very characteristic), the presence in the spot of hair turned white, the disease apparently deeper than the outer or scarf skin, a reddish-white colour of the surface, and a tendency to spread. The presence of "raw flesh" is mentioned (ver. 10) as an indication of a leprosy already somewhat advanced, "an old leprosy." In cases of doubt, the suspected case is to be isolated for a period of seven or, if need be, fourteen days, at the expiration of which the priest's verdict is to be given, as the symptoms may then indicate.

Two cases are mentioned which the priest is not to regard as leprosy. The first (vv. 12, 13) is that in which the plague "covers all the skin of him that hath the plagues from his head even to his feet, as far as appeareth to the priest," so that he "is all turned white." At first thought, this seems quite unaccountable, seeing that leprosy finally affects the whole body. But the solution of the difficulty is not far to seek. For the next verse provides that, in such a case, if "raw flesh" appear, he shall be held to be unclean. The explanation of this provision of ver. 12 is therefore apparently this: that if an eruption had so spread as to cover the whole body, turning it white, and yet no raw flesh had appeared in any place, the disease could not be true leprosy; as, if it were, then, by the time that it had so extended, "raw flesh" would certainly have appeared somewhere. The disease indicated by this exception was indeed well known to the ancients, as it is also to the moderns as the "dry tetter;" which, although an affection often of long duration, frequently disappears spontaneously, and is never malignant.

The second case which is specified as not to be mistaken for leprosy is mentioned in vv. 38, 39, where it is described as marked by bright spots of a dull whiteness, but without the white hair, and other characteristic signs of leprosy. The Hebrew word by which it is designated is rendered in the Revised Version "tetter;" and the disease, a non-malignant tetter or *eczema*, is still known in the East under the same name (*bohak*) which is here used.

Verses 45, 46, give the law for him who has been by the priest adjudged to be a leper. He must go with clothes rent, with his hair neglected, his lip covered, crying, "Unclean! unclean!" without the camp, and there abide alone for so long as he continues to be afflicted with the disease. In other words, he is to assume all the ordinary signs of mourning for the dead; he is to regard himself, and all others are to regard him, as a dead man. As it were, he is a continual mourner at his own funeral.

Wherein lay the reason for this law? One might answer, in general, that the extreme loathsomeness of the disease, which made the presence of those who had it to be abhorrent even to their nearest friends, would of itself make it only fitting, however distressing might be the necessity, that such persons should be excluded from every possibility of appearing, in their revolting corruption, in the sacred and pure precincts of the tabernacle of the holy God, as also from mingling with His people. Many, however, have seen in the regulation only a wise law of public hygiene. That a sanitary intent may very probably have been included in the purpose of this law, we are by no means inclined to deny. In earlier times, and all through the middle ages, the disease was regarded as contagious; and lepers were accordingly segregated, as far as practicable, from the people. In modern times, the weight of opinion until recent years has been against this older view; but the tendency of medical authority now appears to be to reaffirm the older belief. The alarming increase of this horrible disease in all parts of the world, of late, following upon a general relaxation of those precautions against contagion which were formerly thought necessary, certainly supports this judgment; and it may thus be easily believed that there was just sanitary ground for the rigid regulations of the Mosaic code. And just here it may be remarked, that if indeed there be any degree of contagiousness, however small, in this plague, no one who has ever seen the disease, or understands anything of its incomparable horror and loathsomeness, will feel that there is any force in the objections which have been taken to this part of the Mosaic law as of inhuman harshness toward the sufferers. Even were the risk of contagion but small, as it probably is, still, so terrible is the disease that one would more justly say that the only inhumanity were to allow those afflicted with it unrestricted intercourse with their fellow-men. The truth is, that the Mosaic law concerning the treatment of the leper, when compared with regulations touching lepers which have prevailed among other nations, stands contrasted with them by its comparative leniency. The Hindoo law, as is well known, even insists that the leper ought to put himself out of existence, requiring that he shall be buried alive.

But if there be included in these regulations a sanitary intent, this certainly does not exhaust their significance. Rather, if this be admitted, it only furnishes the basis, as in the case of the laws concerning clean and unclean meats, for still more profound spiritual teaching. For, as remarked before, it is one of the fundamental thoughts of the Mosaic law, that death, as being the extreme visible manifestation of the presence of sin in the race, and a sign of the consequent holy wrath of God against sinful man, is inseparably connected with legal uncleanness. But all disease is a forerunner of death, an incipient dying; and is thus, no less really than actual death, a visible manifestation of the presence and power of sin working in the body through death. And yet it is easy to see that it would have been quite impracticable to carry out a law that therefore all disease should render the sick person ceremonially unclean; while, on the other hand, it was of consequence that Israel, and we as well, should be kept in remembrance of this connection between sin and disease, as death beginning. What could have been more fitting, then, than this, that the one disease which, without exaggeration, is of all diseases the most loathsome, which is most manifestly a visible representation of that which is in a measure true of all disease, that it is death working in life, that disease which is, not in a merely rhetorical sense, but in fact, a living image of death,—should be selected from all others for the illustration of this principle: to be to Israel and to us, a visible, perpetual, and very awful parable of the nature and the working of sin?

And this is precisely what has been done. This explains, as sanitary considerations alone do not, not merely the separation of the leper from the holy people, but also the solemn symbolism which required him to assume the appearance of one mourning for the dead; as also the symbolism of his cleansing, which, in like manner, corresponded very closely with that of the ritual of cleansing from defilement by the dead. Hence, while all sickness, in a general way, is regarded in the Holy Scriptures as a fitting symbol of sin, it has always been recognised that, among all diseases, leprosy is this in an exceptional and pre-eminent sense. This thought seems to have been in the mind of David, when, after his murder of Uriah and adultery with Bathsheba, bewailing his iniquity (Psalm li. 7), he prayed, "Purge me with hyssop, and I shall be clean." For the only use of the hyssop in the law, which could be alluded to in these words, is that which is enjoined (xiv. 4-7) in the law for the cleansing of the leper, by the sprinkling of the man to be cleansed with blood and water with a hyssop branch.

And thus we find that, again, this elaborate ceremonial contains, not merely an instructive lesson in public sanitation, and practical suggestions in hygiene for our modern times; but also lessons, far more profound and momentous, concerning that spiritual malady with which the whole human race is burdened,—lessons therefore of the gravest personal consequence for every one of us.

From among all diseases, leprosy has been selected by the Holy Ghost to stand in the law as the supreme type of sin, as seen by God! This is the very solemn fact which is brought before us in this chapter. Let us well consider it, and see that we receive the lesson, however humiliating and painful, in the spirit of meekness and penitence. Let us so study it that we shall with great earnestness and true faith resort to the true and heavenly High Priest, who alone can cleanse us of this sore malady. And in order to do this, we must carefully consider what is involved in this type.

In the first place, leprosy is undoubtedly selected to be a special type of sin, on account of its extreme *loathsomeness*. Beginning, indeed, as an insignificant spot, "a bright place," a mere scale on the skin, it goes on spreading, progressing ever from worse to worse, till at last limb drops from limb, and only the hideous mutilated remnant of what was once a man is left. A vivid picture of the horrible reality has been given by that veteran missionary and very accurate observer, the Rev. William Thomson, D.D., who writes thus: "As I was approaching Jerusalem, I was startled by the sudden apparition of a crowd of beggars, sans eyes, sans nose, sans hair, sans everything.... They held up their handless arms, unearthly sounds gurgled through throats without palates,—in a word, I was horrified."[29] Too horrible is this to be repeated or thought of? Yes! But then all the more solemnly instructive is it that the Holy Spirit should have chosen this disease, the most loathsome of all, as the most fatal of all, to symbolise to us the true nature of that spiritual malady which affects us all, as it is seen by the omniscient and most holy God.

But it will very naturally be rejoined by some; Surely it were gross exaggeration to apply this horrible symbolism to the case of many who, although indeed sinners, unbelievers also in Christ, yet certainly exhibit truly lovely and attractive characters. That this is true regarding many who, according to the Scriptures, are yet unsaved, cannot be denied. We read of one such in the Gospel,—a young man, unsaved, who yet was such that "Jesus looking upon him loved him" (Mark x. 21). But this fact only makes the leprosy the more fitting symbol of sin. For another characteristic of the disease is its *insignificant and often even imperceptible beginning*. We are told that in the case of those who inherit the taint, it frequently remains quite dormant in early life, only gradually appearing in later years. How perfectly the type, in this respect, then, symbolises sin! And surely any thoughtful man will confess that this fact makes the presence of the infection not less alarming, but more so. No comfort then can be rightly had from any complacent comparison of our own characters with those of many, perhaps professing more, who are much worse than we, as the manner of some is. No one who knew that from his parents he had inherited the leprous taint, or in whom the leprosy as yet appeared as only an insignificant bright spot, would comfort himself greatly by the observation that other lepers were much worse; and that he was, as yet, fair and goodly to look upon. Though the leprosy were in him but just begun, that would be enough to fill him with dismay and consternation. So should it be with regard to sin.

And it would so affect such a man the more surely, when he knew that the disease, however slight in its beginnings, was certainly *progressive*. This is one of the unfailing marks of the disease. It may progress slowly, but it progresses surely. To quote again the vivid and truthful description of the above-named writer, "It comes on by degrees in different parts of the body: the hair falls from the head and eyebrows; the nails loosen, decay, and drop off; joint after joint of the fingers and toes shrinks up and slowly falls away; the gums are absorbed, and the teeth disappear; the nose, the eyes, the tongue, and the palate are slowly consumed; and, finally, the wretched victim sinks into the earth and disappears."

In this respect again the fitness of the disease to stand as an eminent type of sin is undeniable. No man can morally stand still. No one has ever retained the innocence of childhood. Except as counteracted by the efficient grace of the Holy Spirit in the heart, the Word (2 Tim. iii. 13) is ever visibly fulfilled, "evil men wax worse and worse." Sin may not develop in all with equal rapidity, but it does progress in every natural man, outwardly or inwardly, with equal certainty.

It is another mark of leprosy that sooner or later it *affects the whole man*; and in this, again, appears the sad fitness of the disease to stand as a symbol of sin. For sin is not a partial disorder, affecting only one class of faculties, or one part of our nature. It disorders the judgment; it obscures our moral perceptions; it either perverts the affections, or unduly stimulates them in one direction, while it deadens them in another; it hardens and quickens the will for evil, while it paralyses its power for the volition of that which is holy. And not only the Holy Scripture, but observation itself, teaches us that sin, in many cases, also affects the body of man, weakening its powers, and bringing in, by an inexorable law, pain, disease, and death. Sooner or later, then, sin affects the whole man. And for that reason, again, is leprosy set forth as its pre-eminent symbol.

It is another remarkable feature of the disease that, as it progresses from bad to worse, the victim becomes more and more *insensible*. This numbness or insensibility of the spots affected—in one most common variety at least—is a constant feature. In some cases it becomes so extreme that a knife may be thrust into the affected limb, or the diseased flesh may be burnt with fire, and yet the leper feels no pain. Nor is the insensibility confined to the body, but, as the leprosy extends, the mind is affected in an analogous manner. A recent writer says: "Though a mass of bodily corruption, at last unable to leave his bed, the leper seems happy and contented with his sad condition." Is anything more characteristic than this of the malady of sin? The sin which, when first committed, costs a keen pang, afterward, when frequently repeated, hurts not the conscience at all. Judgments and mercies, which in earlier life affected one with profound emotion, in later life leave the impenitent sinner as unmoved as they found him. Hence we all recognise the fitness of the common expression, "a seared conscience," as also of the Apostle's description of advanced sinners as men who are "past feeling" (Eph. iv. 19). Of this moral insensibility which sin produces, then, we are impressively reminded when the Holy Spirit in the Word holds before us leprosy as a type of sin.

Another element of the solemn fitness of the type is found in the persistently *hereditary* nature of leprosy. It may indeed sometimes arise of itself, even as did sin in the case of certain of the holy angels, and with our first parents; but when once it is introduced, in the case of any person, the terrible infection descends with unfailing certainty to all his descendants; and while, by suitable hygiene, it is possible to alleviate its violence, and retard its development, it is not possible to escape the terrible inheritance. Is anything more uniformly characteristic of sin? We may raise no end of metaphysical difficulties about the matter, and put unanswerable questions about freedom and responsibility; but there is no denying the hard fact that since sin first entered the race, in our first parents, not a child of man, of human father begotten, has escaped the taint. If various external influences, as in the case of leprosy, may, in some instances, modify its manifestations, yet no individual, in any class or condition of mankind, escapes the taint. The most cultivated and the most barbarous alike, come into the world so constituted that, quite antecedent to any act of free choice on their part, we know that it is not more certain that they will eat than that, when they begin to exercise freedom, they will, each and every one, use their moral freedom wrongly,—in a word, will sin. No doubt, then, when such prominence is given to leprosy among diseases, in the Mosaic symbolism and elsewhere, it is with intent, among other truths, to keep before the mind this very solemn and awful fact with regard to the sin which it so fitly symbolises.

And, again, we find yet another analogy in the fact that, among the ancient Hebrews, the disease was regarded as *incurable* by human means; and, notwithstanding occasional announcements in our day that a remedy has been discovered for the plague, this seems to be the verdict of the best authorities in medical science still. That in this respect leprosy perfectly represents the sorer malady of the soul, every one is witness. No possible effort of will or fixedness of determination has ever availed to free a man from sin. Even the saintliest Christian has often to confess with the Apostle Paul (Rom. vii. 19), "The evil which I would not, that I practise." Neither is culture, whether intellectual or religious, of any more avail. To this all human history testifies. In our day, despite the sad lessons of long experience, many are hoping for much from improved government, education, and such like means; but vainly, and in the face of the most patent facts. Legislation may indeed impose restrictions on the more flagrant forms of sin, even as it may be of service in restricting the devastations of leprosy, and ameliorating the condition of lepers. But to do away with sin, and abolish crime by any conceivable legislation, is a dream as vain as were the hope of curing leprosy by a good law or an imperial proclamation. Even the perfect law of God has proved inadequate for this end; the Apostle (Rom. viii. 3) reminds us that in this it has failed, and could not but fail, "in that it was weak through the flesh." Nothing can well be of more importance than that we should be keenly alive to this fact; that so we may not, through our present apparently tolerable condition, or by temporary alleviations of the trouble, be thrown off our guard, and hope for ourselves or for the world, upon grounds which afford no just reason for hope.

Last of all, the law of leprosy, as given in this chapter, teaches the supreme lesson, that as with the symbolic disease of the body, so with that of the soul, sin *shuts out from God and from the fellowship of the holy*. As the leper was excluded from the camp of Israel and from the tabernacle of Jehovah, so must the sinner, except cleansed, be shut out of the Holy City, and from the glory of the heavenly temple. What a solemnly significant parable is this exclusion of the leper from the camp! He is thrust forth from the congregation of Israel, wearing the insignia of mourning for the dead! Within the camp, the multitude of them that go to the sanctuary of God, and that joyfully keep holy day; without, the leper dwelling alone, in his incurable corruption and never-ending mourning! And so, while we do not indeed deny a sanitary intention in these regulations of the law, but are rather inclined to affirm it; yet of far more consequence is it that we heed the spiritual truth which this solemn symbolism teaches. It is that which is written in the Apocalypse (xxi. 27; xxii. 15) concerning the New Jerusalem: "There shall in no wise enter into it anything unclean.... Without are the dogs, and the sorcerers, and the fornicators, and the murderers, and the idolaters, and every one that loveth and maketh a lie."

In view of all these correspondences, one need not wonder that in the symbolism of the law leprosy holds the place which it does. For what other disease can be named which combines in itself, as a physical malady, so many of the most characteristic marks of the malady of the soul? In its intrinsic loathsomeness, its insignificant beginnings, its slow but inevitable progress, in the extent of its effects, in the insensibility which accompanies it, in its hereditary character, in its incurability, and, finally, in the fact that according to the law it involved the banishment of the leper from the camp of Israel,—in all these respects, it stands alone as a perfect type of sin; it is sin, as it were, made visible in the flesh.

This is indeed a dark picture of man's natural state, and very many are exceedingly loth to believe that sin can be such a very serious matter. Indeed, the fundamental postulate of much of our nineteenth-century thought, in matters both of politics and religion, denies the truth of this representation, and insists, on the contrary, that man is naturally not bad, but good; and that, on the whole, as the ages go by, he is gradually becoming better and better. But it is imperative that our views of sin and of humanity shall agree with the representations held before us in the Word of God. When that Word, not only in type, as in this chapter, but in plain language (Jer. xvii. 9, R.V.), declares that "the heart is deceitful above all things, and it is *desperately sick*," it must be a very perilous thing to deny this.

It is a profoundly instructive circumstance that, according to this typical law, the case of the supposed leper was to be judged by the priest (vv. 2, 3, *et passim*). All turned for him upon the priest's verdict. If he declared him clean, it was well; but if he pronounced him unclean, it made no difference that the man did not believe it, or that his friends did not believe it; or that he or they thought better in any respect of his case than the priest,—out of the camp he must go. He might plead that he was certainly not nearly in so bad a case as some of the poor, mutilated, dying creatures outside the camp; but that would have no weight, however true. For still he, no less really than they, was a leper; and, until made whole, into the fellowship of lepers he must go and abide. Even so for us all; everything turns, not on our own opinion of ourselves, or on what other men may think of us; but solely on the verdict of the heavenly Priest.

The picture thus set before us in the symbolism of this chapter is sad enough; but it would be far more sad did the law not now carry forward the symbolism into the region of redemption, in making provision for the cleansing of the leper, and his re-admission into the fellowship of the holy people. To this our attention is called in the next chapter.

CHAPTER XVIII
THE CLEANSING OF THE LEPER

Lev. xiv. 1-32.

The ceremonies for the restoration of the leper, when healed of his disease, to full covenant privileges, were comprehended in two distinct series. The first part of the ceremonial took place without the camp, and sufficed only to terminate his condition as one ceremonially dead, and allow of his return into the camp, and his association, though still under restriction, with his fellow-Israelites. The second part of the ceremonial took up his case on the eighth day thereafter, where the former ceremonial had left him, as a member, indeed, of the holy people, but a member still under defilement such as debarred him from approach to the presence of Jehovah; and, by a fourfold offering and an anointing, restored him to the full enjoyment of all his covenant privileges before God.

This law for the cleansing of the leper certainly implies that the disease, although incurable by human skill, yet, whether by the direct power of God, as in several instances in Holy Scripture, or for some cause unknown, might occasionally cease its ravages. In this case, although the visible effects of the disease might still remain, in mutilations and scars, yet he would be none the less a healed man. That occasionally instances have occurred of such arrest of the disease, is attested by competent observers, and the law before us thus provides for the restoration of the leper in such cases to the position from which his leprosy had excluded him.

The first part of the ceremonial (vv. 3-9) took place without the camp; for until legally cleansed the man was in the sight of the law still a leper, and therefore under sentence of banishment from the congregation of Israel. Thus, as the outcast could not go to the priest, the priest, on receiving word of his desire, went to him. For the ceremony which was to be performed, he provided himself with two living, clean birds, and with cedar-wood, and scarlet, and hyssop; also he took with him an earthen vessel filled with living water,—*i.e.*, with water from some spring or flowing stream, and therefore presumably pure and clean. One of the birds was then killed in such a manner that its blood was received into the vessel of water; then the living bird and the hyssop—bound, as we are told, with the scarlet band to the cedar-wood—were dipped into the mingled blood and water, and by them the leper was sprinkled therewith seven times by the priest, and was then pronounced clean; when the living bird, stained with the blood of the bird that was killed, was allowed to fly away. Thereupon, the leper washed his clothes, shaved off all his hair, bathed in water, and entered the camp. This completed the first stadium of his restoration.

Certain things about this symbolism seem very clear. First of all, whereas the leper, afflicted, as it were, with a living death, had become, as regards Israel, a man legally dead, the sprinkling with blood, in virtue of which he was allowed to take his place again in the camp as a living Israelite, symbolized the impartation of life; and, again, inasmuch as death is defiling, the blood was mingled with water, the uniform symbol of cleansing. The remaining symbols emphasise thoughts closely related to these. The cedar-wood (or juniper), which is almost incorruptible, signified that with this new life was imparted also freedom from corruption. Scarlet, as a colour, is the constant symbol, again, like the blood, of life and health. What the hyssop was is still in debate; but we can at least safely say that it was a plant supposed to have healing and purifying virtues.

So far all is clear. But what is the meaning of the slaying of the one bird, and the loosing afterward of the other, moistened with the blood of its fellow? Some have said that both of the birds symbolised the leper: the one which was slain, the leper as he was,—namely, as one dead, or under sentence of death by his plague; the other, naturally, then, the leper as healed, who, even as the living bird is let fly whither it will, is now set at liberty to go where he pleases. But when we consider that it is by means of being sprinkled with the blood of the slain bird that the leper is cleansed, it seems quite impossible that this slain bird should typify the leper in his state of defilement. Indeed, if this bird symbolised him as under his disease, this supposition seems even absurd; for the blood which cleansed must then have represented his own blood, and his blood as diseased and unclean!

Neither is it possible that the other bird, which was set at liberty, should represent the leper as healed, and its release, his liberation; however plausible, at first thought, this explanation may seem. For the very same ceremony as this with the two birds was also to be used in the cleansing of a leprous house (vv. 50-53), where it is evident that the loosing of the living bird could not have any such significance; since the notion of a liberty given would be wholly inapplicable in the case of a house. But whatever the true meaning of the symbolism may be, it is clear that it must be one which will apply equally well in each of the two cases, the cleansing of the leprous house, no less than that of the leprous person.

We are therefore compelled to regard the slaying of the one bird as a true sacrifice. No doubt there are difficulties in the way, but they do not seem insuperable, and are, in any case, less than those which beset other suppositions. It is true that the birds are not presented before Jehovah in the tabernacle; but as the ceremony took place outside the camp, and therefore at a distance from the tabernacle, this may be explained as merely because of the necessity of the case. It is true, again, that the choice of the bird was not limited, as in the tabernacle sacrifices, to the turtle-dove or pigeon; but it might easily be that when, as in this case, the sacrifice was elsewhere than at the tabernacle, the rules for service there did not necessarily apply. Finally and decisively, when we turn to the law for the cleansing of the leprous house, we find that atoning virtue is explicitly ascribed to this rite with the birds (ver. 53): "He shall make atonement for the house."

But sacrifice is here presented in a different aspect from elsewhere in the law. In this ceremonial the central thought is not consecration through sacrifice, as in the burnt-offering; nor expiation of guilt through sacrifice, as in the sin-offering; nor yet satisfaction for trespass committed, as in the guilt-offering. It is sacrifice as procuring for the man for whom it is offered purity and life, which is the main thought.

But, according to vv. 52, 53, the atonement is made with both the dead and the living bird. The special thought which is emphasised by the use of the latter, seems to be merely the full completeness of the work of cleansing which has been accomplished through the death of the other bird. For the living bird was represented as ideally identified with the bird which was slain, by being dipped in its blood; and in that it was now loosed from its captivity, this was in token of the fact that the bird, having now given its life to impart cleansing and life to the leper, has fully accomplished that end.

Obviously, this explanation is one that will apply no less readily to the cleansing of the leprous house than of the leprous person. For the leprosy in the house signifies the working of corruption and of decay and death in the wall of the house, in a way adapted to its nature, as really as in the case of the person; and the ceremonial with the birds and other material prescribed means the same with it as with the other,—namely, the removal of the principle of corruption and disease, and impartation of purity and wholesomeness. In both cases the sevenfold sprinkling, as in analogous cases elsewhere in the law, signified the completeness of the cleansing, to which nothing was lacking, and also certified to the leper that by this impartation of new life, and by his cleansing, he was again brought into covenant relations with Jehovah.

With these ceremonies, the leper's cleansing was now in so far effected that he could enter the camp; only he must first cleanse himself and his clothes with water and shave his hair,—ceremonies which, in their primary meaning, are most naturally explained by the importance of an actual physical cleansing in such a case. Every possible precaution must be taken that by no chance he bring the contagion of his late disease into the camp. Of what special importance in this connection, besides the washing, is the shaving of the hair, will be apparent to all who know how peculiarly retentive is the hair of odours and infections of every kind.

The cleansed man might now come into the camp; he is restored to his place as a living Israelite. And yet he may not come to the tabernacle. For even an Israelite might not come, if defiled for the dead; and this is precisely the leper's status at this point. Though delivered from the power of death, there is yet persisting such a connection of his new self with his old leprous self as precludes him from yet entering the more immediate presence of God. The reality of this analogy will appear to any one who compares the rites which now follow (vv. 10-20) with those appointed for the Nazarite, when defiled by the dead (Numb. vi. 9-12).

Seven days, then, as in that case, he remains away from the tabernacle. On the seventh day, he again shaves himself even to the eyebrows, thus ensuring the most absolute cleanness, and washes himself and his clothes in water. The final restoration ceremonial took place on the eighth day,—the day symbolic of the new creation,—when he appeared before Jehovah at the tent of meeting with a he-lamb for a guilt-offering, and another for a sin-offering, and a ewe-lamb for a burnt-offering; also a meal-offering of three tenth-deals, one tenth for each sacrifice, mingled with oil, and a log (3·32 qts.) of oil. The oil was then waved for a wave-offering before the Lord, as also the whole lamb of the guilt-offering (an unusual thing), and then the lamb was slain and offered after the manner of the guilt-offering.

And now followed the most distinctive part of the ceremonial. As in the case of the consecration of the priests was done with the blood of the peace-offering and with the holy oil, so was it done here with the blood of the guilt-offering and with the common oil—now by its waving consecrated to Jehovah—which the cleansed leper had brought. The priest anoints the man's right ear, the thumb of his right hand, and the great toe of his right foot, first with the blood of the guilt-offering, and then with the oil, having previously sprinkled of the oil seven times with his finger before the Lord. The remnant of the oil in the hand of the priest he then pours upon the cleansed leper's head; then offers for him the sin-offering, the burnt-offering, and the meal-offering; and therewith, at last, the atonement is complete, and the man is restored to his full rights and privileges as a living member of the people of the living God.

The chief significance of this ceremonial lies in the prominence given to the guilt-offering. This is evidenced, not only by the special and peculiar use which is made of its blood, in applying it to the leper, but also in the fact that in the case of the poor man, while the other offerings are diminished, there is no diminution allowed as regards the lamb of the guilt-offering, and the log of oil. Why should the guilt-offering have received on this occasion such a place of special prominence? The answer has been rightly given by those who point to the significance of the guilt-offering as representing reparation and satisfaction for loss of service due. By the fact of the man's leprosy, and consequent exclusion from the camp of Israel, God had been, for the whole period of his excision, defrauded, so to speak, of His proper dues from him in respect of service and offerings; and the guilt-offering precisely symbolised satisfaction made for this default in service which he had otherwise been able to render.

Nor is it a fatal objection to this understanding of the matter that, on this principle, he also that for a long time had had an issue should have been required, for his prolonged default of service, to bring a guilt-offering in order to his restoration; whereas from him no such demand was made. For the need, before the law, for the guilt-offering lay, not in the duration of the leprosy, as such apprehend it, but in the nature of the leprosy, as being, unlike any other visitation, in a peculiar sense, a death in life. Even when the man with an issue was debarred from the sanctuary, he was not, like the leper, regarded by the law as a dead man; but was still counted among them that were living in Israel. And if precluded for an indefinite time from the service and worship of God at the tabernacle, he yet, by his public submission to the demands of the law, in the presence of all, rendered still to God the honour due from a member of the living Israel. But in that the leper, unlike any other defiled person, was reckoned ceremonially dead, obviously consistency in the symbolism made it impossible to regard him as having in any sense rendered honour or service to God so long as he continued a leper, any more than if he had been dead and buried. Therefore he must bring a guilt-offering, as one who had, however unavoidably, committed "a trespass in the holy things of the Lord." And so this guilt-offering, in the case of the leper, as in all others, represented the satisfaction of debt; and as the reality or the amount of a debt cannot be affected by the poverty of the debtor, the offering which symbolised satisfaction for the debt must be the same for the poor leper as for the rich leper.

And the application of the blood to ear, hand, and foot meant the same as in the case of the consecration of the priests. Inducted, as one now risen from the dead, into the number of the priestly people, he receives the priestly consecration, devoting ear, hand, and foot to the service of the

Lord. And as it was fitting that the priests, because brought into a relation of special nearness to God, in order to be ministers of reconciliation to Israel, should therefore be consecrated with the blood of the peace-offering, which specially emphasised the realisation of reconciliation,—so the cleansed leper, who was re-established as a living member of the priestly nation, more especially by the blood of the guilt-offering, was therefore fittingly represented as consecrated in virtue, and by means of that fact.

So, like the priests, he also was anointed by the priest with oil; not indeed with the holy oil, for he was not admitted to the priestly order; yet with common oil, sanctified by its waving before God, in token of his consecration as a member of the priestly people. Especially suitable in his case was this anointing, that the oil constantly stands as a symbol of healing virtue, which in his experience he had so wondrously received.

Remembering in all this how the leprosy stands as a pre-eminent type of sin, in its aspect as involving death and corruption, the application of these ceremonies to the antitypical cleansing, at least in its chief aspects, is almost self-evident. As in all the Levitical types, so in this case, at the very entrance on the redeemed life stands the sacrifice of a life, and the service of a priest as mediator between God and man. Blood must be shed if the leper is to be admitted again into covenant standing with God; and the blood of the sacrifice in the law ever points to the sacrifice of Christ. But that great Sacrifice may be regarded in various aspects. Sin is a many-sided evil, and on every side it must be met. As often repeated, because sin as guilt requires expiation, hence the type of the sin-offering; in that it is a defrauding of God of His just rights from us, satisfaction is required, hence the type of the guilt-offering; as it is absence of consecration, life for self instead of life for God, hence the type of the burnt-offering. And yet the manifold aspects of sin are not all enumerated. For sin, again, is spiritual death; and, as death, it involves corruption and defilement. It is with special reference to this fact that the work of Christ is brought before us here. In the clean bird, slain that its blood may be applied to the leper for cleansing, we see typified Christ, as giving Himself, that His very life may be imparted to us for our life. In that the blood of the bird is mingled with water, the symbol of the Word of God, is symbolised the truth, that with the atoning blood is ever inseparably united the purifying energy of the Holy Ghost through the Word. Not the water without the blood, nor the blood without the water, saves, but the blood with the water, and the water with the blood. So it is said of Him to whom the ceremony pointed (1 John v. 6): "This is He that came by water and blood, even Jesus Christ; not with the water only, but with the water and with the blood."

But the type yet lacks something for completeness; and for this reason we have the second bird, who, when by his means the blood has been sprinkled on the leper, and the man is now pronounced clean, is released and flies away heavenward. What a beautiful symbol of that other truth, without which even the atonement of the Lord were nought, that He who died, having by that death for us procured our life, was then released from the bonds of death, rising from the dead on the third day, and ascending to heaven, like the freed bird, in token that His life-giving, cleansing work was done. Thus the message which, as the liberated bird flies carolling away, sweet as a heavenly song, seems to fall upon the ear, is this, "Delivered up for our trespasses, and raised for our justification" (Rom. iv. 25; see *Gr.*).

But although thus and then restored to his standing as a member of the living people of God, not yet was the cleansed leper allowed to appear in the presence of God at the tent of meeting. There was a delay of a week, and only then, on the eighth day, the day typical of resurrection and new creation, does He appear before God. Is there typical meaning in this delay? We would not be too confident. It is quite possible that this delay of a week, before the cleansed man was allowed to present himself for the completion of the ceremonial which reinstated him in the plenary enjoyment of all the rights and privileges of a child of Israel, may have been intended merely as a precautionary rule, of which the purpose was to guard against the possibility of infection, and the defilement of the sanctuary by his presence, through renewed activity of the disease; while, at the same time, it would serve as a spiritual discipline to remind the man, now cleansed, of the extreme care and holy fear with which, after his defilement, he should venture into the presence of the Holy One of Israel; and thus, by analogy, it becomes a like lesson to the spiritually cleansed in all ages.

But perhaps we may see a deeper significance in this week of delay, and his appointed appearance before the Lord on the eighth day. If the whole course of the leper, from the time of his infection till his final reappearing in the presence of Jehovah at the tent of meeting, be intended to typify the history and experience of a sinner as saved from sin; and if the cleansing of the leper without the camp, and his reinstatement thereupon as a member of God's Israel, represents in type the judicial reinstatement of the cleansed sinner, through the application of the blood and Spirit of Christ, in the number of God's people; one can then hardly fail to recognise in the week's delay appointed to him, before he could come into the immediate presence of God, an adumbration of the fact that between the sinner's acceptance and the appointed time of his appearing, finally and fully cleansed, before the

Lord, on the resurrection morning, there intervenes a period of delay, even the whole lifetime of the believer here in the flesh and in the disembodied state. For only thereafter does he at last, wholly perfected, appear before God in the heavenly Zion. But before thus appearing, the accepted man once and again had to cleanse his garments and his person, that so he might remove everything in which by any chance uncleanness might still lurk. Which, translated into New Testament language, gives us the charge of the Apostle Paul (2 Cor. vii. 1) addressed to those who had indeed received the new life, but were still in the flesh: "Let us cleanse ourselves from all defilement of flesh and spirit, perfecting holiness in the fear of God."

But, at last, the week of delay is ended. After its seventh day follows an eighth, the first-day morning of a new week, the morning typical of resurrection and therewith completed redemption, and the leper now, completely restored, appears before God in the holy tabernacle. Even so shall an eighth-day morning dawn for all who by the cleansing blood have been received into the number of God's people. And when that day comes, then, even as when the cleansed man appeared at the tent of meeting, he presented guilt-offering, sin-offering, and burnt-offering, as the warrant for his presence there, and the ground of his acceptance, so shall it be in that day of resurrection, when every one of God's once leprous but now washed and accepted children shall appear in Zion before Him. They will all appear there as pleading the blood, the precious blood of Christ; Christ, at last apprehended and received by them in all His fulness, as expiation, satisfaction, and righteousness. For so John represents it in the apocalyptic vision of the blood-washed multitude in the heavenly glory (Rev. vii. 14, 15): "These are they which come out of the great tribulation, and they washed their robes, and made them white in the blood of the Lamb. *Therefore* are they before the throne of God; and they serve Him day and night in His temple."

And as it is written (Rom. viii. 11) that the final quickening of our mortal bodies shall be accomplished by the Spirit of God, so the leper, now in God's presence, receives a special anointing; a type of the unction of the Holy Ghost in resurrection power, consecrating the once leprous ear, hand, and foot, and therewith the whole body, now cleansed from all defilement, to the glad service of Jehovah our God and our Redeemer.

Such, in outline at least, appears to be the typical significance of this ceremonial of the cleansing of the leper. Some details are indeed still left unexplained, but, probably, the whole reason for some of the regulations is to be found in the immediate practical necessities of the leper's condition.

Of Leprosy in a Garment or House.

xiii. 47-59; xiv. 33-53.

"The garment also that the plague of leprosy is in, whether it be a woollen garment, or a linen garment; whether it be in warp, or woof; of linen, or of woollen; whether in a skin, or in any thing made of skin; if the plague be greenish or reddish in the garment, or in the skin, or in the warp, or in the woof, or in any thing of skin; it is the plague of leprosy, and shall be shewed unto the priest: and the priest shall look upon the plague, and shut up that which hath the plague seven days: and he shall look on the plague on the seventh day: if the plague be spread in the garment, either in the warp, or in the woof, or in the skin, whatever service skin is used for; the plague is a fretting leprosy; it is unclean. And he shall burn the garment, whether the warp or the woof, in woollen or in linen, or any thing of skin, wherein the plague is: for it is a fretting leprosy; it shall be burnt in the fire. And if the priest shall look, and, behold, the plague be not spread in the garment, either in the warp, or in the woof, or in any thing of skin; then the priest shall command that they wash the thing wherein the plague is, and he shall shut it up seven days more: and the priest shall look, after that the plague is washed: and, behold, if the plague have not changed its colour, and the plague be not spread, it is unclean; thou shalt burn it in the fire: it is a fret, whether the bareness be within or without. And if the priest look, and, behold, the plague be dim after the washing thereof, then he shall rend it out of the garment, or out of the skin, or out of the warp, or out of the woof: and if it appear still in the garment, either in the warp, or in the woof, or in any thing of skin, it is breaking out: thou shalt burn that wherein the plague is with fire. And the garment, either the warp, or the woof, or whatsoever thing of skin it be, which thou shalt wash, if the plague be departed from them, then it shall be washed the second time, and shall be clean. This is the law of the plague of leprosy in a garment of woollen or linen, either in the warp, or the woof, or any thing of skin, to pronounce it clean, or to pronounce it unclean.... And the Lord spake unto Moses and unto Aaron, saying, When ye be come into the land of Canaan, which I give to you for a possession, and I put the plague of leprosy in a house of the land of your possession;

then he that owneth the house shall come and tell the priest, saying, There seemeth to me to be as it were a plague in the house: and the priest shall command that they empty the house, before the priest go in to see the plague, that all that is in the house be not made unclean: and afterward the priest shall go in to see the house: and he shall look on the plague, and, behold, if the plague be in the walls of the house with hollow strakes, greenish or reddish, and the appearance thereof be lower than the wall; then the priest shall go out of the house to the door of the house, and shut up the house seven days: and the priest shall come again the seventh day, and shall look: and, behold, if the plague be spread in the walls of the house; then the priest shall command that they take out the stones in which the plague is, and cast them into an unclean place without the city: and he shall cause the house to be scraped within round about, and they shall pour out the mortar that they scrape off without the city into an unclean place: and they shall take other stones, and put them in the place of those stones; and he shall take other mortar, and shall plaister the house. And if the plague come again, and break out in the house, after that he hath taken out the stones, and after he hath scraped the house, and after it is plaistered; then the priest shall come in and look, and, behold, if the plague be spread in the house, it is a fretting leprosy in the house: it is unclean. And he shall break down the house, the stones of it, and the timber thereof, and all the mortar of the house; and he shall carry them forth out of the city into an unclean place. Moreover he that goeth into the house all the while that it is shut up shall be unclean until the even. And he that lieth in the house shall wash his clothes; and he that eateth in the house shall wash his clothes. And if the priest shall come in, and look, and, behold, the plague hath not spread in the house, after the house was plaistered; then the priest shall pronounce the house clean, because the plague is healed. And he shall take to cleanse the house two birds, and cedar wood, and scarlet, and hyssop: and he shall kill one of the birds in an earthen vessel over running water: and he shall take the cedar wood, and the hyssop, and the scarlet, and the living bird, and dip them in the blood of the slain bird, and in the running water, and sprinkle the house seven times: and he shall cleanse the house with the blood of the bird, and with the running water, and with the living bird, and with the cedar wood, and with the hyssop, and with the scarlet: but he shall let go the living bird out of the city into the open field: so shall he make atonement for the house: and it shall be clean."

There has been much debate as to what we are to understand by the leprosy in the garment or in a house. Was it an affection identical in nature with the leprosy of the body? or was it merely so called from a certain external similarity to that plague?

However extraordinary the former supposition might once have seemed, in the present state of medical science we are at least able to say that there is nothing inconceivable in it. We have abundant experimental evidence that a large number of diseases, and, not improbably, leprosy among them, are caused by minute parasitic forms of vegetable life; and, also, that in many cases these forms of life may, and do, exist and multiply in various other suitable media besides the fluids and tissues of the human body. If, as is quite likely, leprosy be caused by some such parasitic life in the human body, it is then evidently possible that such parasites, under favourable conditions of heat, moisture, etc., should exist and propagate themselves, as in other analogous cases, outside the body; as, for instance, in cloth, or leather, or in the plaster of a house; in which case it is plain that such garments or household implements, or such dwellings, as might be thus infected, would be certainly unwholesome, and presumably capable of communicating the leprosy to the human subject. But we have not yet sufficient scientific observation to settle the question whether this is really so; we can, however, safely say that, in any case, the description which is here given indicates a growth in the affected garment or house of some kind of mould or mildew; which, as we know, is a form of life produced under conditions which always imply an unwholesome state of the article or house in which it appears. We also know that if such growths be allowed to go on unchecked, they involve more or less rapid processes of decomposition in that which is affected. Thus, even from a merely natural point of view, one can see the high wisdom of the Divine King of Israel in ordering that, in all such cases, the man whose garment or house was thus affected should at once notify the priest, who was to come and decide whether the appearance was of a noxious and unclean kind or not, and then take action accordingly.

Whether the suspicious spot were in a house or in some article it contained, the article or house (the latter having been previously emptied) was first shut up for seven days (xiii. 50; xiv. 38). If in the garment or other article affected it was found then to have spread, it was without any further ceremony to be burnt (xiii. 51, 52). If it had not spread, it was to be washed and shut up seven days more, at the end of which time, even though it had not spread, if the greenish or reddish colour remained unchanged, it was still to be adjudged unclean, and to be burned (xiii. 55). If, on the other hand, the colour had somewhat "dimmed," the part affected was to be cut out; when, if it spread no further, it was to be washed a second time, and be pronounced clean (xiii. 58). If, however, after the excision of the affected part, the spot appeared again, the article, without further delay, was to be burned (xiii. 57).

The law, in the case of the appearing of a leprosy in a house (xiv. 33-53), was much more elaborate. As in the former case, when the occupant of the house suspects, "as it were a plague in the house," he is to go and tell the priest; who is, first of all, to order the emptying of the house before he goes in, lest that which is in the house, should it prove to be the plague, be made unclean (ver. 36). The diagnosis reminds us of that of the leprosy in the body; greenish or reddish streaks, in appearance "lower than the wall," *i.e.*, deep-seated (ver. 37). Where this is observed, the empty house is to be shut up for seven days (ver. 38); and at the end of that time, if the spot has spread, "the stones in which the plague is" are to be taken out, the plaster scraped off the walls of the house, and all carried out into an unclean place outside of the city, and new stones and new plaster put in the place of the old (vv. 40-42). If, after this, the plague yet reappear, the house is to be adjudged unclean, and is to be wholly torn down, and all the material carried into an unclean place without the city (vv. 44, 45). If, on the other hand, after this renewal of the interior of the house, the spots do not reappear, the priest "shall pronounce the house clean, because the plague is healed" (ver. 48). But, unlike the case of the leprous garment, this does not end the ceremonial. It is ordered that the priest shall take to cleanse (*lit.* "to purge the house from sin") (ver. 49) two birds, scarlet, cedar, and hyssop, which are then used precisely as in the case of the purgation of the leprous man; and at the end, "he shall let go the living bird out of the city into the open field: so shall he make atonement for the house: and it shall be clean" (vv. 50-53).

For the time then present, one can hardly fail to see in this ceremonial, first, a merciful sanitary intent. By the observance of these regulations not only was Israel to be saved from many sicknesses and various evils, but was to be constantly reminded that Israel's God, like a wise and kind Father, had a care for everything that pertained to their welfare; not only for their persons, but also for their dwellings, and even all the various articles of daily use. The lesson is always in force, for God has not changed. He is not a God who cares for the souls of men only, but for their bodies also, and everything around them. His servants do well to remember this, and in this imitate Him, as happily many are doing more and more. Bibles and tracts are good, and religious exhortation; but we have here left us a Divine warrant not to content ourselves with these things alone, but to have a care for the clothing and the homes of those we would reach with the Gospel. In all the large cities of Christendom it must be confessed that the principle which underlies these laws concerning houses and garments, is often terribly neglected. Whether the veritable plague of leprosy be in the walls of many of our tenement houses or not, there can be no doubt that it could not be much worse if it were; and Christian philanthropy and legislation could scarcely do better in many cases than vigorously to enforce the Levitical law, tear down, re-plaster, or, in many cases, destroy from the foundation, tenement houses, which could, with little exaggeration, be justly described as leprous throughout.

But all which is in this law cannot be thus explained. Even the Israelite must have looked beyond this for the meaning of the ordinance of the two birds, the cedar, scarlet, and hyssop, and the "atonement" for the house. He would have easily perceived that not only leprosy in the body, but this leprosy in the garment and the house, was a sign that both the man himself, and his whole environment as well, was subject to death and decay; that, as already he would have learned from the Book of Genesis, even nature was under a curse because of man's sin; and that, as in the Divine plan, sacrificial cleansing was required for the deliverance of man, so also it was somehow mysteriously required for the cleansing of his earthly abode and surroundings, in default of which purgation they must be destroyed.

And from this to the antitypical truth prefigured by these laws it is but a step; and a step which we take with full New Testament light to guide us. For if the leprosy in the body visibly typified the working of sin and death in the soul of man, then, as clearly, the leprosy in the house must in this law be intended to symbolise the working of sin in the material earthly creation, which is man's abode. The type thus brings before us the truth which is set forth by the Apostle Paul in Rom. viii. 20-22, where we are taught in express words that, not man alone, but the whole creation also, because of sin, has come under a "bondage of corruption." "The creation was subjected to vanity, not of its own will, but by reason of him who subjected it.... For we know that the whole creation groaneth and travaileth in pain together until now." This is one truth which is shadowed forth in this type.

But the type also shows us how, as Scripture elsewhere clearly teaches, if after such partial purgation as was effected by means of the deluge the bondage of corruption still persist, then the abode of man must itself be destroyed; "the earth and the works that are therein shall be burned up" (2 Peter iii. 10). Nothing less than fire will suffice to put an end to the working in material nature of this mysterious curse. And yet beyond the fire is redemption. For the atonement shall avail not only for the leprous man, but for the purifying of the leprous abode. The sprinkling of sacrificial blood and water by means of the cedar, and hyssop, and scarlet, and the living bird, which effected the deliverance of the leper, are used also in the same way and for the same end, for the leprous house. And so "according to his promise, we look for new heavens and a new earth, wherein dwelleth righteousness" (2 Peter iii. 13); and it shall be brought in through the virtue of atonement made by a Saviour slain, and applied by a Saviour alive from the dead; so that, as the free bird flies away in token of the full completion of deliverance from the curse, so "the creation itself also shall be delivered from the bondage of corruption into the liberty of the glory of the children of God" (Rom. viii. 21).

But there was also a leprosy of the garment. If the leprosy in the body typified the effect of sin in the soul, and the leprosy in the house, the effect of sin in the earthly creation, which is man's home; the leprosy of the garment can scarcely typify anything else than the presence and effects of sin in those various relations in life which constitute our present environment. Whenever, in any of these, we suspect the working of sin, first of all we are to lay the case before the heavenly Priest. And then, if He with the "eyes like a flame of fire" (Rev. i. 14; ii. 18) declare anything unclean, then that in which the stain is found must be without hesitation cut out and thrown away. And if still, after this, we find the evil reappearing, then the whole garment must go, fair and good though the most of it may still appear. In other words, those relations and engagements in which, despite all possible care and precaution, we find manifest sin persistently reappearing, as if there were in them, however inexplicably, an ineradicable tendency to evil,—these we must resolutely put away, "hating even the garment spotted by the flesh."

The leprous garment must be burnt. For its restoration or purification the law made no provision. For here, in the antitype, we are dealing with earthly relationships, which have only to do with the present life and order. "The fashion of this world passeth away" (1 Cor. vii. 31). There shall be "new heavens and a new earth," but in that new creation the old environment shall be found no longer. The old garments, even such as were best, shall be no longer used. The redeemed shall walk with the King and Redeemer, clothed in the white robes which He shall give. No more leprosy then in person, house, or garment! For we shall be set before the presence of the Father's glory, without blemish, in exceeding joy, "not having spot, or wrinkle, or any such thing." Wherefore "to the only God our Saviour, through Jesus Christ our Lord, be glory, majesty, dominion and power, before all time, and now, and for evermore. Amen."

CHAPTER XIX
OF HOLINESS IN EATING

Lev. xvii. 1-16.

With this chapter begins another subdivision of the law. Hitherto we have had before us only sacrificial worship and matters of merely ceremonial law. The law of holy living contained in the following chapters (xvii.-xx.), on the other hand, has to do for the most part with matters rather ethical than ceremonial, and consists chiefly of precepts designed to regulate morally the ordinary engagements and relationships of every-day life. The fundamental thought of the four chapters is that which is expressed, *e.g.*, in xviii. 3: Israel, redeemed by Jehovah, is called to be a holy people; and this holiness is to be manifested in a total separation from the ways of the heathen. This principle is enforced by various specific commands and prohibitions, which naturally have particular regard to the special conditions under which Israel was placed, as a holy nation consecrated to Jehovah, the one, true God, but living in the midst of nations of idolaters.

The whole of chapter xvii., with the exception of vv. 8, 9, has to do with the application of this law of holy living to the use even of lawful food. At first thought, the injunctions of the chapter might seem to belong rather to ceremonial than to moral law; but closer observation will show that all the injunctions here given have direct reference to the avoidance of idolatry, especially as connected with the preparation and use of food.

It was not enough that the true Israelite should abstain from food prohibited by God, as in chap. xii.; he must also use that which was permitted in a way well-pleasing to God, carefully shunning even the appearance of any complicity with surrounding idolatry, or fellowship with the heathen in their unholy fashions and customs. Even so for the Christian: it is not enough that he abstain from what is expressly forbidden; even in his use of lawful food, he must so use it that it shall be to him a means of grace, in helping him to maintain an uninterrupted walk with God.

In vv. 1-7 is given the law to regulate the use of such clean animals for food as could be offered to God in sacrifice; in vv. 10-16, of such as, although permitted for food, were not allowed for sacrifice.

The directions regarding the first class may be summed up in this: all such animals were to be treated as peace-offerings. No private person in Israel was to slaughter any such animal anywhere in the camp or out of it, except at the door of the tent of meeting. Thither they were to be brought "unto the priest," and offered for peace-offerings (ver. 5); the blood must be sprinkled on the altar of burnt-offering; the fat parts burnt "for a sweet savour unto the Lord" (ver. 6); and then only, the priest having first taken his appointed portions, the remainder might now be eaten by the Israelite, as given back to him by God, in peaceful fellowship with Him.

The law could not have been burdensome, as some might hastily imagine. Even when obtainable, meat was probably not used as food by them so freely as with us; and in the wilderness the lack of flesh, it will be remembered, was so great as to have occasioned at one time a rebellion among the people, who fretfully complained (Numb. xi. 4): "Who shall give us flesh to eat?"

Even the uncritical reader must be able to see how manifest is the Mosaic date of this part of Leviticus. The terms of this law suppose a camp-life; indeed, the camp is explicitly named (ver. 3). That which was enjoined was quite practicable under the conditions of life in the wilderness, when, at the best, flesh was scarce, and the people dwelt compactly together; but would have been utterly inapplicable and impracticable at a later date, after they were settled throughout the land of Canaan, when to have slaughtered all beasts used for food at the central sanctuary would have been impossible. Hence we find that, as we should expect, the modified law of Deuteronomy (xii. 15, 16, 20-24), assuming the previous existence of this earlier law, explicitly repeals it. To suppose that forgers of a later day, as, for instance, of the time of Josiah, or after the Babylonian exile, should have needlessly invented a law of this kind, is an hypothesis which is rightly characterised by Dillmann as "simply absurd."[30]

This regulation for the wilderness days is said (vv. 5, 7) to have been made "to the end that the children of Israel may bring their sacrifices, which they sacrifice in the open field ... unto the Lord, ... and sacrifice them for sacrifices of peace offerings unto the Lord.... And they shall no more sacrifice their sacrifices unto the he-goats, after whom they go a whoring."

There can be no doubt that in the last sentence, "he-goats," as in the Revised Version, instead of "devils," as in the Authorised, is the right rendering. The worship referred to was still in existence in the days of the monarchy; for it is included in the charges against "Jeroboam, the son of Nebat, who made Israel to sin" (2 Chron. xi. 15), that "he appointed him priests, ... for the he-goats, and for the calves which he had made." Nor can here we agree with Dillmann[31] that in this worship of he-goats here referred to, there is "no occasion to think of the goat-worship of Egypt." For inasmuch as we know that the worship of the sacred bull and that of the he-goat prevailed in Egypt in those days, and inasmuch as in Ezekiel xx. 6, 7, 15-18, repeated reference is made to Israel's having worshipped "the idols of Egypt," one can hardly avoid combining these two facts, and thus connecting the goat-worship to which allusion is here made, with that which prevailed at Mendes, in Lower Egypt. This cult at that place was accompanied with nameless revolting rites, such as give special significance to the description of this worship (ver. 7) as "a whoring" after the goats; and abundantly explain and justify the severity of the penalty attached to the violation of this law (ver. 4) in cutting off the offender from this people; all the more when we observe the fearful persistency of this horrible goat-worship in Israel, breaking out anew, as just remarked, some five hundred years later, in the reign of Jeroboam.

The words imply that the ordinary slaughter of animals for food was often connected with some idolatrous ceremony related to this goat-worship. What precisely it may have been, we know not; but of such customs, connecting the preparation of the daily food with idolatry, we have abundant illustration in the usages of the ancient Persians, the Hindoos, and the heathen Arabs of the days before Mohammed. The law was thus intended to cut out this every-day idolatry by the root. With these "field-devils," as Luther renders the word, the holy people of the Lord were to have nothing to do.

Very naturally, the requirement to present all slaughtered animals as peace-offerings to Jehovah gives occasion to turn aside for a little from the matter of food, which is the chief subject of the chapter, in order to extend this principle beyond animals slaughtered for food, and insist particularly that all burnt-offerings and sacrifices of every kind should be sacrificed at the door of the tent of meeting, and nowhere else. This law, we are told (ver. 8), was to be applied, not only to the Israelites themselves, but also to "strangers" among them; such as, *e.g.*, were the Gibeonites. No idolatry, nor anything likely to be associated with it, was to be tolerated from any one in the holy camp.

The principle which underlies this stringent law, as also the reason which is given for it, is of constant application in modern life. There was nothing wrong in itself in slaying an animal in one place more than another. It was abstractly possible—as, likely enough, many an Israelite may have said to himself—that a man could just as really "eat unto the Lord" if he slaughtered and ate his animal in the field, as anywhere else. Nevertheless this was forbidden under the heaviest penalties. It teaches us that he who will be holy must not only abstain from that which is in itself always wrong, but must carefully keep himself from doing even lawful or necessary things in such a way, or under such associations and circumstances, as may outwardly compromise his Christian standing, or which may be proved by experience to have an almost unavoidable tendency toward sin. The laxity in such matters which prevails in the so-called "Christian world" argues little for the tone of spiritual life in our day in those who indulge in it, or allow it, or apologise for it. It may be true enough, in a sense, that as many say, there is no harm in this or that. Perhaps not; but what if experience have shown that, though in itself not sinful, a certain association or amusement almost always tends to worldliness, which is a form of idolatry? Or—to use the apostle's illustration—what if one be seen, though with no intention of wrong, "sitting at meat in an idol's temple," and he whose conscience is weak be thereby emboldened to do what to him is sin? There is only one safe principle, now as in the days of Moses: everything must be brought "before the Lord;" used as from Him and for Him, and therefore used under such limitations and restrictions as His wise and holy law imposes. Only so shall we be safe; only so abide in living fellowship with God.

Very beautiful and instructive, again, was the direction that the Israelite, in the cases specified, should make his daily food a peace-offering. This involved a dedication of the daily food to the Lord; and in his receiving it back again then from the hand of God, the truth was visibly represented that our daily food is from God; while also, in the sacrificial acts which preceded the eating, the Israelite was continually reminded that it was upon the ground of an accepted atonement that even these every-day mercies were received. Such also should be, in spirit, the often neglected prayer before each of our daily meals. It should be ever offered with the remembrance of the precious blood which has purchased for us even the most common mercies; and should thus sincerely recognise what, in the confusing complexity of the second causes through which we receive our daily food, we so easily forget: that the Lord's prayer is not a mere form of words when we say, "Give us this day our daily bread;" but that working behind, and in, and with, all these second causes, is the kindly Providence of God, who, opening His hand, supplies the want of every living thing. And so, eating in grateful, loving fellowship with our Heavenly Father that which His bounty gives us, to His glory, every meal shall become, as it were, a sacramental remembrance of the Lord. We may have wondered at what we have read of the world-wide custom of the Mohammedan, who, whenever the knife of slaughter is lifted against a beast for food, utters his "*Bism allàh*," "In the name of the most merciful God;" and not otherwise will regard his food as being made *halàl*, or "lawful;" and, no doubt, in all this, as in many a Christian's prayer, there may often be little heart. But the thought in this ceremony is even this of Leviticus, and we do well to make it our own, eating even our daily food "in the name of the most merciful God," and with uplifting of the heart in thankful worship toward Him.

But there were many beasts which, although they might not be offered to the Lord in sacrifice, were yet "clean," and permitted to the Israelites as food. Such, in particular, were clean animals that are taken in the hunt or chase. In vv. 10-16 the law is given for the use of these. It is prefaced by a very full and explicit prohibition of the eating of blood;[32] for while, as regards the animals to be offered to the Lord, provision was made with respect to the blood, that it was to be sprinkled around the altar, there was the danger that in other cases, where this was not permissible, the blood might be used for food. Hence the prohibition against eating "any manner of blood," on a twofold ground: first (vv. 11, 14), that the life of the flesh is the blood; and second (ver. 11), that, for this reason, God had chosen the blood to be the symbol of life substituted for the life of the guilty in atoning sacrifice: "I have given it to you upon the altar to make atonement for your souls." Hence, in order that this relation of the blood to the forgiveness of sins might be constantly kept before the mind, it was ordained that never should the Israelite eat of flesh except the blood should first have been carefully drained out. And it was to be treated with reverence, as having thus a certain sanctity; when the beast was taken in hunting, the Israelite must (ver. 13) "pour out the blood thereof, and cover it with dust;"—an act by which the blood, the life, was symbolically returned to Him who in the beginning said (Gen. i. 24), "Let the earth bring forth the living creature after its kind." And because, in the case of "that which dieth of itself," or is "torn of beasts," the blood would not be thus carefully drained off, all such animals (ver. 15) are prohibited as food.

It is profoundly instructive to observe that here, again, we come upon declarations and a command, the deep truth and fitness of which is only becoming clear now after three thousand years. For, as the result of our modern discoveries with regard to the constitution of the blood, and the exact nature of its functions, we in this day are able to say that it is not far from a scientific statement of the facts, when we read (ver. 14), "As to the life of all flesh, the blood thereof is all one with the life thereof." For it is in just this respect that the blood is most distinct from all other parts of the body; that, whereas it conveys and mediates nourishment to all, it is itself nourished by none; but by its myriad cells brought immediately in contact with the digested food, directly and immediately assimilates it to itself. We are compelled to say that as regards the physical life of man—which alone is signified by the original term here—it is certainly true of the blood, as of no other part of the organism, that "the life of all flesh is the blood thereof."

And while it is true that, according to the text, a spiritual and moral reason is given for the prohibition of the use of blood as food, yet it is well worth noting that, as has been already remarked in another connection, the prohibition, as we are now beginning to see, had also a hygienic reason. For Dr. de Mussy, in his paper before the French Academy of Medicine already referred to, calls attention to the fact that, not only did the Mosaic laws exclude from the Hebrew dietary animals "particularly liable to parasites;" but also that "it is in the blood," so rigidly prohibited by Moses as food, "that the germs or spores of infectious disease circulate." Surely no one need fear, with some expositors, lest this recognition of a sanitary intent in these laws shall hinder the recognition of their moral and spiritual purport, which in this chapter is so expressly taught. Rather should this cause us the more to wonder and admire the unity which thus appears between the demands and necessities of the physical and the moral and spiritual life; and, in the discovery of the marvellous adaptation of these ancient laws to the needs of both, to find a new confirmation of our faith in God and in His revealed Word. For thus do they appear to be laws so far beyond the wisdom of that time, and so surely beneficent in their working, that in view of this it should be easy to believe that it must indeed have been the Lord God, the Maker and Preserver of all flesh, who spake all these laws unto His servant Moses.

The moral and spiritual purpose of this law concerning the use of blood was apparently twofold. In the first place, it was intended to educate the people to a reverence for life, and purify them from that tendency to bloodthirstiness which has so often distinguished heathen nations, and especially those with whom Israel was to be brought in closest contact. But secondly, and chiefly, it was intended, as in the former part of the chapter, everywhere and always to keep before the mind the sacredness of the blood as being the appointed means for the expiation of sin; given by God upon the altar to make atonement for the soul of the sinner, "by reason of the life" or soul with which it stood in such immediate relation. Not only were they therefore to abstain from the blood of such animals as could be offered on the altar, but even from that of those which could not be offered. Thus the blood was to remind them, every time that they ate flesh, of the very solemn truth that without shedding of blood there was no remission of sin. The Israelite must never forget this; even in the heat and excitement of the chase, he must pause and carefully drain the blood from the creature he had slain, and reverently cover it with dust;—a symbolic act which should ever put him in mind of the Divine ordinance that the blood, the life, of a guiltless victim must be given, in order to the forgiveness of sin.

A lesson lies here for us regarding the sacredness of all that is associated with sacred things. All that is connected with God, and with His worship, especially all that is connected with His revelation of Himself for our salvation, is to be treated with the most profound reverence. Even though the blood of the deer killed in the chase could not be used in sacrifice, yet, because it was blood, was in its essential nature like unto that which was so used, therefore it must be treated with a certain respect, and be always covered with earth. It is the fashion of our age—and one which is increasing in an alarming degree—to speak lightly of things which are closely connected with the revelation and worship of the holy God. Against everything of this kind the spirit of this law warns us. Nothing which is associated in any way with what is sacred is to be spoken of or treated irreverently, lest we thus come to think lightly of the sacred things themselves. This irreverent treatment of holy things is a crying evil in many parts of the English-speaking world, as also in continental Christendom. We need to beware of it. After irreverence, too often, by no obscure law, comes open denial of the Holy One and of His holy Son, our Lord and Saviour. The blood of Christ, which represented that holy life which was given on the cross for our sins, is holy—an infinitely holy thing! And what is God's estimate of its sanctity we may perhaps learn—looking through the symbol to that which was symbolised—from this law; which required that all blood, because outwardly resembling the holy blood of sacrifice, and, like it, the seat and vehicle of life, should be treated with most careful reverence. And it is safe to say that just those most need the lesson taught by this command who find it the hardest to appreciate it, and to whom its injunctions still seem regulations puerile and unworthy, according to their fancy, of the dignity and majesty of God.

CHAPTER XX
THE LAW OF HOLINESS: CHASTITY

Lev. xviii. 1-30.

Chapters xviii., xix., and xx., by a formal introduction (xviii. 1-5) and a formal closing (xx. 22-26), are indicated as a distinct section, very commonly known by the name, "the Law of Holiness." As this phrase indicates, these chapters—unlike chap. xvii., which as to its contents has a character intermediate between the ceremonial and moral law—consist substantially of moral prohibitions and commandments throughout. Of the three, the first two contain the prohibitions and precepts of the law; the third (xx.), the penal sanctions by which many of these were to be enforced.

The section opens (vv. 1, 2) with Jehovah's assertion of His absolute supremacy, and a reminder to Israel of the fact that He had entered into covenant relations with them: "I am the Lord your God." With solemn emphasis the words are again repeated, ver. 4; and yet again in ver. 5: "I am the Lord."[34] They would naturally call to mind the scene at Sinai, with its august and appalling grandeur, attesting amid earthquake and fire and tempest at once the being, power, and unapproachable holiness of Him who then and there, with those stupendous solemnities, in inexplicable condescension, took Israel into covenant with Himself, to be to Himself "a kingdom of priests and a holy nation." There could be no question as to the right of the God thus revealed to impose law; no question as to the peculiar obligation upon Israel to keep His law; no question as to His intolerance of sin, and full power and determination, as the Holy One, to enforce whatever He commanded. All these thoughts—thoughts of eternal moment—would be called up in the mind of every devout Israelite, as he heard or read this preface to the law of holiness.

The prohibitions which we find in chap. xviii. are not given as an exhaustive code of laws upon the subjects traversed, but rather deal with certain gross offences against the law of chastity, which, as we know from other sources, were horribly common at that time among the surrounding nations. To indulge in these crimes, Israel, as the later history sadly shows, would be especially liable; so contagious are evil example and corrupt associations! Hence the general scope of the chapter is announced in this form (ver. 3): "After the doings of the land of Egypt, wherein ye dwelt, shall ye not do: and after the doings of the land of Canaan, whither I bring you, shall ye not do: neither shall ye walk in their statutes."

Instead of this, they were (ver. 4) to do God's judgments, and keep His statutes, to walk in them, bearing in mind whose they were. And as a further motive it is added (ver. 5): "which if a man do, he shall live in them;" that is, as the Chaldee paraphrast, Onkelos, rightly interprets in the Targum, "with the life of eternity." Which far-reaching promise is sealed by the repetition, for the third time, of the words, "I am the Lord." That is enough; for what Jehovah promises, that shall certainly be!

The law begins (ver. 6) with a general statement of the principle which underlies all particular prohibitions of incest: "None of you shall approach to any that is near of kin to him, to uncover their nakedness;" and then, for the fourth time, are iterated the words, "I am the Lord." The prohibitions which follow require little special explanation. As just remarked, they are directed in particular to those breaches of the law of chastity which were most common with the Egyptians, from the midst of whom Israel had come; and with the Canaanites, to whose land they were going. This explains, for instance, the fulness of detail in the prohibition of incestuous union with a sister or half-sister (vv. 9, 11),—an iniquity very common in Egypt, having the sanction of royal custom from the days of the Pharaohs down to the time of the Ptolemies. The unnatural alliance of a man with his mother, prohibited in ver. 8, of which Paul declared (1 Cor. v. 1) that in his day it did not exist among the Gentiles, was yet the distinguishing infamy of the Medes and Persians for many centuries. Union with an aunt, by blood or by marriage, prohibited in vv. 12-14,—a connection less gross, and less severely to be punished than the preceding,—seems to have been permitted even among the Israelites themselves while in Egypt, as is plain from the case of Amram and Jochebed (Exod. vi. 20). To the law forbidding connection with a brother's wife (ver. 16), the later Deuteronomic law (Deut. xxv. 5-10), made an exception, permitting that a man might marry the widow of his deceased brother, when the latter had died without children, and "raise up seed unto his brother." In this, however, the law but sanctioned a custom which—as we learn from the case of Onan (Gen. xxxviii.)—had been observed long before the days of Moses, both by the Hebrews and other ancient nations, and, indeed, even limited and restricted its application; with good reason providing for exemption of the surviving brother from this duty, in cases where for any reason it might be repugnant or impracticable.

The case of a connection with both a woman and her daughter or granddaughter is next mentioned (ver. 17); and, with special emphasis, is declared to be "wickedness," or "enormity."

The prohibition (ver. 18) of marriage with a sister-in-law, as is well known, has been, and still is, the occasion of much controversy, into which it is not necessary here to enter at length. But, whatever may be thought for other reasons as to the lawfulness of such a union, it truly seems quite singular that this verse should ever have been cited as prohibiting such an alliance. No words could well be more explicit than those which we have here, in limiting the application of the prohibition to the life-time of the wife: "Thou shalt not take a woman to her sister, *to be a rival to her*, to uncover her nakedness, beside the other *in her life time*" (R.V.). The law therefore does not touch the question for which it is so often cited, but was evidently only intended as a restriction on prevalent polygamy. Polygamy is ever likely to produce jealousies and heart-burnings; but it is plain that this phase of the evil would reach its most extreme and odious expression when the new and rival wife was a sister to the one already married; when it would practically annul sisterly love, and give rise to such painful and peculiarly humiliating dissensions as we read of between the sisters Leah and Rachel. The sense of the passage is so plain, that we are told that this interpretation "stood its ground unchallenged from the third century B.C. to the middle of the sixteenth century *A.D.*" Whatever opinion any may hold therefore as to the expediency, upon other grounds, of this much debated alliance, this passage, certainly, cannot be fairly cited as forbidding it; but is far more naturally understood as by natural implication permitting the union, after the decease of the first wife. The laws concerning incest therefore terminate with ver. 17; and ver. 18, according to this interpretation, must be regarded as a restriction upon polygamous connections, as ver. 19 is upon the rights of marriage.

It seems somewhat surprising that the question should have been raised, even theoretically, whether the Mosaic law, as regards the degrees of affinity prohibited in marriage, is of permanent authority. The reasons for these prohibitions, wherever given, are as valid now as then; for the simple reason that they are grounded fundamentally in a matter of fact,—namely, the nature of the relation between husband and wife, whereby they become "one flesh," implied in such phraseology as we find in ver. 16; and also the relation of blood between members of the same family, as in vv. 10, etc. Happily, however, whatever theory any may have held, the Church in all ages has practically recognised every one of these prohibitions, as binding on all persons; and has rather been inclined to err, if at all, by extending, through inference and analogy, the prohibited degrees even beyond the

Mosaic code. So much, however, by way of guarding against excess in such inferential extensions of the law, we must certainly say: according to the law itself, as further applied in chap. xxi. 1-4, and limited in Deut. xxv. 5-10, relationship by marriage is not to be regarded as precisely equivalent in degree of affinity to relationship by blood. We cannot, for instance, conceive that, under any circumstances, the prohibition of the marriage of brothers and sisters should have had any exception; and yet, as we have seen, the marriage between brother and sister-in-law is explicitly authorised, in the case of the levirate marriage, and by implication allowed in other cases, by the language of ver. 18 of this chapter.

But in these days, when there is such a manifest inclination in Christendom, as especially in the United States and in France, to ignore the law of God in regard to marriage and divorce, and regulate these instead by a majority vote, it assuredly becomes peculiarly imperative that, as Christians, we exercise a holy jealousy for the honour of God and the sanctity of the family, and ever refuse to allow a majority vote any authority in these matters, where it contravenes the law of God. While we must observe caution that in these things we lay no burden on the conscience of any, which God has not first placed there, we must insist—all the more strenuously because of the universal tendency to license—upon the strict observance of all that is either explicitly taught or by necessary implication involved in the teachings of God's Word upon this question. Nothing more fundamentally concerns the well-being of society than the relation of the man and the woman in the constitution of the family; and while, unfortunately, in our modern democratic communities, the Church may not be able always to control and determine the civil law in these matters, she can at least utterly refuse any compromise where the civil law ignores what God has spoken; and with unwavering firmness deny her sanction, in any way, to any connection between a man and a woman which is not according to the revealed will of God, as set before us in this most holy, good, and beneficent law.

The chapter before us casts a light upon the moral condition of the most cultivated heathen peoples in those days, among whom many of the grossest of these incestuous connections, as already remarked, were quite common, even among those of the highest station. There are many in our day more or less affected with the present fashion of admiration for the ancient (and modern) heathenisms, who would do well to heed this light, that their blind enthusiasm might thereby be somewhat tempered.

On the other hand, these laws show us, in a very striking contrast, the estimate which God puts upon the maintenance of holiness, purity, and chastity between man and woman; and His very jealous regard for the sanctity of the family in all its various relations. Even in the Old Testament we have hints of a reason for this, deeper than mere expediency,—hints which receive a definite form in the clearer teaching of the New Testament, which tells us that in the Divine plan it is ordained that in these earthly relations man shall be the shadow and image of God. If, as the Apostle tells us (Eph. iii. 15, R.V.), "every family in heaven and on earth" is named from the Father; and if, as he again teaches (Eph. v. 29-32), the relation of husband and wife is intended to be an earthly type and symbol of the relation between the Lord Jesus Christ and His Church, which is His Bride,—then we cannot wonder at the exceedingly strong emphasis which marks these prohibitions. Everything must be excluded which would be incompatible with this holy ideal of God for man; that not only in the constitution of his person, but in these sacred relations which belong to his very nature, as created male and female, he should be the image of the invisible God.

Thus, he who is a father is ever to bear in mind that in his fatherhood he is appointed to shadow forth the ineffable mystery of the eternal relation of the only-begotten and most holy Son to this everlasting Father. As husband, the man is to remember that since he who is joined to his wife becomes with her "one flesh," therefore this union becomes, in the Divine ordination, a type and pattern of the yet more mysterious union of life between the Son of God and the Church, which is His Bride. As brothers and sisters, again, the children of God are to remember that brotherly love, in its purity and unselfish devotion, is intended of God to be a living illustration of the love of Him who has been made of God to be "the firstborn among many brethren" (Rom. viii. 29). And thus, with the family life pervaded through and through by these ideas, will license and impurity be made impossible, and, as happily now in many a Christian home, it will appear that the family, no less truly than the Church, is appointed of God to be a sanctuary of purity in a world impure and corrupt by wicked works, and, no less really than the Church, to be an effective means of Divine grace, and of preparation for the eternal life of the heavenly kingdom, when all of God's "many sons" shall have been brought to glory, the "many brethren" of the First-Begotten, to abide with Him in the Father's house for ever and ever.

After the prohibition of adultery in ver. 20, we have what at first seems like a very abrupt introduction of a totally different subject; for ver. 21 refers, not to the seventh, but to the second, and, therewith also, to the sixth commandment. It reads: "Thou shalt not give any of thy seed to make them pass through the fire to Molech, neither shalt thou profane the name of thy God."

But the connection of thought is found in the historical relation of the licentious practices prohibited in the preceding verses to idolatry, of which this Molech-worship is named as one of the most hideous manifestations. Some, indeed, have supposed that this frequently recurring phrase does not designate an actual sacrifice of the children, but only their consecration to Molech by some kind of fire-baptism. But certainly such passages as 2 Kings xvii. 31, Jer. vii. 31, xix. 5, distinctly require us to understand an actual offering of the children as "burnt-offerings." They were not indeed burnt alive, as a late and untrustworthy tradition has it, but were first slain, as in the case of all burnt-sacrifices, and then burnt. The unnatural cruelty of the sacrifice, even as thus made, was such, that both here and in xx. 3 it is described as in a special sense a "profaning" of God's holy name,—a profanation, in that it represented Him, the Lord of love and fatherly mercy, as requiring such a cruel and unnatural sacrifice of parental love, in the immolation of innocent children.

The inconceivably unnatural crimes prohibited in vv. 22, 23 were in like manner essentially connected with idolatrous worship: the former with the worship of Astarte or Ashtoreth; the latter with the worship of the he-goat at Mendes in Egypt, as the symbol of the generative power in nature. What a hideous perversion of the moral sense was involved in these crimes, as thus connected with idolatrous worship, is illustrated strikingly by the fact that men and women, thus prostituted to the service of false gods, were designated by the terms *qádesh* and *qádesháh*, "sacred," "holy"![35] No wonder that the sacred writer brands these horrible crimes as, in a peculiar and almost solitary sense, "abomination," "confusion."

In these days of ours, when it has become the fashion among a certain class of cultured writers—who would still, in many instances, apparently desire to be called Christian—to act as the apologists of idolatrous, and, according to Holy Scripture, false religions, the mention of these crimes in this connection may well remind the reader of what such seem to forget, as they certainly ignore; namely, that in all ages, in the modern heathenism no less than in the ancient, idolatry and gross licentiousness ever go hand in hand. Still, to-day, even in Her Majesty's Indian Empire, is the most horrible licentiousness practised as an office of religious worship. Nor are such revolting perversions of the moral sense confined to the "Maharájás" of the temples in Western India, who figured in certain trials in Bombay a few years ago; for even the modern "reformed" Hindooism, from which some hope so much, has not always been able to shake itself free from the pollution of these things, as witness the argument conducted in recent numbers of the *Árya Patriká* of Lahore, to justify the infamous custom known as *Niyoga*, practised to this day in India, *e.g.*, by the Panday Brahmans of Allahabad;—a practice which is sufficiently described as being adultery arranged for, under certain conditions, by a wife or husband, the one for the other. One would fain charitably hope, if possible, that our modern apologists for Oriental idolatries are unaccountably ignorant of what all history should have taught them as to the inseparable connection between idolatry and licentiousness. Both Egypt and Canaan, in the olden time,—as this chapter with all contemporaneous history teaches,—and also India in modern times, read us a very awful lesson on this subject. Not only have these idolatries led too often to gross licentiousness of life, but in their full development they have, again and again, in audacious and blasphemous profanation of the most holy God, and defiance even of the natural conscience, given to the most horrible excesses of unbridled lust the supreme sanction of declaring them to be religious obligations. Assuredly, in God's sight, it cannot be a trifling thing for any man, even through ignorance, to extol, or even apologise for, religions with which such enormities are both logically and historically connected. And so, in these stern prohibitions, and their heavy penal sanctions, we may find a profitable lesson for even the cultivated intellect of the nineteenth century!

The chapter closes with reiterated charges against indulgence in any of these abominations. Israel is told (vv. 25, 28) that it was because the Canaanites practised these enormities that God was about to scourge them out of their land;—a judicial reason which, one would think, should have some weight with those whose sympathies are so drawn out with commiseration for the Canaanites, that they find it impossible to believe that it can be true, as we are told in the Pentateuch, that God ordered their extermination. Rather, in the light of the facts, would we raise the opposite question: whether, if God indeed be a holy and righteous Governor among the nations, He could do anything else either in justice toward the Canaanites, or in mercy toward those whom their horrible example would certainly in like manner corrupt, than, in one way or another, effect the extermination of such a people?

Israel is then solemnly warned (ver. 28) that if they, notwithstanding, shall practise these crimes, God will not spare them any more than He spared the Canaanites. No covenant of His with them shall hinder the land from spueing them out in like manner. And though the nation, as a whole, give not itself to these things, each individual is warned (ver. 29), "Whosoever shall commit any of these abominations, even the souls that do them shall be cut off from among their people;" that is, shall be outlawed and shut out from all participation in covenant mercies. And therewith this part of the law of holiness closes, with those pregnant words, repeated now in this chapter for the fifth time: "I am the Lord (Heb. Jehovah) your God!"

CHAPTER XXI
THE LAW OF HOLINESS (CONCLUDED)

Lev. xix. 1-37.

We have in this chapter a series of precepts and prohibitions which from internal evidence appear to have been selected by an inspired redactor of the canon from various original documents, with the purpose, not of presenting a complete enumeration of all moral and ceremonial duties, but of illustrating the application in the everyday life of the Israelite of the injunction which stands at the beginning of the chapter (ver. 2): "Ye shall be holy: for I the Lord your God am holy."

Truly strange it is, in the full light of Hebrew history, to find any one, like Kalisch, representing this conception of holiness, so fundamental to this law, as the "ripest fruit of Hebrew culture"! For it is insisted by such competent critics, as Dillmann, that we have not in this chapter a late development of Hebrew thought, but "ancient," "the most ancient" material;[36]—we shall venture to say, dating even from the days of Moses, as is declared in ver. 1. And we may say more. For if such be the antiquity of this law, it should be easy even for the most superficial reader of the history to see how immeasurably far was that horde of almost wholly uncultured fugitives from Egyptian bondage from having attained through any culture this Mosaic conception of holiness. For "Hebrew culture," even in its latest maturity, has, at the best, only tended to develop more and more the idea, not of holiness, but of legality,—a very different thing! The ideal expressed in this command, "Ye shall be holy," must have come, not from Israel, not even from Moses, as if originated by him, but from the Holy God Himself, even as the chapter in its first verse testifies.

The position of this command at the head of the long list of precepts which follows, is most significant and instructive. It sets before us the object of the whole ceremonial and moral law, and, we may add, the supreme object of the Gospel also, namely, to produce a certain type of moral and spiritual character, a HOLY manhood; it, moreover, precisely interprets this term, so universally misunderstood and misapplied among all nations, as essentially consisting in a spiritual likeness to God: "Ye shall be holy: for I the Lord your God am holy." These words evidently at once define holiness and declare the supreme motive to the attainment and maintenance of a holy character. This then is brought before us as the central thought in which all the diverse precepts and prohibitions which follow find their unity; and, accordingly, we find this keynote of the whole law echoing, as it were, all through this chapter, in the constant refrain, repeated herein no less than fourteen—twice seven—times: "I am the Lord (Heb. Jehovah)!" "I am the Lord your God!"

The first division of the law of holiness which follows (vv. 3-8), deals with two duties of fundamental importance in the social and the religious life: the one, honour to parents; the other, reverence to God.

If we are surprised, at first, to see this place of honour in the law of holiness given to the fifth commandment (ver. 3), our surprise will lessen when we remember how, taking the individual in the development of his personal life, he learns to fear God, first of all, through fearing and honouring his parents. In the earliest beginnings of life, the parent—to speak with reverence—stands to his child, in a very peculiar sense, for and in the place of God. We gain the conception of the Father in heaven first from our experience of fatherhood on earth; and so it may be said of this commandment, in a sense in which it cannot be said of any other, that it is the foundation of all religion. Alas for the child who contemns the instruction of his father and the command of his mother! for by so doing he puts himself out of the possibility of coming into the knowledge and experience of the Fatherhood of God.

The principle of reverence toward God is inculcated, not here by direct precept, but by three injunctions, obedience to which presupposes the fear of God in the heart. These are, first (ver. 3), the keeping of the sabbaths; the possessive, "My sabbaths," reminding us tersely of God's claim upon the seventh part of all our time as His time. Then is commanded the avoidance of idolatry (ver. 4); and, lastly (vv. 5-8), a charge as to the observance of the law of the peace-offering.

One reason seems to have determined the selection of each of these three injunctions, namely, that Israel would be more liable to fail in obedience to these than perhaps any other duties of the law. As for the sabbath, this, like the law of the peace-offering, was a positive, not a moral law; that is, it depended for its authority primarily on the explicit ordinance of God, instead of the intuition of the natural conscience. Hence it was certain that it would only be kept in so far as man retained a vivid consciousness of the Divine personality and moral authority. Moreover, as all history has shown, the law of the sabbath rest from labour constantly comes into conflict with man's love of gain and eager haste to make money. It is a life-picture, true for men of every generation, when Amos (viii. 5) brings before us the Israelites of his day as saying, in their insatiate worldly greed, "When will the sabbath be gone, that we may set forth wheat?" As regards the selection of the second commandment, one can easily see that Israel's loyalty, surrounded as they were on every side with idolaters, was to be tested with peculiar severity on this point, whether they would indeed worship the living God alone and without the intervention of idols.

The circumstances, as regards the peace-offering, were different; but the same principle of choice can be discovered in this also. For among all the various ordinances of sacrificial worship there was none in which the requisitions of the law were more likely to be neglected; partly because these were the most frequent of all offerings, and also because the Israelite would often be tempted, through a short-sighted economy and worldly thriftiness, to use the meat of the peace-offering for food, if any remained until the third day, instead of burning it, in such case, as the Lord commanded. Hence the reminder of the law on this subject, teaching that he who will be holy must not seek to save at the expense of obedience to the holy God.

The second section of this chapter (vv. 9-18) consists of five groups, each of five precepts, all relating to duties which the law of holiness requires from man to man, and each of them closing with the characteristic and impressive refrain, "I am the Lord."

The first of these pentads (vv. 9, 10) requires habitual care for the poor: we read, "Thou shalt not wholly reap the corners of thy field, neither shalt thou gather the gleaning of thy harvest. And thou shalt not glean thy vineyard, neither shalt thou gather the fallen fruit of thy vineyard; thou shalt leave them for the poor and for the stranger."

The law covers the three chief products of their agriculture: the grain, the product of the vine, and the fruit of the trees,—largely olive-trees, which were often planted in the vineyard. So often as God blessed them with the harvest, they were to remember the poor, and also "the stranger," who according to the law could have a legal claim to no land in Israel. Apart from the benefit to the poor, one can readily see what an admirable discipline against man's natural selfishness, and in loyalty to God, this regulation, faithfully observed, must have been. Behind these commands lies the principle, elsewhere explicitly expressed (xxv. 23), that the land which the Israelite tilled was not his own, but the Lord's; and it is as the Owner of the land that He thus charges them that as His tenants they shall not regard themselves as entitled to everything that the land produces, but bear in mind that He intends a portion of every acre of each Israelite to be reserved for the poor. And so the labourer in the harvest-field was continually reminded that in his husbandry he was merely God's steward, bound to apply the product of the land, the use of which was given him, in such a way as should please the Lord.

If the law is not in force as to the letter, let us not forget that it is of full validity as to its spirit. God is still the God of the poor and needy; and we are still every one, as truly as the Hebrew in those days, the stewards of God. And the poor we have with us always; perhaps never more than in these days, in which so great masses of helpless humanity are crowded together in our immense cities, did the cry of the poor and needy so ascend to heaven. And that the Apostles, acting under Divine direction, and abolishing the letter of the theocratic law, yet steadily maintained the spirit and intention of that law in care for the poor, is testified with abundant fulness in the New Testament. One of the firstfruits of Pentecost in the lives of believers was just this, that "all that believed ... had all things common" (Acts ii. 44, 45), so that, going even beyond the letter of the old law, "they sold their possessions and goods, and parted them to all, according as any man had need." And the one only charge which the Apostles at Jerusalem gave unto Paul is reported by him in these words (Gal. ii. 10): "Only they would that we should remember the poor; which very thing I was also zealous to do." Let the believer then remember this who has plenty: the corners of his fields are to be kept for the poor, and the gleanings of his vineyards; and let the believer also take the peculiar comfort from this law, if he is poor, that God, his heavenly Father, has a kindly care, not merely for his spiritual wants, but also for his temporal necessities.

The second pentad (vv. 11, 12) in the letter refers to three of the ten commandments, but is really concerned, primarily, with stealing and defrauding; for the lying and false swearing is here regarded only as commonly connected with theft and fraud, because often necessary to secure the result of a man's plunder. The pentad is in this form: "Ye shall not steal; neither shall ye deal falsely, nor lie one to another. And ye shall not swear by My name falsely, so that thou profane the name of thy God: I am the Lord!"

Close upon stinginess and the careless greed which neglects the poor, with eager grasping after the last grape on the vine, follows the active effort to get, not only the uttermost that might by any stretch of charity be regarded as our own, but also to get something more that belongs to our neighbour. There is thus a very close connection in thought, as well as in position, in these two groups of precepts. And the sequence of thought in this group suggests what is, indeed, markedly true of stealing, but also of other sins. Sin rarely goes alone; one sin, by almost a necessity, leads straight on to another sin. He who steals, or deals falsely in regard to anything committed to his trust, will most naturally be led on at once to lie about it; and when his lie is challenged, as it is likely to be, he is impelled by a fatal pressure to go yet further, and fortify his lie, and consummate his sin, by appealing by an oath to the Holy God, as witness to the truth of his lie. Thus, the sin which in the beginning is directed only toward a fellow-man, too often causes one to sin immediately against God, in profanation of the name of the God of truth, by calling on Him as witness to a lie! Of this tendency of sin, stealing is a single illustration; but let us ever remember that it is a law of all sin that sin ever begets more sin.

This second group has dealt with injury to the neighbour in the way of guile and fraud; the third pentad (vv. 13, 14), progressing further, speaks of wrong committed in ways of oppression and violence. "Thou shalt not oppress thy neighbour, nor rob him: the wages of a hired servant shall not abide with thee all night until the morning. Thou shalt not curse the deaf, nor put a stumbling-block before the blind, but thou shalt fear thy God: I am the Lord!" In these commands, again, it is still the helpless and defenceless in whose behalf the Lord is speaking. The words regard a man as having it in his power to press hard upon his neighbour; as when an employer, seeing that a man must needs have work at any price, takes advantage of his need to employ him at less than fair wages; or as when he who holds a mortgage against his neighbour, seeing an opportunity to possess himself of a field or an estate for a trifle, by pressing his technical legal rights, strips his poor debtor needlessly. No end of illustrations, evidently, could be given out of our modern life. Man's nature is the same now as in the days of Moses. But all dealings of this kind, whether then or now, the law of holiness sternly prohibits.

So also with the injunction concerning the retention of wages after it is due. I have not fulfilled the law of love toward the man or woman whom I employ merely by paying fair wages; I must also pay promptly. The Deuteronomic law repeats the command, and, with a peculiar touch of sympathetic tenderness, adds the reason (xxiv. 15): "for he is poor, and setteth his heart upon it." I must therefore give the labourer his wages "in his day." A sin this is, of the rich especially, and, most of all, of rich corporations, with which the sense of personal responsibility to God is too often reduced to a minimum. Yet it is often, no doubt, committed through sheer thoughtlessness. Men who are themselves blessed with such abundance that they are not seriously incommoded by a delay in receiving some small sum, too often forget how a great part of the poor live, as the saying is, "from hand to mouth," so that the failure to get what is due to them at the exact time appointed is frequently a sore trial; and, moreover, by forcing them to buy on credit instead of for cash, of necessity increases the expense of their living, and so really robs them of that which is their own.

The thought is still of care for the helpless, in the words concerning the deaf and the blind, which, of course, are of perpetual force, and, in the principle involved, reach indefinitely beyond these single illustrations. We are not to take advantage of any man's helplessness, and, especially, of such disabilities as he cannot help, to wrong him. Even the common conscience of men recognises this as both wicked and mean; and this verdict of conscience is here emphasised by the reminder "I am the Lord,"—suggesting that the labourer who reaps the fields, yea, the blind also and the deaf, are His creatures; and that He, the merciful and just One, will not disown the relation, but will plead their cause.

Each of these groups of precepts has kept the poor and the needy in a special way, though not exclusively, before the conscience. And yet no man is to imagine that therefore God will be partial toward the poor, and that hence, although one may not wrong the poor, one may wrong the rich with impunity. Many of our modern social reformers, in their zeal for the betterment of the poor, seem to imagine that because a poor man has rights which are too frequently ignored by the rich, and thus often suffers grievous wrongs, therefore a rich man has no rights which the poor man is bound to respect. The next pentad of precepts therefore guards against any such false inference from God's special concern for the poor, and reminds us that the absolute righteousness of the Holy One requires that the rights of the rich be observed no less than the rights of the poor, those of the employer no less than those of the employed. It deals especially with this matter as it comes up in questions requiring legal adjudication. We read (vv. 15, 16), "Ye shall do no unrighteousness in judgment: thou shalt not respect the person of the poor, nor honour the person of the mighty: but in righteousness shalt thou judge thy neighbour. Thou shalt not go up and down as a talebearer among thy people: neither shalt thou stand against the blood of thy neighbour: I am the Lord!"

A plain warning lies here for an increasing class of reformers in our day, who loudly express their special concern for the poor, but who in their zeal for social reform and the diminishing of poverty are forgetful of righteousness and equity. It applies, for instance, to all who would affirm and teach with Marx that "capital is robbery;" or who, not yet quite ready for so plain and candid words, yet would, in any way, in order to right the wrongs of the poor, advocate legislation involving practical confiscation of the estates of the rich.

In close connection with the foregoing, the next precept forbids, not precisely "tale-bearing," but "slander," as the word is elsewhere rendered, even in the Revised Version. In the court of judgment, slander is not to be uttered nor listened to. The clause which follows is obscure; but means either, "Thou shalt not, by such slanderous testimony, seek in the court of judgment thy neighbour's life," which best suits the parallelism; or, perhaps, as the Talmud and most modern Jewish versions interpret, "Thou shalt not stand silent by, when thy neighbour's life is in danger in the court of judgment, and thy testimony might save him." And then again comes in the customary refrain, reminding the Israelite that in every court, noting every act of judgment, and listening to every witness, is a Judge unseen, omniscient, absolutely righteous, under whose final review, for confirmation or reversal, shall come all earthly decisions: "I," who thus speak, "am the Lord!"

The fifth and last pentad (vv. 17, 18) fitly closes the series, by its five precepts, of which, three, reaching behind all such outward acts as are required or forbidden in the foregoing, deal with the state of the heart toward our neighbour which the law of holiness requires, as the soul and the root of all righteousness. It closes with the familiar words, so simple that all can understand them, so comprehensive that in obedience to them is comprehended all morality and righteousness toward man: "Thou shalt love thy neighbour as thyself." The verses read, "Thou shalt not hate thy brother in thine heart: thou shalt surely rebuke thy neighbour, and not bear sin because of him. Thou shalt not take vengeance, nor bear any grudge against the children of thy people, but thou shalt love thy neighbour as thyself: I am the Lord!"

Most instructive it is to find it suggested by this order, as the best evidence of the absence of hate, and the truest expression of love to our neighbour, that when we see him doing wrong we shall rebuke him. The Apostle Paul has enjoined upon Christians the same duty, indicating also the spirit in which it is to be performed (Gal. vi. 1): "Brethren, even if a man be overtaken in any trespass, ye which are spiritual, restore such a one in a spirit of meekness; looking to thyself, lest thou also be tempted." Thus, if we will be holy, it is not to be a matter of no concern to us that our neighbour does wrong, even though that wrong do not directly affect our personal well-being. Instead of this, we are to remember that if we rebuke him not, we ourselves "bear sin, because of him;" that is, we ourselves, in a degree, become guilty with him, because of that wrong-doing of his which we sought not in any way to hinder. But although, on the one hand, I am to rebuke the wrong-doer, even when his wrong does not touch me personally, yet, the law adds, I am not to take into my own hands the avenging of wrongs, even when myself injured; neither am I to be envious and grudge any neighbour the good he may have; no, not though he be an ill-doer and deserve it not; but be he friend or foe, well-doer or ill-doer, I must love him as myself.

What an admirable epitome of the whole law of righteousness! a Mosaic anticipation of the very spirit of the Sermon on the Mount. Evidently, the same mind speaks in both alike; the law the same, the object and aim of the law the same, both in Leviticus and in the Gospel. In this law we hear: "Ye shall be holy: for I the Lord your God am holy;" in the Sermon on the Mount: "Ye shall be perfect, as your heavenly Father is perfect."

The third division of this chapter (vv. 19-32) opens with a general charge to obedience: "Ye shall keep My statutes;" very possibly, because several of the commands which immediately follow might seem in themselves of little consequence, and so be lightly disobeyed. The law of ver. 19 prohibits raising hybrid animals, as, for example, mules; the next command apparently refers to the chance, through sowing a field with mingled seed, of giving rise to hybrid forms in the vegetable kingdom. The last command in this verse is obscure both in meaning and intention. It reads (R.V.), "Neither shall there come upon thee a garment of two kinds of stuff mingled together." Most probably the reference is to different materials, interwoven in the yarn of which the dress was made; but a difficulty still remains in the fact that such admixture was ordered in the garments of the priests. Perhaps the best explanation is that of Josephus, that the law here was only intended for the laity; which, as no question of intrinsic morality was involved, might easily have been. But when we inquire as to the reason of these prohibitions, and especially of this last one, it must be confessed that it is hard for us now to speak with confidence. Most probable it appears that they were intended for an educational purpose, to cultivate in the mind of the people the sentiment of reverence for the order established in nature by God. For what the world calls the order of nature is really an order appointed by God, as the infinitely wise and perfect One; hence, as nature is thus a manifestation of God, the Hebrew was forbidden to seek to bring about that which is not according to nature, unnatural commixtures; and from this point of view, the last of the three precepts appears to be a symbolic reminder of the same duty, namely, reverence for the order of nature, as being an order determined by God.

The law which is laid down in vv. 20-22, regarding the sin of connection with a bond-woman betrothed to a husband, apparently refers to such a case as is mentioned in Exod. xxi. 7, 8, where the bond-maid is betrothed to her master, while yet, because of her condition of bondage, the marriage has not been consummated. For the same sin in the case of a free woman, where both were proved guilty, for each of them the punishment was death (Deut. xxii. 23, 24). In this case, because the woman's position, inasmuch as she was not free, was rather that of a concubine than of a full wife, the lighter penalty of scourging is ordered for both of the guilty persons. Also, since this was a case of trespass as well, in which the rights of the master to whom she was espoused were involved, a guilt-offering was in addition required, as the condition of pardon.

It will be said, and truly, that by this law slavery and concubinage are to a certain extent recognised by the law; and upon this fact has been raised an objection bearing on the holiness of the law-giver, and, by consequence, on the Divine origin and inspiration of the law. Is it conceivable that the holy God should have given a law for the regulation of two so evil institutions? The answer has been furnished us, in principle, by our Lord (Matt. xix. 8), in that which He said concerning the analogous case of the law of Moses touching divorce; which law, He tells us, although not according to the perfect ideal of right, was yet given "because of the hardness of men's hearts." That is, although it was not the best law ideally, it was the best practically, in view of the low moral tone of the people to whom it was given. Precisely so it was in this case. Abstractly, one might say that the case was in nothing different from the case of a free woman, mentioned Deut. xxii. 23, 24, for which death was the appointed punishment; but practically, in a community where slavery and concubinage were long-settled institutions, and the moral standard was still low, the cases were not parallel. A law which would carry with it the moral support of the people in the one case, and which it would thus be possible to carry into effect, would not be in like manner supported and carried into effect in the other; so that the result of greater strictness in theory would, in actual practice, be the removal thereby of all restriction on license. On the other hand, by thus appointing herein a penalty for both the guilty parties such as the public conscience would approve, God taught the Hebrews the fundamental lesson that a slave-girl is not regarded by God as a mere chattel; and that if, because of the hardness of their hearts, concubinage was tolerated for a time, still the slave-girl must not be treated as a thing, but as a person, and indiscriminate license could not be permitted. And thus, it is of greatest moment to observe, a principle was introduced into the legislation, which in its ultimate logical application would require and effect—as in due time it has—the total abolition of the institution of slavery wherever the authority of the living God is truly recognised.

The principle of the Divine government which is here illustrated is one of exceeding practical importance as a model for us. We live in an age when, everywhere in Christendom, the cry is "Reform;" and there are many who think that if once it be proved that a thing is wrong, it follows by necessary consequence that the immediate and unqualified legal prohibition of that wrong, under such penalty as the wrong may deserve, is the only thing that any Christian man has a right to think of. And yet, according to the principle illustrated in this legislation, this conclusion in such cases can by no means be taken for granted. That is not always the best law practically which is the best law abstractly. That law is the best which shall be most effective in diminishing a given evil, under the existing moral condition of the community; and it is often a matter of such exceeding difficulty to determine what legislation against admitted sins and evils, may be the most productive of good in a community whose moral sense is dull concerning them, that it is not strange that the best of men are often found to differ. Remembering this, we may well commend the duty of a more charitable judgment, in such cases, than one often hears from such radical reformers, who seem to imagine that in order to remove an evil all that is necessary is to pass a law at once and for ever prohibiting it; and who therefore hold up to obloquy all who doubt as to the wisdom and duty of so doing, as the enemies of truth and of righteousness. Moses, acting under direct instruction from the God of supreme wisdom and of perfect holiness, was far wiser than such well-meaning but sadly mistaken social reformers, who would fain be wiser than God.

Next follows a law (vv. 23-25) directing that when any fruit tree is planted, the Israelite shall not eat of its fruit for the first three years; that the fruit of the fourth year shall be wholly consecrated to the Lord, "for giving praise unto Jehovah;" and that only after that, in the fifth year of its bearing, shall the husbandman himself first eat of its fruit.

The explanation of this peculiar regulation is to be found in a special application of the principle which rules throughout the law; that the first-fruit, whether the first-born of man or beast, or the first-fruits of the field, shall always be consecrated unto God. But in this case the application of the principle is modified by the familiar fact that the fruit of a young tree, for the first few years of its bearing, is apt to be imperfect; it is not yet sufficiently grown to yield its best possible product. Because of this, in those years it could not be given to the Lord, for He must never be served with any but the best of everything; and thus until the fruit should reach its best, so as to be worthy of presentation to the Lord, the Israelite was meanwhile debarred from using it. During these three years the trees are said to be "as uncircumcised;" *i.e.*, they were to be regarded as in a condition analogous to that of the child who has not yet been consecrated, by the act of circumcision, to the Lord. In the fourth year, however, the trees were regarded as having now so grown as to yield fruit in perfection; hence, the principle of the consecration of the first-fruit now applies, and all the fourth year's product is given to the Lord, as an offering of thankful praise to Him whose power in nature is the secret of all growth, fruitfulness, and increase. The last words of this law, "that it may yield unto you its increase," evidently refer to all that precedes. Israel is to obey this law, using nothing till first consecrated to the Lord, in order to a blessing in these very gifts of God.

The moral teaching of this law, when it is thus read in the light of the general principle of the consecration of the first-fruits, is very plain. It teaches, as in all analogous cases, that God is always to be served before ourselves; and that not grudgingly, as if an irksome tax were to be paid to the Majesty of heaven, but in the spirit of thanksgiving and praise to Him, as the Giver of "every good and perfect gift." It further instructs us in this particular instance, that the people of God are to recognise this as being true even of all those good things which come to us under the forms of products of nature.

The lesson is not an easy one for faith; for the constant tendency, never stronger than in our own time, is to substitute "Nature" for the God of nature, as if nature were a power in itself and apart from God, immanent in all nature, the present and efficient energy in all her manifold operations. Very fittingly, thus, do we find here again (ver. 25) the sanction affixed to this law, "I am the Lord your God!" Jehovah, your God who redeemed you, who therefore am worthy of all thanksgiving and praise! Jehovah, your God in covenant, who gives the fruitful seasons, filling your hearts with joy and gladness! Jehovah, your God, who as the Lord of Nature, and the Power in nature, am abundantly able to fulfil the promise affixed to this command!

The next six commands are evidently grouped together as referring to various distinctively heathenish customs, from which Israel, as a people holy to the Lord, was to abstain. The prohibition of blood (ver. 26) is repeated again, not, as has been said, in a stronger form than before, but, probably, because the eating of blood was connected with certain heathenish ceremonies, both among the Shemitic tribes and others. The next two precepts (ver. 26) prohibit every kind of divination and augury;

practices notoriously common with the heathen everywhere, in ancient and in modern times. The two precepts which follow, forbidding certain fashions of trimming the hair and beard, may appear trivial to many, but they will not seem so to any one who will remember how common among heathen peoples has been the custom, as in those days among the Arabs, and in our time among the Hindoos, to trim the hair or beard in a particular way, in order thus visibly to mark a person as of a certain religion, or as a worshipper of a certain god. The command means that the Israelite was not only to worship God alone, but he was not to adopt a fashion in dress which, because commonly associated with idolatry, might thus misrepresent his real position as a worshipper of the only living and true God.

"Cutting the flesh for the dead" (ver. 28) has been very widely practised by heathen peoples in all ages. Such immoderate and unseemly expressions of grief were prohibited to the Israelite, as unworthy of a people who were in a blessed covenant relation with the God of life and of death. Rather, recognising that death is of God's ordination, he was to accept in patience and humility the stroke of God's hand; not, indeed, without sorrow, but yet in meekness and quietness of spirit, trusting in the God of life. The thought is only a less clear expression of the New Testament word (1 Thess. iv. 13) that the believer "sorrow not, even as the rest, which have no hope." Also, probably, in this prohibition, as certainly in the next (ver. 28), it is suggested that as the Israelite was to be distinguished from the heathen by full consecration, not only of the soul, but also of the body, to the Lord, he was by that fact inhibited from marring or defacing in any way the integrity of his body.

In general, we may say, then, that the central thought which binds this group of precepts together, is the obligation, not merely to abstain from everything directly idolatrous, but also from all such customs as are, in fact, rooted in or closely associated with idolatry. On the same principle, the Christian is to beware of all fashions and practices, even though they may be in themselves indifferent, which yet, as a matter of fact, are specially characteristic of the worldly and ungodly element in society. The principle assumed in these prohibitions thus imposes upon all who would be holy to the Lord, in all ages, a firm restriction. The thoughtless desire of many, at any risk, to be "in the fashion," must be unwaveringly denied. The reason which is so often given by professing Christians for indulgence in such cases, that "all the world does so," may often be the strongest possible reason for declining to follow the fashion. No servant of God should ever be seen in any part of the livery of Satan's servants. That God does not think these "little things" always of trifling consequence, we are reminded by the repetition here, for the tenth time in this chapter, of the words, "I am the Lord!"

Next (ver. 29) follows the prohibition of the horrible custom, still practised among heathen peoples, of the prostitution of a daughter by a parent. It is here enforced by the consideration of the public weal: "lest the land fall to whoredom, and the land become full of wickedness." Assuredly, that a land in which such harlotry as this, in which all the most sacred relations of life are trampled in the mire, would be nothing less than a land full of wickedness, is so evident as to require no comment.

Herewith now begins the fourth and last division of this chapter (vv. 30-37), with a repetition of the injunction to keep the Sabbaths of the Lord, and reverence His sanctuary. The emphasis on this command, shown by its repetition in this chapter, and the very prominent place which it occupies both in the law and the prophets, certainly suggests that in the mind of God, reverence for the Sabbath and for the place where God is worshipped, has much to do with the promotion of holiness of life, and the maintenance of a high degree of domestic and social morality. Nor is it difficult to see why this should be so. For however the day of holy rest may be kept, and the place of Divine worship be regarded with only an outward reverence by many, yet the fact cannot be disputed, that the observance of a weekly sabbatic rest from ordinary secular occupations, and the maintenance of a spirit of reverence for sacred places or for sacred times, has, and must have, a certain and most happy tendency to keep the God of the Sabbath and the God of the sanctuary before the mind of men, and thus imposes an effective check upon unrestrained godlessness and reckless excesses of iniquity. The diverse condition of things in various parts of modern Christendom, as related to the more or less careful observance of the weekly religious rest, is full of both instruction and warning to any candid mind upon this subject. There is no restraint on immorality like the frequent remembrance of God and the spirit of reverence for Him.

Verse 31 prohibits all inquiring of them that "have familiar spirits," and of "wizards," who pretend to make revelations through the help of supernatural powers. According to 1 Sam. xxviii. 7-11, and Isa. viii. 19, the "familiar spirit" is a supposed spirit of a dead man, from whom one professes to be able to give communications to the living. This pretended commerce with the spirits of the dead has been common enough in heathenism always, and it is not strange to find it mentioned here, when Israel was to be in so intimate relations with heathen peoples. But it is truly most extraordinary that in Christian lands, as especially in the United States of America, and that in the full light, religious and intellectual, of the last half of the nineteenth century, such a prohibition should be fully as pertinent as in Israel! For no words could more precisely describe the pretensions of the so-called modern spiritualism, which within the last half century has led away hundreds of thousands of deluded souls, and those, in many cases, not from the ignorant and degraded, but from circles which boast of more than average culture and intellectual enlightenment. And inasmuch as experience sadly shows that even those who profess to be disciples of Christ are in danger of being led away by our modern wizards and traffickers with familiar spirits, it is by no means unnecessary to observe that there is not the slightest reason to believe that this which was rigidly forbidden by God in the fifteenth century B.C., can now be well-pleasing to Him in the nineteenth century A.D. And those who have most carefully watched the moral developments of this latter-day delusion, will most appreciate the added phrase which speaks of this as "defiling" a man.

Verse 32 enjoins reverence for the aged, and closely connects it with the fear of God. "Thou shalt rise up before the hoary head, and honour the face of the old man, and thou shalt fear thy God: I am the Lord."

A virtue this is which—it must be with shame confessed—although often displayed in an illustrious manner among the heathen, in many parts of Christendom has sadly decayed. In many lands one only needs to travel in any crowded conveyance to observe how far it is from the thoughts of many of the young "to rise up before the hoary head, and honour the face of the old man." So manifest are the facts that one hears from competent and thoughtful observers of the tendencies of our times no lamentation more frequently than just this, for the concurrent decay of reverence for the aged and reverence for God. No more beautiful remarks on these words have we found than the words quoted by Dr. H. Bonar, commenting on this verse: "Lo! the shadow of eternity! for one cometh who is almost in eternity already. His head and his beard, white as snow, indicate his speedy appearance before the Ancient of Days, the hair of whose head is as pure wool."

In this last command is also, no doubt, contained the thought of the comparative weakness and physical infirmity of the aged, which is thus commended in a special way to our tender regard. And thus this sentiment of kindly sympathy for all who are subject to any kind of disability naturally prepares the way for the injunction (vv. 33, 34) to regard "the stranger" in the midst of Israel, who was debarred from holding land, and from many privileges, with special feelings of good-will. "If a stranger sojourn with thee in your land, ye shall not do him wrong. The stranger that sojourneth with you shall be unto you as the home-born among you, and thou shalt love him as thyself; for ye were strangers in the land of Egypt: I am the Lord your God."

The Israelite was not to misinterpret, then, the restrictions which the theocratic law imposed upon such. These might be no doubt necessary for a moral reason; but, nevertheless, no man was to argue that the law justified him in dealing hardly with aliens. So far from this, the Israelite was to regard the stranger with the same kindly feelings as if he were one of his own people. And it is most instructive to observe that this particular case is made the occasion of repeating that most perfect and comprehensive law of universal love, "Thou shalt love thy neighbour as thyself;" and this the more they were to do that they too had been "strangers in the land of Egypt."

Last of all the injunctions in this chapter (vv. 35, 36) comes the command to absolute righteousness in the administration of justice, and in all matters of buying and selling; followed (ver. 37) by a concluding charge to obedience, thus: "Ye shall do no unrighteousness in judgment, in meteyard, in weight, or in measure. Just balances, just weights, a just ephah, and a just hin, shall ye have: I am the Lord your God, which brought you out of the land of Egypt. And ye shall observe all My statutes, and all My judgments, and do them: I am the Lord."

The ephah is named here, of course, as a standard of dry measure, and the hin as a standard of liquid measure. These commandments are illustrated in a graphic way by the parallel passage in Deut. xxv. 13, 14, which reads: "Thou shalt not have in thy bag divers weights, a great and a small. Thou shalt not have in thine house divers measures, a great and a small;" *i.e.*, one set for use in buying, and another set for use in selling. This charge is there enforced by the same promise to honesty in trade which is annexed to the fifth commandment, namely, length of days; and, furthermore, by the declaration that all who thus cheat in trade "are an abomination unto the Lord."

How much Israel needed this law all their history has shown. In the days of Amos it was a part of his charge against the ten tribes (viii. 5), for which the Lord declares that He will "make the land to tremble, and every one in it to mourn," that they "make the ephah small, and the shekel great," and "deal falsely with balances of deceit." So also Micah, a little later, represents the Lord as calling Judah to account for supposing that God, the Holy One, can be satisfied with burnt-offerings and guilt-offerings; indignantly asking (vi. 10, 11), "Are there yet the treasures of wickedness in the house of the wicked, and the scant measure that is abominable?"

But it is not Israel alone which has needed, and still needs, to hear iterated this command, for the sin is found in every people, even in every city, one might say in every town, in Christendom; and—we have to say it—often with men who make a certain profession of regard for religion. All such, however religious in certain ways, have special need to remember that "without holiness no man shall see the Lord;" and that holiness is now exactly what it was when the Levitical law was given out. As, on the one side, it is inspired by reverence and fear toward God, so, on the other hand, it requires love to the neighbour as to one's self, and such conduct as that will secure. It is of no account, therefore, to keep the Sabbath—in a way—and reverence—outwardly—the sanctuary, and then on the week-day water milk, adulterate medicines, sugars, and other foods, slip the yard-stick in measuring, tip the balance in weighing, and buy with one weight or measure and sell with another, "water" stocks and gamble in "margins," as the manner of many is. God hates, and even honest atheists despise, religion of this kind. Strange notions, truly, of religion have men who have not yet discovered that it has to do with just such commonplace, every-day matters as these, and have never yet understood how certain it is that a religion which is only used on Sundays has no holiness in it; and therefore, when the day comes, as it is coming, that shall try every man's work as by fire, it will, in the fierce heat of Jehovah's judgment, be shrivelled into ashes as a spider's web in a flame, and the man and his work shall perish together.

And herewith this chapter closes. Such is the law of holiness! Obligatory, let us not forget, in the spirit of all its requirements, to-day, unchanged and unchangeable, because the Holy God, whose law it is, is Himself unchangeable. Man may be sinful, and because of sin be weak; but there is not a hint of compromise with sin, on this account, by any abatement of its claims. At every step of life this law confronts us. Whether we be in the House of God, in acts of worship, it challenges us there; or in the field, at our work, it commands us there; in social intercourse with our fellow-men, in our business in bank or shop, with our friends or with strangers and aliens, at home or abroad, we are never out of the reach of its requirements. We can no more escape from under its authority than from under the overarching heaven! What sobering thoughts are these for sinners! What self-humiliation should this law cause us, when we think what we are! what intensity of aspiration, when we think of what the Holy One would have us be, holy like Himself!

The closing words above given (ver. 37) assert the authority of the Lawgiver, and, by their reminder of the great deliverance from Egypt, appeal, as a motive to faithful and holy obedience, to the purest sentiment of grateful love for undeserved and distinguishing mercy. And this is only the Old Testament form of a New Testament argument. For we read, concerning our deliverance from a worse than Egyptian bondage (1 Peter i. 15-19): "Like as He which called you is holy, be ye yourselves also holy in all manner of living; because it is written, Ye shall be holy; for I am holy. And if ye call on Him as Father, who without respect of persons judgeth according to each man's work, pass the time of your sojourning in fear: knowing that ye were redeemed, not with corruptible things, as silver or gold, ... but with precious blood, as of a lamb without blemish and without spot, even the blood of Christ."

CHAPTER XXII
PENAL SANCTIONS

Lev. xx. 1-27.

In no age or community has it been found sufficient, to secure obedience, that one should appeal to the conscience of men, or depend, as a sufficient motive, upon the natural painful consequences of violated law. Wherever there is civil and criminal law, there, in all cases, human government, whether in its lowest or in its most highly developed forms, has found it necessary to declare penalties for various crimes. It is the peculiar interest of this chapter that it gives us certain important sections of the penal code of a people whose government was theocratic, whose only King was the Most Holy and Righteous God. In view of the manifold difficulties which are inseparable from the enactment and enforcement of a just and equitable penal code, it must be to every man who believes that Israel, in that period of its history, was, in the most literal sense, a theocracy, a matter of the highest civil and governmental interest to observe what penalties for crime were ordained by infinite wisdom, goodness, and righteousness as the law of that nation.

This penal code (vv. 1-21) is given in two sections. Of these, the first (vv. 1-6) relates to those who give of their seed to Molech, or who are accessory to such crime by their concealment of the fact; and also to those who consult wizards or familiar spirits. Under this last head also comes ver. 27, which appears to have become misplaced, as it follows the formal conclusion of the chapter, and by its subject—the penalty for the wizard, or him who claims to have a familiar spirit—evidently belongs immediately after ver. 6.

The second section (vv. 9-21) enumerates, first (vv. 9-16), other cases for which capital punishment was ordered; and then (vv. 17-21) certain offences for which a lesser penalty is prescribed. These two sections are separated (vv. 7, 8) by a command, in view of these penalties, to sanctification of life, and obedience to the Lord, as the God who has redeemed and consecrated Israel to be a nation to Himself.

These penal sections are followed (vv. 22-26) by a general conclusion to the whole law of holiness, as contained in these three chapters, as also to the law concerning clean and unclean meats (xi.); which would thus appear to have been originally connected more closely than now with these chapters. This closing part of the section consists of an exhortation and argument against disobedience, in walking after the wicked customs of the Canaanitish nations; enforced by the declaration that their impending expulsion was brought about by God in punishment for their practice of these crimes; and, also, by the reminder that God in His special grace had separated them to be a holy nation to Himself, and that He was about to give them the good land of Canaan as their possession.

It is perhaps hardly necessary to observe that the law of this chapter does not profess to give the penal code of Israel with completeness. Murder, for example, is not mentioned here, though death is expressly denounced against it elsewhere (Numb. xxxv. 31). So, again, in the Book of Exodus (xxi. 15) death is declared as the penalty for smiting father or mother. Indeed, the chapter itself contains evidence that it is essentially a selection of certain parts of a more extended code, which has been nowhere preserved in its entirety.

In this chapter death is ordained as the penalty for the following crimes: viz., giving of one's seed to Molech (vv. 2-5); professing to be a wizard, or to have dealings with the spirits of the dead (ver. 27); adultery, incest with a mother or step-mother, a daughter-in-law or mother-in-law (vv. 10-12, 14); and sodomy and bestiality (ver. 13). In a single case—that of incest with a wife's mother—it is added (ver. 14) that both the guilty parties shall be burnt with fire; *i.e.*, after the usual infliction of death by stoning. Of him who becomes accessory by concealment to the crime of sacrifice to Molech, it is said (ver. 5) that God Himself will set His face against that man, and will cut off both the man himself and his family. The same phraseology is used (ver. 6) of those who consult familiar spirits; and the cutting off is also threatened, ver. 18. The law concerning incest with a full- or half-sister requires (ver. 17) that this excision shall be "in the sight of the children of their people;" *i.e.*, that the sentence shall be executed in the most public way, thus to affix the more certainly to the crime the stigma of an indelible ignominy and disgrace. A lesser grade of penalty is attached to an alliance with the wife of an uncle or of a brother; in the latter case (ver. 21) that they shall be childless, in the former (ver. 20), that they shall die childless; that is, though they have children, they shall all be prematurely cut off; none shall outlive their parents. To incest with an aunt by blood no specific penalty is affixed; it is only said that "they shall bear their iniquity," *i.e.*, God will hold them guilty.

The chapter, directly or indirectly, casts no little light on some most fundamental and practical questions regarding the administration of justice in dealing with criminals.

We may learn here what, in the mind of the King of kings, is the primary object of the punishment of criminals against society. Certainly there is no hint in this code of law that these penalties were specially intended for the reformation of the offender. Were this so, we should not find the death-penalty applied with such unsparing severity. This does not indeed mean that the reformation of the criminal was a matter of no concern to the Lord; we know to the contrary. But one cannot resist the conviction in reading this chapter, as also other similar portions of the law, that in a governmental point of view this was not the chief object of punishment. Even where the penalty was not death, the reformation of the guilty persons is in no way brought before us as an object of the penal sentence. In the governmental aspect of the case, this is, at least, so far in the background that it does not once come into view.

In our day, however, an increasing number maintain that the death-penalty ought never to be inflicted, because, in the nature of the case, it precludes the possibility of the criminal being reclaimed and made a useful member of society; and so, out of regard to this and other like humanitarian considerations, in not a few instances, the death penalty, even for wilful murder, has been abrogated. It is thus, to a Christian citizen, of very practical concern to observe that in this theocratic penal code there is not so much as an allusion to the reformation of the criminal, as one object which by means of punishment it was intended to secure. Penalty was to be inflicted, according to this code, without any apparent reference to its bearing on this matter. The wisdom of the Omniscient King of Israel, therefore, must certainly have contemplated in the punishment of crime some object or objects of more weighty moment than this.

What those objects were, it does not seem hard to discern. First and supreme in the intention of this law is the satisfaction of outraged justice, and of the regal majesty of the supreme and holy God, defied; the vindication of the holiness of the Most High against that wickedness of men which would set at nought the Holy One and overturn that moral order which He has established. Again and again the crime itself is given as the reason for the penalty, inasmuch as by such iniquity in the midst of Israel the holy sanctuary of God among them was profaned. We read, for example, "I will cut him off ... because he hath defiled My sanctuary, and hath profaned My holy name;" "they have wrought confusion," *i.e.*, in the moral and physical order of the family; "their blood shall be upon them;" "they have committed abomination; they shall surely be put to death;" "it is a shameful thing; they shall be cut off." Such are the expressions which again and again ring through this chapter; and they teach with unmistakable clearness that the prime object of the Divine King of Israel in the punishment was, not the reformation of the individual sinner, but the satisfaction of justice and the vindication of the majesty of broken law. And if we have no more explicit statement of the matter here, we yet have it elsewhere; as in Numb. xxxv. 33, where we are expressly told that the death-penalty to be visited with unrelenting severity on the murderer is of the nature of an expiation. Very clear and solemn are the words, "Blood, it polluteth the land: and no expiation can be made for the land for the blood that is shed therein, but by the blood of him that shed it."

But if this is set forth as the fundamental reason for the infliction of the punishment, it is not represented as the only object. If, as regards the criminal himself, the punishment is a satisfaction and expiation to justice for his crime, on the other hand, as regards the people, the punishment is intended for their moral good and purification. This is expressly stated, as in ver. 14: "They shall be burnt with fire, that there be no wickedness among you." Both of these principles are of such a nature that they must be of perpetual validity. The government or legislative power that loses sight of either of them is certain to go wrong, and the people will be sure, sooner or later, to suffer in morals by the error.

In the light we have now, it is easy to see what are the principles according to which, in various cases, the punishments were measured out. Evidently, in the first place, the penalty was determined, even as equity demands, by the intrinsic heinousness of the crime. With the possible exception of a single case, it is easy to see this. No one will question the horrible iniquity of the sacrifice of innocent children to Molech; or of incest with a mother, or of sodomy, or bestiality. A second consideration which evidently had place, was the danger involved in each crime to the moral and spiritual well-being of the community; and, we may add, in the third place, also the degree to which the people were likely to be exposed to the contagion of certain crimes prevalent in the nations immediately about them.

But although these principles are manifestly so equitable and benevolent as to be valid for all ages, Christendom seems to be forgetting the fact. The modern penal codes vary as widely from the Mosaic in respect of their great leniency, as those of a few centuries ago in respect of their undiscriminating severity. In particular, the past few generations have seen a great change with regard to the infliction of capital punishment. Formerly, in England, for example, death was inflicted, with intolerable injustice, for a large number of comparatively trivial offences; the death-penalty is now restricted to high treason and killing with malice aforethought; while in some parts of

Christendom it is already wholly abolished. In the Mosaic law, according to this chapter and other parts of the law, it was much more extensively inflicted, though, it may be noted in passing, always without torture. In this chapter it is made the penalty for actual or constructive idolatry, for sorcery, etc., for cursing father or mother, for adultery, for the grosser degrees of incest, and for sodomy and bestiality. To this list of capital offences the law elsewhere adds, not only murder, but blasphemy, sabbath-breaking, unchastity in a betrothed woman when discovered after marriage, rape, rebellion against a priest or judge, and man-stealing.

As regards the crimes specified in this particular chapter, the criminal law of modern Christendom does not inflict the penalty of death in a single possible case here mentioned; and, to the mind of many, the contrasted severity of the Mosaic code presents a grave difficulty. And yet, if one believes, on the authority of the teaching of Christ, that the theocratic government of Israel is not a fable, but a historic fact, although he may still have much difficulty in recognising the righteousness of this code, he will be slow on this account either to renounce his faith in the Divine authority of this chapter, or to impugn the justice of the holy King of Israel in charging Him with undue severity; and will rather patiently await some other solution of the problem, than the denial of the essential equity of these laws. But there are several considerations which, for many, will greatly lessen, if they do not wholly remove, the difficulty which the case presents.

In the first place, as regards the punishment of idolatry with death, we have to remember that, from a theocratic point of view, idolatry was essentially high treason, the most formal repudiation possible of the supreme authority of Israel's King. If, even in our modern states, the gravity of the issues involved in high treason has led men to believe that death is not too severe a penalty for an offence aimed directly at the subversion of governmental order, how much more must this be admitted when the government is not of fallible man, but of the most holy and infallible God? And when, besides this, we recall the atrocious cruelties and revolting impurities which were inseparably associated with that idolatry, we shall have still less difficulty in seeing that it was just that the worshipper of Molech should die. And as decreeing the penalty of death for sorcery and similar practices, it is probable that the reason for this is to be found in the close connection of these with the prevailing idolatry.

But it is in regard to crimes against the integrity and purity of the family that we find the most impressive contrast between this penal code and those of modern times. Although, unhappily, adultery and, less commonly, incest, and even, rarely, the unnatural crimes mentioned in this chapter, are not unknown in modern Christendom, yet, while the law of Moses punished all these with death, modern law treats them with comparative leniency, or even refuses to regard some forms of these offences as crimes. What then? Shall we hasten to the conclusion that we have advanced on Moses? that this law was certainly unjust in its severity? or is it possible that modern law is at fault, in that it has fallen below those standards of righteousness which rule in the kingdom of God?

One would think that by any man who believes in the Divine origin of the theocracy only one answer could be given. Assuredly, one cannot suppose that God judged of a crime with undue severity; and if not, is not then Christendom, as it were, summoned by this penal code of the theocracy—after making all due allowance for different conditions of society—to revise its estimate of the moral gravity of these and other offences? In these days of continually progressive relaxation of the laws regulating the relations of the sexes, this seems indeed to be one of the chief lessons from this chapter of Leviticus; namely, that in God's sight sins against the seventh commandment are not the comparative trifles which much over-charitable and easy-going morality imagines, but crimes of the first order of heinousness. We do well to heed this fact, that not merely unnatural crimes, such as sodomy, bestiality, and the grosser forms of incest, but adultery, is by God ranked in the same category as murder. Is it strange? For what are crimes of this kind but assaults on the very being of the family? Where there is incest or adultery, we may truly say the family is murdered; what murder is to the individual, that, precisely, are crimes of this class to the family. In the theocratic code these were, therefore, made punishable with death; and, we venture to believe, with abundant reason. Is it likely that God was too severe? or must we not rather fear that man, ever lenient to prevailing sins, in our day has become falsely and unmercifully merciful, kind with a most perilous and unholy kindness?

Still harder will it be for most of us to understand why the death-penalty should have been also affixed to cursing or smiting a father or a mother, an extreme form of rebellion against parental authority. We must, no doubt, bear in mind, as in all these cases, that a rough people, like those just emancipated slaves, required a severity of dealing which with finer natures would not be needed; and, also, that the fact of Israel's call to be a priestly nation bearing salvation to mankind, made every disobedience among them the graver crime, as tending to so disastrous issues, not for Israel alone, but for the whole race of man which Israel was appointed to bless. On an analogous principle we justify military authority in shooting the sentry found asleep at his post. Still, while allowing for all this, one can hardly escape the inference that, in the sight of God, rebellion against parents must be a more serious offence than many in our time have been wont to imagine. And the more that we consider how truly basal to the order of government and of society is both sexual purity and the maintenance of a spirit of reverence and subordination to parents, the easier we shall find it to recognise the fact that if in this penal code there is doubtless great severity, it is yet the severity of governmental wisdom and true paternal kindness on the part of the high King of Israel: who governed that nation with intent, above all, that they might become in the highest sense "a holy nation" in the midst of an ungodly world, and so become the vehicle of blessing to others. And God thus judged that it was better that sinning individuals should die without mercy, than that family government and family purity should perish, and Israel, instead of being a blessing to the nations, should sink with them into the mire of universal moral corruption.

And it is well to observe that this law, if severe, was most equitable and impartial in its application. We have here, in no instance, torture; the scourging which in one case is enjoined, is limited elsewhere to the forty stripes save one. Neither have we discrimination against any class, or either sex; nothing like that detestable injustice of modern society which turns the fallen woman into the street with pious scorn, while it often receives the betrayer and even the adulterer—in most cases the more guilty of the two—into "the best society." Nothing have we here, again, which could justify by example the insistence of many, through a perverted humanity, when a murderess is sentenced for her crime to the scaffold, her sex should purchase a partial immunity from the penalty of crime. The Levitical law is as impartial as its Author; even if death be the penalty, the guilty one must die, whether man or woman.

Quite apart, then, from any question of detail, as to how far this penal code ought to be applied under the different conditions of modern society, this chapter of Leviticus assuredly stands as a most impressive testimony from God against the humanitarianism of our age. It is more and more the fashion, in some parts of Christendom, to pet criminals; to lionize murderers and adulterers, especially if in high social station. We have even heard of bouquets and such-like sentimental attentions bestowed by ladies on blood-red criminals in their cells awaiting the halter; and a maudlin pity quite too often usurps among us the place of moral horror at crime and intense sympathy with the holy justice and righteousness of God. But this Divine government of old did not deal in flowers and perfumes; it never indulged criminals, but punished them with an inexorable righteousness. And yet this was not because Israel's King was hard and cruel. For it was this same law which with equal kindness and equity kept a constant eye of fatherly care upon the poor and the stranger, and commanded the Israelite that he love even the stranger as himself. But, none the less, the Lord God who declared Himself as merciful and gracious and of great kindness, also herein revealed Himself, according to His word, as one who would "by no means clear the guilty." This fact is luminously witnessed by this penal code; and, let us note, it is witnessed by that penal law of God which is revealed in nature also. For this too punishes without mercy the drunkard, for example, or the licentious man, and never diminishes one stroke because by the full execution of penalty the sinner must suffer often so terribly. Which is just what we should expect to find, if indeed the God of nature is the One who spake in Leviticus.

Finally, as already suggested, this chapter gives a most weighty testimony against the modern tendency to a relaxation of the laws which regulate the relations of the sexes. That such a tendency is a fact is admitted by all; by some with gratulation, by others with regret and grave concern. French law, for instance, has explicitly legalised various alliances which in this law God explicitly forbids, under heavy penal sanctions, as incestuous; German legislation has moved about as far in the same direction; and the same tendency is to be observed, more or less, in all the English-speaking world. In some of the United States, especially, the utmost laxity has been reached, in laws which, under the name of divorce, legalize gross adultery,— laws which had been a disgrace to pagan Rome. So it goes. Where God denounced the death-penalty, man first apologises for the crime, then lightens the penalty, then abolishes it, and at last formally legalises the crime. This modern drift bodes no good; in the end it can only bring disaster alike to the well-being of the family and of the State. The maintenance of the family in its integrity and purity is nothing less than essential to the conservation of society and the stability of good government.

To meet this growing evil, the Church needs to come back to the full recognition of the principles which underlie this Levitical code; especially of the fact that marriage and the family are not merely civil arrangements, but Divine institutions; so that God has not left it to the caprice of a majority to settle what shall be lawful in these matters. Where God has declared certain alliances and connections to be criminal, we shall permit or condone them at our peril. God rules, whether modern majorities will it or not; and we must adopt the moral standards of the kingdom of God in our legislation, or we shall suffer. God has declared that not merely the material well-being of man, but *holiness*, is the moral end of government and of life; and He will find ways to enforce His will in this respect. "The nation that will not serve Him shall perish." All this is not theology, merely, or ethics, but history. All history witnesses that moral corruption and relaxed legislation, especially in matters affecting the relations of the sexes, bring in their train sure retribution, not in Hades, but here on earth. Let us not miss of taking the lesson by imagining that this law was for Israel, but not for other peoples. The contrary is affirmed in this very chapter (vv. 23, 24), where we are reminded that God visited His heavy judgments upon the Canaanitish nations precisely for this very thing, their doing of these things which are in this law of holiness forbidden. Hence "the land spued them out." Our modern democracies, English, American, French, German, or whatever they be, would do well to pause in their progressive repudiation of the law of God in many social questions, and heed this solemn warning. For, despite the unbelief of multitudes, the Holy One still governs the world, and it is certain that He will never abdicate His throne of righteousness to submit any of His laws to the sanction of a popular vote.

CHAPTER XXIII
THE LAW OF PRIESTLY HOLINESS

Lev. xxi. 1-xxii. 33.

The conception of Israel as a kingdom of priests, a holy nation, was concretely represented in a threefold division of the people,—the congregation, the priesthood, and the high priest. This corresponded to the threefold division of the tabernacle into the outer court, the holy place, and the holy of holies, each in succession more sacred than the place preceding. So while all Israel was called to be a priestly nation, holy to Jehovah in life and service, this sanctity was to be represented in degrees successively higher in each of these three divisions of the people, culminating in the person of the high priest, who, in token of this fact, wore upon his forehead the inscription, "Holiness to Jehovah."

Up to this point the law of holiness has dealt only with such obligations as bore upon all the priestly nation alike; in these two chapters we now have the special requirements of this law in its yet higher demands upon, first, the priests, and, secondly, the high priest.

Abolished as to the letter, this part of the law still holds good as to the principle which it expresses, namely, that special spiritual privilege and honour places him to whom it is given under special obligations to holiness of life. As contrasted with the world without, it is not then enough that Christians should be equally correct and moral in life with the best men of the world; though too many seem to be living under that impression. They must be more than this; they must be holy: God will wink at things in others which He will not deal lightly with in them. And so, again, within the Church, those who occupy various positions of dignity as teachers and rulers of God's flock are just in that degree laid under the more stringent obligation to holiness of life and walk. This most momentous lesson confronts us at the very opening of this new section of the law, addressed specifically to "the priests, the sons of Aaron." How much it is needed is sufficiently and most sadly evident from the condition of baptized Christendom to-day. Who is there that will heed it?

Priestly holiness was to be manifested, first (vv. 1-15), in regard to earthly relations of kindred and friendship. This is illustrated under three particulars, namely, in mourning for the dead (vv. 1-6), in marriage (vv. 7, 8), and (ver. 9) in the maintenance of purity in the priest's family. With regard to the first point, it is ordered that there shall be no defilement for the dead, except in the case of the priest's own family,—father, mother, brother, unmarried sister, son, or daughter.[37] That is, with the exception of these cases, the priest, though he may mourn in his heart, is to take no part in any of those last offices which others render to the dead. This were "to profane himself." And while the above exceptions are allowed in the case of members of his immediate household, even in these cases he is specially charged (ver. 5) to remember, what was indeed elsewhere forbidden to every Israelite, that such excessive demonstrations of grief as shaving the head, cutting the flesh, etc., were most unseemly in a priest. These restrictions are expressly based upon the fact that he is "a chief man among his people;" that he is holy unto God, appointed to offer "the bread of God, the offerings made by fire." And inasmuch as the high priest, in the highest degree of all, represents the priestly idea, and is thus admitted into a peculiar and exclusive intimacy of relation with God, having on him "the crown of the anointing oil of his God," and having been consecrated to put on the "garments for glory and for beauty," worn by none other in Israel, with him the prohibition of all public acts of mourning is made absolute (vv. 10-12). He may not defile himself, for instance, by even entering the house where lies the dead body of a father or a mother!

These regulations, at first thought, to many will seem hard and unnatural. Yet this law of holiness elsewhere magnifies and guards with most jealous care the family relation, and commands that even the neighbour we shall love as ourselves. Hence it is certain that these regulations cannot have been intended to condemn the natural feelings of grief at the loss of friends, but only to place them under certain restrictions. They were given, not to depreciate the earthly relationships of friendship and kindred, but only to magnify the more the dignity and significance of the priestly relation to God, as far transcending even the most sacred relations of earth. As priest, the son of Aaron was the servant of the Eternal God, of God the Holy and the Living One, appointed to mediate from Him the grace of pardon and life to those condemned to die. Hence he must never forget this himself, nor allow others to forget it. Hence he must maintain a special, visible separation from death, as everywhere the sign of the presence and operation of sin and unholiness; and while he is not forbidden to mourn, he must mourn with a visible moderation; the more so that if his priesthood had any significance, it meant that death for the believing and obedient Israelite was death in hope. And then, besides all this, God had declared that He Himself would be the portion and inheritance of the priests. For the priest therefore to mourn, as if in losing even those nearest and dearest on earth he had lost all, were in outward appearance to fail in witness to the faithfulness of God to His promises, and His all-sufficiency as his portion.

Standing here, will we but listen, we can now hear the echo of this same law of priestly holiness from the New Testament, in such words as these, addressed to the whole priesthood of believers: "He that loveth father or mother more than Me is not worthy of Me;" "Let those that have wives be as though they had none, and those that weep as though they wept not;" "Concerning them that fall asleep ... sorrow not, even as the rest, which have no hope." As Christians, we are not forbidden to mourn; but because a royal priesthood to the God of life, who raised up the Lord Jesus, and ourselves looking also for the resurrection, ever with moderation and self-restraint. Extravagant demonstrations of sorrow, whether in dress or in prolonged separation from the sanctuary and active service of God, as the manner of many is, are all as contrary to the New Testament law of holiness as to that of the Old. When bereaved, we are to call to mind the blessed fact of our priestly relation to God, and in this we shall find a restraint and a remedy for excessive and despairing grief. We are to remember that the law for the High Priest is the law for all His priestly house; like Him, they must all be perfected for the priesthood by sufferings; so that, in that they themselves suffer, being tried, they may be able the better to succour others that are tried in like manner (2 Cor. i. 4; Heb. ii. 18). We are also to remember that as priests to God, this God of eternal life and love is Himself our satisfying portion, and with holy care take heed that by no immoderate display of grief we even seem before men to traduce His faithfulness and belie to unbelievers His glorious all-sufficiency.

The holiness of the priesthood was also to be represented visibly in the marriage relation. A priest must marry no woman to whose fair fame attaches the slightest possibility of suspicion,—no harlot, or fallen woman,[38] or a woman divorced (ver. 7); such an alliance were manifestly most unseemly in one "holy to his God." As in the former instance, the high priest is still further restricted; he may not marry a widow, but only "a virgin of his own people" (ver. 14); for virginity is always in Holy Scripture the peculiar type of holiness. As a reason it is added that this were to "profane his seed among his people;" that is, it would be inevitable that by neglect of this care the people would come to regard his seed with a diminished reverence as the separated priests of the holy God. From observing the practice of many who profess to be Christians, one would naturally infer that they can never have suspected that there was anything in this part of the law which concerns the New Testament priesthood of believers. How often we see a young man or a young woman professing to be a disciple of Christ, a member of Christ's royal priesthood, entering into marriage alliance with a confessed unbeliever in Him! And yet the law is laid down as explicitly in the New Testament as in the Old (1 Cor. vii. 39), that marriage shall be only "in the Lord;" so that one principle rules in both dispensations. The priestly line must, as far as possible, be kept pure; the holy man must have a holy wife. Many, indeed, feel this deeply and marry accordingly; but the apparent thoughtlessness on the matter of many more is truly astonishing, and almost incomprehensible.

And the household of the priest were to remember the holy standing of their father. The sin of the child of a priest was to be punished more severely than that of the children of others; a single illustration is given (ver. 9): "The daughter of any priest, if she profane herself by playing the harlot, ... shall be burnt with fire."[39] And the severity of the penalty is justified by this, that by her sin "she profaneth her father." From which it appears that, as a principle of the Divine judgment, if the children of believers sin, their guilt will be judged more heavy than that of others; and that justly, because to their sin this is added, over like sin of others, that they thereby cast dishonour on their believing parents, and in them soil and defame the honour of God. How little is this remembered by many in these days of increasing insubordination even in Christian families!

The priestly holiness was to be manifested, in the second place, in physical, bodily perfection. It is written (ver. 17): "Speak unto Aaron, saying, Whosoever he be of thy seed throughout their generations that hath a blemish, let him not approach to offer the bread of his God."

And then follows (vv. 18-20) a list of various cases in illustration of this law, with the proviso (vv. 21-23) that while such a person might not perform any priestly function, he should not be debarred from the use of the priestly portion, whether of things "holy" or "most holy," as his daily food. The material and bodily is ever the type and symbol of the spiritual; hence, in this case, the spiritual purity and perfection required of him who would draw near to God in the priests' office must be visibly signified by his physical perfection; else the sanctity of the tabernacle were profaned. Moreover, the reverence due from the people toward Jehovah's sanctuary could not well be maintained where a dwarf, for instance, or a humpback, were ministering at the altar. And yet the Lord has for such a heart of kindness; in kindly compassion He will not exclude them from His table. Like Mephibosheth at the table of David, the deformed priest may still eat at the table of God.

There is a thought here which bears on the administration of the affairs of God's house even now. We are reminded that there are those who, while undoubtedly members of the universal Christian priesthood, and thus lawfully entitled to come to the table of the Lord, may yet be properly regarded as disabled and debarred by various circumstances, for which, in many cases, they may not be responsible, from any eminent position in the Church.

In the almost unrestrained insistence of many in this day for "equality," there are indications not a few of a contempt for the holy offices ordained by Christ for His Church, which would admit an equal right on the part of almost any who may desire it, to be allowed to minister in the Church in holy things. But as there were dwarfed and blinded sons of Aaron, so are there not a few Christians who—evidently, at least, to all but themselves—are spiritually dwarfs or deformed; subject to ineradicable and obtrusive constitutional infirmities, such as utterly disqualify, and should preclude, them from holding any office in the holy Church of Christ. The presence of such in her ministry can only now, as of old, profane the sanctuaries of the Lord.

The next section of the law of holiness for the priests (xxii. 1-16) requires that the priests, as holy unto Jehovah, treat with most careful reverence all those holy things which are their lawful portion. If, in any way, any priest have incurred ceremonial defilement,—as, for instance, by an issue, or by the dead,—he is not to eat until he is clean (vv. 2-7). On no account must he defile himself by eating of that which is unclean, such as that which has died of itself, or has been torn by beasts (ver. 8), which indeed was forbidden even to the ordinary Israelite. Furthermore, the priests are charged that they preserve the sanctity of God's house by carefully excluding all from participation in the priests' portion who are not of the priestly order. The stranger or sojourner in the priest's house, or a hired servant, must not be fed from this "bread of God;" not even a daughter, when, having married, she has left the father's home to form a family of her own, can be allowed to partake of it (ver. 12). If, however (ver. 13), she be parted from her husband by death or divorce, and have no child, and return to her father's house, she then becomes again a member of the priestly family, and resumes the privileges of her virginity.

All this may seem, at first, remote from any present use; and yet it takes little thought to see that, in principle, the New Testament law of holiness requires, under a changed form, even the same reverent use of God's gifts, and especially of the Holy Supper of the Lord, from every member of the Christian priesthood. It is true that in some parts of the Church a superstitious dread is felt with regard to approach to the Lord's Table, as if only the conscious attainment of a very high degree of holiness could warrant one in coming. But, however such a feeling is to be deprecated, it is certain that it is a less serious wrong, and argues not so ill as to the spiritual condition of a man as the easy carelessness with which multitudes partake of the Lord's Supper, nothing disturbed, apparently, by the recollection that they are living in the habitual practice of known sin, unconfessed, unforsaken, and therefore unforgiven. As it was forbidden to the priest to eat of those holy things which were his rightful portion, with his defilement or uncleanness on him, till he should first be cleansed, no less is it now a violation of the law of holiness for the Christian to come to the Holy Supper having on his conscience unconfessed and unforgiven sin. No less truly than the violation of this ancient law is this a profanation, and who so desecrates the holy food must bear his sin.

And as the sons of Aaron were charged by this law of holiness that they guard the holy things from the participation of any who were not of the priestly house, so also is the obligation on every member of the New Testament Church, and especially on those who are in official charge of her holy sacraments, that they be careful to debar from such participation the unholy and profane. It is true that it is possible to go to an extreme in this matter which is unwarranted by the Word of God. Although participation in the Holy Supper is of right only for the regenerate, it does not follow, as in some sections of the Church has been imagined, that the Church is therefore required to satisfy herself as to the undoubted regeneration of those who may apply for membership and fellowship in this privilege. So to read the heart as to be able to decide authoritatively on the regeneration of every applicant for Church membership is beyond the power of any but the Omniscient Lord, and is not required in the Word. The Apostles received and baptized men upon their credible profession of faith and repentance, and entered into no inquisitorial cross-examination as to the details of the religious experience of the candidate. None the less, however, the law of holiness requires that the Church, under this limitation, shall to the uttermost of her power be careful that no one unconverted and profane shall sit at the Holy Table of the Lord. She may admit upon profession of faith and repentance, but she certainly is bound to see to it that such profession shall be credible; that is, such as may be reasonably believed to be sincere and genuine. She is bound, therefore, to satisfy herself in such cases, so far as possible to man, that the life of the applicant, at least externally, witnesses to the genuineness of the profession. If we are to beware of imposing false tests of Christian character, as some have done, for instance, in the use or disuse of things indifferent, we are, on the other hand, to see to it that we do apply such tests as the Word warrants, and firmly exclude all such as insist upon practices which are demonstrably, in themselves always wrong, according to the law of God.

No man who has any just apprehension of Scriptural truth can well doubt that we have here a lesson which is of the highest present-day importance. When one goes out into the world and observes the practices in which many whom we meet at the Lord's Table habitually indulge, whether in business or in society,—the crookedness in commercial dealings and sharp dealing in trade, the utter dissipation in amusement, of many Church members,—a spiritual man cannot but ask, Where is the discipline of the Lord's house? Surely, this law of holiness applies to a multitude of such cases; and it must be said that when such eat of the holy things, they "profane them;" and those who, in responsible charge of the Lord's Table, are careless in this matter, "cause them to bear the iniquity that bringeth guilt, when they eat their holy things" (ver. 16). That word of the Lord Jesus certainly applies in this case (Matt. xviii. 7): "It must needs be that occasions of stumbling come; but woe to that man through whom the occasion cometh!"

The last section of the law concerning priestly holiness (xxii. 17-33) requires the maintenance of jealous care in the enforcement of the law of offerings. Inasmuch as, in the nature of the case, while it rested with the sons of Aaron to enforce this law, the obligation concerned every offerer, this section (vv. 17-25) is addressed also (ver. 18) "unto all the children of Israel." The first requirement concerned the perfection of the offering; it must be (vv. 19, 20) "without blemish." Only one qualification is allowed to this law, namely, in the case of the free-will offering (ver. 23), in which a victim was allowed which, otherwise perfect, had something "superfluous or lacking in his parts." Even this relaxation of the law was not allowed in the case of an offering brought in payment of a vow; hence Malachi (i. 14), in allusion to this law, sharply denounces the man who "voweth, and sacrificeth unto the Lord a blemished thing." Verse 25 provides that this law shall be enforced in the case of the foreigner, who may wish to present an offering to Jehovah, no less than with the Israelite.

A third requirement (ver. 27) sets a minimum limit to the age of a sacrificial victim; it must not be less than eight days old. The reason of this law, apart from any mystic or symbolic meaning, is probably grounded in considerations of humanity, requiring the avoidance of giving unnecessary suffering to the dam. A similar intention is probably to be recognised in the additional law (ver. 28) that the cow, or ewe, and its young should not both be killed in one day; though it must be confessed that the matter is somewhat obscure.

Finally, the law closes (vv. 29, 30) with the repetition of the command (vii. 15) requiring that the flesh of the sacrifice of thanksgiving be eaten on the same day in which it is offered. The slightest possibility of beginning corruption is to be precluded in such cases with peculiar strictness.

This closing section of the law of holiness, which so insists that the regulations of God's law in regard to sacrifice shall be scrupulously observed, in its inner principle forbids all departures in matter of worship from any express Divine appointment or command. We fully recognise the fact that, as compared with the old dispensation, the New Testament allows in the conduct and order of worship a far larger liberty than then. But, in our age, the tendency, alike in politics and in religion, is to the confounding of liberty and license. Yet they are not the same, but are most sharply contrasted. Liberty is freedom of action within the bounds of Divine law; license recognises no limitation to human action, apart from enforced necessity,—no law save man's own will and pleasure. It is therefore essential lawlessness,[40] and therefore is sin in its most perfect and consummate expression. But there is law in the New Testament as well as in the Old. Because the New Testament lays down but few laws concerning the order of Divine worship, it does not follow that these few are of no consequence, and that men may worship in all respects just as they choose, and equally please God.

To illustrate this matter. It does not follow, because the New Testament allows large liberty as regards the details of worship, that therefore we may look upon the use of images or pictures in connection with worship as a matter of indifference. If told that these are merely used as an aid to devotion,—the very argument which in all ages has been used by all idolaters,—we reply that, be that as it may, it is an aid which is expressly prohibited under the heaviest penal sanctions in both Testaments. We may take another present-day illustration, which, especially in the American Church, is of special pertinence. One would say that it should be self-evident that no ordinance of the Church should be more jealously guarded from human alteration or modification than the most sacred institution of the sacramental Supper. Surely it should be allowed that the Lord alone should have the right to designate the symbols of His own death in this most holy ordinance. That He chose and appointed for this purpose bread and wine, even the fermented juice of the grape, has been affirmed by the practically unanimous consensus of Christendom for almost nineteen hundred years; and it is not too much to say that this understanding of the Scripture record is sustained by the no less unanimous judgment of truly authoritative scholarship even to-day. Neither can it be denied that Christ ordained this use of wine in the Holy Supper with the most perfect knowledge of the terrible evils connected with its abuse in all ages. All this being so, how can it but contravene this principle of the law of holiness, which insists upon the exact observance of the appointments which the Lord has made for His own worship, when men, in the imagined interest of "moral reform," presume to attempt improvements in this holy ordinance of the Lord, and substitute for the wine which He chose to make the symbol of His precious blood, something else, of different properties, for the use of which the whole New Testament affords no warrant? We speak with full knowledge of the various plausible arguments which are pressed as reasons why the Church should authorise this nineteenth-century innovation. No doubt, in many cases, the change is urged through a misapprehension as to the historical facts, which, however astonishing to scholars, is at least real and sincere. But whenever any, admitting the facts as to the original appointment, yet seriously propose, as so often of late years, to improve on the Lord's arrangements for His own Table, we are bold to insist that the principle which underlies this part of the priestly law of holiness applies in full force in this case, and cannot therefore be rightly set aside. Strange, indeed, it is that men should unthinkingly hope to advance morality by ignoring the primal principle of all holiness, that Christ, the Son of God, is absolute and supreme Lord over all His people, and especially in all that pertains to the ordering of His own house!

We have in these days great need to beseech the Lord that He may deliver us, in all things, from that malign epidemic of religious lawlessness which is one of the plagues of our age; and raise up a generation who shall so understand their priestly calling as Christians, that, no less in all that pertains to the offices of public worship, than in their lives as individuals they shall take heed, above all things, to walk according to the principles of this law of priestly holiness. For, repealed although it be as to the outward form of the letter, yet in the nature of the case, as to its spirit and intention, it abides, and must abide, in force unto the end. And the great argument also, with which, after the constant manner of this law, this section closes, is also, as to its spirit, valid still, and even of greater force in its New Testament form than of old. For we may now justly read it in this wise: "Ye shall not profane My holy name, but I will be hallowed among My people: I am the Lord that hallow you, *that have redeemed you by the cross*, to be your God."

CHAPTER XXIV
THE SET FEASTS OF THE LORD

Lev. xxiii. 1-44.

It is even an instinct of natural religion to observe certain set times for special public and united worship. As we should therefore anticipate, such observances are in this chapter enjoined as a part of the requirement of the law of holiness for Israel.

It is of consequence to observe that the Revisers have corrected the error of the Authorised Version, which renders two perfectly distinct words alike as "feasts;" and have distinguished the one by the translation, "set feasts," the other by the one word, "feasts." The precise sense of the former word is given in the margin "appointed seasons," and it is naturally applied to all the set times of special religious solemnity which are ordained in this chapter. But the other word translated "feast,"—derived from a root meaning "to dance," whence "feast" or "festival,"—is applied to only three of the former six "appointed seasons," namely, the feasts of Unleavened Bread, of Pentecost, and of Tabernacles; as intended to be, in a special degree, seasons of gladness and festivity.

The indication of this distinction is of importance, as completely meeting the allegation that there is in this chapter evidence of a later development than in the account of the feasts given in Exod. xxxiv., where the number of the "feasts," besides the weekly Sabbath, is given as three, while here, as it is asserted, their number has been increased to six. In reality, however, there is nothing here which suggests a later period. For the object of the former law in Exodus was only to name the "feasts" (*haggím*); while that of the chapter before us is to indicate not only these,—which here, as there, are three,—but, in addition to these, all "appointed seasons" for "holy convocations," which, although all *mo'adim*, were not all *haggím*.

The observance of public religious festivals has been common to all the chief religions of the world, both ancient and modern. Very often, though not in all cases, these have been determined by the phases of the moon; or by the apparent motion of the sun in the heavens, as in many instances of religious celebrations connected with the period of the spring and autumnal equinoxes; and thus, very naturally, also with the times of harvest and ingathering. It is at once evident that of these appointed seasons of holy convocation, the three feasts (*haggím*) of the Hebrews also fell at certain points in the harvest season; and with each of these, ceremonies were observed connected with harvest and ingathering; while two, the feast of weeks and that of tabernacles, take alternate names, directly referring to this their connection with the harvest; namely, the feast of firstfruits and that of ingathering. Thus we have, first, the feast of unleavened bread, following passover, which was distinguished by the presentation of a sheaf of the firstfruits of the barley harvest, in the latter part of March, or early in April; then, the feast of weeks, or firstfruits, seven weeks later, marking the completion of the grain harvest with the ingathering of the wheat; and, finally, the feast of tabernacles or ingathering, in the seventh month, marking the harvesting of the fruits, especially the oil and the wine, and therewith the completed ingathering of the whole product of the year.

From these facts it is argued that in these Hebrew feasts we have simply a natural development, with modifications, of the ancient and widespread system of harvest feasts among the heathen; to which the historical element which appears in some of them was only added as an afterthought, in a later period of history. From this point of view, the idea that these feasts were a matter of supernatural revelation disappears; what religious character they have belongs originally to the universal religion of nature.

But it is to be remarked, first, that even if we admit that in their original character these were simply and only harvest feasts, it would not follow that therefore their observance, with certain prescribed ceremonies, could not have been matter of Divine revelation. There is a religion of nature; God has not left Himself without a witness, in that He has given men "rains and fruitful seasons," filling their hearts with food and gladness. And, as already remarked in regard to sacrifice, it is no part of the method of God in revelation to ignore or reject what in this religion of nature may be true and right; but rather to use it, and build on this foundation.

But, again, the mere fact that the feast of unleavened bread fell at the beginning of barley harvest, and that one—though only one—ceremony appointed for that festive week had explicit reference to the then beginning harvest, is not sufficient to disprove the uniform declaration of Scripture that, as observed in Israel, its original ground was not natural, but historical; namely, in the circumstances attending the birth of the nation in their exodus from Egypt.

But we may say more than this. If the contrary were true, and the introduction of the historical element was an afterthought, as insisted by some, then we should expect to find that in accounts belonging to successive periods, the reference to the harvest would certainly be more prominent in the earlier, and the reference of the feast to a historical origin more prominent in the later, accounts of the feasts. Most singular it is then, upon this hypothesis, to find that even accepting the analysis, *e.g.*, of Wellhausen, the facts are the exact reverse. For the only brief reference to the harvest in connection with this feast of unleavened bread is found in this chap. xxiii. of Leviticus, composed, it is alleged, about the time of Ezekiel; while, on the other hand, the narrative in Exod. xii., regarded by all the critics of this school as the earliest account of the origin of the feast of unleavened bread, refers only to the historical event of the exodus, as the occasion of its institution. If we grant the asserted difference in age of these two parts of the Pentateuch, one would thus more naturally conclude that the historical events were the original occasion of the institution of the festival, and that the reference to the harvest, in the presentation of the sheaf of firstfruits, was the later introduction into the ceremonies of the week.

But the truth is that this naturalistic identification of these Hebrew feasts with the harvest feasts of other nations is a mistake. In order to make it out, it is necessary to ignore or pervert most patent facts. These so-called harvest feasts in fact form part of an elaborate system of sacred times,—a system which is based upon the Sabbath, and into which the sacred number seven, the number of the covenant, enters throughout as a formative element. The weekly Sabbath, first of all, was the seventh day; the length of the great festivals of unleavened bread and of tabernacles was also, in each case, seven days. Not only so, but the entire series of sacred times mentioned in this chapter and in chap. xxv. constitutes an ascending series of sacred septenaries, in which the ruling thought is this: that the seventh is holy unto the Lord, as the number symbolic of rest and redemption; and that the eighth, as the first of a new week, is symbolic of the new creation. Thus we have the seventh day, the weekly Sabbath, constantly recurring, the type of each of the series; then, counting from the feast of unleavened bread,—the first of the sacred year,—the fiftieth day, at the end of the seventh week, is signalised as sacred by the feast of firstfruits or of "weeks;" the seventh month, again, is the sabbatic month, of special sanctity, containing as it does three of the annual seasons of holy convocation,—the feast of trumpets on its first day, the great day of atonement on the tenth, and the last of the three great annual feasts, that of tabernacles or ingathering, for seven days from the fifteenth day of the month. Beyond this series of sacred festivals recurring annually, in chap. xxv., the seventh year is appointed to be a sabbatic year of rest to the land, and the series at last culminates at the expiration of seven sevens of years, in the fiftieth year,—the eighth following the seventh seven,—the great year of jubilee, the supreme year of rest, restoration, and release. All these sacred times, differing in the details of their observance, are alike distinguished by their connection with the sacred number seven, by the informing presence of the idea of the Sabbath, and therewith always a new and fuller revelation of God as in covenant with Israel for their redemption.

Now, like to this series of sacred times, in heathenism there is absolutely nothing. It evidently belongs to another realm of thought, ethics, and religion. And so, while it is quite true that in the three great feasts there was a reference to the harvest, and so to fruitful nature, yet the fundamental, unifying idea of the system of sacred times was not the recognition of the fruitful life of nature, as in the heathen festivals, but of Jehovah, as the Author and Sustainer of the life of His covenant people Israel, as also of every individual in the nation. This, we repeat, is the one central thought in all these sacred seasons; not the life of nature, but the life of the holy nation, as created and sustained by a covenant God. The annual processes of nature have indeed a place and a necessary recognition in the system, simply because the personal God is active in all nature; but the place of these is not primary, but secondary and subordinate. They have a recognition because, in the first place, it is through the bounty of God in nature that the life of man is sustained; and, secondly, also because nature in her order is a type and shadow of things spiritual. For in the spiritual world, whether we think of it as made up of nations or individuals, even as in the natural, there is a seed-time and a harvest, a time of firstfruits and a time of the joy and rest of the full ingathering of fruit, and oil, and wine. Hence it was most fitting that this inspired rubric, as primarily intended for the celebration of spiritual things, should be so arranged and timed, in all its parts, as that in each returning sacred season, visible nature should present itself to Israel as a manifest parable and eloquent suggestion of those spiritual verities; the more so that thus the Israelite would be reminded that the God of the Exodus and the God of Sinai was also the supreme Lord of nature, the God of the seed-time and harvest, the Creator and Sustainer of the heavens and the earth, and of all that in them is.

The Weekly Sabbath.

xxiii. 1-3.

"And the Lord spake unto Moses, saying, Speak unto the children of Israel, and say unto them, The set feasts of the Lord, which ye shall proclaim to be holy convocations, even these are My set feasts. Six days shall work be done: but on the seventh day is a sabbath of solemn rest, an holy convocation; ye shall do no manner of work: it is a sabbath unto the Lord in all your dwellings."

The first verse of this chapter announces the purpose of the section as, not to give a complete calendar of sacred times or of seasons of worship,—for the new moons and the sabbatic year and the jubilee are not mentioned,—but to enumerate such sacred times as are to be kept as "holy convocations." The reference in this phrase cannot be to an assembling of the people at the central sanctuary, which is elsewhere ordered (Exod. xxxiv. 23) only for the three feasts of passover, weeks, and atonement; but rather, doubtless, to local gatherings for purposes of worship, such as, at a later day, took form in the institution of the synagogues.

The enumeration of these "set times" begins with the Sabbath (ver. 3), as was natural; for, as we have seen, the whole series of sacred times was sabbatic in character. The sanctity of the day is emphasised in the strongest terms, as a *shabbath shabbathon*, a "sabbath of sabbatism,"—a "sabbath of solemn rest," as it is rendered by the Revisers. While on some other sacred seasons the usual occupations of the household were permitted, on the Sabbath "no manner of work" was to be done; not even was it lawful to gather wood or to light a fire.

For this sanctity of the Sabbath two reasons are elsewhere given. The first of these, which is assigned in the fourth commandment, makes it a memorial of the rest of God, when having created man in Eden, He saw His work which He had finished, that it was very good, and rested from all His work. As created, man was participant in this rest of God. He was indeed to work in tilling the garden in which he had been placed; but from such labour as involves unremunerative toil and exhaustion he was exempt. But this sabbatic rest of the creation was interrupted by sin; God's work, which He had declared "good," was marred; man fell into a condition of wearying toil and unrest of body and soul, and with him the whole creation also was "subjected to vanity" (Gen. iii. 17, 18; Rom. viii. 20). But in this state of things the God of love could not rest; it thus involved for Him a work of new creation, which should have for its object the complete restoration, both as regards man and nature, of that sabbatic state of things on earth which had been broken up by sin. And thus it came to pass that the weekly Sabbath looked not only backward, but forward; and spoke not only of the rest that was, but of the great sabbatism of the future, to be brought in through a promised redemption. Hence, as a second reason for the observance of the Sabbath, it is said (Exod. xxxi. 13) to be a sign between God and Israel through all their generations, that they might know that He was Jehovah which sanctified them, *i.e.*, who had set them apart for deliverance from the curse, that through them the world might be saved.

These are thus the two sabbatic ideas; rest and redemption. They everywhere appear, in one form or another, in all this sabbatic series of sacred times. Some of them emphasise one phase of the rest and redemption, and some another; the weekly Sabbath, as the unit of the series, presents both. For in Deuteronomy (v. 15) Israel was commanded to keep the Sabbath in commemoration of the exodus, as the time when God undertook to bring them into His rest; a rest of which the beginning and the pledge was their deliverance from Egyptian bondage; a rest brought in through a redemption.[41]

The Feast of Passover and Unleavened Bread.

xxiii. 4-14.

"These are the set feasts of the Lord, even holy convocations, which ye shall proclaim in their appointed season. In the first month, on the fourteenth day of the month at even, is the Lord's passover. And on the fifteenth day of the same month is the feast of unleavened bread unto the Lord: seven days ye shall eat unleavened bread. In the first day ye shall have an holy convocation: ye shall do no servile work. But ye shall offer an offering made by fire unto the Lord seven days: in the seventh day is an holy convocation; ye shall do no servile work. And the Lord spake unto Moses, saying, Speak unto the children of Israel, and say unto them, When ye be come into the land which I give unto you, and shall reap the harvest thereof, then ye shall bring the sheaf of the firstfruits of your harvest unto the priest: and he shall wave the sheaf before the Lord, to be accepted for you: on the morrow after the sabbath the priest shall wave it. And in the day when ye wave the sheaf, ye shall offer a he-lamb without blemish of the first year for a burnt offering unto the Lord. And the meal offering thereof shall be two tenth parts of an ephah of fine flour mingled with oil, an offering made by fire unto the Lord for a sweet savour: and the drink offering thereof shall be of wine, the fourth part of an hin. And ye shall eat neither bread, nor parched corn, nor fresh ears, until this selfsame day, until ye have brought the oblation of your God: it is a statute for ever throughout your generations in all your dwellings."

Verses 5-8 give the law for the first of the annual feasts, the passover and unleavened bread. The passover lamb was to be slain and eaten on the evening of the fourteenth day; and thereafter, for seven days, they were all to eat unleavened bread. The first and seventh days of unleavened bread were to be kept as an "holy convocation;" in both of which "servile work," *i.e.*, the usual occupations in the field or in one's handicraft, were forbidden. Further than this the restriction did not extend.

The utter impossibility of making this feast of passover also to have been at first merely a harvest festival is best shown by the signal failure of the many attempts to explain on this theory the name "passover" as applied to the sacrificial victim, and the exclusion of leaven for the whole period. Admit the statements of the Pentateuch on this subject, and all is simple. The feast was a most suitable commemoration by Israel of the solemn circumstances under which they began their national life: their exemption from the plague of the death of the first-born, through the blood of a slain victim; and their exodus thereafter in such haste that they stopped not to leaven their bread.

And there was a deeper spiritual meaning than this. Whereas, secured by the sprinkling of blood, they then fed in safety on the flesh of the victim, by which they received strength for their flight from Egypt, the same two thoughts were thereby naturally suggested which we have seen represented in the peace-offering; namely, friendship and fellowship with God secured through sacrifice, and life sustained by His bounty. And the unleavened bread, also, had more than a historic reference; else it had sufficed to eat it only on the anniversary night, and it had not been commanded also to put away the leaven from their houses. For leaven is the established symbol of moral corruption; and in that, the passover lamb having been slain, Israel must abstain for a full septenary period of a week from every use of leaven, it was signified in symbol that the redeemed nation must not live by means of what is evil, but be a holy people, according to their calling. And the inseparable connection of this with full consecration of person and service, and with the expiation of sin, was daily symbolised (ver. 8) by the "offerings made by fire," burnt-offerings, meal-offerings, and sin-offerings, "offerings made by fire unto the Lord."

On "the morrow after the Sabbath" (ver. 15) of this sacred week, it was ordered (ver. 10) that "the sheaf of the firstfruits of the (barley) harvest" should be brought "unto the priest;" and (ver. 11) that he should consecrate it unto the Lord, by the ceremony of waving it before Him. This wave-offering of the sheaf of firstfruits was to be accompanied (vv. 12, 13) by a burnt-offering, a meal-offering, and a drink-offering of wine. Until all this was done (ver. 14) they were to "eat neither bread, nor parched corn, nor fresh ears" of the new harvest. By the consecration of the firstfruit is ever signified the consecration of the whole, of which it is the first part, unto the Lord. By this act, Israel, at the very beginning of their harvest, solemnly consecrated the whole harvest to the Lord; and are only permitted to use it, when they receive it thus as a gift from Him. This ethical reference to the harvest is here expressly taught; but still more was thereby taught in symbol.

For Israel was declared (Exod. iv. 22) to be God's first-born; that is, in the great redemptive plan of God, which looks forward to the final salvation of all nations, Israel ever comes historically first. "The Jew first, and also the Greek," is the New Testament formula of this fundamental dispensational truth. The offering unto God, therefore, of the sheaf of firstfruits, at the very beginning of the harvest,—in fullest harmony with the historic reference of this feast, which commemorated Israel's deliverance from bondage and separation from the nations, as a firstfruits of redemption,—symbolically signified the consecration of Israel unto God as the first-born unto Him from the nations, the beginning of the world's great harvest.

But this is not all. For in these various ceremonies of this first of the feasts, all who acknowledge the authority of the New Testament will recognise a yet more profound, and prophetic, spiritual meaning. Passover and unleavened bread not only looked backward, but forward. For the Apostle Paul writes, addressing all believers (1 Cor. v. 7, 8): "Purge out the old leaven, that ye may be a new lump, even as ye are unleavened. For our passover also hath been sacrificed, even Christ: wherefore let us keep the feast, not with old leaven, neither with the leaven of malice and wickedness, but with the unleavened bread of sincerity and truth;"—an exposition so plain that comment is scarcely needed. And as following upon the passover, on the morrow after the Sabbath, the first day of the week, the sheaf of firstfruits was presented before Jehovah, so in type is brought before us that of which the same Apostle tells us (1 Cor. xv. 20), that Christ, in that He rose from the dead on the first day after the Sabbath, became "the firstfruits of them that are asleep;" thus, for the first time, finally and exhaustively fulfilling this type, in full accord also with His own representation of Himself (John xii. 24) as "a grain of wheat," which should "fall into the earth and die," and then, living again, "bear much fruit."

The Feast of Pentecost.

xxiii. 15-21.

> "And ye shall count unto you from the morrow after the sabbath, from the day that ye brought the sheaf of the wave offering; seven sabbaths shall there be complete: even unto the morrow after the seventh sabbath shall ye number fifty days; and ye shall offer a new meal offering unto the Lord. Ye shall bring out of your habitations two wave loaves of

two tenth parts of an ephah: they shall be of fine flour, they shall be baken with leaven, for firstfruits unto the Lord. And ye shall present with the bread seven lambs without blemish of the first year, and one young bullock, and two rams: they shall be a burnt offering unto the Lord, with their meal offering, and their drink offerings, even an offering made by fire, of a sweet savour unto the Lord. And ye shall offer one he-goat for a sin offering, and two he-lambs of the first year for a sacrifice of peace offerings. And the priest shall wave them with the bread of the firstfruits for a wave offering before the Lord, with the two lambs: they shall be holy to the Lord for the priest. And ye shall make proclamation on the selfsame day; there shall be an holy convocation unto you: ye shall do no servile work: it is a statute for ever in all your dwellings throughout your generations."

Next in order came the feast of firstfruits, or the feast of weeks, which, because celebrated on the fiftieth day after the presentation of the wave-sheaf in passover week, has come to be known as Pentecost, from the Greek numeral signifying fifty. It was ordered that the fiftieth day after this presentation of the first sheaf of the harvest should be kept as a day of "holy convocation," with abstinence from all "servile work." The former festival had marked the absolute beginning of the harvest with the first sheaf of barley; this marked the completion of the grain harvest with the reaping of the wheat. In the former, the sheaf was presented as it came from the field; in this case, the offering was of the grain as prepared for food. It was ordered (ver. 16) that on this day "a new meal offering" should be offered. It should be brought out of their habitations and be baken with leaven. In both particulars, it was unlike the ordinary meal-offerings, because the offering was to represent the ordinary food of the people. Accompanied with a sevenfold burnt-offering, and a sin-offering, and two lambs of peace-offerings, these were to be waved before the Lord for their acceptance, after the manner of the wave-sheaf (vv. 18-20). On the altar they could not come, because they were baken with leaven.

This festival, as one of the sabbatic series, celebrated the rest after the labours of the grain harvest, a symbol of the great sabbatism to follow that harvest which is "the end of the age" (Matt. xiii. 39). As a consecration, it dedicated unto God the daily food of the nation for the coming year. As passover reminded them that God was the Creator of Israel, so herein, receiving their daily bread from Him, they were reminded that He was also the Sustainer of Israel; while the full accompaniment of burnt-offerings and peace-offerings expressed their full consecration and happy state of friendship with Jehovah, secured through the expiation of the sin-offering.

Was this feast also, like passover, prophetic? The New Testament is scarcely less clear than in the former case. For after that Christ, first having been slain as "our Passover," had then risen from the dead as the "Firstfruits," fulfilling the type of the wave-sheaf on the morning of the Sabbath, fifty days passed; "and when the day of Pentecost was fully come," came that great outpouring of the Holy Ghost, the conversion of three thousand out of many lands (Acts ii.), and therewith the formation of that Church of the New Testament whose members the Apostle James declares (i. 18) to be "a kind of firstfruits of God's creatures." Thus, as the sheaf had typified Christ as "the Firstborn from the dead," the presentation on the day of Pentecost of the two wave-loaves, the product of the sheaf of grain, no less evidently typified the presentation unto God of the Church of the first-born, the first-fruits of Christ's death and resurrection, as constituted on that sacred day. This then was the complete fulfilment of the feast of weeks regarded as a redemptive type, showing how, not only rest, but also redemption was comprehended in the significance of the sabbatic idea. And yet, that complete redemption was not therewith attained by that Church of the first-born on Pentecost was presignified in that the two wave-loaves were to be baken with leaven. The feast of unleavened bread had exhibited the ideal of the Christian life; that of firstfruits, the imperfection of the earthly attainment. On earth the leaven of sin still abides.

The Feast of Trumpets.

xxiii. 23-25.

"And the Lord spake unto Moses, saying, Speak unto the children of Israel, saying, In the seventh month, in the first day of the month, shall be a solemn rest unto you, a memorial of blowing of trumpets, an holy convocation. Ye shall do no servile work: and ye shall offer an offering made by fire unto the Lord."

By a very natural association of thought, in ver. 22 the direction to leave the gleaning of the harvest for the poor and the stranger is repeated verbally from chap. xix. 9, 10. Thereupon we pass from the feast of the seventh week to the solemnities of the seventh month, in which the series of annual sabbatic seasons ended. It was thus, by eminence, the sabbatic season of the year. Of the "set times" of this chapter, three fell in this month, and of these, two—the day of atonement and tabernacles—were of supreme significance: the former being distinguished by the most august religious solemnity of the year, the entrance of the high priest into the Holy of Holies to make atonement for the sins of the nation; the latter marking the completion of the ingathering of the products of the year, with the fruit, the oil, and the wine.

Of this sabbatic month, it is directed (vv. 23-25) that the first day be kept as a *shabbathon*, "a solemn rest," marked by abstinence from all the ordinary business of life, and a holy convocation. The special ceremony of the day, which gave it its name, is described as a "memorial of blowing of trumpets." This "blowing of trumpets" was a reminder, not from Israel to God, as some have fancied, but from God to Israel. It was an announcement from the King of Israel to His people that the glad sabbatic month had begun, and that the great day of atonement, and the supreme festivity of the feast of tabernacles, was now at hand.

That the first day of this sabbatic month should be thus sanctified was but according to the Mosaic principle that the consecration of anything signifies the consecration unto God of the whole. "If the firstfruit is holy, so also the lump;" in like manner, if the first day, so is the month. Trumpets— though not the same probably as used on this occasion—were also blown on other occasions, and, in particular, at the time of each new moon; but, according to tradition, these only by the priests and at the central sanctuary; while in this feast of trumpets every one blew who would, and throughout the whole land.

The Day of Atonement.

xxiii. 26-32.

> "And the Lord spake unto Moses, saying, Howbeit on the tenth day of this seventh month is the day of atonement: it shall be an holy convocation unto you, and ye shall afflict your souls; and ye shall offer an offering made by fire unto the Lord. And ye shall do no manner of work in that same day: for it is a day of atonement, to make atonement for you before the Lord your God. For whatsoever soul it be that shall not be afflicted in that same day, he shall be cut off from his people. And whatsoever soul it be that doeth any manner of work in that same day, that soul will I destroy from among his people. Ye shall do no manner of work: it is a statute for ever throughout your generations in all your dwellings. It shall be unto you a sabbath of solemn rest, and ye shall afflict your souls: in the ninth day of the month at even, from even unto even, shall ye keep your sabbath."

After this festival of annunciation, followed, on the tenth day of the month, the great annual day of atonement. This has already come before us (chap. xiii.) in its relation to the sacrificial system, of which the sin-offering of this day was the culmination. But this chapter brings it before us in another aspect, namely, in its relation to the annual septenary series of sacred seasons, the final festival of which it preceded and introduced.

Its significance, as thus coming in this final seventh and sabbatic month of the ecclesiastical year, lay not merely in the strictness of the rest which was commanded (vv. 28-30) from every manner of work, but, still more, in that it expressed in a far higher degree than any other festival the other sabbatic idea of complete restoration brought in through expiation for sin. This was indeed the central thought of the whole ceremonial of the day,—the complete removal of all those sins of the nation which stood between them and God, and hindered complete restoration to God's favour. And while this restoration was symbolised by the sacrifice of the sin-offering, and its presentation and acceptance before Jehovah in the Holy of Holies; yet, that none might hence argue from the fact of atonement to license to sin, it was ordained (ver. 27) that the people should "afflict their souls," namely, by fasting,[42] in token of their penitence for the sins for which atonement was made; and the absolute necessity of this condition of repentance in order to any benefit from the high-priestly sacrifice and intercession was further emphasised by the solemn threat (ver. 29): "Whatsoever soul it be that shall not be afflicted in that same day, he shall be cut off from his people."

These then were the lessons—lessons of transcendent moment for all people and all ages—which were set forth in the great atonement of the sabbatic month,—the complete removal of sin by an expiatory offering, conditioned on the part of the worshipper by the obedience of faith and sincere repentance for the sin, and issuing in rest and full establishment in God's loving favour.

The Feast of Tabernacles.

xxiii. 33-43.

"And the Lord spake unto Moses, saying, Speak unto the children of Israel, saying, On the fifteenth day of this seventh month is the feast of tabernacles for seven days unto the Lord. On the first day shall be an holy convocation: ye shall do no servile work. Seven days ye shall offer an offering made by fire unto the Lord: on the eighth day shall be an holy convocation unto you; and ye shall offer an offering made by fire unto the Lord: it is a solemn assembly; ye shall do no servile work. These are the set feasts of the Lord, which ye shall proclaim to be holy convocations, to offer an offering made by fire unto the Lord, a burnt offering, and a meal offering, a sacrifice, and drink offerings, each on its own day: beside the sabbaths of the Lord, and beside your gifts, and beside all your vows, and beside all your freewill offerings, which ye give unto the Lord. Howbeit on the fifteenth day of the seventh month, when ye have gathered in the fruits of the land, ye shall keep the feast of the Lord seven days: on the first day shall be a solemn rest, and on the eighth day shall be a solemn rest. And ye shall take you on the first day the fruit of goodly trees, branches of palm trees, and boughs of thick trees, and willows of the brook; and ye shall rejoice before the Lord your God seven days. And ye shall keep it a feast unto the Lord seven days in the year: it is a statute for ever in your generations: ye shall keep it in the seventh month. Ye shall dwell in booths seven days; all that are homeborn in Israel shall dwell in booths: that your generations may know that I made the children of Israel to dwell in booths, when I brought them out of the land of Egypt: I am the Lord your God."

The sin of Israel having been thus removed, the last and the greatest of all the feasts followed—the feast of tabernacles or ingathering. It occupied a full week (ver. 34), from the fifteenth to the twenty-second of the month, the first day being signalised by a holy convocation and abstinence from all servile work (ver. 35). Two reasons are indicated, here and elsewhere, for the observance: the one, natural (ver. 39), the completed ingathering of the products of the year; the other, historical (vv. 42, 43),—it was to be a memorial of the days when Israel dwelt in booths in the wilderness. Both ideas were represented in the direction (ver. 40) that they should take on the first day "the fruit of goodly trees, branches of palm trees, and boughs of thick trees, and willows of the brook," fitly symbolising the product of the vine and the fruit-trees which were harvested in this month; and, making booths of these, all were to dwell in these tabernacles, and "rejoice before the Lord their God seven days." And to this the historical reason is added, "that your generations may know that I made the children of Israel to dwell in booths, when I brought them out of the land of Egypt."

No one need feel any difficulty in seeing in this a connection with similar harvest and vintage customs among other peoples of that time. That other nations had festivities of this kind at that time, was surely no reason why God should not order these to be taken up into the Mosaic law, elevated in their significance, and sanctified to higher ends. Nothing could be more fitting than that the completion of the ingathering of the products of the year should be celebrated as a time of rejoicing and a thanksgiving day before Jehovah. Indeed, so natural is such a festivity to religious minds, that—as is well known—in the first instance, New England, and then, afterward, the whole United States, and also the Dominion of Canada, have established the observance of an annual "Thanksgiving Day" in the latter part of the autumn, which is observed by public religious services, by suspension of public business, and as a glad day of reunion of kindred and friends. It is interesting to observe how this last feature of the day is also mentioned in the case of this Hebrew feast, in the later form of the law (Deut. xvi. 13-15): "After that thou hast gathered in from thy threshing-floor and from thy winepress ... thou shalt rejoice in thy feast, thou, and thy son, and thy daughter, and thy manservant, and thy maidservant, and the Levite, and the stranger, and the fatherless, and the widow, that are within thy gates, ... and thou shalt be altogether joyful."

The chief sentiment of the feast was thus joy and thanksgiving to God as the Giver of all good. Yet the joy was not to be merely natural and earthly, but spiritual; they were to rejoice (ver. 40) "before the Lord." And the thanksgiving was not to be expressed merely in words, but in deeds. The week, we are elsewhere told, was signalised by the largest burnt-offerings of any of the feasts, consisting of a total of seventy bullocks, beginning with thirteen on the first day, and diminishing by one each day; while these again were accompanied daily by burnt-offerings of fourteen lambs and two rams, the double of what was enjoined even for the week of unleavened bread, with meal-offerings and drink-offerings in proportion. Nor was this outward ritual expression of thanksgiving enough; for their gratitude was to be further attested by taking into their glad festivities the Levite who had no portion, the fatherless and the widow, and even the stranger.

It is not hard to see the connection of all this with the historical reference to the days of their wilderness journeyings. Lest they might forget God in nature, they were to recall to mind, by their dwelling in booths, the days when they had no houses, and no fields nor crops, when, notwithstanding, none the less easily the Almighty God of Israel fed them with manna which they knew not, that He might make them to "know that man doth not live by bread only, but by every thing that proceedeth out of the mouth of the Lord" (Deut. viii. 3). There is, indeed, no better illustration of the intention of this part of the feast than those words with their context as they occur in Deuteronomy.

The ceremonies of the feast of tabernacles having been completed with the appointed seven days, there followed an eighth day,—an holy convocation, a festival of solemn rest (vv. 36, 39). This last day of holy solemnity and joy, to which a special name is given, is properly to be regarded, not as a part of the feast of tabernacles merely, but as celebrating the termination of the whole series of sabbatic times from the first to the seventh month. No ceremonial is here enjoined except the holy convocation, and the offering of "an offering made by fire unto the Lord," with abstinence from all servile work.

Typical Meaning of the Feasts of the Seventh Month.

We have already seen that the earlier feasts of the year were also prophetic; that Passover and Unleavened Bread pointed forward to Christ, our Passover, slain for us; Pentecost, to the spiritual ingathering of the firstfruits of the world's harvest, fifty days after the presentation of our Lord in resurrection, as the wave-sheaf of the firstfruits. We may therefore safely infer that these remaining feasts of the seventh month must be typical also. But, if so, typical of what? Two things may be safely said in this matter. The significance of the three festivals of this seventh month must be interpreted in harmony with what has already passed into fulfilment; and, in the second place, inasmuch as the feast of trumpets, the day of atonement, and the feast of tabernacles all belong to the seventh and last month of the ecclesiastical year, they must find their fulfilment in connection with what Scripture calls "the last times."

Keeping the first point in view, we may then safely say that if Pentecost typified the firstfruits of the world's harvest in the ingathering of an election from all nations, the feast of tabernacles must then typify the completion of that harvest in a spiritual ingathering, final and universal. Not only so, but, inasmuch as in the antitypical fulfilment of the wave-sheaf in the resurrection of our Lord, we were reminded that the consummation of the new creation is in resurrection from the dead, and that in regeneration is therefore involved resurrection, hence the feast of tabernacles, as celebrating the absolute completion of the year's harvest, must typify also the resurrection season, when all that are Christ's shall rise from the dead at His coming. And, finally, whereas this means for the now burdened earth permanent deliverance from the curse, and the beginning of a new age thus signalised by glorious life in resurrection, in which are enjoyed the blessed fruits of life's labours and pains for Christ, this was shadowed forth by the ordinance that immediately upon the seven days of tabernacles should follow a feast of the eighth day, the first day of a new week, in celebration of the beginning season of rest from all the labours of the field.

Most beautifully, thus regarded, does all else connected with the feast of tabernacles correspond, as type to antitype, to the revelation of the last things, and therein reveal its truest and deepest spiritual significance: the joy, the reunion, the rejoicing with son and with daughter, the fulness of gladness also for the widow and the fatherless; and this, not only for those in Israel, but also for the stranger, not of Israel, — for Gentile as well as Israelite was to have part in the festivity of that day; and, again, the full attainment of the most complete consecration, signified in the ten-fold burnt-offering;—all finds its place here. And so now we can see why it was that our Saviour declared (Matt. xiii. 39) that the end of this present age should be the time of harvest; and how Paul, looking at the future spiritual ingathering, places the ingathering of the Gentiles (Rom. xi. 25) as one of the last things. In full accord with this interpretation of the typical significance of this feast it is that in Zech. xiv. we find it written that in the predicted day of the Lord, when (ver. 5) the Lord "shall come, and all the holy ones" with Him, and (ver. 9) "the Lord shall be King over all the earth; ... the Lord ... one, and His name one," then (ver. 16) "every one that is left of all the nations ... shall go up from year to year to worship the King, the Lord of hosts, and to keep the feast of tabernacles;" and, moreover, that so completely shall consecration be realised in that day that (ver. 20) even upon the bells of the horses shall the words be inscribed, "Holy unto the Lord!"

But before the joyful feast of tabernacles could be celebrated, the great, sorrowful day of atonement must be kept,—a season marked, on the one hand, by affliction of soul throughout all Israel; on the other, by the complete putting away of the sin of the nation for the whole year, through the presentation of the blood of the sin-offering by the high priest, within the veil before the mercy seat. Now, if the feast of tabernacles has been correctly interpreted, as presignifying in symbol the completion of the great world harvest in the end of the age, does the prophetic word reveal anything in connection with the last things as preceding that great harvest, and, in some sense, preparing for and ushering in that day, which should be the antitype of the great day of atonement?

One can hardly miss of the answer. For precisely that which the prophets and apostles both represent as the event which shall usher in that great day of final ingathering and of blessed resurrection rest and joy in consummated redemption, is the national repentance of Israel, and the final cleansing of their age-long sin. In the type, two things are conspicuous: the great sorrowing of the nation and the great atonement putting away all Israel's sin. And two things, in like manner, are conspicuous in the prophetic pictures of the antitype, namely, Israel's heart-broken repentance, and the removal thereupon of Israel's sin; their cleansing in the "fountain opened for sin and for uncleanness." As Zechariah puts it (xii. 10, xiii. 1), "I will pour upon the house of David, and upon the inhabitants of Jerusalem, the spirit of grace and of supplication; and they shall look unto me whom they have pierced: and they shall mourn for him, as one mourneth for his only son;" and "in that day there shall be a fountain opened to the house of David and to the inhabitants of Jerusalem, for sin and for uncleanness." And the relation of this cleansing of Israel to the days of blessing which follow is most explicitly set forth by the Apostle Paul, in these words concerning Israel (Rom. xi. 12, 15), "If their fall is the riches of the world, and their loss the riches of the Gentiles; how much more their fulness? If the casting away of them is the reconciling of the world, what shall the receiving of them be, but life from the dead?"

So far, then, all seems clear. But the feast of trumpets yet remains to be explained. Has Holy Scripture predicted anything, falling in the period between Pentecost and the repentance of Israel, but specially belonging to the last things, which might with reason be regarded as the antitype of this joyful feast of trumpets? Here, again, it is not easy to go far astray. For the essential idea of the trumpet call is announcement, proclamation. From time to time all through the year the trumpet-call was heard in Israel; but on this occasion it became the feature of the day, and was universal throughout their land. And, as we have seen, its special significance for that time was to announce that the day of atonement and the feast of ingathering, which typified the full consummation of the kingdom of God, were now at hand. One can thus hardly fail to think at once of that other event which, according to our Lord's express word (Matt. xxiv. 14), is immediately to precede "the end," namely, the universal proclamation of the Gospel: "This gospel of the kingdom shall be preached in the whole world for a testimony unto all the nations; and then shall the end come." As throughout the year, from time to time, the trumpet call was heard in Israel, but only in connection with the central sanctuary; but now in all the land, as the chief thing in the celebration of the day which ushered in the final sabbatic month, precisely so in the antitype. All through the ages has the Gospel been sounded forth, but in a partial and limited way; but at "the time of the end" the proclamation shall become universal. And thus and then shall the feast of trumpets also, like Passover and Pentecost, pass into complete fulfilment, and be swiftly followed by Israel's repentance and restoration, and the consequent reappearing, as Peter predicts (Acts iii. 19-21 R.V.), of Israel's High Priest from within the veil, and thereupon the harvest of the world, the resurrection of the just, and the consummation upon earth of the glorified kingdom of God.

Of many thoughts of a practical kind which this chapter suggests, we may perhaps well dwell especially on one. The ideal of religious life, which these set times of the Lord kept before Israel, was a religion of joy. Again and again is this spoken of in the accounts of these feasts. This is true even of Passover, with which we oftener, though mistakenly, connect thoughts of sadness and gloom. Yet Passover was a feast of joy; it celebrated the birthday of the nation, and a deliverance unparalleled in history. The only exception to this joyful character in all these sacred times is found in the day of atonement; but it is itself instructive on the same point, teaching most clearly that in the Divine order, as in the necessity of the case, the joy in the Lord, of which the feast of ingathering was the supreme expression, must be preceded by and grounded in an accepted expiation and true penitence for sin.

So it is still with the religion of the Bible: it is a religion of joy. God does not wish us to be gloomy and sad. He desires that we should ever be joyful before Him, and thus find by blessed experience that "the joy of the Lord is our strength." Also, in particular, we do well to observe further that, inasmuch as all these set times were sabbatic seasons, joyfulness is inseparably connected with the Biblical conception of the Sabbath. This has been too often forgotten; and the weekly day of sabbatic rest has sometimes been made a day of stern repression and forbidding gloom. How utterly astray are such conceptions from the Divine ideal, we shall perhaps the more clearly see when we call to mind the thought which appears more or less distinctly in all these sabbatic seasons, that every Sabbath points forward to the eternal joy of the consummated kingdom, the sabbath rest which remaineth for the people of God (Heb. iv. 9).

CHAPTER XXV
THE HOLY LIGHT AND THE SHEW-BREAD: THE BLASPHEMER'S END

Lev. xxiv. 1-23.

It is not easy to determine with confidence the association of thought which occasioned the interposition of this chapter, with its somewhat disconnected contents, between chap. xxiii., on the set times of holy convocation, and chap. xxv., on the sabbatic and jubilee years, which latter would seem most naturally to have followed the former immediately, as relating to the same subject of sacred times. Perhaps the best explanation of the connection with the previous chapter is that which finds it in the reference to the olive oil for the lamps and the meal for the shew-bread. The feast of tabernacles, directions for which had just been given, celebrated the completed ingathering of the harvest of the year, both of grain and of fruit; and here Israel is told what is to be done with a certain portion of each.

The Ordering of the Light in the Holy Place.

xxiv. 1-4.

"And the Lord spake unto Moses, saying, Command the children of Israel, that they bring unto thee pure olive oil beaten for the light, to cause a lamp to burn continually. Without the veil of the testimony, in the tent of meeting, shall Aaron order it from evening to morning before the Lord continually: it shall be a statute for ever throughout your generations. He shall order the lamps upon the pure candlestick before the Lord continually."

First (vv. 1-4) is given the direction for the ordering of the daily light, which was to burn from evening until morning in the holy place continually. The people themselves are to furnish the oil for the seven-branched candlestick out of the product of their olive yards. The oil is to be "pure," carefully cleansed from leaves and all impurities; and "beaten," that is, not extracted by heat and pressure, as are inferior grades, but simply by beating and macerating the olives with water,—a process which gives the very best. The point in these specifications is evidently this, that for this, as always, they are to give to God's service the very best,—an eternal principle which rules in all acceptable service to God. The oil is to come from the people in general, so that the illuminating of the Holy Place, although specially tended by the high priest, is yet constituted a service in which all the children of Israel have some part. The oil was to be used to supply the seven lamps upon the golden candlestick which was placed on the south side of the Holy Place, without the veil of the testimony, in the tent of meeting. This Aaron was to "order from evening to morning before the Lord continually." According to Exod. xxv. 31-40, this candlestick—or, more properly, lampstand—was made of a single shaft, with three branches on either side, each with a cup at the end like an almond blossom; so that, with that on the top of the central shaft, it was a stand of seven lamps, in a conventional imitation of an almond tree.

The significance of the symbol is brought clearly before us in Zech. iv. 1-14, where the seven-branched candlestick symbolises Israel as the congregation of God, the giver of the light of life to the world. And yet a lamp can burn only as it is supplied with oil and trimmed and cared for. And so in the symbol of Zechariah the prophet sees the golden candlestick supplied with oil conveyed through two golden pipes into which flowed the golden oil, mysteriously self-distilled from two olive trees on either side the candlestick. And the explanation given is this: "Not by might, nor by power, but by My Spirit," saith the Lord. Thus we learn that the golden seven-branched lampstand denotes Israel, more precious than gold in God's sight, appointed of Him to be the giver of light to the world. And yet by this requisition of oil for the golden candlestick the nation was reminded that their power to give light was dependent upon the supply of the heavenly grace of God's Spirit, and the continual ministrations of the priest in the Holy Place. And how this ordering of the light might be a symbolic act of worship, we can at once see, when we recall the word of Jesus (Matt. v. 14, 16): "Ye are the light of the world.... Let your light shine before men, that they may see your good works, and glorify your Father which is in heaven."

How pertinent for instruction still in all its deepest teaching is this ordinance of the lamp continually burning in the presence of the Lord, is vividly brought before us in the Apocalypse (i. 12, 13), where we read that seven candlesticks appeared in vision to the Apostle John; and Christ, in His glory, robed in high-priestly vesture, was seen walking up and down, after the manner of Aaron, in the midst of the seven candlesticks, in care and watch of the manner of their burning. And as to the significance of this vision, the Apostle was expressly told (ver. 20) that the seven candlesticks were the seven Churches of Asia,—types of the collective Church in all the centuries. Thus, as in the language of this Levitical symbol, we are taught that in the highest sense it is the office of the Church to give light in darkness; but that she can only do this as the heavenly oil is supplied, and each lamp is cared for, by the high-priestly ministrations of her risen Lord.

The "Bread of the Presence."

xxiv. 5-9.

> "And thou shall take fine flour, and bake twelve cakes thereof: two tenth parts of an ephah shall be in one cake. And thou shalt set them in two rows, six on a row, upon the pure table before the Lord. And thou shalt put pure frankincense upon each row, that it may be to the bread for a memorial, even an offering made by fire unto the Lord. Every sabbath day he shall set it in order before the Lord continually; it is on the behalf of the children of Israel, an everlasting covenant. And it shall be for Aaron and his sons; and they shall eat it in a holy place: for it is most holy unto him of the offerings of the Lord made by fire by a perpetual statute."

Next follows the ordinance for the preparation and presentation of the "shew-bread," *lit.*, "bread of the Face," or "Presence," *sc.* of God. This was to consist of twelve cakes, each to be made of two tenth parts of an ephah of fine flour, which was to be placed in two rows or piles, "upon the pure table" of gold that stood before the Lord, in the Holy Place, opposite to the golden candlestick. On each pile was to be placed (ver. 7) "pure frankincense," — doubtless, as tradition says, placed in the golden spoons, or little cups (Exod. xxxvii. 16). Every sabbath (vv. 8, 9) fresh bread was to be so placed, when the old became the food of Aaron and his sons only, as belonging to the order of things "most holy;" the frankincense which had been its "memorial" having been first burned, "an offering made by fire unto the Lord" (ver. 7). Tradition adds that the bread was always unleavened; a few have called this in question, but this has been only on theoretic grounds, and without evidence; and when we remember how stringent was the prohibition of leaven even in any offerings made by fire upon the altar of the outer court, much less is it likely that it could have been tolerated here in the Holy Place immediately before the veil.

This bread of the Presence must be regarded as in its essential nature a perpetual meal-offering, — the meal-offering of the Holy Place, as the others were of the outer court.[43] The material was the same, cakes of fine flour; to this frankincense must be added as a "memorial," as in the meal-offerings of the outer court. Such part of the offering as was not burned, as in the case of the others, was to be eaten by the priests only, as a thing "most holy." It differed from those in that there were always the twelve cakes, one for each tribe; and in that while they were repeatedly offered, this lay before the Lord continually. The altar of burnt-offering might sometimes be empty of the meal-offering, but the table of shew-bread, "the table of the Presence," never.

In general, therefore, the meaning of the offering of the shew-bread must be the same as that of the meal-offerings; like them it symbolised the consecration unto the Lord of the product of the labour of the hands, and especially of the daily food as prepared for use. But in this, by the twelve cakes for the twelve tribes it was emphasised that God requires, not only such consecration of service and acknowledgment of Him from individuals, as in the law of chap. ii., but from the nation in its collective and organised capacity; and that not merely on such occasions as pious impulse might direct, but continuously.

In these days, when the tendency among us is to an extreme individualism, and therewith to an ignoring or denial of any claim of God upon nations and communities as such, it is of great need to insist upon this thought thus symbolised. It was not enough in God's sight that individual Israelites should now and then offer their meal-offerings; the Lord required a meal-offering "on behalf of the children of Israel" *as a whole*, and of each particular tribe of the twelve, each in its corporate capacity. There is no reason to think that in the Divine government the principle which took this symbolical expression is obsolete. It is not enough that individuals among us consecrate the fruit of their labours to the Lord. The Lord requires such consecration of every nation collectively; and of each of the subdivisions in that nation, such as cities, towns, states, provinces, and so on. Yet where in the wide world can we see one such consecrated nation? Can we find one such consecrated province or state, or even such a city or town? Where then, from this biblical and spiritual point of view, is the ground for the religious boasting of the Christian progress of our day which one sometimes hears? Must we not say, "It is excluded"?

Typically, the shew-bread, like the other meal-offerings with their frankincense, must foreshadow the work of the Messiah in holy consecration; and, in particular, as the One in whom the ideal of Israel was perfectly realised, and who thus represented in His person the whole Israel of God. But the bread of the Presence represents His holy obedience in self-consecration, not merely, as in the other meal-offerings, presented in the outer court, in the sight of men, as in His earthly life; but here, rather, as continually presented before the "Face of God," in the Holy Place, where

Christ appears in the presence of God for us. And in this symbolism, which has been already justified, we may recognise the element of truth that there is in the view held by Bähr,[44] apparently, as by others, that the shew-bread typified Christ Himself regarded as the bread of life to His people. Not indeed, precisely, that Christ Himself is brought before us here, but rather His holy obedience, continually offered unto God in the heavenly places, in behalf of the true Israel, and as sealing and confirming the everlasting covenant;—this is what this symbol brings before us. And it is as we by faith appropriate Him, as thus ever presenting His holy life to God for us, that He becomes for us the Bread of Life.

The Penalty of Blasphemy.

xxiv. 10-23.

"And the son of an Israelitish woman, whose father was an Egyptian, went out among the children of Israel: and the son of the Israelitish woman and a man of Israel strove together in the camp; and the son of the Israelitish woman blasphemed the Name, and cursed: and they brought him unto Moses. And his mother's name was Shelomith, the daughter of Dibri, of the tribe of Dan. And they put him in ward, that it might be declared unto them at the mouth of the Lord. And the Lord spake unto Moses, saying, Bring forth him that hath cursed without the camp; and let all that heard him lay their hands upon his head, and let all the congregation stone him. And thou shalt speak unto the children of Israel, saying, Whosoever curseth his God shall bear his sin. And he that blasphemeth the name of the Lord, he shall surely be put to death; all the congregation shall certainly stone him: as well the stranger, as the homeborn, when he blasphemeth the name of the Lord, shall be put to death. And he that smiteth any man mortally shall surely be put to death; and he that smiteth a beast mortally shall make it good: life for life. And if a man cause a blemish in his neighbour; as he hath done, so shall it be done to him; breach for breach, eye for eye, tooth for tooth: as he hath caused a blemish in a man, so shall it be rendered unto him. And he that killeth a beast shall make it good: and he that killeth a man shall be put to death. Ye shall have one manner of law, as well for the stranger, as for the homeborn: for I am the Lord your God. And Moses spake to the children of Israel, and they brought forth him that had cursed out of the camp, and stoned him with stones. And the children of Israel did as the Lord commanded Moses."

The connection of this section with the preceding context is now impossible to determine. Very possibly its insertion here may be due to the occurrence here described having taken place at the time of the delivery of the preceding laws concerning the oil for the golden lampstand and the shew-bread. However, the purport and intention of the narrative is very plain, namely, to record the law delivered by the Lord for the punishment of blasphemy; and therewith also His command that the penalty of broken law, both in this case and in others specified, should be exacted both from native Israelites and from foreigners alike.

The incident which was the occasion of the promulgation of these laws was as follows. The son of an Israelitish woman by an Egyptian husband fell into a quarrel in the camp. As often happens in such cases, the one sin led on to another and yet graver sin; the half-caste man "blasphemed the Name, and cursed;" whereupon he was arrested and put into confinement until the will of the Lord might be ascertained in his case. "The Name" is of course the name of God; the meaning is that he used the holy name profanely in cursing. The passage, together with ver. 16, is of special and curious as upon these two the Jews have based their well-known belief that it is unlawful to utter the Name which we commonly vocalise as Jehovah; whence it has followed that wherever in the Hebrew text the Name occurs it is written with the vowels of *Adonáy*, "Lord," to indicate to the reader that this word was to be substituted for the proper name,—a usage which is represented in the Septuagint by the appearance of the Greek word *Kurios*, "Lord," in all places where the Hebrew has Jehovah (or Yáhveh); and which, in both the authorised and revised versions, is still maintained in the retention of "Lord" in all such cases,—a relic of Jewish superstition which one could greatly wish that the Revisers had banished from the English version, especially as in many passages it totally obscures to the English reader the exact sense of the text, wherever it turns upon the choice of this name. It is indeed true that the word rendered "blaspheme" has the meaning "to pronounce," as the Targumists and other Hebrew writers render it; but that it also means simply to "revile," and in many places cannot possibly be rendered "to pronounce," is perforce admitted even by Jewish scholars.[45] To give it the other meaning here were so plainly foreign to the spirit of the Old Testament, debasing reverence to superstition, that no argument against it will be required with any but a Jew.

And this young man, in the heat of his passion, "reviled the Name." The words "of the Lord" are not in the Hebrew; the name "Jehovah" is thus brought before us expressively as The Name, *par excellence*, of God, as revealing Himself in covenant for man's redemption.[46] Horrified at the man's wickedness, "they brought him unto Moses;" and "they put him in ward" (ver. 12), "that it might be declared unto them at the mouth of the Lord" what should be done unto him. This was necessary because the case involved two points upon which no revelation had been made: first, as to what should be the punishment of blasphemy; and secondly, whether the law in such cases applied to a foreigner as well as to the native Israelite. The answer of God decided these points. As to the first (ver. 15), "Whosoever curseth his God shall bear his sin," *i.e.*, he shall be held subject to punishment; and (ver. 16), "He that blasphemeth the name of the Lord, he shall surely be put to death; all the congregation shall certainly stone him." And as to the second point, it is added, "as well the stranger, as the homeborn, when he blasphemeth the Name, shall be put to death."

Then follows (vv. 17-21) a declaration of penalties for murder, for killing a neighbour's beast, and for inflicting a bodily injury on one's neighbour. These were to be settled on the principle of the *lex talionis*, life for life, "breach for breach, eye for eye, tooth for tooth;" in the case of the beast killed, its value was to be made good to the owner. All these laws had been previously given (Exod. xxi. 12, 23-36); but are repeated here plainly for the purpose of expressly ordering that these laws, like that now declared for blasphemy, were to be applied alike to the home-born and the stranger (ver. 22).

Much cavil have these laws occasioned, the more so that Christ Himself is cited as having condemned them in the Sermon on the Mount (Matt. v. 38-42). But how little difficulty really exists here will appear from the following considerations. The Jews from of old have maintained that the law of "an eye for eye," as here given, was not intended to authorise private and irresponsible retaliation in kind, but only after due trial and by legal process. Moreover, even in such cases, they have justly remarked that the law here given was not meant to be applied always with the most exact literality; but that it was evidently intended to permit the commutation of the penalty by such a fine as the judges might determine. They justly argue from the explicit prohibition of the acceptance of any such satisfaction in commutation in the case of a murderer (Numb. xxxv. 31, 32) that this implies the permission of it in the instances here mentioned;—a conclusion the more necessary when it is observed that the literal application of the law in all cases would often result in defeating the very ends of exact justice which it was evidently intended to secure. For instance, the loss by a one-eyed man of his only eye, under such an interpretation, would be much more than an equivalent for the loss of an eye which he had inflicted upon a neighbour who had both eyes. Hence, Jewish history contains no record of the literal application of the law in such cases; the principle is applied as often among ourselves, in the exaction from an offender of a pecuniary satisfaction proportioned to the degree of the disability he has inflicted upon his neighbour. Finally, as regards the words of our Saviour, that He did not intend His words to be taken in their utmost stretch of literality in all cases, is plain from His own conduct when smitten by the order of the high priest (John xviii. 23), and from the statement that the magistrate is endowed with the sword, as a servant of God, to be a terror to evil-doers (Rom. xiii. 4); from which it is plain that Christ did not mean to prohibit the resort to judicial process under all circumstances, but rather the spirit of retaliation and litigation which sought to justify itself by a perverse appeal to this law of "an eye for eye;"—a law which, in point of fact, was given, as Augustine has truly observed, not "as an incitement to, but for the mitigation of wrath."

The narrative then ends with the statement (ver. 23) that Moses delivered this law to the children of Israel, who then, according to the commandment of the Lord, took the blasphemer out of the camp, when all that heard him blaspheme laid their hands upon his head, in token that they thus devolved on him the responsibility for his own death; and then the congregation stoned the criminal with stones that he died (ver. 23).

The chief lesson to be learned from this incident and from the law here given is very plain. It is the high criminality in God's sight of all irreverent use of His holy name. To a great extent in earlier days this was recognised by Christian governments; and in the Middle Ages the penalty of blasphemy in many states of Christendom, as in the Mosaic code and in many others, although not death, was yet exceedingly severe. The present century, however, has seen a great relaxation of law, and still more of public sentiment, in regard to this crime,—a change which, from a Christian point of view, is a matter for anything but gratulation. Reverence for God lies at the very foundation of even common morality. Our modern atheism and agnosticism may indeed deny this, and yet, from the days of the French Revolution to the present, modern history has been presenting, in one land and another, illustrations of the fact which are pregnant with most solemn warning. And while no one could wish that the crime of blasphemy should be punished with torture and cruelty, as in some instances in the Middle Ages, yet the more deeply one thinks on this subject in the light of the Scripture and of history, the more, if we mistake not, will it appear that it might be far better for us, and might argue a far more hopeful and wholesome condition of the public sentiment than that which now exists, if still, as in Mosaic days and sometimes in the Middle Ages, death were made the punishment for this crime;—a crime which not only argues the extreme of depravity in the criminal, but which, if overlooked by the State, or expiated with any light penalty, cannot but operate most fatally by breaking down in the public conscience that profound reverence toward God which is the most essential condition of the maintenance of all private and public morality.

In this point of view, not to speak of other considerations, it is not surprising that the theocratic law here provides that blasphemy shall be punished with death in the case of the foreigner as well as the native Israelite. This sin, like those of murder and violence with which it is here conjoined, is of such a kind that to every conscience which is not hopelessly hardened, its wickedness must be manifest even from the very light of nature. Nature itself is sufficient to teach any one that abuse and calumny of the Supreme God, the Maker and Ruler of the world,—a Being who, if He exist at all, must be infinitely good,—must be a sin involving quite peculiar and exceptional guilt. Hence, absolute equity, no less than governmental wisdom, demanded that the law regarding blasphemy, as that with respect to the other crimes here mentioned, should be impartially enforced upon both the native Israelite and the foreigner.

CHAPTER XXVI
THE SABBATIC YEAR AND THE JUBILEE

Lev. xxv. 1-55.

The system of annually recurring sabbatic times, as given in chap. xxiii., culminated in the sabbatic seventh month. But this remarkable system of sabbatisms extended still further, and, besides the sacred seventh day, the seventh week, and seventh month, included also a sabbatic seventh year; and beyond that, as the ultimate expression of the sabbatic idea, following the seventh seven of years, came the hallowed fiftieth year, known as the jubilee. And the law concerning these two last-named periods is recorded in this twenty-fifth chapter of Leviticus.

First (vv. 1-5), is given the ordinance of the sabbatic seventh year, in the following words: "When ye come into the land which I give you, then shall the land keep a sabbath unto the Lord. Six years thou shalt sow thy field, and six years thou shalt prune thy vineyard, and gather in the fruits thereof; but in the seventh year shall be a sabbath of solemn rest for the land, a sabbath unto the Lord: thou shalt neither sow thy field, nor prune thy vineyard. That which groweth of itself of thy harvest thou shalt not reap, and the grapes of thy undressed vine thou shalt not gather: it shall be a year of solemn rest for the land."

This sacred year is thus here described as a sabbath for the land unto the Lord,—a *shabbath shabbathon*; that is, a sabbath in a special and eminent sense. No public religious gatherings were ordered, however, neither was labour of every kind prohibited. It was strictly a year of rest for the land, and for the people in so far as this was involved in that fact. There was to be no sowing or reaping, even of what might grow of itself; no pruning of vineyard or fruit trees, nor gathering of their fruit. These regulations thus involved the total suspension of agricultural labour for this entire period.

It was further ordered (vv. 6, 7) that during this year the spontaneous produce of the land should be equally free to all, both man and beast: "The sabbath of the land shall be for food for you; for thee, and for thy servant and for thy maid, and for thy hired servant and for thy stranger that sojourn with thee; and for thy cattle, and for the beasts that are in thy land, shall all the increase thereof be for food."

That this cannot be regarded as merely a regulation of a communistic character, designed simply to affirm the absolute equality of all men in right to the product of the soil, is evident from the fact that the beasts also are included in the terms of the law. The object was quite different, as we shall shortly see.

That it should be regarded as possible for a whole people thus to live off the spontaneous produce of self-sowed grain may seem incredible to us who dwell in less propitious lands; and yet travellers tell us that in the Palestine of to-day, with its rich soil and kindly climate, the various food grains continuously propagate themselves without cultivation; and that in Albania, also, two and three successive harvests are sometimes reaped as the result of one sowing. So, even apart from the special blessing from the Lord promised to them if they would obey this command, the supply of at least the necessities of life was possible from the spontaneous product of the sabbath of the land. Though less than usual, it might easily be sufficient. In Deut. xv. 1-11 it is ordered also that the seventh year should be "a year of release" to the debtor; not indeed as regards all debts, but loans only; nor, apparently, that even these should be released absolutely, but that throughout the seventh year the claim of the creditor was to be in abeyance. The regulation may naturally be regarded as consequent upon this fundamental law regarding the sabbath of the land. The income of the year being much less than usual, the debtor, presumably, might often find it difficult to pay; whence this restriction on collection of debt during this period.

The central thought of this ordinance then is this, that man's right in the soil and its product, originally granted from God, during this sabbatic year reverted to the Giver; who, again, by ordering that all exclusive rights of individuals in the produce of their estates should be suspended for this year, placed, for so long, the rich and the poor on an absolute equality as regards means of sustenance.

The Jubilee.

xxv. 8-12.

> "And thou shalt number seven sabbaths of years unto thee, seven times seven years; and there shall be unto thee the days of seven sabbaths of years, even forty and nine years. Then shalt thou send abroad the loud trumpet on the tenth day of the seventh month; in the day of atonement shall ye send

abroad the trumpet throughout all your land. And ye shall hallow the fiftieth year, and proclaim liberty throughout the land unto all the inhabitants thereof: it shall be a jubilee unto you; and ye shall return every man unto his possession, and ye shall return every man unto his family. A jubilee shall that fiftieth year be unto you: ye shall not sow, neither reap that which groweth of itself in it, nor gather the grapes in it of the undressed vines. For it is a jubilee; it shall be holy unto you: ye shall eat the increase thereof out of the field."

The remainder of this chapter, vv. 8-55, is occupied with this ordinance of the jubilee year; an observance absolutely without a parallel in any nation, and which has to do with the solution of some of the most difficult social problems, not only of that time, but also of our own. Seven weeks of years, each terminating with the sabbatic year of solemn rest for the land, were to be numbered, *i.e.*, forty-nine full years, of which the last was a sabbatic year, beginning, as always, with the feast of atonement in the tenth day of the seventh month. And then when, at its expiration, the day of atonement came round again, at the beginning of the fiftieth year of this reckoning, at the close, as would appear, of the solemn expiatory ritual of the day, throughout all the land of Israel the loud trumpet was to be sounded, proclaiming "liberty throughout the land unto all the inhabitants thereof." The ordinance is given in vv. 8-12 above.

It appears that the liberty thus proclaimed was threefold: (1) liberty to the man who, through the reverses of life, had become dispossessed from his family inheritance in the land, to return to it again; (2) liberty to every Hebrew slave, so that in the jubilee he became a free man again; (3) the liberty of release from toil in the cultivation of the land,—a feature, in this case, even more remarkable than in the sabbatic year, because already one such sabbatic year had but just closed when the jubilee year immediately succeeded.

Why this year should be called a jubilee (Heb. *yobel*) is a vexed question, on which scholars are far from unanimous; but as it is of no practical importance, there is no need to enter on the discussion here. To suppose that these enactments should have originated, as the radical critics claim, in post-exilian days, when, under the existing social and political conditions, their observance was impossible, is utterly absurd.[47] Not only so, but in view of the admitted neglect even of the sabbatic year,—an ordinance certainly less difficult to carry out in practice,—during four hundred and ninety years of Israel's history, the supposition that the law of the jubilee should have been first promulgated at any earlier post-Mosaic period is scarcely less incredible.

The Jubilee and the Land.

xxv. 13-28.

"In this year of jubilee ye shall return every man unto his possession. And if thou sell aught unto thy neighbour, or buy of thy neighbour's hand, ye shall not wrong one another: according to the number of years after the jubilee thou shalt buy of thy neighbour, and according unto the number of years of the crops he shall sell unto thee. According to the multitude of the years thou shalt increase the price thereof, and according to the fewness of the years thou shalt diminish the price of it; for the number of the crops doth he sell unto thee. And ye shall not wrong one another; but thou shalt fear thy God: for I am the Lord your God. Wherefore ye shall do My statutes, and keep My judgments and do them; and ye shall dwell in the land in safety. And the land shall yield her fruit, and ye shall eat your fill, and dwell therein in safety. And if ye shall say, What shall we eat the seventh year? behold, we shall not sow, nor gather in our increase: then I will command My blessing upon you in the sixth year, and it shall bring forth fruit for the three years. And ye shall sow the eighth year, and eat of the fruits, the old store; until the ninth year, until her fruits come in, ye shall eat the old store. And the land shall not be sold in perpetuity; for the land is Mine: for ye are strangers and sojourners with Me. And in all the land of your possession ye shall grant a redemption for the land. If thy brother be waxen poor, and sell some of his possession, then shall his kinsman that is next unto him come, and shall redeem that which his brother hath sold. And if a man have no one to redeem it, and he be waxen rich and find sufficient to redeem it; then let him count the years of the sale thereof, and restore the overplus unto the man to whom he sold it; and he shall return unto his possession. But if he be not able to get it back for himself, then that which he hath sold shall remain in the hand of him that hath bought it until the year of jubilee: and in the jubilee it shall go out, and he shall return unto his possession."

The remainder of the chapter (vv. 13-55) deals with the practical application of this law of the jubilee to various cases. In vv. 13-28 we have the application of the law to the case of property in *land*; in vv. 29-34, to sales of *dwelling houses*; and the remaining verses (35-55) deal with the application of this law to the institution of *slavery*.

As regards the first matter, the transfers of right in land, these in all cases were to be governed by the fundamental principle enounced in ver. 23: "The land shall not be sold in perpetuity; for the land is Mine: for ye are strangers and sojourners with Me."

Thus in the theocracy there was no such thing as either private or communal ownership in land. Just as in some lands to-day the only owner of the land is the king, so it was in Israel; but in this case the King was Jehovah. From this it follows, evidently, that properly speaking, according to this law, there could be no such thing in Israel as a sale or purchase of land. All that any man could buy or sell was the right to its products, and that, again, only for a limited time; for every fiftieth year the land was to revert to the family to whom its use had been originally assigned. Hence the regulations (vv. 14-19) regarding such transfers of the right to the use of the land. They are all governed by the simple and equitable principle that the price paid for the usufruct of the land was to be exactly proportioned to the number of years which were to elapse between the date of the sale and the reversion of the land, which would take place in the jubilee. Thus, the price for such transfer of right in the first year of the jubilee period would be at its maximum, because the sale covered the right to the produce of the land for forty-nine years; while, on the other hand, in the case of a transfer made in the forty-eighth year, the price would have fallen to a very small amount, as only the product of one year's cultivation remained to be sold, and after the ensuing sabbatic year the land would revert in the jubilee to the original holder. The command to keep in mind this principle, and not wrong one another, is enforced (vv. 17-19) by the injunction to do this because of the fear of God; and by the promise that if Israel will obey this law, they shall dwell in safety, and have abundance.

In vv. 24-28, after the declaration of the fundamental law that the land belongs only to the Lord, and that they are to regard themselves as simply His tenants, "sojourners with Him," a second application of the law is made. First, it is ordered that in every case, and without reference to the year of jubilee, every landholder who through stress of poverty may be obliged to sell the usufruct of his land shall retain the right to redeem it. Three cases are assumed. First (ver. 25), it is ordered that if the poor man have lost his land, and have a kinsman who is able to redeem it, he shall do so. Secondly (ver. 26), if he have no such kinsman, but himself become able to redeem it, it shall be his privilege to do so. In both cases alike, "the overplus," *i.e.*, the value of the land for the years still remaining till the jubilee, for which the purchaser had paid, is to be restored to him, and then the land reverts at once, without waiting for the jubilee, to the original proprietor. The third case (ver. 28) is that of the poor man who has no kinsman to buy back his landholding, and never becomes able to do so himself. In such a case, the purchaser was to hold it until the jubilee year, when the land reverted without compensation to the family of the poor man who had transferred it. That this was strictly equitable is self-evident, when we remember that, according to the law previously laid down, the purchaser had only paid for the value of the product of the land until the jubilee year; and when he had received its produce for that time, naturally and in strict equity his right in the land terminated.

The Jubilee and Dwelling Houses.

xxv. 29-34.

"And if a man sell a dwelling house in a walled city, then he may redeem it within a whole year after it is sold; for a full year shall he have the right of redemption. And if it be not redeemed within the space of a full year, then the house that is in the walled city shall be made sure in perpetuity to him that bought it, throughout his generations: it shall not go out in the jubilee. But the houses of the villages which have no wall round about them shall be reckoned with the fields of the country: they may be redeemed, and they shall go out in the jubilee. Nevertheless the cities of the Levites, the houses of the cities of their possession, may the Levites redeem at any time. And if one of the Levites redeem [not], then the house that was sold, and the city of his possession, shall go out in the jubilee: for the houses of the cities of the Levites are their possession among the children of Israel. But the field of the suburbs of their cities may not be sold; for it is their perpetual possession."

In vv. 29-34 is considered the application of the jubilee ordinance to the sale of dwelling houses: first (vv. 29-31), to such sale in case of the people generally; secondly (vv. 32-34), to sales of houses by the Levites. Under the former head we have first the law as regards sales of dwelling houses in "walled cities;" to which it is ordered that the law of reversion in the jubilee shall not apply, and for which the right of redemption was only to hold valid for one year. The obvious reason for exempting houses in cities from the law of reversion is that the law has to do only with land such as may be used in a pastoral or agricultural way for man's support. And this explains why, on the other hand, it is next ordered (ver. 31) that in the case of houses in unwalled villages the law of redemption and reversion in the jubilee shall apply as well as to the land. For the inhabitants of the villages were the herdsmen and cultivators of the soil; and the house was regarded rightly as a necessary attachment to the land, without which its use would not be possible. But inasmuch as God had assigned no landholding to the Levites in the original distribution of the land,—and apart from their houses they had no possession (ver. 33),—in order to secure them in the privilege of a permanent holding, such as others enjoyed in their lands, it was ordered that in their case their houses, as being their only possession in real estate, should be treated as were the landholdings of members of the other tribes. [48]

The relation of the jubilee law to personal rights in the land having been thus determined and expounded, in the next place (vv. 35-55) is considered the application of the law to slavery. Quite naturally, this section begins (vv. 35-37) with a general injunction to assist and deal mercifully with any brother who has become poor. "If thy brother be waxen poor, and his hand fail with thee; then thou shalt uphold him: as a stranger and a sojourner shall he live with thee. Take thou no usury of him or increase; but fear thy God: that thy brother may live with thee. Thou shalt not give him thy money upon usury, nor give him thy victuals for increase."

The evident object of this law is to prevent, as far as possible, that extreme of poverty which might compel a man to sell himself in order to live. Debt is a burden in any case, to a poor man especially; but debt is the heavier burden when to the original debt is added the constant payment of interest. Hence, not merely "usury" in the modern sense of *excessive* interest, but it is forbidden to claim or take any interest whatever from any Hebrew debtor. On the same principle, it is forbidden to take increase for food which may be lent to a poor brother; as when one lets a man have twenty bushels of wheat on condition that in due time he shall return for it twenty-two. This command is enforced (ver. 38) by reminding them from whom they have received what they have, and on what easy terms, as a gift; from their covenant God, who is Himself their security that by so doing they shall not lose: "I am the Lord your God, which brought you forth out of the land of Egypt, to give you the land of Canaan, to be your God." They need not therefore have recourse to the exaction of interest and increase from their poor brethren in order to make a living, but are to be merciful, even as Jehovah their God is merciful.

The Jubilee and Slavery.

xxv. 39-55.

"And if thy brother be waxen poor with thee, and sell himself unto thee; thou shalt not make him to serve as a bondservant: as an hired servant, and as a sojourner, he shall be with thee; he shall serve with thee unto the year of jubilee: then shall he go out from thee, he and his children with him, and shall return unto his own family, and unto the possession of his fathers shall he return. For they are My servants, which I brought forth out of the land of Egypt: they shall not be sold as bondmen. Thou shalt not rule over him with rigour; but shalt fear thy God. And as for thy bondmen, and thy bondmaids, which thou shalt have; of the nations that are round about you, of them shall ye buy bondmen and bondmaids. Moreover of the children of the strangers that do sojourn among you, of them shall ye buy, and of their families that are with you, which they have begotten in your land: and they shall be your possession. And ye shall make them an inheritance for your children after you, to hold for a possession; of them shall ye take your bondmen for ever: but over your brethren the children of Israel ye shall not rule, one over another, with rigour. And if a stranger or sojourner with thee be waxen rich, and thy brother be waxen poor beside him, and sell himself unto the stranger or sojourner with thee, or to the stock of the stranger's family: after that he is sold he may be redeemed; one of his brethren may redeem him: or his uncle, or his uncle's son, may redeem him, or any that is nigh of kin unto him of his family may redeem him; or if he be waxen rich, he may redeem himself. And he shall reckon with him that bought him from the year that he sold himself to him unto the year of jubilee: and the price of his sale shall be according unto the number of years; according to the time of an hired servant shall he be with him. If there be yet many years, according unto them he shall give back the price of his redemption out of the money that he was bought for. And if there remain but few years unto the year of jubilee, then he shall reckon with him; according unto his years shall he give back the price of his redemption. As a servant hired year by year shall he be with him: he shall not rule with rigour over him in thy sight. And if he be not redeemed by these means, then he shall go out in the year of jubilee, he, and his children with him. For unto Me the children of Israel are servants; they are My servants whom I brought forth out of the land of Egypt: I am the Lord your God."

Even with the burdensomeness of debt lightened as above, it was yet possible that a man might be reduced to poverty so extreme that he should feel compelled to sell himself as a slave. Hence arises the question of slavery, and its relation to the law of the jubilee. Under this head two cases were possible: the first, where a man had sold himself to a fellow-Hebrew (vv. 39-46); the second, where a man had sold himself to a foreigner resident in the land (vv. 47-55).

With the Hebrews and all the neighbouring peoples, slavery was, and had been from of old, a settled institution. Regarded simply as an abstract question of morals, it might seem as if the Lord might once for all have abolished it by an absolute prohibition; after the manner in which many modern reformers would deal with such evils as the liquor traffic, etc. But the Lord was wiser than many such. As has been remarked already, in connection with the question of concubinage, that law is not in every case the best which may be the best intrinsically and ideally. That law is the best which can be best enforced in the actual moral status of the people, and consequent condition of public opinion. So the Lord did not at once prohibit slavery; but He ordained laws which would restrict it, and modify and ameliorate the condition of the slave wherever slavery was permitted to exist; laws, moreover, which have had such an educational power as to have banished slavery from the Hebrew people.

In the first place, slavery, in the unqualified sense of the word, is allowed only in the case of non-Israelites. That it was permitted to hold these as bondmen is explicitly declared (vv. 44-46). It is, however, important, in order to form a correct idea of Hebrew slavery, to observe that, according to Exod. xxi. 16, man-stealing was made a capital offence; and the law also carefully guarded from violence and tyranny on the part of the master the non-Israelite slave lawfully gotten, even decreeing his emancipation from his master in extreme cases of this kind (Exod. xxi. 20, 21, 26, 27).

With regard to the Hebrew bondman, the law recognises no property of the master in his person; that a servant of Jehovah should be a slave of another servant of Jehovah is denied; because they are His servants, no other can own them (vv. 42, 55). Thus, while the case is supposed (ver. 39) that a man through stress of poverty may sell himself to a fellow-Hebrew as a bondservant, the sale is held as affecting only the master's right to his service, but not to his person. "Thou shalt not make him to serve as a bondservant: as an hired servant, and as a sojourner, he shall be with thee."

Further, it is elsewhere provided (Exod. xxi. 2) that in no case shall such sale hold valid for a longer time than six years; in the seventh year the man was to have the privilege of going out free for nothing. And in this chapter is added a further alleviation of the bondage (vv. 40, 41): "He shall serve with thee unto the year of jubilee: then shall he go out from thee, he and his children with him, and shall return unto his own family, and unto the possession of his fathers shall he return. For they are My servants, which I brought forth out of the land of Egypt: they shall not be sold as bondmen."

That is, if it so happened that before the six years of his prescribed service had been completed the jubilee year came in, he was to be exempted from the obligation to service for the remainder of that period.

The remaining verses of this part of the law (vv. 44-46) provide that the Israelite may take to himself bondmen of "the children of the strangers" that sojourn among them; and that to such the law of the periodic release shall not be held to apply. Such are "bondmen for ever." "Ye shall make them an inheritance for your children after you, to hold for a possession; of them shall ye take your bondmen for ever."

It is to be borne in mind that even in such cases the law which commanded the kind treatment of all the strangers in the land (xix. 33, 34) would apply; so that even where permanent slavery was allowed it was placed under humanising restriction.

In vv. 47-55 is taken up, finally, the case where a poor Israelite should have sold himself as a slave to a foreigner resident in the land. In all such cases it is ordered that the owner of the man must recognise the right of redemption. That is, it was the privilege of the man himself, or of any of his near kindred, to buy him out of bondage. Compensation to the owner however, enjoined in such cases according to the number of the years remaining to the next jubilee, at which time he would be obliged to release him (ver. 54), whether redeemed or not. Thus we read (vv. 50-52): "He shall reckon with him that bought him from the year that he sold himself to him unto the year of jubilee: and the price of his sale shall be according unto the number of years; according to the time of an hired servant shall he be with him. If there be yet many years, according unto them he shall give back the price of his redemption out of the money that he was bought for. And if there remain but few years unto the year of jubilee, then he shall reckon with him; according unto his years shall he give back the price of his redemption. As a servant hired year by year shall he be with him."

Furthermore, it is commanded (ver. 53) that the owner of the Israelite, for so long time as he may remain in bondage, shall "not rule over him with rigour;" and by the addition of the words "in thy sight" it is intimated that God would hold the collective nation responsible for seeing that no oppression was exercised by any alien over any of their enslaved brethren. To which it should also be added, finally, that the regulations for the release of the slave carefully provided for the maintenance of the family relation. Families were not to be parted in the emancipation of the jubilee; the man who went out free was to take his children with him (vv. 41, 54). In the case, however, where the wife had been given him by his master, she and her children remained in bondage after his emancipation in the seventh year; but of course only until she had reached her seventh year of service. But if the slave already had his wife when he became a slave, then she and their children went out with him in the seventh year (Exod. xxi. 3, 4). The contrast in the spirit of these laws with that of the institution of slavery as it formerly existed in the Southern States of America and elsewhere in Christendom, is obvious.

These, then, were the regulations connected with the application of the ordinance of the jubilee year to rights of property, whether in real estate or in slaves. In respect to the cessation from the cultivation of the soil which was enjoined for the year, the law was essentially the same as that for the sabbatic year, except that, apparently, the right of property in the spontaneous produce of the land, which was in abeyance in the former case, was in so far recognised in the latter that each man was allowed to "eat the increase of the jubilee year out of the field" (ver. 12).

Practical Objects of the Sabbatic Year and Jubilee Law.

Such was this extraordinary legislation, the like of which will be sought in vain in any other people. It is indeed true that, in some instances, ancient lawgivers decreed that land should not be permanently alienated, or that individuals should not hold more than a certain amount of land. Thus, for example, the Lacedemonians were forbidden to sell their lands, and the Dalmatians were wont to redistribute their lands every eight years. But laws such as these only present accidental coincidences with single features of the jubilee year; an agreement to be accounted for by the fact that the aim of such lawgivers was, in so far, the same as that of the Hebrew code, that they sought thus to guard against excessive accumulations of property in the hands of individuals, and those consequent great inequalities in the distribution of wealth which, in all lands and ages, and never more clearly than in our own, have been seen to be fraught with the gravest dangers to the highest interests of society. Beyond this single point we shall search in vain the history of any other people for an analogy to these laws concerning the sabbatic and the jubilee year.

What was the immediate object of this remarkable legislation? It is not irrelevant to observe that in so far as regards the prescription of a periodic rest to the land, agricultural science recognises that this is an advantage, especially in places where it may be difficult to obtain fertilisers for the soil in adequate amount. But it cannot be supposed that this was the chief object of these ordinances, not even in so far as they had respect to the land. We shall not err in regarding them as intended, like all in the Levitical system, to make Israel to be in reality, what they were called to be, a people holy, *i.e.*, fully consecrated to the Lord. The bearing of these laws on this end is not hard to perceive.

In the first place, the law of the sabbatic year and the jubilee was a most impressive lesson as to the relation of God to what men call their property; and, in particular, as to His relation to man's property in land. By these ordinances every Israelite was to be reminded in a most impressive way that the land which he tilled, or on which he fed his flocks and herds, belonged, not to himself, but to God. Just as God taught him that his time belonged to Him, by putting in a claim for the absolute consecration to Himself of every seventh day, so here He reminded Israel that the land belonged to Him, by asserting a similar claim on the land every seventh year, and twice in a century for two years in succession.

No one will pretend that the law of the sabbatic year or the jubilee is binding on communities now. But it is a question for our times as to whether the basal principle regarding the relation of God to land, and by necessary consequence the right of man regarding land, which is fundamental to these laws, is not in its very nature of perpetual force. Surely, there is nothing in Scripture to suggest that God's ownership of the land was limited to the land of Palestine, or to that land only during Israel's occupancy of it. Instead of this, Jehovah everywhere represents Himself as having given the land to Israel, and therefore by necessary implication as having a like right over it while as yet the Canaanites were dwelling in it. Again, the purpose of God's dealing with Egypt is said to be that Pharaoh might know this same truth: that the earth (or land) was the Lord's (Exod. ix. 29); and in Psalm xxiv. 1 it is stated, as a broad truth, without qualification or restriction, that the earth is the Lord's, as well as that which fills it. It is true that there is no suggestion in any of these passages that the relation of God to the earth or to the land is different from His relation to other property; but it is intended to emphasise the fact that in the use of land, as of all else, we are to regard ourselves as God's stewards, and hold and use it as in trust from Him.

The vital relation of this great truth to the burning questions of our day regarding the rights of men in land is self-evident. It does not indeed determine how the land question should be dealt with in any particular country, but it does settle it that if in these matters we will act in the fear of God, we must keep this principle steadily before us, that, primarily, the land belongs to the Lord, and is to be used accordingly. How, as a matter of fact, God did order that the land should be used, in the only instance when He has condescended Himself to order the political government of a nation, we have already seen, and shall presently consider more fully.

It is obvious that the natural and therefore intended effect of these regulations, if obeyed, would have been to impose a constant and powerful check upon man's natural covetousness and greed of gain. Every seventh year the Hebrew was to pause in his toil for wealth, and for one whole year he was to waive even his ordinary right to the spontaneous produce of his fields; which year of abstinence from sowing and reaping once in fifty years was doubled. Add to this the strict prohibition of lending money upon interest to a fellow-Israelite, and we can see how far-reaching and effective, if obeyed, were such regulations likely to be in restraining that insatiate greed for riches which ever grows the more by that which feeds it.

Yet again; the law of the sabbatic year and the jubilee was adapted to serve also as a singularly powerful discipline in that faith toward God which is the soul of all true religion. In this practical way every Hebrew was to be taught that "man doth not live by bread alone, but by every word that proceedeth out of the mouth of God." The lesson is ever hard to learn, though none the less necessary. This thought is alluded to in ver. 20, where it is supposed that a man might raise the very natural objection to these laws, "What shall we eat the seventh year?" To which the answer is given, with reference even to the extreme case of the jubilee year: "I will command My blessing upon you in the sixth year, and it shall bring forth fruit for the three years; until the ninth year ... ye shall eat the old store."

But probably the most prominent and important object of the regulations in this chapter was to secure, as far as possible, the equal distribution of wealth, by preventing excessive accumulations either of land or of capital in the hands of a few, while the mass should be sunk in poverty. It is certain that these laws, if carried out, would have had a marvellous effect in this respect. As for capital, we all know what an important factor in the production of wealth is accumulation by interest on loans, especially when the interest is constantly compounded. There can be no doubt of its immense power as an instrument for at once enriching the lender and in proportion impoverishing the borrower. But among the Israelites, to receive interest or its equivalent was prohibited. One other chief cause of the excessive wealth of individuals among us, as in all ages, is the acquirement in perpetuity by individuals of a disproportionate amount of the public land. The condition of things in the United Kingdom is familiar to all, with its inevitable effect on the condition of large masses of people; and in parts of the United States there are indications of a like tendency working toward the similar disadvantage of many small landholders and cultivators. But in Israel, if these laws should be carried into effect, such a state of things, so often witnessed among other nations, was made for ever impossible. Individual ownership in the land itself was forbidden; no man was allowed more than a leasehold right;

nor could he, even by adding largely to his leaseholds, increase his wealth indefinitely, so as to transmit a fortune to his children, to be still further augmented by a similar process in the next and succeeding generations; for every fifty years the jubilee came around, and whatever leaseholds he might have acquired from less fortunate brethren, reverted unconditionally to the original owner or his legal heirs.

However impracticable such arrangements may seem to us under the conditions of modern life, yet it must be confessed that in the case of a nation just starting on its career in a new country, as was Israel at that time, nothing could well be thought of more likely to be effective toward securing, along with careful regard to the rights of property, an equal distribution of wealth among the people, than the legislation which is placed before us in this chapter.

It deserves to be specially noticed by how exact equity the laws are distinguished. While, on the one hand, excessive accumulations, either of capital or of land, were thus made impossible, there is here nothing of the destructive communism advocated by many in our day. These laws put no premium on laziness; for if a man, through indolence or vice, was compelled to sell out his right in his land, he had no security of obtaining it again until the jubilee; that is to say, upon an average, during his working lifetime. On the other hand, encouragement was given to industry, as a man who was thrifty might, by purchase of leaseholds, materially increase his wealth and comfort in life. And the effect on inheritance is evident. There could, on the one hand, be no inheritance of such colossal and overgrown fortunes as are possible in our modern states,—no blessing, certainly, in many cases, to the heirs; and neither, on the other hand, could there be any inheritance of hopeless and degrading poverty. A man might have had an indolent or a vicious father, who had thus forfeited his landholding; but while the father would doubtless suffer deserved poverty during his active life, the young man, when the jubilee returned, and the lost paternal inheritance reverted to him, would have the opportunity to see whether he might not, with his father's experience before him as a warning, do better, and retrieve the fortunes of the family. In any case, he would not start upon the work of life weighted, as are multitudes among us, with a crushing and almost irremovable burden of poverty.

It is certain, no doubt, that these laws are not morally binding now; and no less certain, probably, that failing, as they did, to secure observance in Israel, such laws, even if enacted, could not in our day be practically carried out any more than then. Nevertheless, so much we may safely say, that the intention and aim of these laws as regards the equal distribution of wealth in the community ought to be the aim of all wise legislation now. It is certain that all good government ought to seek in all righteous and equitable ways to prevent the formation in the community of classes, either of the excessively rich or of the excessively poor. Absolute equality in this respect is doubtless unattainable, and in a world intended for purposes of moral training and discipline were even undesirable; but extreme wealth or extreme poverty are certainly evils to the prevention of which our legislators may well give their minds. Only it needs also to be kept in mind that these Hebrew laws no less distinctly teach us that this end is to be sought only in such a way as shall neither, on the one hand, put a premium on laziness and vice, nor, on the other, deny to the virtuous and industrious the advantage which industry and virtue deserve, of additional wealth, comfort, and exemption from toilsome drudgery.

In close connection with all this it will be observed that all this legislation, while guarding the rights of the rich, is evidently inspired by that same merciful regard for the poor which marks the Levitical law throughout. For in all these regulations it is assumed that there would still be poor in the land; but the law secured to the poor great mitigations of poverty. Every seventh year the produce of the land was to be free alike to all; if one were poor his brother was to uphold him; when lending him, he was not to add to the debt the burden of interest or increase. And then there was to the poor man the ever-present assurance, which alone would take off half the bitterness of poverty, that through the coming of the jubilee the children at least would have a new chance, and start life on an equality, in respect of inheritance in land, with the sons of the richest. And when we remember the close connection between extreme poverty and every variety of crime, it is plain that the whole legislation is as admirably adapted to the prevention of crime as of abject and hopeless poverty. Well might Asaph use the words which he employs, with evident allusion to the trumpet sound which ushered in the jubilee: "Happy the people that know the joyful sound!" *i.e.*, that have the blessed experience of the jubilee, that supreme earthly sabbatism of the people of God.[49]

Most significant and full of instruction, no less to us than to Israel, was the ordinance that both the sabbatic and the jubilee years should date from the day of Atonement. It was when, having completed the solemn ritual of that day, the high priest put on again his beautiful garments and came forth, having made atonement for all the transgressions of Israel, that the trumpet of the jubilee was to be sounded. Thus was Israel reminded in the most impressive manner possible that all these social, civil, and communal blessings were possible only on condition of reconciliation with God through atoning blood; atonement in the highest and fullest sense, which should reach even to the Holy of Holies, and place the blood on the very mercy-seat of Jehovah. This is true still, though the nations have yet to learn it. The salvation of nations, no less than that of individuals, is conditioned by national fellowship with God, secured through the great Atonement of the Lord. Not until the nations learn this lesson may we expect to see the crying evils of the earth removed, or the questions of property, of land-holding, of capital and labour, justly and happily solved.

Typical Significance of the Sabbatic and Jubilee Years.

But we must not forget that the sabbatic year and the year of jubilee, following the seventh seven of years, are the two last members of a sabbatic system of septenary periods, namely, the sabbath of the seventh day, the feast of Pentecost, following the expiry of the seventh week from Passover, and then the still more sacred seventh month, with its two great feasts, and the day of atonement intervening. But, as we have seen, we have good scriptural authority for regarding all these as typical. Each in succession brings out another stage or aspect of the great Messianic redemption, in a progressive revelation historically unfolding. In all of these alike we have been able to trace thoughts connected with the sabbatic idea, as pointing forward to the final rest, redemption, and consummated restoration, the sabbatism that remaineth to the people of God. To these preceding sabbatic periods these last two are closely related. Both alike began on the great day of atonement, in which all Israel was to afflict their souls in penitence for sin; and on that day they both began when the high priest came out from within the veil, where, from the time of his offering the sin-offering, he had been hidden from the sight of Israel for a season; and both alike were ushered in with a trumpet blast.

We shall hardly go amiss if we see in both of these—first in the sabbatic year, and still more clearly in the year of jubilee—a prophetic foreshadowing in type of that final repentance of the children of Israel in the latter days, and their consequent re-establishment in their land, which the prophets so fully and explicitly predict. In that day they are to return, as the prophets bear witness, every man to the land which the Lord gave for an inheritance to their fathers. Indeed, one might say with truth that even the lesser restoration from Babylon was prefigured in this ordinance; but, without doubt, its chief and supreme reference must be to that greater restoration still in the future, of which we read, for example, in Isa. xi. 11, when "the Lord shall set His hand again the *second* time to recover the remnant of His people, which shall remain, from Assyria, and from Egypt, ... and from the islands of the sea."

But the typical reference of these sacred years of sabbatism reaches yet beyond what pertains to Israel alone. For not only, according to the prophets and apostles, is there to be a restoration of Israel, but also, as the

Apostle Peter declared to the Jews (Acts iii. 19-21), closely connected with and consequent on this, a "restoration of all things." And it is in this great, final, and exceedingly glorious restoration of the time of the end that we recognise the ultimate antitype of these sabbatic seasons. When read in the light of later predictions they appear to point forward with singular distinctness to what, according to the Holy Word, shall be when Jesus Christ, the heavenly High Priest, shall come forth from within the veil; when the last trumpet shall sound, and He who was "once offered to bear the sins of many" shall appear a second time, apart from sin, to them that wait for Him, unto salvation (Heb. ix. 28).

Even in the beginning of the Pentateuch (Gen. iii. 17-19) it is explicitly taught that because of Adam's sin, the curse of God, in some mysterious way, fell even upon the material earthly creation. We read that the Lord said unto Adam: "Cursed is the ground for thy sake; in toil shalt thou eat of it all the days of thy life; thorns also and thistles shall it bring forth to thee; and thou shalt eat the herb of the field; in the sweat of thy face shalt thou eat bread, till thou return unto the ground." It is because of sin, then, that man is doomed to labour, toilsome and imperfectly requited by an unwilling soil. It lies immediately before us that both the sabbatic year and the year of jubilee, by the ordinance regarding the rest for the land, and the special promise of sufficiency without exhausting labour, involved for Israel a temporary suspension of the full operation of this curse. The ordinance therefore points unmistakably in a prophetic way to what the New Testament explicitly predicts—the coming of a day when, with man redeemed, material nature also shall share the great deliverance. In a word, in the sabbatic year, and in a yet higher form in the year of jubilee, we have in symbol the wonderful truth which in the most didactic language is formally declared by the Apostle Paul in these words (Rom. viii. 19-22): "The earnest expectation of the creation waiteth for the revealing of the sons of God. For the creation was subjected to vanity, not of its own will, but by reason of him who subjected it, in hope that the creation itself also shall be delivered from the bondage of corruption into the liberty of the glory of the children of God. For we know that the whole creation groaneth and travaileth in pain together until now."

The jubilee year contained in type all this, and more. Where the sabbatic year had typically pointed only to a coming rest of the earth from the primeval curse, the jubilee, falling, not on a seventh, but on an eighth year, following immediately on the sabbatic seventh, pointed also to the permanence of this blessed condition. It is the festival, by eminence, of the new creation, of paradise completely and for ever restored.

Moreover, as falling in the fiftieth year, and therefore on an eighth year of the sabbatic calendar, the jubilee was to the week of years as the Lord's day to the week of days. Like that, it is the festival of resurrection. This is as clearly foreshadowed in the type as the other. For in the year of jubilee not only was the land to rest, but every bond-slave was to be released, and to return to his inheritance and to his family. In the light of what has preceded, and of other revelations of Scripture, we can hardly miss of perceiving the typical meaning of this. For what is the great event which the Apostle Paul, in the passage just cited, associates in time with the deliverance of the earthly creation, but "the redemption of the body," as the final issue of the atoning work of Christ? For as yet even believers are in bondage to death and the grave; but the day which is coming, the day of earth's redemption, shall bring to all that are Christ's, all that are Israelites indeed, deliverance "from the bondage of corruption into the liberty of the glory of the children of God."

And as the slave who was freed in the year of jubilee therewith also returned to his forfeited inheritance, so also shall it be in that day. For precisely this is given us by the Holy Spirit in the New Testament (1 Peter i. 4, 5), as another aspect of the day when the heavenly Aaron shall come forth from the Holiest. For we are begotten *unto an inheritance*, reserved in heaven for us, "who by the power of God are guarded through faith unto a salvation ready to be revealed in the last time." Cast out through death from the inheritance of the earth, which in the beginning was given by God to our first father, and to his seed in him, but which was lost to him and to his children through his sin, the great jubilee of the future shall bring us again, every man who is in Christ by faith, into the lost inheritance, redeemed and glorified citizens of a redeemed and glorified earth. Hence it is that in Rev. xxii. we are shown in vision, first, the new earth, delivered from the curse, and then the New Jerusalem, the Church of the risen and glorified saints of God, descending from God out of heaven, to assume possession of the purchased inheritance.

And the law adds also: "Ye shall return every man unto his family;" which gives the last feature here prefigured of that supreme sabbatism which remaineth for the people of God (Heb. iv. 9). It shall bring the reunion of those who had been parted and scattered. The day of resurrection is accordingly spoken of (2 Thess. ii. 1) as a day of "gathering together" of all who, though one in Christ, have been rudely parted by death. And yet more, it will be "the day of our gathering together unto Him," even the blessed Lord Jesus Christ, the "*Goel*," the Kinsman-Redeemer of the ruined bondsmen and their lost inheritance: "Whom not having seen, we love," but then expect to see even as He is, and beholding Him, be like Him, and be with Him for ever and for ever. Who should not long for the day?—the day when for the first time, this last type of Leviticus shall pass into complete fulfilment in the antitype; the day of "the restoration of all things;" the day of the deliverance of the material creation from her present bondage to corruption; the day also of the release of every true Israelite from the bondage of death, and the eternal establishment of all such with the Elder Brother, the First-begotten, in the enjoyment of the inheritance of the saints in light.

"Love, rest, and home!

Sweet hope!

Lord! tarry not, but COME!"

PART III
CONCLUSION AND APPENDIX

XXVI., XXVII.

1. Conclusion: Promises and Threatenings: xxvi.

2. Appendix: Concerning Vows: xxvii.

CHAPTER XXVII
THE PROMISES AND THREATS OF THE COVENANT

Lev. xxvi. 1-46.

One would have expected that this chapter would have been the last in the book of Leviticus, for it forms a natural and fitting close to the whole law as hitherto recorded. But whatever may have been the reason of its present literary form, the fact remains that while this chapter is, in outward form, the conclusion of the Levitical law, another chapter follows it in the manner of an appendix.

Chapter xxvi. opens with these words (vv. 1, 2): "Ye shall make you no idols, neither shall ye rear you up a graven image, or a pillar, neither shall ye place any figured stone in your land, to bow down unto it: for I am the Lord your God. Ye shall keep My sabbaths, and reverence My sanctuary: I am the Lord."

These verses, as they stand in the English versions as a preface to this chapter, at first sight seem but distantly related to what follows; and the Chaldee paraphrast and others have therefore appended them to the preceding chapter. But with that they have even less evident connection. The thought of the editor of this part of the canon, however, seems to have been that the three commands which are here repeated might be regarded as presenting a compendious summary, in its fundamental principles, of the whole law, the promises and threatenings attached to which immediately follow. And the more we think upon these commands and what they involve, the more evident will appear the fitness of their selection from the whole law to introduce this chapter.

The commands which are here repeated are three: namely, (1) a detailed prohibition of idolatry in the forms then chiefly prevalent; (2) an injunction to observe God's sabbaths; and (3) to reverence His sanctuary. Inasmuch as the various forms of idol-worship, which are here forbidden, all involved the recognition of gods other than Jehovah, it is plain that ver. 1 is in effect inclusive of the first and second commandments of the decalogue. The injunction to keep God's sabbaths, although in principle including all the sabbatic times previously appointed, evidently refers especially to the weekly sabbath of the fourth commandment; while the command to reverence the sanctuary of Jehovah covers in principle the ground of the third. And thus, in fact, these three injunctions essentially include the four commands of the decalogue which have to do with man's duty to God, and are thus fundamental to all other duties, both to God and man. Very appropriately, then, are these verses given here as a brief summary of the law to which the following promises and threatenings are annexed. And their suitableness to that which follows is the more clear when we remember that the weekly sabbath, in particular, is elsewhere (Exod. xxxi. 12-17) declared to be a sign of God's covenant with Israel, to which these promises and threats belong; and that the presence of Jehovah's sanctuary also, which they are here charged to reverence, was a continual visible witness among them of the special presence of God in Israel in pursuance of that covenant.

After this pertinent summation of the most fundamental commands of the law, the remainder of the chapter contains, first (vv. 3-13), promises of blessing from God, in case they shall obey this law; secondly (vv. 14-39), threats of chastising judgment, in case they disobey; and, thirdly (vv. 40-45), a prediction of their final repentance, and promise of their gracious restoration thereupon to the favour of God, and the everlasting endurance of God's covenant to preserve them in existence as a nation. The chapter then closes (ver. 46) with the declaration: "These are the statutes and judgments and laws, which the Lord made between Him and the children of Israel in mount Sinai by the hand of Moses."

The Promises of the Covenant.

xxvi. 3-13.

"If ye walk in My statutes, and keep My commandments, and do them; then I will give you rains in their season, and the land shall yield her increase, and the trees of the field shall yield their fruit. And your threshing shall reach unto the vintage, and the vintage shall reach unto the sowing time: and ye shall eat your bread to the full, and dwell in your land safely. And I will give peace in the land, and ye shall lie down, and none shall make you afraid: and I will cause evil beasts to cease out of the land, neither shall the sword go through your land. And ye shall chase your enemies, and they shall fall before you by the sword. And five of you shall chase an hundred, and an hundred of you shall chase ten thousand: and your enemies shall fall before you by the sword. And I will have respect unto you, and make you fruitful, and multiply you; and I will establish My covenant with you. And ye shall eat old store long kept, and ye shall bring forth the old because of the new. And I will set My tabernacle among you: and My soul shall not abhor you. And I will walk among you, and will be your God, and ye shall be My people. I am the Lord your God, which brought you forth out of the land of Egypt, that ye should not be their bondmen; and I have broken the bars of your yoke, and made you go upright."

The promises of the covenant are thus to the effect that if Israel shall keep the law, God will give them rain and fruitful seasons, harvests so abundant that the "threshing shall reach unto the vintage, and the vintage shall reach unto the sowing time;" internal security; deliverance from the wild beasts, which are still such a scourge in many parts of the East; and such power and spirit, that no enemy shall be able to stand before them, but five of them shall chase an hundred, and an hundred chase ten thousand. Then (ver. 9) is renewed the promise, given long before to Abraham, of a great increase in their numbers; and thereupon, very naturally, is repeated the promise of abundant harvests, so that notwithstanding they shall be so multiplied, one year's harvest should not be consumed before it would have to be removed from the granaries to make room for the new (ver. 10). And then this section ends with the assurance, which secures all other blessings, temporal and spiritual, that God will abide among them in His tabernacle, and will be their God, and they shall be His people. And the fulfilment of all this is guaranteed by the person, the purpose, and the past dealing of the Promiser; Himself, Jehovah; His purpose, to deliver them from bondage; and His past mercy, in breaking the bands of their yoke.

"The Vengeance of the Covenant."

xxvi. 14-46.

"But if ye will not hearken unto Me, and will not do all these commandments; and if ye shall reject My statutes, and if your soul abhor My judgments, so that ye will not do all My commandments, but break My covenant; I also will do this unto you; I will appoint terror over you, even consumption and fever, that shall consume the eyes, and make the soul to pine away: and ye shall sow your seed in vain for your enemies shall eat it. And I will set My face against you and ye shall be smitten before your enemies: they that hate you shall rule over you; and ye shall flee when none pursueth you. And if ye will not yet for these things hearken unto me, then I will chastise you seven times more for your sins. And I will break the pride of your power; and I will make your heaven as iron, and your earth as brass: and your strength shall be spent in vain: for your land shall not yield her increase, neither shall the trees of the land yield their fruit. And if ye walk contrary unto Me, and will not hearken unto Me; I will bring seven times more plagues upon you according to your sins. And I will send the beast of the field among you, which shall rob you of your children, and destroy your cattle, and make you few in number; and your ways shall become desolate. And if by these things ye will not be reformed unto Me, but will walk contrary unto Me; then will I also walk contrary unto you; and I will smite you, even I, seven times for your sins. And I will bring a sword upon you, that shall execute the vengeance of the covenant; and ye shall be gathered together within your cities: and I will send the pestilence among you; and ye shall be delivered into the hand of the enemy. When I break your staff of bread, ten women shall bake your bread in one oven, and they shall deliver your bread again by weight: and ye shall eat, and not be satisfied. And if ye will not for all this hearken unto Me, but walk contrary unto Me; then I will walk contrary unto you in fury; and I also will chastise you seven times for your sins. And ye shall eat the flesh of your sons, and the flesh of your daughters shall ye eat. And I will destroy your high places, and cut down your sun-images, and cast your carcases upon the carcases of your idols; and My soul shall abhor you. And I will make your cities a waste, and will bring your sanctuaries unto desolation, and I will not smell the savour of your sweet odours. And I will bring the land into desolation: and your enemies which dwell therein shall be astonished at it. And you will I scatter among the nations, and I will draw out the sword after you: and your land shall be a desolation, and your cities shall be a waste. Then shall the land enjoy her sabbaths, as long as it lieth desolate, and ye be in your enemies' land; even then shall the land rest, and enjoy her sabbaths. As long as it lieth desolate it shall have rest; even the rest which it had not in your sabbaths, when ye dwelt upon it. And as for them that are left of you I will send a faintness into their heart in the lands of their enemies: and the sound of a driven leaf shall chase them; and they shall flee, as one fleeth from the sword; and they shall fall when none pursueth. And they shall stumble one upon another, as it were before the sword, when none pursueth: and ye shall have no power to stand before your enemies. And ye shall perish among the nations, and the land of your enemies shall eat you up. And they that are left of you shall pine away in their iniquity in your enemies' lands; and also in the iniquities of their fathers shall they pine away with them. And they shall confess their iniquity, and the iniquity of their fathers, in their trespass which they trespassed against Me, and also that because they have walked contrary unto Me, I also walked contrary unto them, and brought them into the land of their enemies: if then their uncircumcised heart be humbled, and they then accept of the punishment of their iniquity; then will I remember My covenant with Jacob; and also My covenant with Isaac, and also My covenant with Abraham will I remember; and I will remember the land. The land also shall be left of them, and shall enjoy her sabbaths, while she lieth desolate without them; and they shall accept of the punishment of their iniquity: because, even because they rejected My judgments, and their soul abhorred My statutes. And yet for all that, when they be in the land of their enemies, I will not reject them, neither will I abhor them, to destroy them utterly, and to break My covenant with them: for I am the Lord their God: but I will for their sakes remember the covenant of their ancestors, whom I brought forth out of the land of Egypt in the sight of the nations, that I might be their God: I am the Lord. These are the statutes and judgments and laws, which the Lord made between Him and the children of Israel in mount Sinai by the hand of Moses."

So, if Israel should not obey the commandments of the Lord, but break that covenant which they had made with Him, when they had said unto the Lord (Exod. xxiv. 7): "All that the Lord hath spoken will we do, and be obedient;" then they are threatened, first in a general way (vv. 14-17) with terrible judgments, which shall reverse, and more than reverse, all the blessings. God will appoint over them "terror;" disease shall ravage them, consumption and fever; their enemies shall lay waste the land, defeat them in battle, and rule over them; and instead of five of them chasing an hundred, they should flee when none was pursuing (vv. 17, 18). Then follow four series of threats, each conditioned by the supposition that through what they should have already experienced of Jehovah's judgment, they should not repent; each also introduced by the formula, "I will chastise (or "smite") you seven times for your sins." In this four times repeated series of denunciations, thus introduced, we are not to insist that numerical precision was intended; neither can we, with some, give to the "seven times" a numerical or temporal reference. The thought which runs through all these denunciations, and determines the form which they take, is this: that the judgments threatened as to follow each new display of hardness and impenitence on the part of Israel shall be marked by continually increasing severity; and the phrase "seven times," by the reference to the sacred number "seven," intimates that the vengeance should be "the vengeance of the covenant" (ver. 25), and also the awful thoroughness and completeness with which the threatened judgments, in case of their continued obduracy, would be inflicted.

This interpretation is sustained by the details of each section. The first series (vv. 18-20), in which the threatenings of vv. 14-17 are developed, adds to what had been previously threatened, the withholding of harvest for lack of rain. He who had promised to send the rains "in their season," if they were obedient, now declares that if they will not hearken unto Him for the other chastisements before denounced, He will "make their heaven as iron, and their earth as brass." The second series threatens in addition their devastation by wild beasts, which shall rob them of their children and their cattle; and also, in consequence of these great judgments, with a great diminution of their numbers. The third series (vv. 23-26) repeats, under forms still more intense, the threats of sword, pestilence, and famine. The staff of bread shall be broken, and when, stricken with pestilence, they are gathered together in their cities, one oven shall suffice ten women for their baking, and bread shall be distributed by rations and in insufficient quantity (vv. 25, 26).

It is intimated that with these extraordinary judgments it shall become increasingly evident that it is Jehovah who is thus dealing with them for the breach of His covenant. This is suggested (ver. 24) by the emphatic use of the personal pronoun in the Hebrew, only to be rendered in English by a stress of voice; and by the declaration (ver. 25) that the sword which should be brought upon them should "execute the vengeance of the covenant."

The same remark applies with still more emphasis to the next and last of these sub-sections (vv. 27-39), the terrific denunciations of which are introduced by these words, which almost seem to flash with the fire of God's avenging wrath: "If ... ye will walk contrary unto Me; then I will walk contrary unto you in fury (*lit.*, "I will walk with you in fury of opposition"); and I also will chastise you seven times for your sins." All that has been threatened before is here repeated with every circumstance which could add terror to the picture. Was famine threatened? it shall be so awful in its severity that they shall eat the flesh of their own sons and daughters. The high places which had been the scenes of their licentious worship should be destroyed, and the "sun-images" which they had worshipped, going after Baal, should be cut down; and, in visible sign of the Divine wrath and of God's holy contempt for the impotent idols for which they had forsaken the Lord, upon the fallen idols should lie the dead corpses of their worshippers. The sanctuaries (with special,—though, perhaps, not exclusive,—reference, as the following words show, to the holy places of Jehovah's tabernacle or temple) should become a desolation; the sweet savour of their sacrifices should be rejected. The holy people should be scattered into other lands; the land should become so desolate that those of their enemies who should dwell in it should themselves be astonished at its transformation. And so, while they should be scattered in their enemies' land, the land would "enjoy her sabbaths;"[50] *i.e.*, it should thus, untilled and desolate, enjoy the rest which Jehovah had commanded them to give the land each seventh year, which they had not observed. Meanwhile, the condition of the banished nation in the lands of their captivity should be most pitiful: minished in number, those that were left alive should pine away in their iniquities, and in the iniquity of their fathers; timid and broken-spirited, they should flee before the sound of a broken leaf, and the land of their enemies should "eat them up."

And herewith ends the second section of this remarkable prophecy. Promising Israel the highest prosperity in the land of Canaan, if they will keep the words of this covenant, it threatens them with successive judgments of sword, famine, and pestilence, of continually increasing severity, to culminate, if they yet persist in disobedience, in their expulsion from the land for a prolonged period; and predicts their continued existence, despite the most distressing conditions, in the lands of their enemies, while their own land meanwhile lies desolate and untilled without them.

The fundamental importance and instructiveness of this prophecy is evident from the fact that all later predictions concerning the fortunes of Israel are but its more detailed exposition and application to successive historical conditions. Still more evident is its profound significance when we recall to mind the fact, disputed by none, that not only is it an epitome of all later prophecy of Holy Scripture concerning Israel, but, no less truly, an epitome of Israel's history. So strictly true is this that we may accurately describe the history of that nation, from the days of Moses until now, as but the translation of this chapter from the language of prediction into that of history.

The facts which illustrate this statement are so familiar that one scarcely needs to refer to them. The numerous visitations in the days of the Judges, when again and again the people were given into the hands of their enemies for their sins, and so often as then they repented, were again and again delivered; the heavier judgments of later days, first in the days of the earlier kings, and afterwards culminating in the captivity of the ten tribes, following the siege and capture of Samaria, 721 B.C.; and still later, the terrible siege and capture of Jerusalem by Nebuchadnezzar, 586 B.C., to the horrors of which the Lamentations of Jeremiah bear most sorrowful witness;—what were all these events, with others of lesser importance, but an historical unfolding of this twenty-sixth chapter of Leviticus?

And how, since Old Testament days, this prophecy has been continually illustrated in Israel's history, is, or should be, familiar to all. As apostasy has succeeded to apostasy, judgment has followed upon judgment. To a Nebuchadnezzar succeeded an Antiochus Epiphanes; and, after the Greco-Syrian judgment, then, following the supreme national crime of the rejection and crucifixion of their promised Messiah, came the Roman captivity, the most terrible of all; a judgment continued even until now in the eighteen hundred years of Israel's exile from the land of the covenant, and their scattering among the nations,—eighteen hundred years of tragic suffering, such as no other nation has ever known, or, knowing, has yet survived; sufferings which are still exhibited before the eyes of all the world to-day in the bitter experiences of the four millions of Jews in the Empire of the Czar, and the persecutions of Anti-Shemitism in other lands.

Existing, rather than living, under such conditions for centuries, as a natural result, the Jewish people became few in number, as here predicted; having been reduced from not less than seven or eight millions in the days of the kingdom, to a minimum, about two hundred years ago, of not more than three millions.[51] And, strangest of all, throughout this time the once fertile land has lain desolate, for the Gentiles have never settled in it in any great number; and in place of a population of five hundred to the square mile in the days of Solomon, we find now only a few hundred thousand miserable people, and the most of the land, for lack of cultivation, in such a condition that nothing can easily exceed its desolation. And when we have said all this, and much more that might be said without exaggeration, we have but simply testified that vv. 31-34 of this chapter have in the fullest possible sense become historical fact. For it was written (vv. 32-34): "I will bring the land into desolation: and your enemies which dwell therein shall be astonished at it. And you will I scatter among the nations, and I will draw out the sword after you: and your land shall be a desolation, and your cities shall be a waste. Then shall the land enjoy her sabbaths, as long as it lieth desolate, and ye be in your enemies' land; even then shall the land rest, and enjoy her sabbaths."

These facts make this chapter to be an apologetic of prime importance. It is this, because we have here evidence of foreknowledge, and therefore of the supernatural inspiration of the Holy Spirit of God in the prophecy here recorded. The facts cannot be adequately explained, either on the supposition of fortunate guessing or of accidental coincidence. It was not indeed impossible to forecast on natural grounds that Israel would become corrupt, or that, if so, they should experience disaster in consequence of their moral depravation. For God has not one law for Israel and another for other nations. Nor does the argument rest on the details of these threatened judgments, as consisting in the sword, famine, and pestilence; for other nations have experienced these calamities, though, indeed, few in equal measure with Israel; and of these one has a natural dependence on another.

But setting aside these elements of the prophecy, as of less apologetic significance, two particulars yet remain in which this predicted experience has been unique, and antecedently to the event in so high degree improbable, that we can reasonably think here neither of shrewd human forecast nor of chance agreement of prediction and fulfilment. The one is the predicted survival of exiled Israel as a nation in the land of their enemies, their indestructibility throughout centuries of unequalled suffering; the other, the extraordinary fact that their land, so rich and fertile, which was at that time and for centuries afterwards one of the principal highways of the world's commerce and travel, the coveted possession of many nations from a remote antiquity, should during the whole period of Israel's banishment remain comparatively unoccupied and untilled.

As regards the former particular, we may search history in vain for a similar phenomenon. Here is a people who, at their best, as compared with many other nations, such as the Egyptians, Babylonians, and Romans, were few in number and in material resources; who now have been scattered from their land for centuries, crushed and oppressed always, in a degree and for a length of time never experienced by any other people; yet never merging in the nations with whom they were mingled, or losing in the least their peculiar racial characteristics and distinct national identity. This, although now for a long time matter of history, was yet, *à priori*, so improbable that all history records no other instance of the kind; and yet all this had to be if those words of ver. 44 were to prove true: "When they be in the land of their enemies, I will not reject them, neither will I abhor them, to destroy them utterly." With abundant reason has Professor Christlieb referred to this fact as an unanswerable apologetic, thus: "We point to the people of Israel as a perennial historical miracle. The continued existence of this nation up to the present day, the preservation of its national peculiarities throughout thousands of years, in spite of all dispersion and oppression, remains so unparalleled a phenomenon, that without the special providential preparation of God, and His constant interference and protection, it would be impossible for us to explain it. For where else is there a people over which such judgments have passed, and yet not ended in destruction?"[52]

No less remarkable and significant is the long-continued depopulation of the land of Israel. For it was and is by nature a richly fertile land; and at the time of this prediction—whether it be assigned to an earlier or a later period—it was upon one of the chief commercial and military routes of the world, and its possession has thus been an object of ambition to all the dominant nations of history. Surely, one would have expected that if Israel should be cast out of such a land, it would at once and always be occupied by others who should cultivate its proverbially productive soil. But it was not to be so, for it had been otherwise written. And yet it seems as if it had scarcely been possible that through all these later centuries of the history of Christendom, the land could have thus lain desolate, except for the so momentous discovery in 1497 of the Cape route to India, by which event— which no one could in so remote days have well anticipated—the tide of commerce with the East was turned away from Egypt, Syria, and Palestine, to the Atlantic and the Indian Oceans; so that the land of Israel was left, like a city made to stand solitary in a desert by the shifting of the channel of a river; and its predicted desolation thus went on to receive its most complete, consummate, and now long-realised fulfilment.

So, then, stands the case. It is truly difficult to understand how one can fairly escape the inference from these facts, namely, that they imply in this chapter such a prescience of the future as is not possible to man, and therefore demonstrate that the Spirit of God must, in the deepest and truest sense, have been the author of these predictions of the future of the chosen people and their land.

And it is of the very first importance, with reference to the controversies of our day regarding this question, that we note the fact that the argument is of such a nature that it is not in the least dependent upon the date that any may have assigned to the origin of this chapter. Even though we should, with Graf and Wellhausen, attribute its composition to exilian or post-exilian times, it would still remain true that the chapter contained unmistakable predictions regarding the nation and the land; predictions which, if fulfilled, no doubt, in a degree, in the days of the Babylonian exile and the return, were yet to receive a fulfilment far more minute, exhaustive, and impressive, in centuries which then were still in a far distant future. But if this be granted, it is plain that these facts impose a limitation upon the conclusions of criticism. That only is true science which takes into view *all* the facts with respect to any phenomenon for which one seeks to account; and in this case the facts which are to be explained by any theory, are not merely peculiarities of style and vocabulary, etc., but also this phenomenon of a demonstrably predictive element in the chapter; a phenomenon which requires for its explanation the assumption of a supernatural inspiration as one of the factors in its authorship. But if this is so, how can we reconcile with such a Divine inspiration any theory which makes the last statement of the chapter, that "these are the statutes which the Lord made ... in mount Sinai by the hand of Moses," to be untrue, and the preceding "laws" to be thus, in plain language, a forgery of exilian or post-exilian times?

The Promised Restoration.

xxvi. 40-45.

> "And they shall confess their iniquity, and the iniquity of their fathers, in their trespass which they trespassed against Me, and also that because they have walked contrary unto Me, I also walked contrary unto them, and brought them into the land of their enemies: if then their uncircumcised heart be humbled, and they then accept of the punishment of their iniquity; then will I remember My covenant with Jacob; and also My covenant with Isaac, and also My covenant with Abraham will I remember; and I will remember the land. The land also shall be left of them, and shall enjoy her

sabbaths, while she lieth desolate without them; and they shall accept of the punishment of their iniquity: because, even because they rejected My judgments, and their soul abhorred My statutes. And yet for all that, when they be in the land of their enemies, I will not reject them, neither will I abhor them, to destroy them utterly, and to break My covenant with them: for I am the Lord their God: but I will for their sakes remember the covenant of their ancestors, whom I brought forth out of the land of Egypt in the sight of the nations, that I might be their God: I am the Lord."

This closing section of this extraordinary chapter yet remains to be considered. It is the most remarkable of all, whether from a historical or a religious point of view. It declares that even under so extreme visitations of Divine wrath, and howsoever long Israel's stubborn rebellion and impenitence should continue, yet the nation should never become extinct and pass away. Very impressive are the words (vv. 43-45) which emphasise this prediction: "The land also shall be left of them, and shall enjoy her sabbaths, while she lieth desolate without them; and they shall accept[53] of the punishment of their iniquity: because, even because they rejected My judgments, and their soul abhorred My statutes. And yet for all that, when they be in the land of their enemies, I will not reject them, neither will I abhor them, to destroy them utterly, and to break My covenant with them: for I am the Lord their God: but I will for their sakes remember the covenant of their ancestors, whom I brought forth out of the land of Egypt in the sight of the nations, that I might be their God: I am the Lord."

As to what is included in this promise of everlasting covenant mercy, we are told explicitly (ver. 40)[54] that as the final result of these repeated and long-continued judgments, the children of Israel "shall confess their iniquity, and the iniquity of their fathers, in their trespass which they trespassed" against the Lord. Also they will acknowledge (ver. 41) that all these calamities have been sent upon them by the Lord; that it is because they have walked contrary unto Him that He has also walked contrary unto them, and brought them into the land of their enemies. And then follows the great promise (vv. 41, 42): "If then their uncircumcised heart be humbled, and they then accept of the punishment of their iniquity; then will I remember My covenant with Jacob; and also My covenant with Isaac, and also My covenant with Abraham will I remember; and I will remember the land."

These words are very full and explicit. That they have had already a partial and inadequate fulfilment in the restoration from Babylon, and the spiritual quickening by which it was accompanied, is not to be denied. But one only needs to refer to the covenants to which reference is made, and especially the covenant with Abraham, as recorded in the book of Genesis,[55] to see that by no possibility can that Babylonian restoration be said to have exhausted this prophecy. Since those earlier days Israel has again forsaken the Lord, and committed the greatest of all their national sins in the rejection and crucifixion of the promised Messiah; and therefore, again, according to the threat of the earlier part of this chapter, they have been cast out of their land and scattered among the nations, and the land, again, for centuries has been left a desolation. But for all this, God's covenant with Israel has not lapsed, nor, as we are here formally assured, can it ever lapse. To imagine, with some, that because of the new dispensation of grace to the Gentiles which has come in, therefore the promises of this covenant have become void, is a mistake which is fatal to all right understanding of the prophetic word. As for the spiritual blessing of true repentance and a national turning unto God, Zechariah, after the Babylonian captivity, represents the prediction as yet to have a larger and far more blessed fulfilment, in a day which, beyond all controversy, has never yet risen on the world. For it is written (Zech. xii. 8-14; xiii. 1): "In that day ... I will pour upon the house of David, and upon the inhabitants of Jerusalem, the spirit of grace and of supplication; and they shall look unto Me whom they have pierced: and they shall mourn for Him, as one mourneth for his only son, and shall be in bitterness for Him, as one that is in bitterness for his firstborn; ... all the families that remain, every family apart, and their wives apart. In that day there shall be a fountain opened to the house of David and to the inhabitants of Jerusalem, for sin and for uncleanness." And that this great promise, which implies by its very terms the previous "piercing" of the Messiah, is still valid for the nation in the new dispensation, is expressly testified by the Apostle Paul, who formally teaches, with regard to Israel, that "God did not cast off His people which He foreknew;" that "the gifts and calling of God are without repentance;" and that therefore the days are surely coming when "all Israel shall be saved" (Rom. xi. 2, 29, 26).

And while nothing is said in this chapter of Leviticus as to the relation of this future repentance of Israel to the establishment of the kingdom of God, we only speak according to the express teaching both of the later prophets and of the apostles, when we add that we are not to think of this covenant of God concerning Israel as of little consequence to our faith and hope as Christians. For we are plainly taught, with regard to the present exclusion and impenitence of Israel (Rom. xi. 15), that "the receiving of them" again shall be as "life from the dead;" which, again, is only what long before had been declared in the Old Testament (Psalm cii. 13-16); that when God shall arise and have mercy upon Zion, and the set time to have pity upon her shall come, the nations shall fear the name of the Lord, and all the kings of the earth His glory.

And while we may grant that the matter is in itself of less moment, it is yet of importance to observe that the very covenant which promises spiritual mercy to the people, as explicitly assures us (ver. 42) that, when Israel confesses its sin, God "will remember the land" as well as the people. All that has been said for the present and unchangeable validity of the former part of this promise, is of necessity true for this latter part also. To affirm the former, and on that ground maintain the faith and expectation of the future repentance of Israel, and yet deny the latter part of this promise, which is no less verbally explicit, regarding the land of Israel, is an inconsistency of interpretation which is as astonishing as it is common. For the restoration of the scattered nation to their land is repeatedly promised, as here, in connection with, and yet in clear distinction from, their conversion, by both the pre- and post-exilian prophets. And if, for reasons not hard to discover, the promise concerning the land is not in so many words repeated in the New Testament, its future fulfilment is yet, to say the least, distinctly assumed in the prediction of Christ (Luke xxi. 24), that Israel, because of their rejection of Him, should be "led captive into all the nations, and Jerusalem be trodden down of the Gentiles,"—not for ever, but only—"until the times of the Gentiles be fulfilled." Surely these words of our Lord imply that, whenever these "times of the Gentiles" shall have run their course, their present domination over the Holy City and the Holy Land shall end.

Nor is such a restoration of Israel to their land, with all that it implies, inconsistent, as some have urged, with the spirit and principles of the Gospel. Many a Gentile nation is greatly favoured of the Lord, and, as one mark of that favour, is permitted to abide in peace and prosperity in their own land. Why should it be any more alien to the spirit of the Gospel that penitent Israel should be blessed in like manner, and, upon their turning unto the Lord, also, like many other nations, be permitted to dwell in peace and safety in that land which lies almost empty and desolate for them until this day? And if it be urged that, admitting this interpretation, we shall also be obliged to admit that Israel is in the future to be exalted to a position of pre-eminence among the nations, which, again, is inconsistent, it is said, with the principles of the Gospel dispensation, we must again deny this last assertion, and for a similar reason. If not inconsistent with the Gospel that the British nation, for example, should to-day hold a position of exceptional eminence and world-wide influence among the nations, how can it be inconsistent with the Gospel that Israel, when repentant before God, should be in like manner exalted of Him to national eminence and glory?

While in itself this question may be of little consequence, yet in another aspect it is of no small moment that we steadfastly affirm the permanent validity of this part of the promise of the covenant with Israel as given in this chapter. For it is not too much to say that the logic and the exegesis which make the promise to have become void with regard to Israel's land, if accepted, would equally justify one in affirming the abrogation of the promise of Israel's final repentance, if the exigencies of any eschatological theory should seem to require it. Either both parts of this promise in ver. 42 are still valid, or neither is now valid; and if either is still in force, the other is in force also. These two, the promise concerning the people, and the promise concerning the land, stand or fall together.

CHAPTER XXVIII
CONCERNING VOWS

Lev. xxvii. 1-34.

As already remarked, the book of Leviticus certainly seems, at first sight, to be properly completed with the previous chapter; and hence it has been not unnaturally suggested that this chapter has by some editor been transferred, either of intention or accident, from an earlier part of the book— as, *e.g.*, after chapter XXV. The question is one of no importance; but it is not hard to perceive a good reason for the position of this chapter after not only the rest of the law, but also after the words of promise and threatening which conclude and seal its prescriptions. For what has preceded has concerned duties of religion which were obligatory upon all Israelites; the regulations of this chapter, on the contrary, have to do with special vows, which were obligatory on no one, and concerning which it is expressly said (Deut. xxiii. 22): "If thou shalt forbear to vow, it shall be no sin in thee." To these, therefore, the promises and threats of the covenant could not directly apply, and therefore the law which regulates the making and keeping of vows is not unfitly made to follow, as an appendix, the other legislation of the book.

Howsoever the making of vows be not obligatory as a necessary part of the religious life, yet, in all ages and in all religions, a certain instinct of the heart has often led persons, either in order to procure something from God, or as a thank-offering for some special favour received, or else as a spontaneous expression of love to God, to "make a special vow." But just in proportion to the sincerity and depth of the devout feeling which suggests such special acts of worship and devotion, will be the desire to act in the vow, as in all else, according to the will of God, so that the vow may be accepted of Him. What then may one properly dedicate to God in a vow? And, again, if by any stress of circumstances a man feels compelled to seek release from a vow, is he at liberty to recall it? and if so, then under what conditions? Such are the questions which in this chapter were answered for Israel.

As for the matter of a vow, it is ruled that an Israelite might thus consecrate unto the Lord either persons, or of the beasts of his possession, or his dwelling, or the right in any part of his land. On the other hand, "the firstling among beasts" (vv. 26, 27), any "devoted thing" (vv. 28, 29), and the tithe (vv. 30-33) might not be made the object of a special vow, for the simple reason that on various grounds each of these belonged unto the Lord as His due already. Under each of these special heads is given a schedule of valuation, according to which, if a man should wish for any reason to redeem again for his own use that which, either by prior Divine claim or by a special vow, had been dedicated to the Lord, he might be permitted to do so.

Of the Vowing of Persons.

xxvii. 1-8.

"And the Lord spake unto Moses, saying, Speak unto the children of Israel, and say unto them, When a man shall accomplish a vow, the persons shall be for the Lord by thy estimation. And thy estimation shall be of the male from twenty years old even unto sixty years old, even thy estimation shall be fifty shekels of silver, after the shekel of the sanctuary. And if it be a female, then thy estimation shall be thirty shekels. And if it be from five years old even unto twenty years old, then thy estimation shall be of the male twenty shekels, and for the female ten shekels. And if it be from a month old even unto five years old, then thy estimation shall be of the male five shekels of silver, and for the female thy estimation shall be three shekels of silver. And if it be from sixty years old and upward; if it be a male, then thy estimation shall be fifteen shekels, and for the female ten shekels. But if he be poorer than thy estimation, then he shall be set before the priest, and the priest shall value him; according to the ability of him that vowed shall the priest value him."

First, we have the law (vv. 2-8) concerning the vowing of persons. In this case it does not appear that it was intended that the personal vow should be fulfilled by the actual devotement of the service of the person to the sanctuary. For such service abundant provision was made by the separation of the Levites, and it can hardly be imagined that under ordinary conditions it would be possible to find special occupation about the sanctuary for all who might be prompted thus to dedicate themselves by a vow to the Lord.

Moreover, apart from this, we read here of the vowing to the Lord of young children, from five years of age down to one month, from whom tabernacle service is not to be thought of.

The vow which dedicated the person to the Lord was therefore usually discharged by the simple expedient of a commutation price to be paid into the treasury of the sanctuary, as the symbolic equivalent of the value of his self-dedication. The persons thus consecrated are said to be "for the Lord," and this fact was to be recognised and their special dedication to Him discharged by the payment of a certain sum of money. The amount to be paid in each instance is fixed by the law before us, with an evident reference to the labour value of the person thus given to the Lord in the vow, as determined by two factors—the sex and the age. Inasmuch as the woman is inferior in strength to the man, she is rated lower than he is. As affected by age, persons vowed are distributed into four classes: the lowest, from one month up to five years; the second, from five years to twenty; the third, from twenty to sixty; the fourth, from sixty years of age and upwards.

The law takes first (vv. 3, 4) the case of persons in the prime of their working powers, from twenty to sixty years old, for whom the highest commutation rate is fixed; namely, fifty shekels for the male and thirty for a female, "after the shekel of the sanctuary," *i.e.*, of full standard weight. If younger than this, obviously the labour value of the persons service would be less; it is therefore fixed (ver. 5) at twenty shekels for the male and ten for the female, if the age be from five to twenty; and if the person be over sixty, then (ver. 7), as the feebleness of age is coming on, the rate is fifteen shekels for the male and ten for the female.[56] In the case of a child from one month to five years old, the rate is fixed (ver. 6) at five, or, in a female, then at three shekels. In this last case it will be observed that the rate for the male is the same as that appointed (Numb. xviii. 15, 16) for the redemption of the firstborn, "from a month old," in all cases. As in that ordinance, so here, the payment was merely a symbolic recognition of the special claim of God on the person, without any reference to a labour value.

But although the sum was so small that even at the most it could not nearly represent the actual value of the labour of such as were able to labour, yet one can see that cases might occur when a man might be moved to make such a vow of dedication of himself or of a child to the Lord, while he was yet too poor to pay even such a small amount. Hence the kindly provision (ver. 8) that if any person be poorer than this estimation, he shall not therefore be excluded from the privilege of self-dedication to the Lord, but "he shall be set before the priest, and the priest shall value him; according to the ability of him that vowed shall the priest value him."

Of the Vowing of Domestic Animals.

xxvii. 9-13.

"And if it be a beast, whereof men offer an oblation unto the Lord, all that any man giveth of such unto the Lord shall be holy. He shall not alter it, nor change it, a good for a bad, or a bad for a good: and if he shall at all change beast for beast, then both it and that for which it is changed shall be holy. And if it be any unclean beast, of which they do not offer an oblation unto the Lord, then he shall set the beast before the priest: and the priest shall value it, whether it be good or bad: as thou the priest valuest it, so shall it be. But if he will indeed redeem it, then he shall add the fifth part thereof unto thy estimation."

This next section concerns the vowing to the Lord of domestic animals (vv. 9-13). If the animal thus dedicated to the Lord were such as could be used in sacrifice, then the animal itself was taken for the sanctuary service, and the vow was unalterable and irrevocable. If, however, the animal vowed was "any unclean beast," then the priest (ver. 12) was to set a price upon it, according to its value; for which, we may infer, it was to be sold and the proceeds devoted to the sanctuary.

In this case, the person who had vowed the animal was allowed to redeem it to himself again (ver. 13) by payment of this estimated price and one-fifth additional, a provision which was evidently intended to be of the nature of a fine, and to be a check upon the making of rash vows.

Of the Vowing of Houses and Fields.

xxvii. 14-25.

"And when a man shall sanctify his house to be holy unto the Lord, then the priest shall estimate it, whether it be good or bad: as the priest shall estimate it, so shall it stand. And if he that sanctified it will redeem his house, then he shall add the fifth part of the money of thy estimation unto it, and it shall be his. And if a man shall sanctify unto the Lord part of the field of his possession, then thy estimation shall be according to the sowing thereof: the sowing of a homer of barley shall be valued at fifty shekels of silver. If he sanctify his field from the year of jubilee, according to thy estimation it shall stand. But if he sanctify his field after the jubilee, then the priest shall reckon unto him the money according to the years that remain unto the year of jubilee, and an abatement shall be made from thy estimation. And if he that sanctified the field will indeed redeem it, then he shall add the fifth part of the money of thy estimation unto it, and it shall be assured to him. And if he will not redeem the field, or if he have sold the field to another man, it shall not be redeemed any more: but the field, when it goeth out in the jubilee, shall be holy unto the Lord, as a field devoted; the possession thereof shall be the priest's. And if he sanctify unto the Lord a field which he hath bought, which is not of the field of his possession; then the priest shall reckon unto him the worth of thy estimation unto the year of jubilee: and he shall give thine estimation in that day, as a holy thing unto the Lord. In the year of jubilee the field shall return unto him of whom it was bought, even to him to whom the possession of the land belongeth. And all thy estimations shall be according to the shekel of the sanctuary: twenty gerahs shall be the shekel."

The law regarding the consecration of a man's house unto the Lord by a vow (vv. 14, 15) is very simple. The priest is to estimate its value, without right of appeal. Apparently, the man might still live in it, if he desired, but only as one living in a house belonging to another; presumably, a rental was to be paid, on the basis of the priest's estimation of value, into the sanctuary treasury. If the man wished again to redeem it, then, as in the case of the beast that was vowed, he must pay into the treasury the estimated value of the house, with the addition of one-fifth.

In the case of the "sanctifying" or dedication of a field by a special vow two cases might arise, which are dealt with in succession. The first case (vv. 16-21) was the dedication to the Lord of a field which belonged to the Israelite by inheritance; the second (vv. 22-24), that of one which had come to him by purchase. In the former case, the priest was to fix a price upon the field on the basis of fifty shekels for so much land as would be sown with a *homer*—about eight bushels—of barley. In case the dedication took effect from the year of jubilee, this full price was to be paid into the Lord's treasury for the field; but if from a later year in the cycle, then the rate was to be diminished in proportion to the number of years of the jubilee period which might have already passed at the date of the vow. Inasmuch as in the case of a field which had been purchased, it was ordered that the price of the estimation should be paid down to the priest "in that day" (ver. 23) in which the appraisal was made, it would appear as if, in the present case, the man was allowed to pay it annually, a shekel for each year of the jubilee period, or by instalments otherwise, as he might choose, as a periodic recognition of the special claim of the Lord upon that field, in consequence of his vow.

Redemption of the field from the obligation of the vow was permitted under the condition of the fifth added to the priest's estimation, *e.g.* on the payment of sixty instead of fifty shekels (ver. 19).

If, however, without having thus redeemed the field, the man who vowed should sell it to another man, it is ordered that the field, which otherwise would revert to him again in full right of usufruct when the jubilee year came round, should be forfeited; so that when the jubilee came the exclusive right of the field would henceforth belong to the priest, as in the case of a field devoted by the ban. The intention of this regulation is evidently penal; for the field, during the time covered by the vow, was in a special sense the Lord's; and the man had the use of it for himself only upon condition of a certain annual payment; to sell it, therefore, during that time, was, in fact, from the legal point of view, to sell property, absolute right in which he had by his vow renounced in favour of the Lord.

The case of the dedication in a vow of a field belonging to a man, not as a paternal inheritance, but by purchase (vv. 22-24), only differed from the former in that, as already remarked, immediate payment in full of the sum at which it was estimated was made obligatory; when the jubilee year came, the field reverted to the original owner, according to the law (xxv. 28). The reason for thus insisting on full immediate payment, in the case of the dedication of a field acquired by purchase, is plain, when we refer to the law (xxv. 25), according to which the original owner had the right of redemption guaranteed to him at any time before the jubilee. If, in the case of such a dedicated field, any part of the amount due to the sanctuary were still unpaid, obviously this, as a lien upon the land, would stand in the way of such redemption. The regulation of immediate payment is therefore intended to protect the original owner's right to redeem the field.

Ver. 25 lays down the general principle that in all these estimations and commutations the shekel must be "the shekel of the sanctuary," twenty gerahs to the shekel;—words which are not to be understood as pointing to the existence of two distinct shekels as current, but simply as meaning that the shekel must be of full weight, such as only could pass current in transactions with the sanctuary.

The "Vow" in New Testament Ethics.

Not without importance is the question whether the vow, as brought before us here, in the sense of a voluntary promise to God of something not due to Him by the law, has, of right, a place in New Testament ethics and practical life. It is to be observed in approaching this question, that the Mosaic law here simply deals with a religious custom which it found prevailing, and while it gives it a certain tacit sanction, yet neither here or elsewhere ever recommends the practice; nor does the whole Old Testament represent God as influenced by such a voluntary promise, to do something which otherwise He would not have done. At the same time, inasmuch as the religious impulse which prompts to the vow, howsoever liable to lead to an abuse of the practice, may be in itself right, Moses takes the matter in hand, as in this chapter and elsewhere, and deals with it simply in an educational way. If a man will vow, while it is not forbidden, he is elsewhere (Deut. xxii. 22) reminded that there is no special merit in it; if he forbear, he is no worse a man.

Further, the evident purpose of these regulations is to teach that, whereas it must in the nature of the case be a very serious thing to enter into a voluntary engagement of anything to the holy God, it is not to be done hastily and rashly; hence a check is put upon such inconsiderate promising, by the refusal of the law to release from the voluntary obligation, in some cases, upon any terms; and by its refusal, in any case, to release except under the condition of a very material fine for breach of promise. It was thus taught clearly that if men made promises to God, they must keep them. The spirit of these regulations has been precisely expressed by the Preacher (Eccl. v. 5, 6): "Better is it that thou shouldest not vow, than that thou shouldest vow and not pay. Suffer not thy mouth to cause thy flesh to sin; neither say thou before the messenger [of God],[57] that it was an error: wherefore should God be angry at thy voice, and destroy the work of thine hands?" Finally, in the careful guarding of the practice by the penalty attached also to change or substitution in a thing vowed, or to selling that which had been vowed to God, as if it were one's own; and, last of all, by insisting that the full-weight shekel of the sanctuary should be made the standard in all the appraisals involved in the vow, — the law kept steadily and uncompromisingly before the conscience the absolute necessity of being strictly honest with God.

But in all this there is nothing which necessarily passes over to the new dispensation, except the moral principles which are assumed in these regulations. A hasty promise to God, in an inconsiderate spirit, even of that which ought to be freely promised Him, is sin, as much now as then; and, still more, the breaking of any promise to Him when once made. So we may take hence to ourselves the lesson of absolute honesty in all our dealing with God, — a lesson not less needed now than then.

Yet this does not touch the central question: Has the vow, in the sense above defined — namely, the promise to God of something not due to Him in the law — a place in New Testament ethics? It is true that it is nowhere forbidden; but as little is it approved. The reference of our Lord (Matt. xv. 5, 6) to the abuse of the vow by the Pharisees to justify neglect of parental claims does not imply the propriety of vows at present; for the old dispensation was then still in force. The vows of Paul (Acts xviii. 18; xxi. 24-26) apparently refer to the vow of a Nazarite, and in no case present a binding example for us, inasmuch as they are but illustrations of his frequent conformity to Jewish usages in things involving no sin, in which he became a Jew that he might gain the Jews. On the other hand, the New Testament conception of Christian life and duty seems clearly to leave no room for a voluntary promise to God of what is not due, seeing that, through the transcendent obligation of grateful love to the Lord for His redeeming love, there is no possible degree of devotement of self or of one's substance which could be regarded as not already God's due. "He died for all, that they which live should no longer live unto themselves, but unto Him who for their sakes died and rose again." The vow, in the sense brought before us in this chapter, is essentially correlated to a legal system such as the Mosaic, in which dues to God are prescribed by rule. In New Testament ethics, as distinguished from those of the Old, we must therefore conclude that for the vow there is no logical place.

The question is not merely speculative and unpractical. In fact, we here come upon one of the fundamental points of difference between Romish and Protestant ethics. For it is the Romish doctrine that, besides such works as are essential to a state of salvation, which are by God made obligatory upon all, there are other works which, as Rome regards the matter, are not commanded, but are only made matters of Divine counsel, in order to the attainment, by means of their observance, of a higher type of Christian life. Such works as these, unlike the former class, because not of universal obligation, may properly be made the subject of a vow. These are, especially, the voluntary renunciation of all property, abstinence from marriage, and the monastic life. But this distinction of precepts and counsels, and the theory of vows, and of works of supererogation, which Rome has based upon it, all Protestants have with one consent rejected, and that with abundant reason. For not only do we fail to find any justification for these views in the New Testament, but the history of the Church has shown, with what should be convincing clearness, that, howsoever we may gladly recognise in the monastic communities of Rome, in all ages, men and women living under special vows of poverty, obedience, and chastity, whose purity of life and motive, and sincere devotion to the Lord, cannot be justly called in question, it is none the less clear that, on the whole, the tendency of the system has been toward either legalism on the one hand, or a sad licentiousness of life on the other. In this matter of vows, as in so many things, it has been the fatal error of the Roman Church that, under the cover of a supposed Old Testament warrant, she has returned to "the weak and beggarly elements" which, according to the New Testament, have only a temporary use in the earliest childhood of religious life.

Exclusions from the Vow.

xxvii. 26-33.

"Only the firstling among beasts, which is made a firstling to the Lord, no man shall sanctify it; whether it be ox or sheep, it is the Lord's. And if it be of an unclean beast, then he shall ransom it according to thine estimation, and shall add unto it the fifth part thereof: or if it be not redeemed, then it shall be sold according to thy estimation. Notwithstanding, no devoted thing, that a man shall devote unto the Lord of all that he hath, whether of man or beast, or of the field of his possession, shall be sold or redeemed: every devoted thing is most holy unto the Lord. None devoted, which shall be devoted of men, shall be ransomed; he shall surely be put to death. And all the tithe of the land, whether of the seed of the land, or of the fruit of the tree, is the Lord's: it is holy unto the Lord. And if a man will redeem aught of his tithe, he shall add unto it the fifth part thereof. And all the tithe of the herd or the flock, whatsoever passeth under the rod, the tenth shall be holy unto the Lord. He shall not search whether it be good or bad, neither shall he change it: and if he change it at all, then both it and that for which it is changed shall be holy; it shall not be redeemed."

The remaining verses of this chapter specify three classes of property which could not be dedicated by a special vow, namely, "the firstling among beasts" (ver. 26); any "devoted thing" (vv. 28, 29), *i.e.*, anything which had been devoted to the Lord by the ban—as, *e.g.*, all the persons and property in the city of Jericho by Joshua (vii. 17); and, lastly, "the tithe of the land" (ver. 30). The reason for prohibiting the vowing of any of these is in every case one and the same; either by the law or by a previous personal act they already belonged to the Lord. To devote them in a vow would therefore be to vow to the Lord that over which one had no right. As for the firstborn, the Lord had declared His everlasting claim on these at the time of the Exodus (Exod. xiii. 12-15); to vow to give the Lord His own, had been absurd. To the law previously given, however, concerning the firstling of unclean beasts (Exod. xiii. 13), it is here added that, if a man wish to redeem such a firstling, the same law shall apply as in the redemption of what has been vowed; namely, the priest was to appraise it, and then the man whose it had been might redeem it by the payment of the amount thus fixed, increased by one-fifth.

The Law of the Ban.

xxvii. 28, 29.

"Notwithstanding, no devoted thing, that a man shall devote unto the Lord of all that he hath, whether of man or beast, or of the field of his possession, shall be sold or redeemed: every devoted thing is most holy unto the Lord. None devoted, which shall be devoted of men, shall be ransomed; he shall surely be put to death."

Neither could any "devoted thing" be given to the Lord by a vow, and for the same reason—that it belonged to Him already. But it is added that, unlike that which has been vowed, the Lord's firstlings and the tithes, that which has been devoted may neither be sold nor redeemed. If it be a person which is thus "devoted," "he shall surely be put to death" (ver. 29). The reason of this law is found in the nature of the *herem* or ban. It devoted to the Lord only such persons and things as were in a condition of irreformable hostility and irreconcilable antagonism to the kingdom of God. By the ban such were turned over to God, in order to the total nullification of their power for evil; by destroying whatever was capable of destruction, as the persons and all living things that belonged to them; and by devoting to the Lord's service in the sanctuary and priesthood such of their property as, like silver, gold, and land, was in its nature incapable of destruction. In such devoted persons or things no man therefore was allowed to assert any personal claim or interest, such as the right of sale or of redemption would imply. Elsewhere the Israelite is forbidden even to desire the silver or gold that was on the idols in devoted cities (Deut. vii. 25), or to bring it into his house or tent, on penalty of being himself banned or devoted like them; a threat which was carried out in the case of Achan (Josh. vii.), who, for appropriating a wedge of gold and a garment which had been devoted, according to the law here and elsewhere declared, was summarily put to death.

This is not the place to enter fully into a discussion of the very grave questions which arise in connection with this law of the ban, in which it is ordered that "none devoted," "whether of man or beast," "shall be ransomed," but "shall be surely put to death." The most familiar instance of its application is furnished by the case of the Canaanitish cities, which Joshua, in accordance with this law of Lev. xxvii. 28, 29, utterly destroyed, with their inhabitants and every living thing that was in them. There are many sincere believers in Christ who find it almost impossible to believe that it can be true that God commanded such a slaughter as this; and the difficulty well deserves a brief consideration. It may not indeed be possible wholly to remove it from every mind; but one may well call attention, in connection with these verses, to certain considerations which should at least suffice very greatly to relieve its stress.

In the first place, it is imperative to remember that, if we accept the teaching of Scripture, we have before us in this history, not the government of man, but the government of God, a true theocracy. Now it is obvious that if even fallible men may be rightly granted power to condemn men to death, for the sake of the public good, much more must this right be conceded, and that without any limitation, to the infinitely righteous and infallible King of kings, if, in accord with the Scripture declarations, He was, literally and really, the political Head (if we may be allowed the expression) of the Israelitish nation. Further, if this absolute right of God in matters of life and death be admitted, as it must be, it is plain that He may rightly delegate the execution of His decrees to human agents. If this right is granted to one of our fellow-men, as to a king or a magistrate, much more to God.

Granting that the theocratic government of Israel was a historical fact, the only question then remaining as to the right of the ban, concerns the justice of its application in particular cases. With regard to this, we may concede that it was quite possible that men might sometimes apply this law without Divine authority; but we are not required to defend such cases, if any be shown, any more than to excuse the infliction of capital punishment in America sometimes by lynch law. These cases furnish no argument against its infliction after due legal process, and by legitimate governmental authority. As to the terrible execution of this law of the ban, in the destruction of the inhabitants of the Canaanitish cities, if the fact of the theocratic authority be granted, it is not so difficult to justify this as some have imagined. Nor, conversely, when the actual facts are thoroughly known, can the truth of the statement of the Scripture that God commanded this terrible destruction, be regarded as irreconcilable with those moral perfections which Scripture and reason alike attribute to the Supreme Being.

The researches and discoveries of recent years have let in a flood of light upon the state of society prevailing among those Canaanitish tribes at the date of their destruction; and they warrant us in saying that in the whole history of our race it would be hard to point to any civilized community which has sunken to such a depth of wickedness and moral pollution. As we have already seen, the book of Leviticus gives many dark hints of unnamable horrors among the Canaanitish races: the fearful cruelties of the worship of Molech, and the unmentionable impurities of the cult of Ashtoreth; the prohibition among some of these of female chastity, requiring that all be morally sacrificed[58]—one cannot go into these things. And when now we read in Holy Scripture that the infinitely pure, holy, and righteous God commanded that these utterly depraved and abandoned communities should be extirpated from the face of the earth, is it, after all, so hard to believe that this should be true? Nay, may we not rather with abundant reason say that it would have been far more difficult to reconcile with the character of God, if He had suffered them any longer to exist?

Nor have we yet fully stated the case. For we must, in addition, recall the fact that these corrupt communities, which by this law of the ban were devoted to utter destruction, were in no out-of-the-way corner of the world, but on one of its chief highways. The Phœnicians, for instance, more than any people of that time, were the navigators and travellers of the age; so that from Canaan as a centre this horrible moral pestilence was inevitably carried by them hither and thither, a worse than the "black death," to the very extremities of the known world. Have we then so certainly good reason to call in question the righteousness of the law which here ordains that no person thus devoted should be ransomed, but be surely put to death? Rather are we inclined to see in this law of the theocratic kingdom, and its execution in Canaan—so often held up as an illustration of the awful cruelty of the old theocratic *régime*—not only a conspicuous vindication of the righteousness and justice of God, but a no less illustrious manifestation of His mercy;—of His mercy, not merely to Israel, but to the whole human race of that age, who because of this deadly infection of moral evil had otherwise again everywhere sunk to such unimaginable depths of depravity as to have required a second flood for the cleansing of the world. This certainly was the way in which the Psalmist regarded it, when (Psalm cxxxvi. 17-22) he praised Jehovah as One who "smote great kings, and slew famous kings, and gave their land for an heritage, even an heritage unto Israel His servant: for HIS MERCY endureth for ever;" a thought which is again more formally expressed (Psalm lxii. 12) in the words: "Unto Thee, O Lord, belongeth mercy: for Thou renderest to every man according to his work."

Nor can we leave this law of the ban without noting the very solemn suggestion which it contains that there may be in the universe persons who, despite the great redemption, are morally irredeemable, hopelessly obdurate; for whom, under the government of a God infinitely righteous and merciful, nothing remains but the execution of the ban—the "eternal fire which is prepared for the devil and his angels" (Matt. xxv. 41); "a fierceness of fire which shall devour the adversaries" (Heb. x. 27). And this, not merely although, but BECAUSE God's "mercy endureth for ever."

The Law of the Tithe.

xxvi. 30-33.

"And all the tithe of the land, whether of the seed of the land, or of the fruit of the tree, is the Lord's: it is holy unto the Lord. And if a man will redeem aught of his tithe, he shall add unto it the fifth part thereof. And all the tithe of the herd or the flock, whatsoever passeth under the rod, the tenth shall be holy unto the Lord. He shall not search whether it be good or bad, neither shall he change it: and if he change it at all, then both it and that for which it is changed shall be holy; it shall not be redeemed."

Last of all these exclusions from the vow is mentioned the tithe. "Whether of the seed of the land, or of the herd, or of the flock," it is declared to be "holy unto the Lord;" "it is the Lord's." That because of this it cannot be given to the Lord by a special vow, although not formally stated, is self-evident. No man can give away what belongs to another, or give God what He has already. In Numb. xviii. 21 it is said that this tenth should be given "unto the children of Levi ... for the service of the tent of meeting."

Most extraordinary is the contention of Wellhausen and others, that since in Deuteronomy no tithe is mentioned other than of the product of the land, therefore, because of the mention here also of a tithe of the herd and the flock, we must infer that we have here a late interpolation into the "priest-code," marking a time when now the exactions of the priestly caste had been extended to the utmost limit. This is not the place to go into the question of the relation of the law of Deuteronomy to that which we have here; but we should rather, with Dillmann,[59] from the same premises argue the exact opposite, namely, that we have here the very earliest form of the tithe law. For that an ordinance so extending the rights of the priestly class should have been "smuggled" into the Sinaitic laws after the days of Nehemiah, as Wellhausen, Reuss, and Kuenen suppose, is simply "unthinkable;"[60] while, on the other hand, when we find already in Gen. xxviii. 22 Jacob promising unto the Lord the tenth of all that He should give him, at a time when he was living the life of a nomad herdsman, it is inconceivable that he should have meant "all, *excepting* the increase of the flocks and herds," which were his chief possession.

The truth is that the dedication of a tithe, in various forms, as an acknowledgment of dependence upon and reverence to God, is one of the most widely-spread and best-attested practices of the most remote antiquity. We read of it among the Romans, the Greeks, the ancient Pelasgians, the Carthaginians, and the Phœnicians; and in the Pentateuch, in full accord with all this, we find not only Jacob, as in the passage cited, but, at a yet earlier time, Abraham, more than four hundred years before Moses, giving tithes to Melchizedek. The law, in the exact form in which we have it here, is therefore in perfect harmony with all that we know of the customs both of the Hebrews and surrounding peoples, from a time even much earlier than that of the Exodus.

Very naturally the reference to the tithe, as thus from of old belonging to the Lord, and therefore incapable of being vowed, gives occasion to other regulations respecting it. Like unclean animals, houses, and lands which had been vowed, so also the tithe, or any part of it, might be redeemed by the individual for his own use, upon payment of the usual mulct of one-fifth additional to its assessed value. So also it is further ordered, with special regard to the tithe of the herd and the flock, "that whatsoever passeth under the rod," *i.e.*, whatever is counted, as the manner was, by being made to pass into or out of the fold under the herdsman's staff, "the tenth"—that is, every tenth animal as in its turn it comes—"shall be holy to the Lord." The owner was not to search whether the animal thus selected was good or bad, nor change it, so as to give the Lord a poorer animal, and keep a better one for himself; and if he broke this law, then, as in the case of the unclean beast vowed, as the penalty he was to forfeit to the sanctuary both the original and its attempted substitute, and also lose the right of redemption.

A very practical question emerges just here, as to the continued obligation of this law of the tithe. Although we hear nothing of the tithe in the first Christian centuries, it began to be advocated in the fourth century by Jerome, Augustine, and others, and, as is well known, the system of ecclesiastical tithing soon became established as the law of the Church. Although the system by no means disappeared with the Reformation, but passed from the Roman into the Reformed Churches, yet the modern spirit has become more and more adverse to the mediæval system, till, with the progressive hostility in society to all connection of the Church and the State, and in the Church the development of a sometimes exaggerated voluntaryism, tithing as a system seems likely to disappear altogether, as it has already from the most of Christendom.

But in consequence of this, and the total severance of the Church from the State, in the United States and the Dominion of Canada, the necessity of securing adequate provision for the maintenance and extension of the Church, is more and more directing the attention of those concerned in the practical economics of the Church, to this venerable institution of the tithe as the solution of many difficulties. Among such there are many who, while quite opposed to any enforcement of a law of tithing for the benefit of the Church by the civil power, nevertheless earnestly maintain that the law of the tithe, as we have it here, is of permanent obligation and binding on the conscience of every Christian. What is the truth in the matter? In particular, what is the teaching of the New Testament?

In attempting to settle for ourselves this question, it is to be observed, in order to clear thinking on this subject, that in the law of the tithe as here declared there are two elements—the one moral, the other legal,—which should be carefully distinguished. First and fundamental is the principle that it is our duty to set apart to God a certain fixed proportion of our income. The other and—technically speaking—*positive* element in the law is that which declares that the proportion to be given to the Lord is precisely one-tenth. Now, of these two, the first principle is distinctly recognised and reaffirmed in the New Testament as of continued validity in this dispensation; while, on the other hand, as to the precise proportion of our income to be thus set apart for the Lord, the New Testament writers are everywhere silent.

As regards the first principle, the Apostle Paul, writing to the Corinthians, orders that "on the first day of the week"—the day of the primitive Christian worship—"every one" shall "lay by him in store, as God hath prospered him." He adds that he had given the same command also to the Churches of Galatia (1 Cor. xvi. 1, 2). This most clearly gives apostolic sanction to the fundamental principle of the tithe, namely, that a definite portion of our income should be set apart for God. While, on the other hand, neither in this connection, where a mention of the law of the tithe might naturally have been expected, if it had been still binding as to the letter, nor in any other place does either the Apostle Paul or any other New Testament writer intimate that the Levitical law, requiring the precise proportion of a tenth, was still in force;—a fact which is the more noteworthy that so much is said of the duty of Christian benevolence.

To this general statement with regard to the testimony of the New Testament on this subject, the words of our Lord to the Pharisees (Matt. xxiii. 23), regarding their tithing of "mint and anise and cummin"—"these ye ought to have done"—cannot be taken as an exception, or as proving that the law is binding for this dispensation; for the simple reason that the present dispensation had not at that time yet begun, and those to whom He spoke were still under the Levitical law, the authority of which He there reaffirms. From these facts we conclude that the law of these verses, in so far as it requires the setting apart to God of a certain definite proportion of our income, is doubtless of continued and lasting obligation; but that, in so far as it requires from all alike the exact proportion of one-tenth, it is binding on the conscience no longer.

Nor is it difficult to see why the New Testament should not lay down this or any other precise proportion of giving to income, as a universal law. It is only according to the characteristic usage of the New Testament law to leave to the individual conscience very much regarding the details of worship and conduct, which under the Levitical law was regulated by specific rules; which the Apostle Paul explains (Gal. iv. 1-5) by reference to the fact that the earlier method was intended for and adapted to a lower and more immature stage of religious development; even as a child, during his minority, is kept under guardians and stewards, from whose authority, when he comes of age, he is free.

But, still further, it seems to be often forgotten by those who argue for the present and permanent obligation of this law, that it was here for the first time formally appointed by God as a binding law, in connection with a certain divinely instituted system of theocratic government, which, if carried out, would, as we have seen, effectively prevent excessive accumulations of wealth in the hands of individuals, and thus secure for the Israelites, in a degree the world has never seen, an equal distribution of property. In such a system it is evident that it would be possible to exact a certain fixed and definite proportion of income for sacred purposes, with the certainty that the requirement would work with perfect justice and fairness to all. But with us, social and economic conditions are so very different, wealth is so very unequally distributed, that no such law as that of the tithe could be made to work otherwise than unequally and unfairly. To the very poor it must often be a heavy burden; to the very rich, a proportion so small as to be a practical exemption. While, for the former, the law, if insisted on, would sometimes require a poor man to take bread out of the mouth of wife and children, it would still leave the millionaire with thousands to spend on needless luxuries. The latter might often more easily give nine-tenths of his income than the former could give one-twentieth.

It is thus no surprising thing that the inspired men who laid the foundations of the New Testament Church did not reaffirm the law of the tithe as to the letter. And yet, on the other hand, let us not forget that the law of the tithe, as regards the moral element of the law, is still in force. It forbids the Christian to leave, as so often, the amount he will give for the Lord's work, to impulse and caprice. Statedly and conscientiously he is to "lay by him in store as the Lord hath prospered him." If any ask how much should the proportion be, one might say that by fair inference the tenth might safely be taken as an *average minimum* of giving, counting rich and poor together. But the New Testament (2 Cor. viii. 7, 9) answers after a different and most characteristic manner: "See that ye abound in this grace.... For ye know the grace of our Lord Jesus Christ, that, though He was rich, yet for your sakes

He became poor, that ye through His poverty might become rich." Let there be but regular and systematic giving to the Lord's work, under the law of a fixed proportion of gifts to income, and under the holy inspiration of this sacred remembrance of the grace of our Lord, and then the Lord's treasury will never be empty, nor the Lord be robbed of His tithe.

And so hereupon the book of Leviticus closes with the formal declaration—referring, no doubt, strictly speaking, to the regulations of this last chapter—that "these are the commandments, which the Lord commanded Moses for the children of Israel in mount Sinai." The words as explicitly assert Mosaic origin and authority for these last laws of the book, as the opening words asserted the same for the law of the offerings with which it begins. The significance of these repeated declarations respecting the origin and authority of the laws contained in this book has been repeatedly pointed out, and nothing further need be added here.

To sum up all:—what the Lord, in this book of Leviticus, has said, was not for Israel alone. The supreme lesson of this law is for men now, for the Church of the New Testament as well. For the individual and for the nation, HOLINESS, consisting in full consecration of body and soul to the Lord, and separation from all that defileth, is the Divine ideal, to the attainment of which Jew and Gentile alike are called. And the only *way* of its attainment is through the atoning Sacrifice, and the mediation of the High Priest appointed of God; and the only *evidence* of its attainment is a joyful obedience, hearty and unreserved, to all the commandments of God. For us all it stands written: "Ye shall be holy; for I, Jehovah, your God, am holy."

FOOTNOTES:

[1] "Genesis may be made up of various documents, and yet have been compiled by Moses; and the same thing is possible, even in the later books of the Pentateuch. If these could be successfully partitioned among different writers, on the score of variety in literary execution, why may not these have been engaged jointly with Moses himself in preparing each his appointed portion, and the whole have been finally reduced by Moses to its present form?... Why might not these continue their work, and record what occurred after Moses was taken away?"—Professor W. H. Green, *Schaff-Herzog Encyclopædia*; article, "The Pentateuch."

[2] "If it be proven that a record was committed to writing at a comparatively late date, it does not necessarily follow that the essential part has not been accurately handed down."—Professor Strack, *ibid*.

[3] Something like this seems to have been the final position of the late Professor Delitzsch, who said: "We hold firmly that Moses laid the foundation of this codification" (of the "priest-code" of Leviticus, etc.), "but it was continued in the post-Mosaic period within the priesthood, to whom was entrusted the transmission, interpretation, and administration of the law. We admit this willingly; and even the participation of Ezra in this codification in itself furnishes no stumbling block for us. For it is not inconceivable that laws which until then had been handed down orally were fixed by him in writing to secure their judicial authority and execution. The most important thing for us is the historico-traditional character of the Pentateuchal legislation, and especially the occasions for (the laws) and the fundamental arrangements in the history of the times. That which we cannot be persuaded to admit is that the so-called Priestly Code is the work of the free invention of the latest date, which takes on the artificial appearance of ancient history."—*The Presbyterian Review*, July 1882; article, "Delitzsch on the Origin and Composition of the Pentateuch," p. 578.

[4] *The Expositor*, January, 1889; article, "The Old Theology and the New," pp. 54, 55.

[5] From the note in xvi. 1 it would appear that this chapter, so different in subject from the five preceding chapters on "Uncleannesses," originally

preceded them, and so followed x., with which it is so closely connected. Its exposition is therefore given immediately after that of x.

[6] This name is often restricted to xviii.-xx.

[7] The usage of the common Hebrew phrase so rendered does not warrant the translation in the old version: "of his voluntary will."

[8] See Psalm lxix. 9, and compare in the Hebrew such expressions as, "the fire hath consumed the burnt-offering;" and Deut. iv. 24, "thy God is a devouring fire," etc., in all which the verb signifying "to eat" is idiomatically used of fire.

[9] Kurtz, "Der Alt-testamentliche Opfercultus," p. 243.

[10] A striking parallel to this ordinance is found in a caste custom in North India, where the caste Hindoo, as I have often seen, if he give you a drink of water in a vessel, will only use an earthen vessel, which, immediately after you have drunk, he breaks, to preclude the possibility of its accidental use thereafter, by which ceremonial defilement might be contracted. For the Hindoo does not regard it as possible so to cleanse a metallic vessel as to remove the defilement thus caused; and as he could not afford to throw it away, he will give one to drink in the cheap earthen vessel, or else no drink at all.

[11] It is to be regretted that the Revisers had not allowed in this case the rendering "trespass-offering" to stand, as in the Authorised Version. For, unlike the more generic term "guilt," our word "trespass" very precisely indicates the class of offences for which this particular offering was ordained. It is indeed true that the Hebrew word so rendered is quite distinct from that rendered "trespass;" yet, in this instance, by the attempt to represent this fact in English, more has been lost than gained.

[12] Even in the burnt-offering, the hide of the victim was assigned to the priest (vii. 8).

[13] See "Die Bücher Exodus und Leviticus," 2 Aufl., p. 462.

[14] Especially striking in this connection is the expression used by the Apostle Paul (Rom. xv. 16), where he speaks of himself as "a minister of Christ Jesus unto the Gentiles, ministering the Gospel of God;" in which last phrase, the Greek word denotes "ministration as a priest." See R.V., margin.

[15] "Commentary on the Epistle to the Hebrews," vol. ii., p. 172.

[16] See, *e.g.*, Exod. xxiv. 10; Ezek. i. 26.

[17] Thus *e.g.*, in Cant. iv. 13, where the Revised Version reads, "Thy shoots are an orchard of pomegranates," the Jewish paraphrast in the Chaldee

Targum renders, "Thy young men are filled with the commandments (of God) like unto pomegranates (*sc.* with their seeds)."

[18] Not, however, as many imagine, in behalf of those who have in this age died in sin, but in ministrations to the living nations in the flesh, in the age to come. We find no ground of hope, in Holy Scripture, for the impenitent dead.

[19] The interposition of chapters xi.-xv. on ceremonial uncleanness, between chapters x. and xvi., which are so closely connected by this historical note in xvi. 1, certainly suggests an editorial redaction—as the phrase is—in which the latter chapter, for whatsoever reason, has been removed from its original context. But that such a redaction, of which we have in the book other traces, does not of necessity affect in the slightest degree the question of its inspiration and Divine authority, should be self-evident.

[20] "Die Bücher Exodus und Leviticus," 2 Aufl., p. 525.

[21] "Symbolik des Mosäischen Cultus," 2 Band., p. 668.

[22] "Biblische Abhandlungen," pp. 239-270.

[23] In *The Nineteenth Century*, September, 1889.

[25] This latter reason, however, would rather appear to have demanded, as in the case of the leper, a guilt-offering.

[26] This word, it should be noted, is now popularly used to denote a disease quite distinct from leprosy, known also as "Barbadoes leg," which consists essentially of an elephantine enlargement of the lower extremities.

[27] This opinion has been ably argued by Sir Risdon Bennett, M.D., LL.D., F.R.S., in "By-paths of Bible Knowledge," vol. ix., "The Diseases of the Bible."

[28] Compare our frequent use of the word to denote paralysis.

[29] "The Land and the Book," vol. i., pp. 530, 531.

[30] "Die Bücher Exodus und Leviticus," 2 Aufl., p. 535.

[31] "Die Bücher Exodus und Leviticus," 2 Aufl., p. 537.

[32] These verses have been partially expounded, indeed, before, in so far as was necessary to a complete exposition of the sin-offering; but in this context the subject is brought forward in another relation, which renders necessary this additional exposition.

[34] It deserves to be noticed that in this phrase, which recurs with such frequency in this "Law of Holiness," the original, with evident allusion to Exod. iii. 15; vi. 2-4, always has the covenant name of God, commonly

anglicised "Jehovah." The retention of the term "Lord" here, as in many other places, is much to be regretted, as seriously weakening and obscuring the sense to the ordinary reader.

[35] See, for example, in the Hebrew text, 1 Kings xiv. 24; Gen. xxxviii. 21; Hosea iv. 14, *et passim.*

[36] "Die Bücher Exodus und Leviticus," 2 Aufl., p. 550.

[37] The wife is not mentioned, but that she would also be included in the exception, in view of her being always regarded in the law as yet nearer to her husband than father or mother, may be safely taken for granted.

[38] See margin (R.V.).

[39] That is, not burnt alive, but after execution.

[40] See 1 John iii. 4 and 2 Thess. ii. 3, 4, 7, 8,—passages which, in view of this most manifest and characteristic tendency of our times, are pregnant with very solemn warning.

[41] See the inspired comment in Heb. iv.

[42] Compare Isa. lviii. 3-7, Zech. vii. 5, where the necessity of the inward sorrow for sin and turning unto God, in connection with this fast of the seventh month, is solemnly urged upon Israel.

[43] See Kurtz, "Der Alttestamentliche Opfercultus," p. 271.

[44] "Symbolik des Mosäischen Cultus," erster Band, pp. 428-432.

[45] See, *e.g.*, Rabbi Dr. J. Levy, "Chaldäisches Wörterbuch," zweiter Band, pp. 301, 302; and compare Numb. xxiii. 8, Prov. xi. 26, xxiv. 24, where the same Hebrew word is used.

[46] *Cf.* the expression used with reference to Jesus Christ, Phil. ii. 9 (R.V.), "the name which is above every name."

[47] Thus Dillmann writes: "That the law (of the jubilee) in its principal features was already issued by Moses does not admit of demonstration to him who wills not to believe it; but that it cannot have been in the first instance the invention of a post-exilian scribe is certain. Only in the simpler communal relations of the more ancient time could a law of such an ideal character have seemed practicable; after the exile, all the presuppositions involved in its promulgation are wanting" ("Die Bücher Exodus und Leviticus," 2 Aufl., p. 608).

[48] The interpretation of ver. 33 presents a difficulty which, if the rendering retained in the text by the Revisers be accepted, is hard to resolve. But if we assume that a negative has fallen out of the first clause in the

received text, and read with the Vulgate, as given in the margin of the Revised Version, "if one of the Levites redeem *not*," all becomes clear. In the exposition we have ventured to assume in this instance the correctness of the Vulgate.

[49] See Psalm lxxxix. 15.

[50] Much has been made of this reference to the neglect of the sabbatic years as evidence of the late composition of the chapter; but surely in this argument there is little force. For, even apart from any question of inspiration, the ordinance of the sabbatic year was of such an extraordinary character, so opposed alike to human selfishness and eagerness for gain, and calling for such faith in God, that it would require no great knowledge of human nature to anticipate its probable neglect, even on natural grounds. But, even were this not so, still an argument of this kind against the Mosaic origin of this minatory section of the covenant can have decisive force for those only who, for whatsoever reason, have come to disbelieve that God can tell beforehand what free agents will do, or that, if He know, He can impart that knowledge to His servants.

[51] So Basnage ("History of the Jews," London, 1700, chap. xxviii., sec. 15) estimated it in his day. Since then, however, their number has materially increased, and is still increasing; a fact the significance of which has been pointed out by the present writer in "The Jews; or, Prediction and Fulfilment" (New York, 1883, pp. 178-83).

[52] "Modern Doubt and Christian Belief," p. 333.

[53] It is the same Hebrew word which is rendered "enjoy" when applied to the land and "accept" when applied to Israel: it might thus be rendered "enjoy" in the latter case—"they shall enjoy the punishment of their iniquity," when the words would express a severe irony, a figure of which we have examples elsewhere in the Scriptures.

[54] The "if" which introduces ver. 40 in the Authorised version has no equivalent in the Hebrew, and should therefore be omitted, as in the revision.

[55] See Gen. xii. 1-3; xiii. 14-17; xv. 5-21; xvii. 2-11; xxii. 15-18.

[56] These commutation rates are so low that it is plain that they could not have represented the actual value of the individual's labour. The highest sum which is named—fifty shekels—as the rate for a man from twenty to sixty years of age, taking the shekel as 2s. 3·37*d*., or $·5474, would only amount to £5 14s. 0¾*d*., or $27·375. Even from this alone it is clear that, as stated above, the chief reference in these figures must have been symbolic

of a claim of God upon the person, graded according to his capacity for service.

[57] So certainly should we render instead of "angel," in accordance with the suggestion of the margin (R.V.). The reference is to the priest, as Mal. ii. 7 makes very clear: "He [the priest] is the messenger of the Lord."

[58] On this subject, among other authorities, see Ebrard, "Apologetik," 2 Theil, pp. 167-90, especially p. 173.

[59] See "Die Bücher Exodus und Leviticus," pp. 635-638.

[60] See "Undenkbar;" so Dillmann, *op. cit.*, p. 638.